Please Don't Lose the Date Card

Wild Cats
of the
World

Wild Cats
of the
World

C. A.W. Guggisberg

Taplinger Publishing Company | New York

First Edition

Published in the United States in 1975 by
TAPLINGER PUBLISHING CO., INC.
New York, New York

Published simultaneously in the Dominion of Canada by
Burns & MacEachern, Ltd, Ontario

Library of Congress Catalog Card Number: 74-21020

ISBN 0-8008-8324-1

Designed by Mollie M. Torras

Contents

The illustrations are grouped following page 106

Wild Cats
of the
World

Wild Cats

The plain of yellow grass resembles an enormous wheat-field as it spreads out under an azure sky with rows of white cumuli floating lazily in the breeze. Unbroken, except for a few piles of huge granite boulders, the plain extends to a faraway range of blue hills on one side, to a long line of trees on the other. These trees, mostly yellow-barked acacias interspersed with a few kigelias (usually called sausage trees), mark the course of a river-bed, which now, in the midst of the dry season, contains nothing but a series of stagnant pools.

Everywhere the plain is dotted with animals. In every direction are herds of round-bellied zebras, bovine wildebeests, and tail-waggling Thomson's gazelles, as well as scattered groups of shiny-coated topi and elegant Grant's gazelles. Toward the river there is a concentration of sleek, reddish-brown impalas, one buck lording it over a harem of nearly a hundred does.

From the top of the nearest granite kopje we might overlook an even wider tract of country, with more game. But it would not be advisable to scramble up over the boulders, for the towering fortress has already been commandeered as a look-out post: on one of its highest battlements stands a big cat, a lioness, her amber eyes sweeping the plain below.

After a few moments she turns round and begins to descend, jumping lightly from one rocky step to the next. She is heading toward a broad bench of granite, jutting out like a platform about half-way down. As we follow her course, we suddenly realize that she is not the sole occupant of the fortress. Five lionesses lie asleep on the stony bench, and a number of cubs of various ages can be seen playing among the surrounding bushes. Two dark-maned males and two more lionesses are stretched out in the shade of an umbrella tree at the foot of the hill.

The sleepers on the platform waken up as the lioness steps into their midst. There is some rubbing of heads—the leonine version of a friendly greeting—but she does not tarry for more than a couple of minutes. Continuing on her way, she is almost immediately followed by two of the five lionesses whose rest she has disturbed. The remaining three watch them go, and after a short while, they, too, get to their feet, yawn, stretch, and then bound down one after the

9

other. They stop at the umbrella tree, and after some more head-rubbing are joined by the two lionesses. The males look after them with an almost reproachful expression on their faces, but before the lionesses have gone forty yards, walking in single file, they rise, first one, then the other, to trot along behind the ladies. Leaving the cubs behind among the bushes and boulders, all the adults of the pride are now moving away from the kopje.

The three lionesses which were the first to set out are well ahead, their eyes fixed on a herd of grazing zebras. Having at first advanced fairly briskly, they now move more and more slowly, adopting a low-slung, almost crouching, gait. For a while, the black spots on the backs of their ears can still be seen among the waving grass as the lionesses deviate more and more to the left, but eventually all three vanish as completely as if they had been swallowed up by the earth.

The main party meanwhile has spread out, its members advancing like skirmishers. They intend to circumvent the herd from the right, but the zebras are by now fully aware of what is happening. They have their heads up and are looking toward the lions, although they do not seem to be in a great hurry to get away. They know exactly how near a lion must get in order to rush them successfully, and for the moment they are quite content simply to observe their enemies. Only when the lions begin to close in, in a wide half-circle, do they move on, at a trot first, and then, seeing some of the hunters advance more quickly, at a gallop. As the zebras move off to the left, a black-tufted tail suddenly jerks up out of the yellow grass, and a lioness from the separate party of three races forward. She misses by a few feet—but at that moment a second tawny shape flashes past and, after a short rush, catches up with a zebra. Over it goes, and for a few seconds its legs can be seen flailing above the grass. The other lions approach at an eager trot. A kill has been made, and soon the vultures will be circling overhead.

All this time, the tawny hunters' strategy has been watched by a spotted cat standing on top of an ant-hill about half a mile away—a female cheetah, whose half-grown cubs are playing nearby. Intent on keeping as great a distance as possible between herself and the lions, she calls the cubs with a birdlike chirp and moves off in the direction of the river. Several herds of Thomson's gazelles take flight at the cheetah family's approach, while a couple of topi, snorting and stamping, watch the passage of the cats and even follow behind for a short stretch until they see the cheetahs disappear among the reeds and bushes fringing the river.

Coming out into the open after having crossed the river-bed, the mother cheetah discovers a dozen Thomson's gazelles. She stops in mid-stride, watching them. They have not seen her emerge from cover, and the wind is such that they cannot get her scent. The cheetah cubs settle down in a patch of scrub, while the mother begins to stalk forward, stiff-legged, head straight out in front. She advances slowly, step by step, and gradually the 120 yards that separated her from the gazelles shrinks to 100, then 80. Suddenly she literally shoots forward, racing at a tremendous speed, straight as an arrow. The thomies have seen her now—they run—but she is already among them and bowls one over. After ten minutes or so she comes back to her cubs, dragging the dead thomie along with her.

About a mile from where the cheetah crossed the river-bed, on one of the yellow-barked acacias, there lies another spotted cat, asleep, chin resting on paw, the hind legs dangling on both sides of the branch, and the long tail hanging below. It is a leopard, a big, beautifully marked male. The afternoon is now well advanced, and the rays of the setting sun have taken on a golden tinge. Dusk is less than an hour away.

The leopard opens his eyes, yawns, gets to his feet, and casts a searching look around. He stretches with luxurious elaboration and, having gone through this relaxing exercise, settles down again, but with his legs drawn up. The paws and shoulders get a few licks, there are some more yawns, and then, getting up for good, he proceeds to walk purposefully along the sloping branch, golden in the evening light. He pauses briefly at the main fork before running down part of the trunk and jumping off elegantly to the ground. Without a moment's hesitation he sets out through the grass, walking more or less parallel to the river-bed.

After covering about a quarter of a mile, the leopard stops dead and raises his head, his alert eyes fixed on a spot close to the river-bank. A solitary reed-buck has come out of cover for its evening grazing. Watching it for some time, motionless except for the nervously twitching tip of the tail, the leopard now begins to stalk through the high grass, keeping his body well down and moving slowly and with utmost deliberation. Some scrub and bushes nearer the river provide him more cover, but the closer he gets to his prospective prey, the slower he moves. Inch by inch he crawls forward, never taking his eyes off the antelope, often waiting several minutes before sliding to the next bit of cover. Now he is in a patch of scrub next to the buck, crouching flat, invisible even to the hammerkop sitting in a near-by tree. For most of the time, the reed-buck has been half-facing in the direction from which the leopard has made his approach, but now it turns its head away to look at a female that has just stepped out of a reed-bed. It is the last thing he will ever do—the leopard pounces from a few yards away, grabs the buck, and drags it down. The hammerkop flies up, calling "kek-kek-kek," and the female, hearing the bird's call, bounds away. For the buck, however, the warning has come too late. It lies dead, with the leopard crouching over it.

The zebra, the gazelle, and the reed-buck—all had to die to give life to animals which do not have access to the primary food supply produced from inorganic matter through the marvel of photosynthesis. Unable to obtain the life-sustaining organic compounds directly from the plants, carnivores must get them from the plant-eaters—and in doing so, they have for ages past preserved the vegetable kingdom from destruction and safeguarded the food-manufacturing process on which all animal life ultimately depends. It it were not for the carnivores, the herbivores would long ago have overrun the earth and turned most of it into a desert.

The scenes just described were not cruel acts of bloody murder, but necessary incidents in the struggle that has to go on if there is to be any sort of ecological balance. Even as these lines are being written, similar incidents involving wild cats are taking place the world over—in northern forests and Indian jungles, on Scottish hillsides, in Arabian deserts, and on the densely wooded banks of the Amazon. The few glimpses of life and death on the African veld might as easily have been other visions: a lynx pouncing on a snow-shoe rabbit, a tiger stalking a cheetal deer, a wildcat grabbing a vole, a sand cat chasing after a jerboa, or a jaguar bounding on the back of a tapir.

The plains of East Africa have been chosen for this first meeting with wild cats in order to present three widely differing species. Taking the cat family as a whole, two of them are definite outsiders—the lion with its sociable habits, and the cheetah, which relies not on stalking ability, but on speed, running down its prey over a considerable distance. The two also differ from other cats in some of their outward characteristics: the cheetah is long-legged and unable to completely withdraw its claws, while the lion has a tuft at the end of the tail in both sexes, and a very well-developed mane which distinguishes the male from the female.

The leopard, however, can stand in for the great majority of cats. It is solitary in its habits, and its appearance is fairly typical of the family. It has a short, roundish head, a lithe, muscular, deep-chested body, strong, relatively short limbs, a long tail, and a short, thick, close coat which is kept sleek and glossy from constant cleaning. The forelimbs are not merely ambulatory—restricted to backward and forward movements—but are capable of free rotatory motion and can therefore be used to catch and hold prey or to fend off an aggressor. The hind limbs provide the motive power behind the amazing jumping feats performed by this and many other species.

The feet are well-haired except for the naked, rubbery pads, which allow a soft and noiseless tread. All cats are digitigrade, walking on their toes, of which there are five on the forefoot, though with the thumb or pollex raised above the other toes and not touching the ground. The hind foot has four toes only, the big toe or hallux being absent. In most cats the large, compressed, and strongly curved claws are only bared for catching prey or in defence. Drawn back into their sheaths by a system of muscles and tendons, they cannot be blunted through contact with the hard ground, and do not, of course, normally show up in the animal's spoor.

Compared with those of a wolf or an African hunting dog, the leopard's jaws are very short. Of its thirty teeth, the incisors are small, unspecialized, and arranged in a horizontal line. Not suitable for any real biting, they are mostly used for gnawing bones or for grabbing very small cubs if they have to be transported to another shelter. The canines, one in each jaw, are long and slightly bent, highly adapted for grabbing an animal and for perforating its skin. They are better developed in the cat family than in any other living carnivores. Of the cheek-teeth, the first upper premolar and the single upper molar are small and practically without function. The other cheek teeth are not developed for crushing (as in dogs, hyenas, and bears), but for cutting, the third upper premolar and the single lower molar—the so-called carnassials—being especially big and sharp-edged. They do not meet, but cut past each other like shears.

The deciduous milk teeth of a cub are twenty-six in number, three incisors and one canine in each jaw, three milk molars in the upper jaw and two in the lower. The second upper and lower milk molars have a certain resemblance to the carnassials of the permanent dentition.

The tongue, too, comes into play while the animal is feeding. Its surface is beset all over with sharp-pointed, recurved horny papillae which make it so rough that it can be used to rasp particles of meat from a bone or to lick the hairs off a dead animal's skin. While not quite as mobile as that of a dog, it moves with great rapidity and precision when a cat is lapping up water. In addition, it is a highly efficient toilet implement used in cleaning and grooming its owner's coat. Cats have the largest eyes of all carnivores, those of a lion, for instance, being bigger than a man's, with a diameter of 37.5 mm (1.48 in) as compared with 23 mm (0.9 in). They are directed forward, and while this position does not give all-round vision, it makes possible the accurate judging of distances, an ability which naturally is of vital importance in stalking and catching prey.

All cats rely greatly on their sense of sight, and with most of them being at least partly nocturnal, night vision is well-developed. To let in the maximum quantity of whatever light there may be, the pupils dilate widely in the dark. In strong light, however, they contract rapidly, retaining their round outlines in the leopard, but becoming oval or turning into vertical slits in other species. Behind the retina there is a reflecting layer, so densely coated with minute particles of guanin that it takes on a gold or silver lustre. It brightens and throws back the limited amount of light falling through the pupils at night, the rays thus coming in contact with the receptor cells twice, first on the way in and then, amplified, on the way out, stimulating them each time. These reflected rays cause a cat's eyes to shine in the beam of a lamp or the glow of a fire. It should hardly be necessary to stress the fact that no animal's eyes "glow" in absolute darkness.

A cat's nose is small in comparison with that of any member of the dog family, but one cannot help feeling that the olfactory sense of the felids has often been underrated. It certainly is of great importance in establishing and keeping up intraspecific contacts, and on occasion it probably plays a not inconsiderable part in locating prey. The whiskers, or vibrissae, so well-developed in all cats, are organs of touch and should be of considerable use on nocturnal prowls or in stalking through thick cover. Hearing is very acute, even though the ears of most cats are relatively short.

The long tail characteristic of a majority of species is said to act as a balancing pole in tree-climbing and as a sort or rudder in jumping. This may well be, but there are cats with very short tails—for example, the lynxes—which do not seem to be in the least hampered in their jumping performances. The positioning of the tail and its movements are highly indicative of an individual's moods and intention, so we may assume it to have an important function in intraspecific communication. It may, in fact, be very significant that in the one really social cat, the lion, a black tuft draws special attention to the tip of the tail. In other species, the end of the tail is made conspicuous by white or black markings, or by a combination of the two colours. Held high enough, it acts as a guide for an individual following another one.

Prey is usually stalked or ambushed, the victim being pounced upon from as near as possible. Only the cheetah, and to a much lesser degree the lion, will pursue a prospective prey over more than a short distance. Small cats catch and kill their prey by a bite into the back of the neck. Big cats may first grab an animal by the nape in order to drag it down, but will then frequently take hold of its throat and kill it by strangulation. The leopard, probably the best stalker among the big cats, often goes straight for the throat. The nape bite also plays a part in mating, males usually grabbing their partners by the back of the neck.

In some species, including the leopard, the females have two pairs of abdominal mammae; in others there are four pairs, of which two are in a pectoral position. Mothers devote a lot of care to their offspring. They keep them clean, attend to the youngsters' toilet until they are able to lick themselves, fetch them back by the loose skin of the neck whenever they go astray, and, of course, bring in prey—or take the cubs to a kill—as soon as they begin to eat meat.

Most wild cats are encountered singly, in couples, or in family groups consisting of a mother with her cubs or kittens. All the species which have so far been studied somewhat more closely have been found to have more or less territorial habits, occupying home ranges which they claim for their own by placing scent marks, also by scratching trees and by uttering certain sounds.

Taxonomically, all cats were originally included in the genus *Felis.* Soon, however, it was realized that even though cats, large or small, striped, spotted, or uniform in colour, had a very distinctive family resemblance, there nevertheless were differences big enough to justify the setting up of several genera. The long-legged cheetah, for instance, with its partly retractile claws, was at an early date in taxonomic history made the sole representative of the genus *Acinonyx,* the genus *Felis* thus being reserved for the "retractile clawed cats." There were, however, groups which did not really fit into the picture of a "cat" as represented by the domestic cat and the European wildcat. The long-legged, stumpy-tailed lynxes had to be split off and placed into a genus of their own. Some zoologists also pointed to fundamental differences between large and small cats.

The wildcat and its many relatives, close and more distant, have pupils contracting into vertical slits, while those of the lion, tiger, leopard, and jaguar remain round. In small cats, the suspension of the hyoid is fully ossified, the larynx or voice organ thus being held near the base of the skull and inhibited in its motion. In the big cats, however, the suspension of the hyoid is incomplete, its lower part consisting of a ligamentous cord. The larynx is not fused to the skull and has greater mobility. Small cats can purr continuously; big cats, when making purring sounds, must pause for breath after each purr. Big cats can roar, while small cats utter high-pitched screams.

In current textbooks, we therefore find the once familiar names *Felis leo, Felis tigris, Felis pardus,* and *Felis onca* (for lion, tiger, leopard, and jaguar) replaced by *Panthera leo, Panthera tigris, Panthera pardus,* and *Panthera onca.*

In recent times the taxonomic subdivision of the cat family has been carried even further, but no two authorities seem to be in entire agreement on generic and subgeneric status.

The Origin and Evolution of Cats

The members of the cat family, or *Felidae,* are the most highly developed of all the present-day terrestrial carnivores—the *Fissipedia* of zoologists. Their perfect adaptation to a hunter's life is the result of a lengthy process of evolution which can be said to have begun when the world was still dominated by giant reptiles. During late Cretaceous times, small, long-nosed creatures, unnoticed by monstrous Triceratops and ferocious Gorgosaurus, scurried around in the shade of ferns, cycads, and ginkgoes, preying upon the already numerous insects. These creatures were placental mammals with rows of tiny, sharply cusped teeth in their jaws, and if we want to get a general idea of their appearance, we must look at the solenodons of Cuba and Hispaniola or at the tree shrews of southeastern Asia.

The saurians became extinct at the end of the Cretaceous Period, and the disappearance of the reptiles from so many of the ecological niches which they had formerly occupied may have been the impulse which sped up the evolution of mammals, so that the Tertiary Period is rightly referred to as the "Age of Mammals." Geologists have subdivided the Tertiary into five periods: the Palaeocene, Eocene, Oligocene, Miocene, and Pliocene. The Palaeocene began about 65 million years ago, the Pliocene ended about 3 million years ago with the advent of the Pleistocene epoch of the Quaternary Age.

Some of the very unspecialized mammals that survived into the Palaeocene from Cretaceous times went on catching insects and have done so right up to the present. Others turned to a herbivorous diet, They became the ancestors of the ungulates, but soon found themselves preyed upon by former insectivores which had so much increased in size that they were now able to overpower their fellow mammals. These earliest carnivores, called *Creodonta* by palaeontologists, had long bodies and short limbs. Their toes were armed with claws, and they had forty-four teeth, differentiated into three incisors, one canine, four premolars, and three molars in each jaw, as shown in the following dental formula: $\frac{3\ 1\ 4\ 3}{3\ 1\ 4\ 3}$. Certain features of their skulls indicate that their jaws were operated by strong muscles. Their brains, however, were small, and by present-day standards the creodonts cannot have been very efficient hunters. They must nevertheless have found it easy enough to kill the slow and equally dull-witted forerunners of the ungulates, for they flourished, splitting up into numerous families and genera, and became the dominant carnivores of the Eocene, with some species attaining the size of a wolf or even a lion. As they evolved into formidable predators, their upper molars and hindmost lower molars showed a tendency to enlarge and to acquire the cutting edge characteristic of the carnassials of present-day carnivores. The creodonts went into decline at the end of the Eocene, although one family, the *Hyenodontidae,* survived through the Oligocene and Miocene, only becoming extinct in the Pliocene.

The place of the *Creodonta* was taken by the *Miacidae,* which can most probably be regarded as having evolved out of some primitive creodont. The earliest known miacids, from the Torrejon deposits of North America, were small animals, probably forest dwellers. They had much bigger brains than the creodonts, whose extinction may well have been due to competition from their more efficient relatives. At a very early point of miacid evolution, the fourth upper premolar and the first lower molar developed into carnassials. As the same teeth form the carnassials of the modern *Fissipedia*—viverrids, hyenas, raccoons, bears, martens, dogs, and cats—we can safely assume all of them to have descended from the miacids.

The *Miacidae* came up rapidly and began to specialize along divergent lines. The forerunners of dogs, martens, viverrids, and cats can, in fact, already be recognized in late Eocene times. Among the carnivores, the canids—dogs, wolves, foxes—and the short-legged viverrids—civet cats, genets, and mongooses—are the *Fissipedia* nearest to the miacid stock, and it seems very probable that the cats originated from a civet-like species. Living viverrids, with few exceptions, have five toes on their forefeet and hind feet. Some are plantigrade like their ancestors, others digitigrade like the cats. The claws of genets and civets are retractile or semiretractile, but not those of the mongooses. Most viverrids have forty teeth, the dental formula being $\frac{3}{3}\frac{1}{1}\frac{4}{4}\frac{2}{2}$. Of the canids, the wolves and foxes have forty-two teeth ($\frac{3}{3}\frac{1}{1}\frac{4}{4}\frac{2}{3}$). In the Indian wild dog or dhole, and in the American bush dog, this number has been reduced to forty and thirty-eight respectively, while the bat-eared fox of Africa has no less than forty-eight teeth. To accommodate a large number of teeth, a jaw has to be of corresponding length, and this explains the pointed muzzles so characteristic of viverrids and canids, so different from the short, rounded profiles of cats. Comparison of a civet skull with that of a leopard will show the number of cheek teeth as greatly reduced in the felid, with the upper jaw lacking one premolar and one molar, while the lower jaw lacks two premolars and one molar. The dental formula of the leopard (and of the majority of cats) thus reads $\frac{3}{3}\frac{1}{1}\frac{3}{2}\frac{1}{1}$ and adds up to a total of thirty teeth. The cats appear to be on the point of gradually losing the first upper premolar, for it is absent in the cheetah, the lynx, and some other species.

The history of the cat family can thus be traced back to when the Eocene merged into the Oligocene, one of its earliest members being *Proailurus* from the Quercy phosphorites of southern France. About the size of a small civet, this animal had relatively long limbs, a very long tail, and combined viverrid with certain felid characteristics. *Proailurus,* or a species closely allied to it, could well have been ancestral to the *Nimravinae,* which must have been common and widely distributed during the Oligocene and Miocene. Their remains, which have been found both in Europe and North America, give evidence of a strong tendency to develop tusklike canines, very much in the line of the sabre-toothed tigers. The nimravids became extinct during the Pliocene, but some species were of so intermediate a character between civet-like *Proailurus* and the true cats that the ancestor of the latter will probably have to be searched for among the early and unspecialized nimravids. *Pseudailurus,* for instance, was a relatively long-limbed animal with partly digitigrade, five-toed feet, and with a dentition more like a true cat's than that of any modern viverrid.

The so-called sabre-toothed tigers—next to the mammoth probably the most popular of extinct mammals—have been a great puzzle to palaeontologists, and their true relationship to the cat family is still very much under discussion. J. R. Hough describes them as "pseudofelids," as a distant offshoot that probably deviated early in the Tertiary Age and followed a line of evolution more or less parallel to that of the *Felidae.* J. Piveteau assumed two lines of evolution, one related to the nimravids and branching off early in the Tertiary, the other a late Tertiary offshoot of the *Felidae.* There is, however, very little relationship among the different genera of sabre-toothed cats (*Megantereon, Homotherium, Machairodus,* and *Smilodon*), and Björn Kurtén may be right in regarding them not as forming one or two homologous groups, but as representing a recurrent adaptive type which evolved independently in several different lineages of the cat family. A tendency to develop tusklike canines existed, after all, among the nimravids, and it has cropped up again in a modern species, the clouded leopard. Long-tusked species existed also among the creodonta, and a Field Museum expedition digging for fossils in northwestern Argentina brought back a skull that could easily have been mistaken for that of a sabre-tooth cat, but came, in fact, from a carnivorous marsupial, *Thylacosmilus.*

Sabre-toothed cats, some of which exceeded present-day lions and tigers in size, have come to light in Europe, China, Africa, and North and South America. It has been suggested that these fearsome-looking creatures were actually scavengers, using their tusks to slit open the carcasses of big herbivores, but most authors regard them as adapted to killing large, thick-skinned animals such as elephants and rhinoceroses. In Friesenhahn Cave in Texas, remains of sabre-toothed cats have been found in association with great numbers of teeth and bones of juvenile elephants, which apparently formed a considerable part of their prey.

The best-known species is the American *Smilodon,* of which abundant remains have been dug up at the late Pleistocene water-holes of Rancho La Brea in California. These pools were treacherous traps, for underneath the water there were deposits of soft tar into which innumerable animals disappeared after having got their limbs inextractably caught. *Smilodon* was about the size of a lion, but with heavier forequarters, light hindquarters, and a short stump of a tail. It cannot have been a very agile predator and may largely have preyed upon the slow-moving giant ground sloths of its time. It survived longest of all sabre-toothed cats, almost to the end of the Pleistocene, if the datings obtained from La Brea material—14,500 years—are correct. Many of the bones recovered from the tar pits give evidence of pathological lesions, especially in the limbs and in the lumbar region, and it could well be that *Smilodon* was a species that had run its course and succumbed to what may be called phylogenetic senescence.

Animals that can be recognized as true cats are known from the early Pliocene, and in the course of this period, the last of the Tertiary subdivisions, many of the genera which we know today must have come into existence. As far as the fossil record goes, big cats resembling lions and tigers turned up quite suddenly during the Villafranchian, as the early Pleistocene is called. There was, for instance, the Tuscany lion, which roamed through northern Italian and central European forests. It was the size of a small lion, but differed from that species in its dentition and may have been more closely related to the leopard. Two possible ancestral forms of the latter—*Panthera pardoides* and *Panthera palaeosinensis*—have come from the Villafranchian of Europe and China respectively. India at that time also had a large cat, *Panthera cristatus,* but it was fairly aberrant and not related to any modern species. Of the lynxes, a species known as *Lynx brevirostris* has been recorded from late Pliocene deposits, while two species have become known from the Villafranchian of Europe (Issoire lynx) and China (Shansi lynx). The cheetah's origin must go back a long way into the Pliocene, for it makes its appearance in the Villafranchian as the very highly specialized giant cheetah (*Acinonyx pardinensis*), which, apart from being as big as a lion, differed from the present-day species only in some minor features of skull and dentition.

During the Middle and Late Pleistocene, the Northern Hemisphere went through a series of glaciations, which, in central Europe, have been given the names of four German rivers: Günz, Mindel, Riss, and Würm (the alphabetical order indicates the chronological sequence). The warm intervals between the main glaciations are known as the Cromer (Günz-Mindel), Holstein (Mindel-Riss), and Eem (Riss-Würm) interglacials. For most of what is popularly referred to as the "Ice Age," Europe was inhabited by cave lions and leopards, China by giant tigers, and North America by giant jaguars. The Issoire lynx held out until the Mid-Pleistocene, while the earliest records of the northern lynx have come from the last or Eemian Interglacial.

There were, of course, a lot more chances for the robust skeletal remains of big cats to be preserved than for the delicate bones of the small ones. We do know that in the European Villafranchian there existed a species, Martelli's wildcat (*Felis lunensis*), of about the same size as the modern wildcat, but its fossil record is exceedingly scanty. It may have survived into the Mid-Pleistocene, where it could have merged into the wildcat, which has certainly been present since the Holstein Interglacial, perhaps even since the Cromer Interglacial. The wildcat was common during the Würm Glaciation, its remains being very well represented in cave deposits of that period. Pallas's cat, now restricted to Central Asia, temporarily spread into Europe during the last glaciation and has been recorded from the famous sites of Schweizersbild and Kesslerloch. A find from Eemian deposits at Untertürkheim near Stuttgart has been somewhat doubtfully referred to as the jungle cat. The jaws of a big felid brought to light from Mid-Pleistocene Bed II of Olduvai Gorge in Tanzania has been described as looking more like that of a tiger than a lion. The tiger, as we know it today, is thought to have originated in northeastern Asia, and it seems unlikely that it should ever have reached East Africa, especially as it apparently began to expand its area of distribution fairly late, at a time when the island of Ceylon was already separated from the Indian mainland. The jaw could, however, have belonged to a species ancestral to both tiger and lion combining the characteristics of both.

In the course of time, the cat family has spread out over Eurasia, Africa, and the whole of America. As far as we know, Africa was penetrated during the Miocene Period, South America during the Pleistocene. Felids other than domestic cats are absent from the West Indies, from Greenland, Iceland, the Falkland Islands, and Madagascar, from New Guinea, Australia, New Zealand, and, of course, Antarctica. They have established themselves on Sumatra, Nias, Java, the Kangean Islands, and Bali, but not on Lombok or any other of the Lesser Sunda Islands. There are cats on Borneo, but not on Celebes or the Moluccas. They occur on Palawan in the Philippines, Formosa (Taiwan), and Sakhalin, but not on the Japanese islands, with the exception of Iriomote at the southwestern end of the Ryukyu Archipelago.

Wildcat
Felis silvestris
(SCHREBER 1777)

The eighteenth century was an age of flowery prose, and when Thomas Pennant wrote his *Tour of Scotland and Voyage to the Hebrides,* he referred to the wildcat: "This animal may be called the British Tiger; it is the fiercest and most destructive beast we have, making dreadful havocke among our poultry, lambs and kids." Pennant did no more than express the general opinion of his time, an opinion that was to endure for another 150 years and help to lead to the extinction of the wildcat in many parts of its area of distribution. Today we know this attractive creature—which Frances Pitt has called a "Highland Gentleman"—somewhat better and we realize that its "dreadful havocke" is mainly confined to the mice and voles against which we humans have long been waging a tiresome and costly war. If, instead of declaring it as "vermin," we had protected the wildcat, it would have fought a considerable part of this war for us!

The wildcat has been a problem animal not only to landowners and gamekeepers, who did their very best to get rid of it once and for all, but also to zoologists interested in its taxonomy and its relationship to other cats. In the tenth edition of his *Systema Naturae,* published in 1758, Linnaeus included the "Cat" under the scientific designation of *Felis catus.* Considering the domestic cat as a direct descendant of the European wildcat, a species which did not occur in his Swedish homeland, he simply based his description of the "Cat" on an ordinary tabby—probably his own. A few years later, however, the German naturalist Schreber produced a *Natural History of Mammals* which was issued in parts; with wildcats available in Germany, a plate illustrating this species was printed in 1775, bearing the caption *"Felis catus Linn. ferus."* The text to go with it appeared in print in 1777, and it looks as if Schreber had meanwhile given the matter of the wildcat's correct scientific name some thought, for he dropped *"Felis catus ferus"* in favour of *Felis silvestris,* the forest cat.

Thus it came about that zoologists of a later age, when taxonomy had evolved into something like a fine art with as rigorous a set of rules as chess, found themselves with three names to choose from for the European wildcat. The one given by Linnaeus (*Felis catus*) could be discarded at once, for it was based on the domestic cat, which had long since been found to have descended not from the

European wildcat, but from the wildcat of Egypt, named *Felis lybica* by Forster in his German translation of Buffon's *Natural History*. But what of those two names of Schreber's? According to the rules of nomenclature, the Linnaean or earliest post-Linnaean name given to a species should be awarded priority, which in this case would be *Felis catus ferus* (or rather, *Felis ferus*). Some authors have, in fact, used this name, but the great majority retained *Felis silvestris,* particularly as, for quite a long time, there were doubts as to whether the caption of Schreber's plate had actually antedated the text referring to it.

With a steadily increasing number of hunters and collectors sending in specimens from all over Asia and Africa, other wildcats were described and named by taxonomists working in the museums of Europe and America. To the Egyptian wildcat of Forster there were added *Felis ocreata* from Abyssinia, *Felis caffer* from the Cape of Good Hope, *Felis ornata* from India, *Felis caudatus* from Russian Asia, and a great many more. Some of these species were divided into subspecies, and the taxonomy of wildcats eventually drifted into a state of utter chaos. Gradually, however, it was realized that most of the wildcat species described since the publication of Schreber's *Natural History of Mammals* were closely related to the European wildcat—so closely, in fact, that there was no justification for regarding them as distinct species. In 1951 R. I. Pocock of the British Museum issued a *Catalogue of the Genus* Felis in which he regarded *Felis silvestris* as a species with forty subspecies, distributed over Europe, Africa, and most of Asia. The main ancestor of the domestic cat thus became *Felis silvestris lybica,* and the other African and Asiatic "species" mentioned above were renamed *Felis silvestris ocreata, Felis silvestris caffer, Felis silvestris ornata,* and *Felis silvestris caudata.* A few years later, Dr. Th. Haltenorth of Munich reduced the number of subspecies to twenty-one, at the same time hinting at the possibility that some of these might eventually also prove to have very little validity. It has now become customary to deal with the wildcat, *Felis silvestris,* under three main types: the European forest wildcat (*Felis silvestris silvestris*), the African wildcat (*Felis silvestris lybica*), and the Asiatic steppe or desert wildcat (*Felis silvestris ornata*).

Once the specific identity of the European forest wildcat and the African wildcat had been recognized, there were suggestions that the name *Felis catus* of Linnaeus ought now to be given priority over *Felis silvestris* of Schreber. There are, however, good reasons for not applying a name given to a domestic animal to its wild ancestor, and it has therefore been decided to restrict the use of *Felis catus* to the "Tiger of the Hearth" in all its colour phases.

Forest Wildcat
Felis silvestris silvestris
(SCHREBER 1777)
and related subspecies (*grampia, caucasica*, etc.)

Characteristics. About a third larger than a domestic cat, the forest wildcat is also more sturdily built, with longer legs, a broader head, and a relatively shorter tail which in adult individuals does not taper to a point but ends bluntly, as if the tip had been chopped off. The ground colour of the dense, long-haired fur is yellowish grey, darker and more greyish on the back, more yellowish, almost cream, on the underside. The throat is whitish. Four or five longitudinal stripes run from the forehead to the nape, merging into a more or less distinct dorsal line which ends at the root or on the upper side of the tail. From this dorsal line, a number of transverse bars run down to the belly. The tail has several dark encircling marks, of which only the last two or three are real rings. Its tip is blackish. The legs are transversely striped, and there is a round black spot at the base of the fifth toe of the hind foot, about 2 cm (0.79 in) in diameter. The nose is always flesh-coloured. There are thirty teeth. The female has eight teats.

Young individuals are much more distinctly marked than adults and have a tapering tail. Between the ages of three and ten months they are easily mistaken for domestic cats, but even in adults the differences are not as clear-cut as might be expected. Early records of wildcats from the Bernese and Pennine Alps of Switzerland, for instance, are now definitely known to have been based on feral domestic cats. There have been many suggestions as to how the two could be distinguished with absolute certainty, but so far none has proved infallible. Paul Schauenberg of Geneva has recently pointed out that a capacity of the brain-case of over 35 cm^3 (14 in^3) indicates a wildcat, of under 32 cm^3 (13 in^3) a domestic cat. For skulls with a brain capacity of between 32 and 35 cm^3 (avg. 14 in^3) he has come up with a craniometrical index which is obtained by dividing the total length of the skull by the capacity of the brain-case. It reads lower than 2.75 in wildcats and higher than this figure in domestic cats.

Measurements. In 102 male Scottish wildcats (*Felis silvestris grampia*) the head and body length varied from 36.5 cm to 65.3 cm (avg. 58.9 cm or 23 in); the tail 21 to 34.2 cm (avg. 31.5 cm or 12 in). Five females had a head and body length of 54.5 to 58.4 cm (avg. 57.1 cm or 22 in.); tail, 29.3 to 33.1 cm (avg. 31.1 cm or 12 in). For the Caucasian wildcat (*Felis silvestris caucasica*), G. A. Novikov gives the head and body length of males as 63 to 75 cm (avg. 27 in); tail, 30 to 34 cm (avg. 12 in). The head and body length of females was 58 to 63 cm (avg. 24 in); tail, 27 to 33 cm (avg. 12 in). The weights of 102 Scottish male wildcats varied from 3 to 6.9 kg (avg. 5.1 kg or 11 lb), of eleven females from 3.2 to 4.5 kg (avg. 4 kg or 9 lb). Caucasian male wildcats are reported to weigh approximately 6 kg (14 lb), females 4 to 5 kg (avg. 10 lb). Some authors have accepted male weights up to 10 (23 lb) and even, in Czechoslovakia, 14.8 kg (33 lb). B. Condé and Schauenberg weighed 177 forest wildcats from France (106 males and 71 females) and obtained an average of about 5 kg (11 lb) for males (with a maximum of 7.7 kg [17 lb]) and of 3.5 kg (8 lb) for females. This result made them doubtful about any report of weights of males over 8 kg (18 lb) and of females over 6 kg (13 lb). In the course of their work with wildcats, Condé and Schauenberg observed daily and seasonal weight fluctuations which in males ranged from 100 to 400 g (avg. 14 oz) and from 1.10 to 2.50 kg (avg. 4 lb) respectively. Heaviest male weights were recorded from September to the end of February. The seasonal variations in females, ranging from 250 g (9 oz) to 2.15 kg (5 lb) were found to be more complex than in males.

Distribution.   At one time, the forest wildcat was found all over England and Scotland, but there seems to be no evidence for its occurrence in Ireland. By the middle of the last century, its extermination south of the Tweed River was practically complete, and it did not take long for the last few individuals lingering in the Welsh mountains and in the Lake District to be accounted for. At the turn of the century the species had become very rare in Scotland, but it made a spectacular comeback when its main enemies, the gamekeepers, were occupied elsewhere during the First World War. With a more enlightened attitude toward so-called "vermin" during the 1920s and 1930s, the wildcat of Scotland managed to maintain this recovery. At the beginning of the 1960s, it was reported as well established in the counties of Ross and Cromarty, Inverness-shire, Moray, Banff, West Aberdeenshire, Argyllshire, and Perth, increasing in Nairn and spreading into Angus, but still uncommon in Caithness and Sutherland.

In Germany the forest wildcat was officially declared as "vermin" in 1848, and within a short time it became extinct in Pomerania,

Württemberg, Baden, and Saxony, where the last one was killed as early as 1850. Hanging on precariously in a few restricted areas, its numbers increased after the Second World War and it is now not uncommon in the Eifel and in the Rhenish Palatinate, in the Weser Bergland, as well as in the forested mountain regions of Hunstük, Taunus, Rhön, Westerwald, Harz, and Thüringerwald. There are no reliable records of its occurrence in the Swiss Alps, nor have any remains of forest wildcats ever been found in alpine caves. The species used to be common on the Central Plateau and especially in the forests of the Jura Mountains, but in Switzerland, too, it was exterminated speedily and efficiently. Odd individuals, however, keep turning up in the Jura forests, most probably migrants from across the French border. Two animals shot in 1969 and 1970 as feral domestic cats at La Moutoie and Bavelier were definitely identified as wildcats at the Berne Natural History Museum.

Wildcats still occur in Spain and Portugal, in France (eastern Pyrenees, Orleans, Ardennes, Champagne, Lorraine, Vosges), Belgium (Ardennes), Italy, Greece, Yugoslavia, Austria (Carinthia, Styria), Czechoslovakia, and Poland. The species once also inhabited southern Sweden, large parts of north-western Russia, and the southern parts of the Ural Mountains, but it was driven out of these regions by a deterioration of climatic conditions which set in about 800 B.C. and continued into early medieval times. In Russia it is at present common in the Caucasus, Lesser Caucasus, and Talysh, while smaller numbers are found in the Dniester region of Odessa, the Vinnitsa and Carpathian regions of the Ukraine, and in the Moldavian forests along the Rivers Prut and Dniester.

Habits. The Scottish wildcat is encountered not only in woodlands, but also in treeless though usually rocky mountain terrain. On the European Continent, extensive and varied forests with plenty of undergrowth, rocky outcrops, and small clearings are the forest wildcat's main habitat. Being highly adaptable, it often visits other types of country, such as more open forests, heaths, moors, marshlands, and it may even settle there if it finds conditions suitable. In southern Europe it is often found in the scrubby type of bush known as *macchia*. In Germany and adjoining countries the wildcat favours coniferous forests, while in the Caucasus it prefers the broad-leaved forest zone.

It is mainly active in the evening and early morning, often taking a rest in the middle of the night. Wildcats occasionally move about in daytime, and they certainly like to sun themselves on a branch or on a secluded boulder. This urge to soak up warmth may support the theory that the forest wildcat's ancestors originally came from the south, invaded Europe a long time ago and adapted themselves successfully to life in a climate much harsher than that of their ancient homeland. Each individual occupies a well-defined home range or territory, which has been estimated to cover about fifty hectares (or 128 acres) in the Carpathian forests, but varies considerably in accordance with local conditions. The male defends this territory against other toms, but does not hesitate to pass far beyond its boundaries when forced to do so by shortage of prey or in order to find a female at mating time. Within its home range, an animal has several dens and resting places, a system of regularly used tracks, and a number of trees against which it stands up to scratch the bark—a gesture usually referred to as "sharpening the claws," which may also be a way of placing territorial markings. The forest wildcat climbs with great agility and takes to a tree when pursued, but it usually comes down the trunk backward, not head-first, an indication that it is not a truly arboreal animal, such as the marten or the squirrel.

In Scotland, mating takes place during the first half of March, in Germany during February and March, somewhat earlier in the pleasantly mild climate of the Rhineland than under the harsher conditions prevailing on the Harz Mountains. The wildcats of the Caucasus, too, mate in February and March. The courtship is a very rowdy affair, accompanied by a lot of mewing, screeching, and caterwauling. Several toms may sit for hours around a female, howling almost incessantly, trying to approach her one after the other, only to be greeted with vicious hisses and discordant yells. The rival suitors often fight violent battles. The female eventually signifies her readiness by rolling around on the ground, and then she crouches down so as to let the favoured tom stand over her. At the moment of mating he bites the back of her neck. The act is of very short duration and is repeated many times in succession.

In the presence of males the female oestrus lasts from two to five, six, or, exceptionally, eight days. The period of gestation has been found to average sixty-six days, with a minimum of sixty-three and a maximum of sixty-nine and a half days. It is somewhat longer than the gestation of the domestic cat, which is given as fifty-eight days by some authors and as sixty-three by others. The three to four (mostly two or three) kittens are born in a hollow tree, a rock cave, in the abandoned hole of a fox or badger. The sex ratio seems to be roughly equal at birth, with just a slight bias toward males. Newborn kittens weigh about 40 g (1.5 oz) and their eyes remain closed for nine to ten days. Lactation lasts about a month. When the kittens have reached an age of four to five weeks, they come out of the den and play around in the open, with the mother frequently joining them in their games or bringing them toys in the shape of live prey. At about twelve weeks they begin to accompany the mother on her hunting trips. She now teaches them to make use of what they learned in play. They quickly become expert stalkers, and the family probably breaks up when they are about five months old.

The mortality rate among kittens is high, with most deaths occurring between the second and fourth months. Young males show the first signs of sexual activity within nine or ten months, while females are able to reproduce at an age of about one year. Toms have always been assumed not to take an active part in rearing the young, and this has now been fully confirmed by Condé and Schauenberg, who observed great numbers of captive wildcats under conditions devised to simulate life in the wild. Most authors state categorically that the female produces only one litter a year, but there have been recurrent rumours of an occasional second litter. As the normal period of sexual activity in males has been found to range from the end of December to the end of June, Condé and Schauenberg do not consider it as altogether impossible for a female to breed twice in the same year.

The dominance of small rodents among the forest wildcat's prey is well exemplified by the stomach contents of twenty-eight eastern Carpathian specimens examined by Waldemar Lindemann: mice and dormice, 65%; squirrels, susliks, and other medium-sized rodents, 12%; hares and rabbits, 5%; roe-deer fawns, 1%; caper-caillie, black cock, hazel-hen, and other game-birds, 8%; small birds (up to the size of a jay), 6%; unidentified, 3%. There are regions where mice and voles make up almost 100% of the prey. Detlev Müller-Using, the game biologist, once took six voles from a single stomach, and a wildcat shot in the Jura Mountains in 1935 was found to have eaten at least ten voles. There is another older and often quoted Swiss record of twenty-six mice taken from the stomach of a wildcat. In Scotland, small rodents and birds make up the bulk of the prey, even though a certain number of mountain hares, rabbits, and grouse are taken, as well as the odd roe-deer fawn or wild grown lamb. Individuals that kill larger animals are usually specialists—somewhat like the man-eaters among the big cats—and should not be allowed to give the species as a whole a bad name.

Forest wildcats stalk their prey, approaching under cover until they can reach their victim in a couple of bounds and grab it by the neck. This method of hunting was well described to J. G. Millais, the naturalist painter, by John Ross, deer-stalker on Lord Lovat's estate:

I was looking over my beat to see what deer were on the ground, when I saw the sun shining on something brown on the open hillside about three-hundred yards below me by the edge of a clump of bracken. . . . I sat down and put the glass on it, and saw that it was a large wildcat. At first it kept slowly moving along the edge of the ferns, but just inside, and when he crossed the least open space he took two or three paces, just as a tame cat does in stalking a sparrow. . . . By and by a rabbit came out into the open about three hundred yards ahead of the cat, and commenced feeding. As the cat advanced nearer and nearer, the rabbit kept moving out to where the grass was better, and each time he ran, the cat made a little run too, . . . As both animals were now within the field of my glass, I could watch the action of both. All of a sudden, the rabbit, which was perhaps twenty yards out in the open, dropped his ears, half squatted, and then began running aimlessly in circles. I could not hear his screams of fear, but could distinctly see his mouth open, and that he was calling in terror. The same moment, the wildcat, with all his hair bristling, burst from the ferns, and making three or four tremendous bounds four or five feet into the air, and going at a great speed, sprang on the back of the rabbit, who seemed paralised and unable to move further.

On another occasion, a wildcat was seen to pounce in quick succession on three blue hares feeding on a mountain slope. After the first one had been killed, the other two simply sat and waited to be slaughtered in their turn.

Apart from man, the most dangerous enemy of the forest wildcat must be the lynx, which is said to hunt and kill it whenever it has a chance. Schauenberg could not find any evidence of foxes ever preying on it. A vixen, however, was once seen fighting hard to keep off a wildcat that was trying to enter a den where she had her cubs. Eagle owls and eagles will sometimes attack a cat, but there are at least two reliable records of golden eagles having come to grief on such occasions. Seton Gordon, the animal photographer, was told of a wildcat that managed to extricate itself from the claws of an eagle, doing so much damage in the process that the bird was found dead a short time later. Sir P. Christison saw an eagle swoop down and settle close to the place where a wildcat was devouring a variable hare. As the cat had no intention of giving up its prey, it went for the marauder. There was a terrific battle, which ended with the eagle's flying up, carrying the cat. When the bird had reached an altitude of 1500 to 2000 feet, Christison saw the cat get loose and fall to its death. On the following day he found the badly wounded eagle about three miles away.

When cornered, the forest wildcat certainly defends itself most gallantly, and there are reliable accounts of men and dogs having been badly clawed. Fighting at close quarters, a wildcat will throw itself on its back and fend off an attacker with all four of its sharply clawed paws.

Even in the depth of the coldest winter it is very rare for a forest wildcat to take shelter within a building. As a rule, this animal shuns man and all his works and keeps as far away from civilization as possible. In captivity, it has proved to be quite untameable. Frances Pitt the well-known naturalist was fully convinced that any wild creature, if caught young enough, would eventually become friendly with those who cared for it. She obtained a half-grown female wildcat from Scotland, but soon had to admit: "Her pale green eyes glared hatred at human beings, and all attempts to establish friendly relations with her failed. She grew less afraid, but as her timidity departed, her savagery increased." Thinking that the animal might have been too old, she repeated the experiment with a very young tom, which she named "Satan." "He was but a wee scrap of yellow-grey tabby fur, as small a kitten as I could desire, but his name was bestowed on sight and never changed. It remained appropriate until the day, six years and nine months later, when an epidemic of 'cat influenza' claimed him. Yet, though there was no reason to change his designation, I believe that Satan became more nearly tame than any previous wild cat." Frances Pitt could only handle him as long as he was weak and small. He grew fast, and with increasing strength he fought like a fury, going into paroxysms of spitting and scratching when she tried to pick him up. He learned to know the members of the family and the staff, came to the side of his cage to get food, and even took it from the hand, though spitting savagely all the time, and never really lost his fundamental ferocity. However, he was all gentleness and devotion to a domestic female kitten who had been put in with him to keep him company. The kittens produced by the pair had the appearance of typical wildcats. One of them, named the "Imp of Satan," followed Frances Pitt around like a dog. The hybrids mated among themselves, and of their offspring some had the characteristics of wildcats, while others looked like domestic cats.

African Wildcat
Felis silvestris lybica
(FORSTER 1780)
and related subspecies

Haltenorth has listed ten subspecies of *Felis silvestris* for Africa and the Near East, but these can be dealt with under the heading of *Felis silvestris lybica*.

Characteristics. The African wildcat is somewhat larger than a domestic cat, more sturdily built, and its coat varies from pale sandy through yellowish grey to greyish brown and dark grey. In many regions, two extreme types occur side by side, one greyish tan, the other iron or silvery-grey, and all possible transitions between the two can usually be encountered. The markings, which may be pale, almost invisible, or rich reddish brown, consist of some tabbylike lines on the face, spots on the fore-parts and on the lower chest, and wavy vertical stripes extending from the spine to the belly. The forelegs and the upper parts of the hind limbs are encircled by broad rings, more distinct than the markings on the body. In a specimen which I obtained from Athi River, near Nairobi, these rings were dark brown, almost black on the inside of the forelegs. The tail is long, thin, and tapering, with a black tip, two or three clearly defined rings, and usually with some more or less indistinct markings. The soles of the feet are black, the backs of the ears usually reddish brown, ochre, or sandy rufous, but they can also be grey, especially in Egyptian specimens. The darkest-coloured individuals are found in forest areas, the palest in semi-deserts.

Measurements. Shoulder height is 35.5 cm (14 in); head and body, 55 to 65 cm (avg. 23 in); tail, 30 to 35 cm (avg. 12 in); and the average weight is about 5.4 kg (12 lb), with the lightest individuals coming from Mauretania, the heaviest from Abyssinia.

Distribution. Cats of the *lybica* group are found in all parts of Africa, except in waterless deserts and in the depth of the equatorial forest belt. The wildcats of the Balearic Islands, Corsica, Sardinia, Sicily, and Crete are intermediate between the forest wildcat and the African wildcat, but more closely allied to the latter. Cats from Sardinia and Sicily (subspecies *sarda*) have been declared as identical to specimens from Morocco, Algeria, Tunisia, Cyrenaica, the Hoggar, Mountains in Algeria, and Tassili-n-Ajjer. They can therefore be considered as definitely belonging to the *lybica* group. The wildcats of Palestine and Arabia (subspecies *iraki*) connect the *lybica* group with the Asiatic steppe wildcats and the Caucasian forest wildcats.

Habits. The African wildcat can be said to thrive in almost any type of country, level or mountainous, open or wooded. In what used to be British Cameroon, it has been reported in secondary and high deciduous forest. In East Africa it occurs wherever there is plenty of cover, be it bush, long grass, or rock. In South Africa it often lurks in reed beds. It is by no means a rare animal, but being solitary and mainly nocturnal in its habits, it is rarely seen. It usually spends the day in a hollow tree, a thicket, or a rock crevice, but will occasionally hunt during the day in cool, cloudy, weather. In almost thirty years of African travel I have only three times had glimpses of wildcats in broad daylight, and one of them was accidentally flushed by a serval I was taking pictures of. However, driving around at night in an area of bush and native plantations on the lower slopes of Mount Kenya, I have seen a good number in just a few nights.

The African wildcat is probably capable of overpowering young dik-diks and duikers, but it feeds mainly on small mammals, especially rodents and hares, also on snakes, lizards, large insects, and on birds up to the size of a guinea fowl. Examining several stomachs at Batinah in Oman during a drought, when there was a scarcity of rodents, David L. Harrison found them to contain scarabid and tenebrionid beetles, grasshoppers, and crickets, the remains of a lizard, some mammalian fur, and a date stone.

The animal utters a rather harsh "mwa, mwa," and at mating time there is a lot of screeching and yowling. The gestation period ranges from fifty-six to sixty days, and is thus closer to that of the domestic cat than to the forest wildcat. The litter consists of two to three, rarely four or five kittens.

Secretive and shy as the African wildcat may be, it nevertheless does not shun man as much as the forest wildcat and often lives close to villages and farms. Kittens are easily reared in captivity and become very docile. Describing the country south of the Bahr el Ghazal, George Schweinfurth, the botanist-explorer, wrote:

> One of the commonest animals hereabouts was the wildcat of the steppes. Although the natives do not breed them as domestic animals, yet they catch them separately when they are quite young and find no dif-

ficulties in reconciling them to a life about their huts and enclosures, where they grow up and wage their natural warfare against the rats. I procured several of these cats, which, after they had been kept tied up for several days, seemed to lose a considerable measure of their ferocity and to adapt themselves to an indoor existence so as to approach in many ways to the habits of the common cat. By night I attached them to my parcels, which were otherwise in jeopardy, and by this means I could go to bed without further fear of any depredation from the rats.

How different a story from what Frances Pitt and others have had to tell of their efforts to subdue to the forest wildcat! The cats of the *lybica* group must, in fact, be regarded as practically predestined to domestication, and it is mainly from the ancient wildcat populations of Palestine and Egypt that the ancestors of our domestic cats came. There is evidence of tabbies roaming the streets of Jericho in the late sixth and early fifth millennium B.C., and the archaeological site of Haçilar in Asia Minor, which dates back to the middle of the sixth millennium, has given us several small statues of women playing with cats. About 2000 B.C., the domestic cat made its appearance in Egypt.

Nobody seems to know just when it was introduced in Europe. Excavations in the Lake Dwellers' settlements of Switzerland and Germany have brought forth unquestionable remains of the forest wildcat, in such quantities that we must assume the animals to have been hunted for food, but no trace of the domestic race. It seems likely that the first Egyptian cats may have reached Greece and Rome around the beginning of the Christian Era. First kept as pets by the wealthy, they demonstrated their well-known independence by spreading out into the rural districts, where they soon replaced the semi-tame martens and weasels which had been tolerated around farms and homesteads in order to keep down mice and voles. Palladius, writing on agricultural topics in A.D. 350, referred to the cat as a widely distributed animal. Investigating a second- and third-century Roman settlement at Stillfried on the March in Austria, archaeologists unearthed bricks showing the footprints of a cat. The animal must have walked over the bricks when they were still soft and laid out to await burning, and in doing so it left the earliest record of the domestic cat's presence in central Europe.

Further progress across Europe seems to have been slow, for cats are said to have been quite rare in England up to the tenth century. We can, however, be sure that as long as forest wildcats were still common, they often mated with the village cats, infusing a considerable amount of their blood into the descendants of the Egyptian immigrants. It is interesting that the domestic cat retained not only its independence of character, but also its outward appearance and did not change as much as the dog, its age-old rival for human affection. A zoologically interested visitor from a faraway planet might at first find it difficult to accept a chihuahua, a poodle, and a St. Bernard as races of one and the same species, but a cat remains unmistakably a cat, whether it is a Siamese, a Persian, a Manx, or an ordinary tabby.

Asiatic Steppe Wildcat, Desert Cat
Felis silvestris ornata
(GRAY 1832)
and related subspecies (*caudata, chutuchta,* and *vellerosa*)

Characteristics. The typical Indian "desert cat" is not much bigger than a domestic cat, pale sandy, fulvescent, grey or isabelline in colour, with the pattern of transverse stripes so characteristic of the forest wildcat and the African wildcat mostly broken up into small round dots of brown, grey, or black. The long, thin, and tapering tail is spotted in its basal part, but ringed toward the black-tipped end. The soles of the feet are black. The desert cat of the southern Gobi (subspecies *chutuchta*) has the stripes unbroken while the Ordos cat (subspecies *vellerosa*) from southeastern Mongolis is quite unmarked and almost as long-haired as an Angora cat.

Measurements. In Indian specimens (typical *ornata*), the head and body length varies from 50 to 65 cm (avg. 23 in); tail, 25 to 30 cm (avg. 11 in); and weight, 3 to 4 kg (avg. 7 lb). Specimens from Turkmenistan and from the Caspian Sea attain a head and body length of from 55 to 63 (avg. 23 in) and even up to 70 cm (27 in); tail, 25 to 33 cm (avg. 11 in).

Distribution. Northwestern India, from the Punjab and Sind to Saugor and Nagpur, but not extending into the valley of the Ganges and rarely south of the Narbada River; westward through Baluchistan and southern Afghanistan to central and southern Iran, merging with the *lybica* group in southern Mesopotamia; northward through Turkmenistan and Kazakhstan, probably linking up with the forest wildcats of the Caucasian type in Azerbaijan and Armenia;

eastward through the Tarim and Lop Nor basin to Mongolia and north-western China.

Habits. In India the desert wildcat is most common on open, sandy plains, while in Kazakhstan it inhabits extensive clay valleys with lakes and isolated rows of sandy mounds, seeking shelter in the belts of bush and reeds fringing the bodies of water. Throughout the foothills of the Tien Shan Mountains it can be encountered in bushy areas and in the undergrowth of apple groves, but not above an elevation over 2000 m (6600 ft). The steppe wildcat occasionally establishes its den in hollow trees or in old buildings, more often in badgers' dens.

Along the Ili River of Kazakhstan, small mammals—muskrats, sand hares, gerbils, house mice, jerboas—have been found to make up 81% of the prey taken by the steppe wildcat. It also catches lizards, insects, and birds up to the size of pheasants, and has been recorded eating the berries of the Russian olive and of the nitre bush, a zygophyllaceous plant. In Central Asia, mating takes place toward the end of January or in February. The gestation period is about two months, and the litter consists of two to five kittens.

Sand-Dune Cat
Felis margarita
(LOCHE 1858)

When the French first explored the Ouargla Oasis of the northern Sahara in 1855 and 1856, Capitaine Victor Loche, attached to the expedition as a naturalist, collected a new species of cat at Ngouça (or Negoussa), which he later named *Felis margarita* after Commandant Margueritte, the leader of the party. In time, a few more specimens of what has become known as the sand-dune cat have been obtained, but it still is a rarity in zoological collections.

In 1927, S. I. Ognev, the Russian mammalogist, described, under the name *Eremaelurus thinobia,* a desert cat from Repetek in Turkmenistan which showed such a remarkable similarity to Loche's sand-dune cat that some taxonomists wondered whether the two might belong to the same species. Taking into consideration the enormous distance separating the two populations, however, this seemed most unlikely, and Pocock suggested that *Felis margarita* and *Eremaelurus thinobia* could well have originated separately from African and Asiatic wildcats and followed parallel lines of evolution in adapting to almost identical desert conditions. The problem was dramatically solved when Wilfred Thesiger, the British explorer, brought back from Ramlat al Ghafa, in the eastern part of the Rub' al Khali, the "Empty Quarter," the skin of a cat which closely resembled both the sand-dune cat of the Sahara and Ognev's Repetek cat. The skin unfortunately was not complete, but a few years later, in 1952, a specimen was caught alive on the southern edge of the Rub' al Khali and sent to the London Zoo, where it lived for seven years. It was unmistakably a sand-dune cat and, with an Arabian population linking the cats of Transcaspia and the Sahara, there was no reason not to consider them as conspecific. Ognev's name *"thinobia"* thus became a synonym for the earlier *margarita.* The species is regarded as closely related to the wildcat.

Characteristics. The sand-dune cat is small, with short limbs, large ears placed rather low on the head, and a broad face adorned with well-developed cheek whiskers. The pelage is soft and dense, mostly pale sandy to grey straw ochre in colour, slightly darker on the back, whitish on the belly. A fulvous reddish streak runs across each cheek from the outer corner of the eyes. The lower half of the face is whitish to pale ochre. The backs of the ears are rufous tawny, tipped with black. There are blackish bars on the limbs, but the stripes running down the flanks are indistinct and almost invisible. The tail is tipped black, with two or three subterminal rings. The soles of the feet are covered with dense mats of hairs, about 2 cm (0.8 in) in length, which completely hide the pads.

Measurements. Shoulder height is about 26 cm (10 in); head and body length, 45 to 57.2 cm (avg. 20 in); tail, 28 to 34.8 cm (avg. 12 in). Loche's type specimen had a head and body length of 45 cm (18 in); tail, 28 cm (11 in).

Distribution. In Africa the sand-dune cat has been recorded from various points in the northern Sahara, from Tassili-n-Ajjer, Air, and Senegal, doubtfully from western Egypt. As far as the Arabian peninsula is concerned, the species has so far been found in the Rub' al Khali and in eastern Saudi Arabia, but it may well be less rare in the great sand deserts of the interior than the small number of specimens would indicate. In Western Asia it occurs in the Kara Kum, Kizil Kum, and Patta Kum deserts (Turkmenistan, Uzbekistan, and Kazahkstan).

Habits. This beautiful little cat shows a definite preference for extremely arid terrain—for *ergs* (regions of shifting sand) in the Sahara, and for sand-dune regions overgrown with saxaul, sand acacias, saltwort, and other desert plants in Transcaspia. In Arabia, too, it seems mainly to inhabit sand-dune country, even though it has also been reported in rocky areas. It is wonderfully well adapted to life in deserts and semi-deserts. The thick padding of the soles facilitates progress over loose surfaces and may also give protection against the heat of rock and sand. Although mainly crepuscular and nocturnal in its habits, spending the hours of fiercely blazing sunshine in a shallow burrow dug into a dune or underneath some scrub, the sand-dune cat must, in an emergency, be able to run about without burning its feet.

It preys on jerboas, sand voles, and other rodents, occasionally on hares, birds, reptiles, and locusts. The low-set ears enable it to flatten itself in such a way that even the scantiest cover can be used. Inhabiting completely waterless regions, the sand-dune cat is apparently able to get along without drinking, as the body juices of its victims probably fully cover its own liquid requirements.

In Transcaspia, the kittens, two to four in number, are born from the first half of April onward. They are about 19 cm (10 in) long at birth, of which 5.8 (2 in) go to the tail. The family remains together until autumn, by which time the kittens are about two-thirds to three-fourths the adult size.

Venomous snakes, large birds of prey, and wolves are the sand-dune cat's main enemies.

Black-Footed Cat

Felis nigripes

(BURCHELL 1822)

The black-footed cat is something like a southern counterpart of the sand-dune cat, a species not far from *Felis silvestris*, but adapted to life in a fairly arid region, in this case the southern dry belt of Africa. It was made known to science by the great naturalist-explorer William Burchell, who obtained several skins at Litakun, not far from present-day Kuruman.

Characteristics. The black-footed cat is the smallest of African felines and can be considered as the smallest wild cat of the world. Its coat varies from dark ochre to pale ochre and sandy, somewhat darker on the back and lighter on the belly.

While the markings of other dry-country cats tend to be pale, sometimes almost invisible, the black-footed cat shows a bold pattern of rounded dark brown to black spots which are arranged in rows on the throat, chest, and belly. There are two streaks across each cheek, two transverse bars on the forelegs, and up to five on the haunches. The backs of the slightly rounded ears are pale brown. The soles of the feet are black. The tail is shortish—only about half the length of the head and body—thin, tapering to a point and tipped black, with two or three black sub-terminal rings, sometimes with a few incomplete rings on the basal part. The black-footed cats of the Karroo are larger, with darker ground colour and spots than the typical form, and have been named as a subspecies, *Felis nigripes thomasi*.

Measurements. Males: head and body length is 42.5 to 50 cm (avg. 18 in); tail, 15 to 20 cm (avg. 7 in). Females: head and body length is 33.7 to 36.8 cm (avg. 14 in); tail, 15.7 to 17 cm (avg. 6 in). Weight is 1.5 to 2.75 kg (avg. 4 lb).

Distribution. The black-footed cat ranges widely throughout Botswana, and its northern limit lies between latitudes 20° and 21° south. In South-West Africa, it is found about as far west as the railway linking Keetmanshoop with Windhoek, the westernmost record being from Quickborn near Okahandja. In the Great Karroo region of the Cape Province, the black-footed cat roams as far south as Fort Beaufort and the Albany District. Eastward it extends to

Griqualand West, part of the Orange Free State, Transvaal, and possibly into the southwestern corner of Rhodesia. It has been reported from Natal, but seems now to be extinct in that province. Its occurrence in the northern section of Kruger National Park has only been established fairly recently.

Habits. The black-footed cat favours dry country ranging from terrain of the Karroo and Kalahari sand-plains type to grassy savannahs. It hides in the burrows of jumping hares and other animals, sometimes in hollow termite hills, and most authors have described it as of mainly nocturnal habits. Park Ranger M. Rowland-Jones, however, reports that in Kruger National Park he often saw it out and about toward evening and early in the morning. In captivity it has been found to be more diurnal than most small cats.

Little is known of its feeding habits in the wild, but it probably preys on ground squirrels, small rodents, birds, and small reptiles. E. Cronje Wilmot, a careful observer of wildlife who was tsetse control officer in Ngamiland, published the following notes on this species:

> A most interesting but locally rather rare small wild feline is the Sebula-bulakwana or black-footed cat. This is the smallest of the African wild cats; but what it lacks in size is fully compensated for by its extreme ferocity. Though its weight is only about a quarter of that of a small sheep, this little feline readily attacks those animals. It fastens on the neck and hangs on until the jugular is pierced. This I have not seen myself, but have so frequently been told the same story by old reliable natives that I cannot doubt the assertion.

The black-footed cat certainly seems to have secured for itself a prominent place in native imagination, for Wilmot goes on, "All Masarwa Bushmen will tell you the absurd story that these little cats will fasten on the neck of a giraffe, just as they do with a sheep or a goat."

The two or three young are said to be usually reared at the bottom of a burrow, but two small kittens found by Rowland-Jones were placed, one under a bush, the other under a thick clump of malaha palms. The kittens spat, uttered plaintive mews, and took chickens and eggs at an early age. Paul Leyhausen has successfully bred and reared this species in captivity, thus adding greatly to our knowledge of its reproduction and habits. While female heat lasts for at least six days in domestic cats and some other species, with frequent matings for three or four days, the period of observed matings was only five to ten hours in the black-footed cat. Most felines tend to be decidedly solitary in their habits, but Leyhausen has described the black-footed cat as more unsociable than any other species he ever had under observation, with even the contact between the two sexes at mating time reduced to an absolute minimum.

The gestation period was found to last from fifty-nine to sixty-eight days, with a mean duration of sixty-three days. It is thus longer than that of the domestic cat and comes close to the gestation period of the forest wildcat. The kittens of three litters—numbering one, two, and two—left the nest twenty-eight to twenty-nine days after birth and took the first solid food when thirty-four to thirty-five days old. They caught their first mice within forty-three to forty-four days, and the permanent upper canines were present at ages ranging from 150 to 158 days. During the early stages of their development, the kittens were thus more advanced than domestic cats of the same age, but they only reached maturity within twenty-one months, which is about twice the normal span in the domestic species.

As soon as the kittens were able to run well, they did not, on being disturbed, dart back to the nest as young domestic cats invariably do. Instead, they displayed a marked tendency to scatter, running away from their mother and from each other to any cover they could find. Then they froze until the mother gave the all clear—a peculiar, almost noiseless staccato, accompanied by synchronous up-and-down movements of the half-flattened ears. On hearing the sound—which Leyhausen never heard in any other feline—the kittens relaxed and ran back to the mother.

The female began carrying prey to the nest a few days before the kittens showed any interest in it. When they were about five weeks old, she brought them live prey. She never injured the mouse nor did she coax the kittens by competing with them. She simply released her victim near the nest, and then sat down to watch. Whenever the rodent tried to escape, she used her paws to drive it back toward the kittens, but never grabbed it as a domestic cat would have done.

Leyhausen's black-footed cats were fed mostly with mice and chicks, sometimes with small rats and guinea pigs. They had a definite liking for insects and consumed amazing quantities of grass, going off their food whenever they did not get enough of it for a long period. They displayed considerable skill and persistence in digging, and Leyhausen suggests that they might dig small mammals out of their shallow burrows. The way captive individuals kept walking and trotting around for hours might be taken as an indication that they were used to covering large distances in their search for prey. Black-footed cats have been reliably reported to interbreed with caffer cats, the South African form of the African wildcat, and Leyhausen had no difficulty in mating his male with a domestic cat.

Pale or Chinese Desert Cat

Felis bieti

(MILNE EDWARDS 1892)

When Prince Henry d'Orleans attempted to cross Tibet at the head of a scientific expedition in 1889, he was stopped near the forbidden city of Lhasa and forced to turn east toward Szechwan. While strolling in the fur markets of Tatsienlu and Torgolo, his zoological collector picked up the first two skins of a feline that was to puzzle taxonomists until a skull became available for examination in 1925. Long thought to stand very near to the jungle cat, the species was eventually found to be allied to the wildcat, so closely, in fact, that the two easternmost forms of the latter, the Gobi cat (subspecies *chutuchta*) and the long-haired Ordos cat (subspecies *vellerosa*), were for some time regarded as identical with the Chinese desert cat.

Characteristics. The Chinese desert cat is fairly large, yellowish grey in colour, somewhat darker on the back, and with practically no markings on the flanks. There usually are two indistinct brownish streaks across each cheek, two or three washed-out, transverse bands on the outer side of the haunches, and a brownish cross-band on the inner side of the forearm. The ears are yellowish brown on the outside, with the tips adorned with short pencils of hairs about 2 cm (0.8 in) in length. The tail is tipped black and has three to four subterminal blackish rings on the basal portion. There are hairy pads on the soles of the feet, though much less developed than in the sand-dune cat.

Measurements. Head and body length is 68.5 to 84.0 cm (avg. 30 in); tail, 29 to 35 cm (avg. 12 in).

Distribution. Specimens of this cat have come from the Tatung Mountains of northwestern Kansu, from Minshan in southern and Kweito in western Kansu, from western Szechwan and from Sungpan in northern Szechwan. The species thus appears to be restricted to the border area between western China and eastern Tibet.

Habits. "Desert cat" is something of a misnomer, for this species has so far always been found in steppe country and on mountains covered with bush and forest. E. Weigold reported that his dog chased a Chinese desert cat at an altitude of 3000 m (9840 ft) east of Sungpan and got the worst of the encounter, coming back with two bites. The life history of this feline is still unknown.

Jungle Cat, Reed Cat

Felis (Chaus) chaus

(GÜLDENSTAEDT 1776)

Two different types of felines can easily be distinguished on the wall paintings of Egyptian monuments—the African wildcat, and the considerably larger species which we now know as the jungle or reed cat. Both of them played an important part in the ancient cults of the Nile Valley, and the reed cat was, in addition, trained for hunting wildfowl.

Zoologists have long regarded this species as closely allied to the lynxes, and while it has now definitely been included in the genus *Felis,* the various points in which it differs from the wildcat and its nearest relatives have been acknowledged by its being made the sole representative of the subgenus *Chaus.*

Characteristics. Larger than the forest wildcat, the jungle cat has long legs, a comparatively short tail, and small pencils of black hairs on its ears. The colour of its coat varies from sandy or yellowish grey to greyish brown and tawny red. Adults usually have no markings on the trunk, but there may be slight traces of transverse bands on the upper parts of the limbs. The backs of the ears are reddish, tipped black, without any trace of white spots or transverse bars. The black-tipped tail is more or less annulated and has an indistinct dorsal stripe. The kittens are striped black, but by the time they reach sexual maturity these markings have almost faded away. The first upper premolar is distinctly developed. F. W. Champion, of the British Indian Forest Service, records seeing a completely black specimen.

Measurements. Shoulder height is 35.5 to 38.10 cm (avg. 14 in). A head and body length of 60 cm (24 in) is usually given for the Indian jungle cat, with a tail length varying from 22.8 to 25.4 cm (avg. 9 in). A specimen obtained in Assam by E. P. Gee had a head and body length of 76.27 cm (30 in) and a tail length of 27.94 cm (11 in). According to Novikov, Central Asian specimens have a head and body length of 73 to 75 cm (avg. 29 in) and a tail length of 25 to 29 cm (avg. 11 in). Weight is 5 to 9 kg (avg. 16 lb) in India, up to 16 kg (36 lb), mostly less, in Central Asia.

Distribution. Lower Egypt, Israel, Jordan, Syria, Iraq, Iran, Asia Minor, eastern Transcaucasia; north along the western shoreline of the Caspian Sea to the lower reaches of the Volga, east through Turkmenistan, Tadzhikistan, and Kazakhstan to Chinese Turkestan; Afghanistan, Baluchistan, Nepal; south throughout the Indian Peninsula to Cape Comorin and Ceylon; also Burma, Siam, Indochina, and possibly Yunnan in western China.

Habits. In many parts of India the jungle cat can be considered as the most common of the small felines. It is found in woodlands, on open plains, in patches of long grass, in reed beds, corn-fields and sugar plantations, from sea-level to 2100 m (6900 ft) and 2400 m (7900 ft) in the Himalayas. It does not shun the vicinity of man and often prowls around in the immediate neighbourhood of villages. In Kashmir it has even been known to take shelter in buildings. In Iraq it is quite common in the tall reed beds fringing the river-banks, which it leaves to go hunting in the crop fields. It shows a preference for dense tamarisk jungles in the Jordan Valley and in Egypt keeps to low marshy ground, reed-beds, cane-fields, and other crops. In a letter to Thomas Pennant, the explorer Peter Simon Pallas wrote that he had found the "Chaus of Güldenstaedt" among the reeds about the Caspian Sea and Lake Aral. Güldenstaedt, who described and named the species, was a junior member of the expedition headed by Pallas from 1768 to 1774.

The jungle cat establishes its den in the disused burrow of a badger, fox, or porcupine, sometimes among reeds or under a bush. It does not restrict its activities to the night and can often be seen hunting in broad daylight. Riding on an elephant, F. W. Champion was sometimes able to approach a jungle cat closely and watch it creep through the long grass, searching for small mammals and birds.

Jungle cats usually move at a slow, careful, and noiseless trot, but can also move at great speed, bounding along at 23 km per hour (14 mph.). They have been seen to execute vertical jumps of an amazing height. Their prey consists mainly of hares and other small mammals, also of game-birds such as pheasants, francolins, and chukor. They are known to kill porcupines, and when hungry will readily take frogs and snakes. Droppings examined by George B. Schaller in Kanha National Park contained remains, of rats, mice, and lizards. The species is powerful enough to be considered as a potential predator on cheetal fawns. T. C. Jerdon, in his classic book on Indian mammals, gives a good indication of its speed, strength, and temerity: "Quite recently I shot a peafowl at the edge of a sugar cane field, when one of these cats sprang out, seized the peafowl, and after a short struggle (for the bird was not dead) carried it off before my astonished eyes and in spite of my running up, made good its escape with my booty." Jungle cats often make a nuisance of themselves by raiding poultry-yards. In Tadzhikistan they have been reported eating the fruits of the Russian olive.

In Russian Central Asia, mating takes place in February and March, accompanied by loud howls of the male. The kittens, three to five in number, are born in May after a gestation period of about sixty-six days, and are well hidden in a nest of dry reeds which may be lined with some fur. In Assam, three-week-old kittens have, however, been found at the end of January and beginning of February, and Schaller thought that congregations of jungle cats on open meadows, which he observed in Kanha National Park during the cool season, might have been part of their mating behaviour. Maturity is attained at the age of eighteen months. The species has often been said to breed twice a year, but so far there exists no definite proof for this assertion. Kittens become tame very quickly and purr like domestic cats. Their inborn savagery, however, comes out at feeding time, and they usually resent the approach of strangers.

Pallas's Cat, Manul
Felis (Otocolobus) manul
(PALLAS 1776)

Pallas's cat has various cranial features in common with the lynxes, and some zoologists therefore regard it as the sole representative of a separate genus *Otocolobus,* which they place close to the genus *Lynx.* Others point to similarities with the wildcats, especially the forest wildcat, and consider *Otocolobus* as a subgenus of *Felis.* It has been suggested that Pallas's cat may actually have evolved out of the wildcat in adaptation to the harsh living conditions predominating in its Central Asian habitats. As implied by its name, this cat was discovered by Peter Simon Pallas, the German naturalist who contributed so much to the scientific exploration of the Russian Empire.

Characteristics. The manul, only slightly larger than a domestic cat, has a massive body, which is carried on short stout legs. The head is short and broad, with very short, bluntly rounded ears, set low and wide apart, protrudingly only slightly from the surrounding fur. The eyes are big, directed straight forward, like an owl's, with pupils that appear spindle-shaped in outline rather than completely round. The cheeks are adorned with small side-whiskers. The coat is longer and more dense than in any other wild cat. Its general colour varies from light grey to yellowish buff and russet, the white tips of the hairs always producing a frosted, silvery appearance. Two dark streaks run obliquely across each cheek. Lips, chin, and throat are white. Traces of transverse stripes may be present on the back, especially on its posterior part, and on the limbs. The dark-tipped tail is encircled by four rings. Kittens have a thick woolly coat, but lack the frosting so characteristic of the adult specimens.

Measurements. Head and body length is 50 to 65 cm (avg. 22 in), tail 21 to 31 cm (avg. 10 in), weight 2.5 to 3.5 kg (avg. 7 lb).

Distribution. From Transcaucasia (one record only) and the eastern shoreline of the Caspian Sea through Turkmenistan, Uzbekistan, eastern and central Kazakhstan, Tibet, and Dzungaria to the Altai, Tuva, Transbaikalia, Mongolia, Kansu, and Szechwan, south to Iran, Afghanistan, and eastern Ladak. Early reports of its occurrence on the Astrakhan Steppe are now considered erroneous.

47

Habits. Within the manul's or Pallas's cat's area of distribution in Russian Asia, places of occurrence are often very far from each other, and there are many regions from which the species is absent or where it is at least extremely rare. It has been reported as common in Tuva, particularly on the southern slopes of the Tannu Ola and in the valley of the Tes-Khem River, also on the Chuya Steppe of Transbaikalia, from where, during the 1930s, about 100 to 150 skins per year reached the fur depots of Kosh-Achach. Pallas's cat is an inhabitant of steppes and deserts, especially of rocky plateaus and treeless, rocky, mountain-sides. It sometimes goes up to 3000 m (9800 ft), and it has been encountered at over 4000 m (13,000 ft) near Yamdok Lake in Ladak.

In the southern parts of the Altai it roams mostly along the rocky streams known locally as *kurumiks*. It is solitary and secretive, choosing as its den the burrows of marmots and other animals, a cave, a rock fissure, or a hollow under a stone slab. It usually emerges from its hiding place at dusk and hunts during the night, but can occasionally be encountered in daytime. In western Transbaikalia, the manul's prey was found to consist mostly of mouse hares or pikas (89%) and to a much lesser degree of murines (4%), ground squirrels, hares, insectivores, and birds. It hunts mainly by sight, and the position of its ears may, as in the sand-dune cat, be an adaptation to stalking in open country where there is very little cover, enabling the animal to peer over a stone, or a small scrubby bush, without displaying too much of its head.

S. U. Stroganov states that Pallas's cat does not hiss when irritated, but produces a shrill sound through almost closed lips. A scream reminiscent of both the barking of a small dog and the cry of an owl may possibly be its sexual call. Reproduction takes place during April and May in Transbaikalia, and captive specimens have produced litters of five to six kittens.

According to Stroganov, Pallas's cat remains wild and vicious in captivity, yet a specimen from Ladak kept by Colonel A. E. Ward became very tame, even though it always disliked strangers. There have been reports of Pallas's cat being kept in a semi-domestic state in various parts of Central Asia. "They differ in many ways from the domestic cat," Pallas wrote, "but they like to mate with him." He suggested that the manul might be the ancestor of the long-haired domestic races, such as the Angoras, and the black, blue, white, and red Persians. Modern zoologists tend to refute this idea, but nobody seems to have undertaken cross-breeding experiments in order to clear up the point once and for all.

Lynx
Lynx lynx
(LINNAEUS 1758)

The peoples of ancient Europe, living close to untamed nature, could not fail to be fascinated by the lynx, the big secretive cat that lurked in the mysterious depths of dark forests, from which it occasionally emerged to make its presence felt by a quick raid on their flocks of sheep and goats. In Teutonic and Scandinavian folk-lore, this bold freebooter was regarded as sacred to Freya, the goddess of love and beauty, and a couple of lynxes (not wildcats, as is often stated) were supposed to have drawn her chariot when she rode into battle. The authors of the Classical Age represented the lynx as sharing with Lyncaeus of Greek mythology the ability to see through stone walls.

Felis lynx was the name Linnaeus gave to the biggest European cat, but the lynx has since been found to differ so much from the wildcat and its cousins, that there is every justification for placing it in a separate genus. Some authors still speak of the lynxes of southern Europe and Canada as specifically different from the northern European lynx, but it seems much more reasonable to regard them as subspecies.

Characteristics. The lynx is a large, powerfully built cat with long sturdy legs, a very short tail, and triangular ears topped by tufts of black hairs about 4 cm (1.6 in) in length. Both sexes carry well-developed side-whiskers, which during winter can take on almost manelike proportions. The paws are large and furred so densely in winter that a remarkably efficient snow-shoe effect is created. There are only two premolars in the upper jaw, not three as in the wildcat, with a total of twenty-eight teeth.

The coat is yellowish brown, marked more or less distinctly with dark spots. Lynxes from the Iberian Peninsula, the Balkans, and Romania have the spots black and very well defined, but those from the Pyrenees and the Carpathian Mountains intergrade with the much more faintly spotted northern lynxes. The isabelline lynx of Tibet, Ladak, and Gilgit is indistinctly spotted on the lower parts and apparently quite unspotted in winter when the coat is thicker. North American specimens often have a hoary appearance, with the spots almost invisible.

49

Measurements. Northern lynx: shoulder height is 60 to 75 cm (avg. 27 in); head and body length, 80 to 130 cm (avg. 41 in); tail, 11 to 24.5 cm (avg. 7 in); weight, 18 to 38 kg (avg. 63 lb). Spanish lynx: shoulder height, 60 to 70 cm (avg. 25 in); head and body length, 85 to 110 cm (avg. 38 in); tail, 12.5 to 13 cm (avg. 5 in). Isabelline lynx: head and body length, 86.36 cm (34 in); tail, 20.3 cm (8 in).

Distribution. The lynx departed from Britain during the last glaciation, never to return. It may not have found the post-glacial Atlantic climate to its liking, for it failed really to establish itself anywhere in westernmost Europe. It has always been rare in the coastal areas of Norway, and in Denmark, where it certainly occurred during the Bronze Age, the lynx does not seem to have been present in historic times. Prehistoric remains of it are scarce in Belgium, and there is no indication of its ever having inhabited Holland. Otherwise, however, the distribution of the lynx once included all of Europe, from Scandinavia south to the Mediterranean, the Black Sea and the Caucasus, and eastward through the Russian forest belt to the Ural Mountains.

Considering that one modern author, Novikov, still refers to it as "undoubtedly a noxious predatory animal," we need not wonder that it gradually disappeared from most of its former haunts. Many governments encouraged its destruction by paying bounties, and during the last century the systematic extermination of the species was greatly speeded up through the rapid increase of human populations, the improvement of fire-arms, and the widespread cutting of forests. In France, for instance, where the eighteenth century had seen its disappearance from the Vosges Mountains and from the Alsace, the last lynx of the Jura was killed in 1845, the last one of the Massif Central in 1875. In the French Alps, a specimen was taken in 1909, and some were seen in 1913. The museum of Hyères has the skeleton of a female said to have been killed in the *département* of Basses-Alpes after 1912. The last unquestioned record for the French Pyrenees is of a lynx shot on Canigou in 1917. Sightings reported in 1957, 1960, and 1963 have met with doubt or open disbelief on the part of most authorities, even though with lynxes apparently still occurring on the Spanish side of the Pyrenees, the probability of one straying over the border does not seem to be so very remote.

As far as Italy is concerned, Professor Toschi has come to the conclusion that all the so-called lynxes of Sardinia, Sicily, and Calabria were nothing but wildcats, and he also considers reports from the Abruzzese as quite unsubstantiated. The lynx did, however, occur in the Italian Alps, especially in the Piedmont, and it was there, in the province of Cuneo, that the last Italian specimens were taken during the first two decades of this century. According to Toschi, there have been no reliable records after 1915. In western Germany, the species was exterminated during the first half of the last century, the last survivor probably being a lynx shot in 1850 on the Zipfelalp in Bavaria. From Eastern Prussia, however, reports of occasional appearances kept coming in during the 1920s and 1930s, and this led to an effort at reestablishing the species with the release of five specimens in 1940 and 1941. They seem to have done well, for in 1959 no less than twelve lynxes were said to be present around Allenstein in former Eastern Prussia.

A lynx presumed shot in the lower Engadine in 1872 has long been considered as the last of its kind reliably recorded in Switzerland, but Schauenberg accepts several later reports. One specimen was apparently taken on the Weisstorpass in the Pennine Alps on August 15, 1894, and the Geneva Museum has the skin of a very young lynx said to have been picked up near Brig in the Rhone Valley in 1902. Since the Second World War there have been various rumours of lynxes having strayed into Switzerland. No specimen was ever obtained, but some of the accounts, especially from the eastern parts of the country, of roe-deer and small stock killed by mysterious predators have the ring of truth and could well point to one or two of those feline raiders having sometimes crossed the Swiss border from Austria.

At present there are resident lynx populations in Spain, Portugal, Norway, Sweden, Finland, in the Baltic States, Poland, Czechoslovakia, Yugoslavia, Greece, Romania, and Russia. The species fortunately displays a high degree of biological dynamism, showing signs of recovery just as soon as human persecution is reduced or ceases altogether. The protection accorded to lynxes in Romania and Czechoslovakia in 1933 and 1934, respectively, brought an immediate response, and populations built up so well that shortly after the Second World War individuals began to migrate away from the Slovakian Carpathians, some of them appearing in central and southern Moravia, in Bohemia, Austria, and possibly Switzerland, others moving northwest through the Moravian Gate into the mountains of the Bohemian-Polish borderland and into Saxony, where the last "native" lynx had been shot in 1743. In 1964, the province of Slovakia had some 500 lynxes inhabiting about 1,371,000 hectares (3,386,000 acres) of forest. Increases in Sweden and Russia led to an influx into Finland, where the species had been practically exterminated. Were it not for the interference of man, the lynx would speedily reconquer most of the territory it has lost. This can be taken as a hopeful augury with regard to recent attempts to reintroduce it into areas from which it long ago disappeared. In Switzerland, for instance, two lynxes purchased from Czechoslovakia were released in 1970 in the canton of Obwalden, within the central part of the Alps.

From Asia Minor and Transcaucasia, the lynx extends south to Iran and to the Kurdish Mountains of northern Iraq. H. B. Tristram, who from 1858 to 1897 made a thorough study of Palestinian natural history, once saw a lynx and also obtained skins from natives who knew the species well. David L. Harrison thinks that it has now become extinct in that region due to the expanding human population and progressive deforestation. Eastward the lynx ranges throughout the Siberian forest belt to the island of Sakhalin, to Mongolia, Manchuria, and possibly northern China. It also occurs in Chinese Turkestan, in the mountain areas of Russian Central Asia, on the Kopet Dhag mountains of Turkmenistan, on the western Pamirs, in Tibet, Ladak, and Gilgit, down to about 1800 m (5900 ft) in the upper Indus Valley.

In North America it is found through Alaska and Canada to Newfoundland, north to the tree-line and south to the Great Lakes, to Pennsylvania in the east and through Oregon to Colorado and the Sierra Nevada in the west. In densely settled areas it has fared as badly as in Europe, and a lynx shot in the Adirondacks in 1952 was the first recorded for New York State in forty-five years.

Habits. Throughout the greater part of its vast area of distribution, the lynx shows a preference for old, high-timbered forests with dense undergrowth and windfalls. Like many other cats, however, it is adaptable enough to colonize a variety of other types of habitat. In the Coto Doñana of Spain, for instance, it has established itself very successfully in the fairly open forests of pines, junipers, and pistachio scrub covering old sand-dune areas, as well as in the almost impenetrable bush along the swamps. In Mongolia and the Gobi Altai, the lynx is a rock dweller, partial to places where stony outcrops alternate with shrubs. In the Altai it does not go much higher than the timber line at 1800 m (5900 ft) and is absent from the vast stretches of high mountain tundra. General Alexander A. A. Kinloch and other sportsmen, however, have encountered it when hunting yak and argali on the bleak and treeless uplands of Ladak and Tibet. "The Tartars have informed me that the lynx frequently killed sheep and goats," Kinloch reported, "and it is certainly armed quite formidable enough to do so. Hares, however, appear to be its favourite food, and as they literally swarm in some places, it can have no difficulty in killing them whenever it likes."

In the North American forests it is the varying hare, also known as the snow-shoe rabbit, that forms the main prey of the lynx. Mice are also taken, as well as grouse, ducks, stranded fish, young deer, and an occasional mountain sheep. Yet so dependent is the big cat on the hares, that its numbers increase and decrease with the regular fluctuations—caused by disease—of the snow-shoe rabbit population. Attention was first drawn to these cycles through the fur returns of the Hudson's Bay Company, which showed the numbers of lynx pelts to vary from about 2000 to 36,000 per annum, with 1831, 1839, 1859, 1868, 1878, 1888, 1897, 1906, and 1916 as years of especially great abundance. The intervals have been calculated to average out at 9.6 years, and it has been found—as was to be expected—that the peaks do not occur at the same time all over Canada. Although the greatest numbers of lynx pelts came in during years of maximum hare abundance, three or four years go by before a rapid decline sets in. In 1907, at a time when snow-shoe rabbits were at a minimum in Alaska, Charles Sheldon, the American sportsman-naturalist, found lynxes still common in the area of present-day Mount McKinley National Park, but they were mostly emaciated and in no condition to withstand the rigours of the northern winter. Some of them had taken to stalking and killing Dall sheep, but it seemed as if the majority would rather starve than turn to other prey, even though mice were extremely abundant.

In the Tatar region of Russian Asia, hares make up 66% of the food taken in winter, followed by murine rodents, water voles, and birds. In the Altai, however, the winter diet consists of 58.9% of roe-deer, followed by maral (Asiatic wapiti), 14.3%; musk-deer, 8.9%; blue hares, 7.1%; carrion, 5.3%; domestic sheep, 3.5%; and capercaillie, 2.0%. Roe-deer top the bill of fare in the Carpathians, and their populations have been noticed to decline sensibly in the presence of lynxes. Hares, chamois, marmots, and game-birds are frequently taken, with red deer and wild boar much more rarely except when young. Examining the stomachs of ninety-three lynxes from Bielowiesa and other parts of Poland, Lindemann was able to compile the following list of prey: hares and variable hares, 50%; game-birds, 15%; mice and other small rodents, 10%; roe-deer, 7%; other mammals (squirrels, marmots, martens, badgers, wildcats, foxes, dogs), 5%; unidentified, 2%. In the Coto Doñana, rabbits are the main prey, with red-legged partridges and fawns of red and fallow deer being taken fairly frequently. A lynx was seen to jump up and seize one of a covey of red-legged partridges passing overhead. The isabelline lynx, according to C. H. Stockley, will do the same, and sometimes strikes down three or four partridges as they rise.

The usual way a lynx makes a kill is by stalking as close as possible to the prospective victim and then to pounce on it in one or two bounds. It has been said to leap down occasionally from a branch onto a passing deer, elk, or musk-deer and to cling to the animal's back, inflicting fatal wounds. Some authors categorically deny the possibility of this ever happening. But why? It is always rash to state that an animal will never do that or always do this. A leopard sometimes kills by dropping on its prey from a tree, so why not a lynx when opportunity favours this kind of attack? As a rule, the lynx is definitely a lone hunter, but here again we must allow for exceptions. Dulkeit, a Russian observer, reported that two lynxes combined forces to kill a young maral stag near Lake Teletskoe. F. D. Shaposhnikov, as quoted by Stroganov, saw tracks of a pair of lynxes hunting a musk-deer, one moving higher up on the slope of the mountain and behind, while the second was lower down and in front. The frightened prey ended up between the two predators. Traders and Indians on the Yukon told Edward W. Nelson, at one time chief of the U.S. Biological Survey, of lynxes, presumably family parties, co-operating in regular rabbit drives during winter.

Few naturalists can have had better opportunities for observing the hunting habits of this secretive cat than Charles Sheldon did when he spent a whole winter in the Mount McKinley region. One day, while watching a group of twelve Dall rams, he suddenly caught sight of a lynx creeping up a rock, from where it closely observed the grazing sheep for about twenty minutes. When they moved on, it followed under cover of a ridge, its gait rapid and crouching, and every few feet the lynx rose to full height in order to look ahead. It finally crept up a rock near the top of the ridge, but when it lifted its head to peer over, the sheep had gone and the lynx gave up. On another occasion, Sheldon came across a young ram, about twenty months old and weighing 52 kg (117 lb), which had just been brought down by a lynx. One eye was bitten out and an ear torn off, but the animal was not dead yet, and Sheldon had to put it out of its misery before reconstructing the way the cat had attacked and overpowered its quarry. The tracks in the snow showed that the lynx had jumped on the sheep's back from a ledge jutting out over a gully, and the two animals had then slid and struggled three hundred feet down a gulch. The lynx was a male, weighing a mere 9.07 kg (20 lb), probably a half-starved animal. A few months later Sheldon found a second-year ewe, weighing between 59 and 68 kg (avg. 144 lb), that had become the victim of a lynx. In this case, the attacker had jumped down from a rock and landed on the sheep's back, fastening its teeth around the left eye. The animals then slid down about fifty yards, and during the ensuing struggle the cat apparently never left the ewe's back. In neither instance had the attacker tried to grab the neck or throat, as a leopard would have done, and, from the long and clumsy struggle necessary to subdue the victims, one imagines that these sturdy Dall sheep were just about the limit of what a lynx could tackle. Had there been a sufficiency of their usual prey—snow-shoe rabbits—they would most probably not have gone in for this type of big-game hunting.

The thick "galoshes" which come with its winter pelage give the lynx a decided advantage on snow with a crusty surface. This is a great hindrance to ungulates, for they keep breaking through and can only struggle along slowly and painfully, often injuring their legs in the process. Under conditions of this kind the biggest game animals are killed. On the Koksha River of Siberia, at a time when the depth of the crusted snow was 90 cm (35 in), Dulkeit came across an adult maral stag that had fallen a victim to lynxes, and he points out that such kills are by no means infrequent. The Siberian winter often creates conditions, however, under which the lynxes find their "snow-shoes" to be of little use, and they have a very marked tendency to avoid forest areas with an abundance of deep, loose snow. Heavy snow-falls may induce them to migrate to more suitable hunting grounds.

In western Siberia the home range of a lynx usually extends over 15 to 25 km² (avg. 8 mi²) and over about 30 km² (12 mi²) under favourable winter conditions. When prey becomes scarce, however, lynxes will stray beyond the borders of their territories and take to roaming far and wide in search of crop lands, where the murine population is higher than in forests, or move into the insular birch groves of the forest steppe. In February 1947 a Siberian lynx was trailed for a distance of no less than 36 km (22 mi) above the timberline from the valley of Lake Teletskoe through the valley of Bolshoi Abakan—and this was only part of its trek. Lynxes are good swimmers and will cross even broad rivers without hesitation. The individual home range naturally varies greatly in accordance with the availability of prey, and the "control" exercised by humans and wolves. In the Carpathian regions most densely populated by lynxes, each animal has a range of about 20 km² (8 mi²). In the forests of northern Russia, Finland, northern Sweden, and Norway, where game is scarce, a single lynx may occupy an area of some 60 to 100 km^2 (avg. 31 mi^2). The lynx territories of the Cota Doñana vary from 4 to 10 km (avg. 4 mi) in diameter in summer, but are somewhat more spacious in winter. A territory usually contains a number of scratching trees, and the owner also takes care regularly to mark certain places with its droppings and urine.

When the lynx population of an area reaches too high a level, some individuals will emigrate, as has been observed in central Europe during the years following the Second World War. The solitary wanderers are so secretive that they would hardly be noticed at all, if they did not leave a trail of kills, especially roe-deer, with perhaps the odd sheep or goat thrown in for good measure. Some lynxes may decapitate their prey, and roe-deer with their heads neatly severed from the body as if cut off with a knife are a good indication of the presence of one of these invisible raiders. The habit does not, however, seem to be so general as is often assumed, for Dr. Butenik, a Czech game biologist with a good knowledge of the lynx, has put it on record that neither he nor any of his Slovak friends have ever come across a decapitated roe.

A lynx hunts by eye and its sight is wonderfully acute. Waldemar Lindemann was able to prove experimentally that his tame lynx could see a mouse at 75 m (250 ft), a hare at 300 m (1000 ft), and a roe-deer at 500 m (1600 ft). The sense of hearing is certainly very well developed, but the sense of smell seems to play almost no part in finding prey. It probably is used mainly for identifying territorial markings and for finding a partner at mating time.

In southern Spain, mating is thought to take place mainly in January. In central Europe, Siberia, and Canada, the mating season falls into February and March, beginning about mid-February in the more northerly regions. Males and females can, during this period, be encountered far outside their usual haunts. Reporting on the reproductive habits of the Carpathian lynx, F. K. Werner states that strong males occupy definite mating territories and are sought out and visited by the females. The master of a mating site that Werner had under observation was an old and powerful male. Several females competed for his attentions, and they often belaboured each other with their claws. No other male dared approach the dominant tom. Some did turn up in the neighbourhood, but took care to keep several kilometres away and contented themselves with courting the females that had been chased away by the dominant male's jealous wives. However, a Russian observer, Yablonski, who studied lynxes in the forests of the Altai, was of the opinion that the males were chasing after the females, and Stroganov quotes him as writing: "I chanced to see five or six males courting one female in the taiga. Fierce fights may occur among the males for the possession of the female."

It is during the mating season that the lynx, usually a silent animal, is most often heard. The challenging cry of the male has been described as a muted, almost bearlike purr. The female's answering call is more of a vibrating whine, something like "e-e-e-eo-ooo-ooeee." Canoeing on an Ontario lake one night, the great pioneer animal photographer George Shiras suddenly spotted a catlike figure sitting upright on the bank, its greenish-yellow eyes glowing brightly in the beam of his jacklight. Shiras pointed his camera, closed his eyes tightly, and fired a magnesium flare. The animal jumped high in the air, and as it struck the ground again, it gave a piercing cry. The French Canadian guide sitting behind Shiras was emphatic that it could not possibly have been a lynx, for he had never before heard one give a howl of this kind. When Shiras developed the plate, there appeared a magnificent Canada lynx, its shape clearly mirrored in the lake—a picture which even now can be rated among the masterpieces of animal photography. The terrifying yell Shiras and his companion heard must have expressed either anger or fear.

The gestation period is of about nine to ten weeks' duration, and the two to three (more rarely one, four, or five) cubs, about 70 g (2 oz) in weight, are born in a natural cave, a badger's set, under an overhanging rock, or in a hollow underneath the gnarled roots of a mighty forest tree. They open their eyes on the sixteenth or seventeenth day. Lactation lasts for roughly five months, but the cubs begin to take meat from the thirtieth day onward. At the age of about forty days their hunting instincts awaken, and they playfully go through the motions of stalking and catching prey. Should there be a serious disturbance, the female will remove her offspring to another den. Soon the youngsters begin to go out hunting with their mother. C. H. Stockley was lucky enough once to come across a female with three cubs in the Hanle District of Ladak, at an altitude of about 5500 m (18,000 ft). "The woolly things played happily within a few yards of me," he writes, "while the mother stood anxiously watching about 60 yards away, occasionally making a mewing noise to call them to her. Eventually they joined her, and the family moved off together." The cubs remain with their mother until they are chased away by her suitors at the beginning of the next mating season. They usually stay together for some time longer, but the group gradually breaks up, each eventually going its own solitary way. Females attain sexual maturity at an age of twenty-one months, males only at thirty-three months.

The Augsburg Zoo had a lynx that lived to an age of at least seventeen years. The normal life-span in the wild is thought to be about thirteen to fourteen years. Apart from man, who in many parts of its range still kills it as a "noxious pest" or for its fur, the main enemy of the lynx is undoubtedly the wolf, for a marked increase in its numbers invariably brings about a rapid decline of the lynx population. When eastern Slovakia was invaded by wolves during the Second World War, the hitherto fairly numerous lynxes moved west and south, and they were noticed to disappear from the Levocskipohori Mountains just as soon as their enemies turned up in strength.

The lynx also gives way to the wolverine or glutton, as Charles Sheldon was able to observe in the Mount McKinley region. Watching a lynx feeding on the carcass of a Dall sheep it had killed two days earlier, he suddenly saw the cat rise and run uphill, apparently greatly alarmed. "At the same time," Sheldon reports, "we saw a wolverine running towards the dead sheep, thus explaining the sudden departure of the lynx—for evidently the relation of a lynx to a wolverine is one of fear. The wolverine leapt to the carcass and began vigorously tearing it and feeding on it." The lynx sat quietly two hundred yards away and made no effort to reclaim its kill.

Bobcat, Bay Lynx
Lynx rufus
(SCHREBER 1777)

Audubon called the animal now generally referred to as bobcat the common American "wildcat." This old name still persists in some parts of North America, often in a rather muddled context, for there are people who insist that bobcats inhabit the low hills, wildcats the mountains, while others use "bobcat" for males and "wildcat" for females. Another piece of "unnatural history" makes the bobcat out to be a cross between the Canada lynx and the domestic cat!

It has been suggested that the bobcat might be nothing but a southern form of the Canada lynx, as the Spanish lynx is of the northern European lynx. But from what we know of the Pleistocene history of the genus *Lynx*, the bobcat seems to have been present in North America long before the northern lynx crossed the Bering Strait and established itself in what is now Alaska and Canada. There is some overlap between the two species, but no cases of hybridization have ever been recorded. Along the southern shore of Lake Superior, especially around Marquette, Michigan, George Shiras noticed a definite tendency of the bobcat to move north and replace the intensively trapped Canada lynx. Up to 1900, he occasionally encountered a Canada lynx but never saw or heard of a bobcat in the area. Thirty years later, however, he was informed that from January 1, 1929, to September 1930, the county of Marquette had paid bounties on 151 bobcats and 13 lynxes.

Characteristics. In average size, the bobcat is smaller than the Canada lynx. The legs are more slender, the feet smaller, and the ears less conspicuously tufted, sometimes not tufted at all. The coat is less long, of various shades of buff and brown, spotted and lined with black and brownish black, and streaked black on the crown. The backs of the ears are heavily marked with black. The short tail is tipped black only on the upper side.

Measurements. Shoulder height is 45 to 58 cm (avg. 21 in); head and body length, 65 to 105 cm (avg. 33 in); tail, 11 to 19 cm (avg. 6 in). Weight is up to 14 kg (32 lb). Bobcats from different regions vary considerably in size, the smallest of the many subspecies being located in southwestern Mexico, the two largest in Nova Scotia

59

and the Rocky Mountains. The biggest bobcat on record, measured by William T. Hornaday, came from Montana. It stood 45.72 cm (18 in) at the shoulders; had a head and body length of 78.74 cm (31 in); tail, 17.78 cm (7 in); weight, 8.17 kg (18 lb).

Distribution. Throughout the United States, north to the Canadian border, crossing into British Columbia in the west and Nova Scotia in the east, and south into Mexico. The species has been exterminated in the most densely populated areas of some of the Eastern and midwestern states.

Habits. The bobcat is much more ubiquitous than the Canada lynx, inhabiting sage-brush country, semi-desert regions, bare mountain-sides, the dense tangles of West Coast chaparral, and woodlands of many types, including subtropical swamp forests and the heavy, humid forests of the Cascade Mountains. In the arid Southwest, it shows a preference for foot-hill bush, but is also quite abundant in open, barren, and rocky areas. Though mainly terrestrial, it climbs trees with ease and takes refuge among their branches when chased by dogs. It is shy and secretive, but more tolerant of man's presence than the lynx, and does not retreat from advancing civilization. It will, in fact, continue its nocturnal activities quite close to human settlements. Sometimes, especially in winter, it hunts during daytime, and in places where it feels safe it leaves its hiding place to sun itself.

The den is usually well concealed in a dense thicket, in a hollow tree or a rocky cavity, quite often in the middle of an almost impenetrable windfall. On the rocky Snake River Plain of southeastern Idaho, where Theodore N. Bailey made a three-year study of bobcats, home ranges were generally too large to be successfully defended. There was, in fact, a considerable degree of overlap, with marginal areas rarely occupied simultaneously by neighbouring animals. Territorial overlap was largest among males, who could range over up to 173.5 km² (67 mi²) of country. The females' territories, with an extent of only up to about 15.5 km² (6 mi²), were much better defined. A male territory could, however, embrace the ranges of several females. At a time of food scarcity in severe winter weather, Bailey once found two adult males and one female inhabiting for two weeks the same rock pile, but each animal had its own separate entrance and hunting area.

Droppings are often deposited on ant-hills, rocks, trails, small clearings, and other significant points. "A bobcat smelling fresh feces," Bailey observes, "apparently knew that the area had recently been visited and could change its movements to avoid an encounter. Females, especially those with young kittens, appeared to mark more intensely." Bailey found urine to be squirted on rocks, snowbanks, and bushes in the vicinity of the dens. Scrapes, too, seemed to serve as means of communication. The presence of small scent glands on each side of the anus makes it probable that scent markings permitting sexual or individual recognition are placed.

Hunting within its range, but without necessarily using every part of it, the bobcat preys mainly on small mammals: in New Mexico, for instance, on rabbits, kangaroo rats, pocket gophers, ground squirrels, and chipmunks, as well as on a large variety of mice and on whatever birds that can be caught. Stomachs examined by Oregon government hunters were found to contain the remains of red squirrels, snow-shoe rabbits, bush rabbits, deer, sheep, and blue grouse. Where the highly destructive jack-rabbits are common, they form the bobcat's favourite food. On the Snake River Plain, Bailey recorded jack-rabbits and cotton-tails to constitute 90% of the prey. Cotton-tails are rather slow, tending to freeze rather than run and preferring rocky, broken habitats where they can easily be stalked, and bobcats catch them with greater facility than the more numerous, but very much swifter, jack-rabbits. On nearby mountain slopes, where rabbits and hares were less common, the bobcat preyed more heavily upon rodents and birds. Foxes, turtles, crayfish, and frogs have also been recorded among the bobcat's prey. Deer are mainly killed in winter when in poor condition. Of twenty-six deer kills examined by Bailey, twenty-three had been eaten as carrion. He could find no remains of sheep in three hundred bobcats' stomachs and feces. Many of the rodents on the bobcat's bill of fare are known carriers of plague and other diseases, and even though the odd individual may make a nuisance of itself by raiding chicken runs or killing a lamb, the species should be given full credit for keeping down these dangerous pests.

Hunting takes place on the ground and in stalking its victims, the bobcat displays great stealth and patience. Edmund C. Jaeger, the well-known American desert specialist, once watched a female catch a gopher.

> I first saw her some distance ahead, lying prone on a slight rise of the ground. I stopped and noted that she was looking intently at a pile of loose earth before her. Not long afterwards she rose in an expectant and tense springing position. It was evident that she saw the gopher coming up to the entrance of the hole with a load of loose earth. A moment later

she leapt forward, thrust her right paw into the burrow and adroitly brought out and pounced upon her prey. Then she bit it several times and carried it off, probably to her kittens.

Bailey once saw an old female that was stalking along a ridge from which she could see a considerable distance, when suddenly she changed her direction and carefully approached the well-worn path of a jack-rabbit. She then went into ambush behind a sage-brush and leaped on the first rabbit that came within six feet of her.

Mating can occur from February to June and is about the only occasion in which males and females are found to associate. Camping among some mesquite thickets during late April, Jaeger obtained a fascinating glimpse of mating bobcats:

> I was awakened near midnight by an interrupted series of ferocious hisses, shrill screams, harsh squalls, and deep-toned yowls [he recounts]. No alley strays could ever have half-equaled this cat concert of the desert wilds. Luckily, it was moonlight, and I was able to see the animals almost perfectly. The female most of the time lay crouched upon the ground, while the big male, which must have weighed twenty pounds, walked menacingly about her. Sometimes they both sat upright, facing each other. The loud and ludicrous serenade was kept up for almost half an hour, and it ended with a dual climax of discordant, frightening squalls as mating took place.

After a gestation period of about fifty days, one to six (most often three) kittens are born in a dark, carefully hidden den, a cave or a rock pile for instance, lined with grass and moss. They open their eyes on the ninth or tenth day, and the mother soon begins to bring them dead prey to be sniffed at and pulled about. As long as they are too young to digest flesh, she herself will then eat the squirrel or whatever else it may be. The kittens, delightful bundles of short, but nevertheless thick and soft fur, express their well-being by purring and utter little plaintive mews when in distress. When five weeks old, they come out of the den, especially between dusk and nightfall, and romp about with considerable zest. At first they quickly tire and may fall asleep in the middle of the game, but they rapidly gain in strength and vigour. They are nursed for about two months, and while they are still small, the mother may restrict her hunting to an area within approximately a one-mile radius around the den. When three to five months old, the kittens are led from the dens and begin to accompany their mother on her forays. On these outings, the female's upturned tail and conspicuous ear patches probably help them to keep her in sight as they trail behind through dense vegetation at night. When the kittens are older and tend to travel separately, contact is retained by means of calls. Bailey wrote:

> Some young bobcats become partially self-sufficient at seven to nine months, spending periods of time alone within their mother's home range, before rejoining her, perhaps after several days of unsuccessful hunting. One mother led one of her kittens, a nine-months old male, out of his familiar range and returned several days later alone. He did not return. No kittens were captured within their mother's home range after she had her next litter. When self-sufficient, all young left their home area, and several were later captured by fur trappers twelve to fifteen miles from their birthplaces. Some bobcats have been known to travel nearly 100 miles searching for a place to live. This innate wandering of sexually immature bobcats is of survival value to the species, because it prevents overcrowding and ensures that new areas will be occupied.

Among the bobcat's enemies can be numbered the puma, which is said to pursue it as unceasingly as the northern lynx of Europe pursues the wildcat.

Caracal, Desert Lynx
Caracal caracal
(SCHREBER 1776)

The caracal is very lynxlike in appearance, long-legged and with tufted ears, but it has a tail considerably longer than that of the true lynxes and is classified as the sole representative of the genus *Caracal* which, of course, is very close to the genus *Lynx*. The name "caracal," first popularized in Europe by Buffon, comes from the Turkish word "Karakal," meaning "black ear."

Characteristics. The caracal is smaller than the lynx, with a long slender body, slim legs, and a tail that tapers sharply at the tip and is about one-third the length of the head and body. The pelage is dense but relatively short, and there are no side-whiskers. The colour is a uniform reddish brown, but white on the chin, throat, and belly. The eye is ringed with white, and there is a small black spot above its anterior corner. A narrow black line runs from the eye to the nose. The narrow, pointed ears, black on the outside, are adorned with black tufts about 4.5 cm (2 in) in length. The tail is reddish brown above and pale sandy below. Black specimens have been recorded from Uganda and from Kaffraria, South Africa. The anterior upper premolar is absent.

Measurements. Shoulder height is 40 to 45 cm (avg. 17 in); head and body length, 66 to 76 cm (avg. 28 in); tail, about 22 cm (9 in); weight, 15 to 18 kg (avg. 37 lb).

Distribution. From central India, Cutch, Punjab, and Sind through Baluchistan, Afghanistan, and Iran into Turkmenistan, where it is occasionally encountered in the Nebi Dagh district; west through Asia Minor, Syria, and Lebanon to Iraq, Kuwait, Jordan, Israel, and the Sinai Peninsula. The species apparently has a fairly wide distribution throughout the Arabian Peninsula, but does not penetrate the interior sand deserts. From Egypt, Libya, Algeria, and Morocco, it ranges south over the whole extent of the African continent with the sole exception of the equatorial rain-forest belt, but it is especially common in South Africa. In East Africa it occurs sparsely in the Mara and Amboseli reserves, and in somewhat greater numbers in the Tsavo National Park and in northern Kenya. A. Blainey Percival, a Kenya game warden with many years' experience, saw it only twice and reports having had ten skins submitted for examination. I think I once caught a very fleeting glimpse of a caracal in the Amboseli Reserve, and I definitely saw one in the northern part of the Serengeti National Park and another in Marsabit Forest—a rather unusual habitat!

Habits. As implied in the name "desert lynx," the caracal is an animal of essentially dry areas. In Africa, for instance, it frequents woodlands, savannahs, and acacia scrub, but does not enter thick tropical or evergreen coastal forests. It is, however, also absent from the more barren parts of the Sahara Desert, and in Arabia, too, it is partial rather to arid, hilly steppes and mountain ranges than to the sterile tracts of true sand desert. In India, the caracal inhabits stony, broken ground with jungle scrub.

The caracal is solitary and mainly nocturnal, but can occasionally be seen trotting along a bush road or native path in broad daylight. It climbs well and takes to trees when pursued by dogs. Its gait is not unlike that of the cheetah, and the caracal can certainly be considered as the fastest feline of its size. It jumps remarkably well, and often catches birds, especially pigeons, by leaping at them to a height of several feet and knocking down a few with well-aimed blows of its paws. As it is easily tamed, the caracal has often been trained for hunting, both in India and in Iran. Edward Blyth as quoted by Jerdon, reported that a brace of them were sometimes pitted against each other, considerable wagers being made as to which of the two would disable the greater number out of a flock of tame feeding pigeons, before the whole mass managed to flutter out of reach. Ten or a dozen birds were usually struck down. In Jerdon's time, the Bheels of Mhowa occasionally used caracals to stalk pea-fowl, kites, crows, cranes, and hares. Colonel Ward knew a Punjabi zemindar who kept a small pack of these felines with which he hunted hares. Provided there were not too many bushes, the results were good, but the hares proved themselves quicker at turning and twisting and often got away. In Africa, the desert lynx preys upon birds up to the size of francolins and guinea fowl, also upon rodents, hyraxes (rock rabbits), klipspringers, dik-diks, duikers, and the fawns of impala, bush-buck, and other antelopes. G. C. Shortridge knew of a young greater kudu's being killed, and there are reports of caracals stalking and catching tawny and martial eagles roosting in trees at night. Lizards are often taken, and a tame specimen has been seen to kill and partially eat a cobra. A kill is occasionally dragged up into the fork of a tree, where it can be devoured at leisure without interference from other predators.

There does not seem to be a very definite time for mating, even though the two to three (more rarely five or six) kittens are mainly born in July and August in South Africa, and from September to December in Rhodesia. The gestation period lasts seventy days, and the female usually chooses a porcupine burrow, a holly tree, a rock crevice, or a dense patch of bush as a den in which to rear her offspring. The kittens are fully finished miniatures of their parents, tawny and with black, pointed ears. When four to five weeks old, they are already very lively, tearing around with great speed and uttering chirping, birdlike noises while romping with each other. They remain with their mother for about a year.

Adult caracals occasionally emit a cry not unlike that of a leopard, though lower in key, but as a whole they are silent animals. They will, of course, hiss, growl, and spit when cornered or disturbed at a kill. From observations made in captivity, the life-span of this species is thought to extend to sixteen or seventeen years.

Serval
Leptailurus serval
(SCHREBER 1776)

The long legs and the shortish tail, about one-third the length of the head and body, give the serval a certain resemblance to the lynxes, but its ears are not tufted and it has the full complement of thirty teeth. The skull is more elongate than that of most cats, and has a very high sagittal crest. There is thus every justification for placing this species in a separate genus. Anybody who has watched a serval in its native habitat will agree to it being the most graceful of the smaller African cats.

Characteristics. The serval is high-legged, lightly built, and can easily be recognized by its very large, oval ears. The coat is pale yellowish buff to reddish yellow, with black markings consisting either of large spots that tend to merge into longitudinal stripes on the neck and back, or of numerous small spots which give the animal a speckled appearance. The two types were originally described as different species, designated "serval" and "servaline." They have since been found to intergrade and must be regarded as mere ecotypes, the large spotted serval inhabiting grasslands, bush, and open savannahs, while the small spotted servaline occurs in fairly dense savannahs, gallery forests, secondary forests, and even in detached patches of rain-forest, without, however, penetrating the depth of the equatorial forest belt. The tail is black-tipped, spotted for about half its length, and ringed in its distal part. The backs of the ears are black with very distinct white spots. Black servals are quite often seen on the moorlands of the Aberdare Mountains, at about 3000 m (9800 ft), and have also been reported from Mount Kenya, the Mau Forest, the Cheringani Hills, and from Kilimanjaro. I have seen a couple of skins of this melanistic variety in the Usambara Mountains of Tanzania, and on one occasion I caught a glimpse of a black serval jumping off a boulder in hilly country near Nuu, Ukamba.

Measurements. Shoulder height is 40 to 65 cm (avg. 21 in); head and body length, 70 to 95 cm (avg. 32 in); tail, 36 to 45 cm (avg. 16 in); weight, 13 to 18 kg (avg. 35 lb). The servaline is said to be somewhat smaller than the large-spotted form.

67

Distribution. The serval is widely distributed throughout sub-Saharan Africa. Heim de Balsac and Jean B. Panouse consider its occurrence in southern Morocco as possible, even though evidence is scanty and based on hearsay only. The species used to be common in the forest areas of the eastern Cape, but is now rare everywhere south of the Orange River. The small-spotted form occurs mainly in the tropical regions of western and central Africa, extending from Senegal to northeastern Angola and across the Congo basin to Uganda and Lake Bangweulu in Zambia.

Habits. The serval can be encountered wherever there is water and a reasonable amount of cover, be it high grass, scrub, undergrowth or reed beds. It is less nocturnal than both the African wildcat and the caracal, and I have often watched it prowling around in broad daylight. However, to get a proper idea of how common these felines really are, one must drive around in the dark and look for them with a spotlight. I have seen up to four or five a night in an area of scrub and native shambas (gardens) on the lower slopes of Mount Kenya. The serval is swift and agile in its movements, and when you put one up, it will usually take flight in a series of wonderfully elastic bounds, each of which lifts the slim, pliable body high above the grass. It is of a solitary disposition and mainly terrestrial, but climbs well and sometimes takes to a tree when chased by dogs. The spoor can show slight indications of claw marks.

For locating prey, the serval seems to depend as much on its sense of hearing as on sight. One day, about mid-morning, I had an excellent view of one of these cats stalking through fairly high grass in Nairobi National Park. It suddenly stopped and tensed, with its big ears inclined forward, obviously listening to some faint, but promising rustle. It stood like this for a few seconds, then pounced and caught a biggish rodent, probably a vlei rat, which it held down with its paws before biting its neck. While hunting, the serval had been too absorbed to pay the slightest attention to my Land-Rover, but as soon as it had killed or at least disabled its prey, it made off at great speed, carrying the rat in its mouth. Vlei rats, grass rats, and similar rodents are sure to make up a large part of the serval's prey. It also kills hares, cane rats, small antelopes, lizards, and birds up to the size of a guinea fowl. Raymond Hook, the well-known Kenya naturalist, suggested that servals might dig out mole rats after having pinpointed their whereabouts by listening to their underground movements. I have seen bat-eared foxes, which have ears of a similar size and shape, catch gerbils in this way.

The serval utters a cry that has been described as a shrill "meoa,

meoa," repeated seven or eight times in succession. In addition, it purrs like a cat and growls ferociously when disturbed while feeding. There is no definite mating season, and the gestation period lasts from sixty-eight to seventy-four days. The kittens, two to four in number, are born in an ant bear's or porcupine's burrow, in the middle of a mealie field, in thick scrub, or in a rock hole. Lactation has been recorded as extending over seven and a half months.

Servals take well to life in captivity. Some friends of mine had a remarkably tame one that lived in an outdoor enclosure during daytime, but was allowed to enter the house through a small door at night. It then walked silently and elegantly round and round the living room, sometimes even jumping onto the back of a settee, without being in any way put out by the presence of strangers.

When cornered, a serval will fight a good deal less fiercely than a caracal, and may, on occasion, be killed by a single, medium-sized dog. Some African tribes consider its flesh a delicacy, while others hunt it for the sake of its pelt, which they use to make the fur cloaks known as "karrosses." No attempts seem ever to have been made to train the serval for sporting purposes.

Marbled Cat
Pardofelis marmorata
(MARTIN 1836)

The skull of the marbled cat is short and broad, more rounded than in most other felines, with the nasal bones very broad and flat. Adults have the eye sockets surrounded by a complete bony ring. The teeth are fairly robust. The anterior upper premolar is often wanting and very small when present at all. The first lower premolar is not very prominent either. The pupils are ovoid in outline.

In 1834, Sir William Jardine described and figured this species in his famous *Naturalist's Library* on the basis of two skins in the Edinburgh Museum which were assumed—wrongly—to have come from Java. He regarded them as specimens of the little-known "Diard's cat" and wrote: "The great discrepancy in our species and the description by Desmoulins of the *Felix diardii* is the great size given of the animal, 5 feet 4 inches, and we must consider that this is some mistake." There certainly was a mistake, for *Felix diardii* is one of the names given to the clouded leopard, the markings of which happen to be very nearly the same as those of the much smaller marbled cat. The specific designation *"marmorata"* was introduced by Martin in the *Proceedings of the Zoological Society of London,* in which so many new animals have been described and named.

Characteristics.   The marbled cat is somewhat larger than a domestic cat, with short, rounded ears and a long bushy tail about three-quarters the length of the head and body, and of the same thickness throughout. The pelt is thick and soft, with well-developed woolly under-fur. The ground colour is brownish grey to bright yellow or rufous brown. The sides of the body are marked with large, irregular blotches of a dark shade, each margined with black, especially on the hind edges. There are solid black dots on limbs and underparts. Some narrow longitudinal black lines on the head and neck merge into an irregular, interrupted dorsal stripe. The black-tipped tail is spotted and coloured dull black on its upper side. The backs of the ears are black with grey median bars.

Measurements.   Head and body are 45.7 to 60.9 cm (avg. 21 in); tail, 35.5 to 40.6 cm (avg. 15 in).

Distribution.   Nepal, Sikkim, Assam, Burma, Malaya, Indochina, Borneo, Sumatra.

Habits.   Few naturalists can boast of having seen this beautiful cat in its native habitat. One, to whom this rare treat came not only once, but twice, was E. P. Stebbing of the Indian Forest Service. "Both the animals I saw were in trees," he wrote, "and one had all the appearance of being engaged in stalking some birds perched on twigs above it. The animal was creeping along a branch in the manner many of us have observed our domestic tabby perform the same feat in a home garden. I watched him for a short time, but not knowing what he would do if he missed his quarry, and fearing to lose him, I brought his stalk to a sudden termination with a charge of shot, and saved the feathered songster for that occasion." We may regret that the interesting observation was cut short in this way, but those were the days of the naturalist-collector, and Stebbing did at least produce a lively sketch of the marbled cat in action, which he published in one of his books.

From what little we know of its life in the hill tracts of northern India, the marbled cat appears to be a forest dweller of mainly arboreal habits. Birds constitute the major part of its prey, but it also catches squirrels, rats, and possibly lizards and frogs. In Sarawak, according to Charles Hose, it is more often found in low country than in mountain areas, and has been known to frequent clearings. Hose also stated that it was very fierce when caught and did not live long in captivity. A more recent observer, E. Banks, considers it as one of the "fiercest of all cats." A specimen which he succeeded in keeping alive for some time ate squirrels, birds, and frogs, but refused to touch carrion. The remains of a rat were found in the stomach of a marbled cat shot at night in cut-over forest, and Banks suggests that in Borneo the species is nocturnal and hunts mainly on the ground. Nothing is known of its reproduction.

Golden Cat
Profelis aurata
(TEMMINCK 1827)

Museum collectors usually find it a great advantage to enroll the help of native hunters in obtaining rare and elusive forest animals. The golden cat of Africa, however, is surrounded by so much tribal superstition that Ivan T. Sanderson, working in what was then British Cameroon, found it almost impossible to get specimens of this species. Whenever he saw pieces of its skin forming part of a chief's ceremonial robe, he was told that they had come from "far, far country," and neither cajoling nor bribing were of any avail. He finally managed to add a few skins to his collection, but not a single skull. Some hunters in his employ did kill a golden cat only three miles from his base camp, but they immediately disappeared into the forest for days and would never show him where the animal had been shot.

The golden cat is "big medicine" also in former French Cameroon. The pygmy tribes, for instance, regard the tail as a talisman that assures good fortune and success in elephant hunting. Such beliefs apparently are not held in the northeastern Congo basin, for during an expedition through the Ituri Forest, I was offered two complete skins of golden cats which had been caught in snares. I did not buy them, for the heads and feet had been badly skinned, and I suspected their general state of preservation to be rather poor. I have often regretted this decision, for some museum might nevertheless have been glad to have these rare specimens.

The skull has the ring around the eye socket open at the back. The anterior upper premolar is very small.

Characteristics. The golden cat, sturdily built, with fairly long legs, big paws, a small head, and a moderately long tail, is about twice the size of a domestic cat. Its colour shows an almost incredible degree of variability, ranging from chestnut through foxy red, fawn, greyish brown, silvery grey, and bluish grey to dark slaty. Cheeks, chin, chest, belly, and the insides of the legs are white. Some specimens are marked all over with dark brown or dark grey dots, while others have the spotting restricted to the belly and the insides of the limbs. The backs of the ears are blackish. The tail has a dark central line along its dorsal surface and a few dark bands are sometimes in-

72

dicated. The skins I saw in the Ituri Forest were both grey, with a slight brownish tinge, unmarked except for a few grey spots on the white belly. The red and grey colour phases have originally been described as distinct species, but they are now known to occur side by side in the same localities and are sure to interbreed. No real proof has yet been obtained to support the suggestion that the pelt might change from red to grey with advancing age. Black specimens have been recorded on various occasions.

Measurements. Shoulder height is 50 cm (20 in); head and body, 65 to 85 cm (avg. 29 in); tail, 24 t 40 cm (avg. 12 in). A specimen with a head and body length of 91 cm (35 in) has been reported from Senegal. The weight is about 15 kg (34 lb).

Distribution. Central Africa, from Casamence in Senegal to southern Cameroon and Gabon, and across the Congo basin to Uganda and Kenya. The golden cat is found on the Virunga Volcanoes, which straddle the western border of Uganda, as well as in the neighbouring parts of Kigezi and Toro. It also occurs on the Ruwenzori Mountains, where it may be fairly common, even though it is hardly ever seen. One specimen, pale ginger in colour, has been obtained near Gulu in the Acholi country. The presence of this species in the Mau Forest of Kenya became known fairly recently, when native hunters were found in possession of two skins. A game warden showed them to an assembly of Kipsigis elders, but only three of them could remember ever having seen similar skins. The golden cat has been vaguely rumoured to occur in the Aberdare Mountains, east of the Rift Valley, but no specimen has yet been obtained. In Uganda it has been recorded up to 3600 m (11,800 ft).

Habits. The golden cat frequents high deciduous forest and is thought to be mainly crepuscular and nocturnal. The few Kipsigis who were aware of the animal's existence in the Mau Forest knew practically nothing of its habits, but described it as powerful and fierce. Liberians questioned by Sir Harry Johnston referred to the golden cat as the leopard's brother and stated it to be very bloodthirsty. According to R. Malbrant and A. Maclatchy, it spends the day high up in a tree.

The golden cat is known to prey on poultry in native villages, and one individual killed in the Senegal had in its stomach the feathers, gizzard, and feet of an unidentified bird. Tree hyraxes and rodents of various kinds are sure to be taken, and the animal is quite powerful enough to kill small- and medium-sized forest ungulates such as duikers, pigmy antelopes, and water chevrotains. Ernst Zwilling, an Austrian hunter and collector who spent a number of years in Cameroon, tells of suddenly seeing a golden cat emerge from the undergrowth while he was trying to attract a duiker by imitating its call. The cat had obviously been heading in the direction of the sound in order to stalk the presumed antelope.

Temminck's Cat, Asiatic Golden Cat

Profelis temmincki

(VIGORS and HORSFIELD 1828)

Temminck's cat, the species most closely related to the African golden cat, occurs in southeastern Asia, and there is a gap of a good 7000 km (4300 mi) between the two forest dwellers. Did a vast expanse of dense rain forest once cover the whole of tropical Africa and Asia? We know for certain that during the Pleistocene Age, Africa at times had a climate considerably more humid than it is today, with the equatorial forest belt extending across the continent to the Indian Ocean. When drier conditions began to prevail, the tropical forests of East Africa were reduced to a few isolated patches situated on mountains and highlands still receiving a considerable amount of precipitation—small areas of refuge to some of the West African animals that had followed the eastward spread of their forest habitat. This, of course, explains the occurrence of the golden cat in the Mau Forest of Kenya. We must assume that at the height of one of the Pleistocene pluvial, or rainy, periods, there was a connection between the African and Asiatic forest areas—across southern Arabia, Mesopotamia, and parts of Iran—which made it possible for the ancestors of the present-day golden cats to range from the Senegal to China and Sumatra. When this link was broken, the Asiatic and African representatives gradually evolved into separate species.

The Asiastic golden cat became known to science through the efforts of Dr. Thomas Horsfield, one of Sir Stamford Raffles' scientific collaborators, and it was named after Coenraad Jacob Temminck, the eminent Dutch naturalist who described and named the African golden cat. The skull has the orbits of the eye sockets nearly closed at the back.

Characteristics. In average size, Temminck's cat is rather larger than the African golden cat, but from one region to another its measurements are likely to vary considerably. The tail, of equal thickness throughout, is about one-half to two-thirds the length of the head and body. The pelt is of moderate length, dense and rather harsh, and varies from golden brown to dark brown, bright golden red and grey in colour. The backs of the short, rounded ears are black with a grizzled central area, and there is a grey patch behind each ear. White lines bordered with black run across the cheeks and from the inner corners of the eyes up to the crown. The underside of the tail is white in its terminal third. Some specimens are unmarked or show only the faintest vestiges of spots on flanks and underparts, while others, especially in the more northern parts of this feline's area of distribution, have a handsome pattern of spots and stripes that closely resembles the markings of the leopard cat. One subspecies, known as Fontainier's cat (*Profelis temmincki tristis*), was in fact long regarded as a form of the leopard cat, and some zoologists believe that the last word on its taxonomic position may not have been spoken yet. Melanistic specimens occur fairly frequently, and many years ago I remember seeing a particularly beautiful, glossy black specimen in the Basel Zoo.

Measurements. Length of the head and body is 79.27 cm (31 in); tail, 48.26 cm (19 in). For Chinese specimens, G. M. Allen gives a head and body length of 73 to 105 cm (avg. 35 in); tail, 48 to 56 cm (20 in).

Distribution. Nepal, Sikkim, Assam, Burma, Tibet, China (Yunnan, Szechwan, east of Fukien, possibly north to Kansu), Indochina, Siam, Malaya, and Sumatra.

Habits. Like its African counterpart, Temminck's cat is a forest dweller, with a predilection for wooded areas interspersed with rocky tracts. In parts of China, it is therefore known as the "shilu-lui," the rock cat. Another Chinese name for the species is "huang poo," yellow leopard, while in Burma it is often called the "fire cat" or "fire Tiger." It probably kills birds of many kinds, as well as mammals up to the size of small deer. It has been known to prey on poultry, sheep, and goats, even on water buffalo calves. It often moves about on the ground, walking along with its tail in the air, and according to the Lushai tribesmen of the Burmese-Assamese borderlands, it does not climb trees at all. However, the first specimen Brian Hodgson, the father of Himalayan natural history, ever obtained was captured in a tree in the midst of an exceedingly dense forest. It bore its captivity very tranquilly, and apart from one excess of fury when a dog approached its cage, gave evidence of a very tractable disposition. A Temminck's cat kept by E. P. Gee was very devoted to its master, jumping into his lap the moment he sat down, suckling the lobes of his ears and licking his head. It played for hours with a domestic cat or with dogs, and at times went off into the forest to hunt, but always returned instantly when called. Gee bought it in April from an Assamese animal dealer who had picked it up as a small kitten in the Garo Hills during February. By November it had become a very handsome, golden-coloured animal. It was later given to the London Zoo. According to information received from members of the Mishmi tribe on the Assamese-Tibetan border, Temminck's cat breeds in a hollow tree and has two kittens. Gee's pet, however, was one of a litter of three.

Bay Cat, Bornean Red Cat
Profelis badia
(GRAY 1874)

The bay cat, originally described by Gray of the British Museum from a very imperfect skin, was at one time regarded as the sole representative of a distinct genus, *Badiofelis*. There can, however, be little doubt about its being closely allied to Temminck's cat, even though it is considerably smaller than this species and has a higher, more rounded skull. The first upper premolar is small and has only one root.

Characteristics. The bay cat, or Bornean red cat, looks like a miniature edition of Temminck's cat. Its pelt is bright chestnut above, paler on the belly, with some obscure spots on underparts and limbs. There occasionally are some faint stripes on the face and cheeks. Specimens of a colour phase ranging from bluish to blackish grey have been reported. The long and tapering tail has a whitish median streak running down the terminal half of its lower surface, becoming pure white at the tip, which is marked by a small black spot. The backs of the rounded ears are blackish brown.

Measurements. Head and body length is 50 to 60 cm (avg. 21 in); tail, 35 to 40 cm (avg. 15 in).

Distribution. Borneo.

Habits. This species is still very imperfectly known. Charles Hose reported it as very rare and only found in dense forest. The only specimen he obtained came from the Suai River in Sarawak. Tom Harrison states it to have a preference for great areas of rocky limestone situated on the edge of the jungle, and to roam to an altitude of about 900 m (2950 ft). He had some evidence of its eating offal as well as small mammals and found it to have a reputation for "viciousness."

Leopard Cat
Prionailurus bengalensis
(KERR 1792)

In 1792 a small Indian cat, yellowish and with black markings, was described by Kerr and named *Felis bengalensis*. As the zoological exploration of southeastern Asia progressed, many similar cats were given specific distinction, and they can be found scattered through the literature of the last century under names such as Sumatra cat, Javan cat, lesser cat, Chinese cat, Elliot's cat, Jerdon's cat, and wagati cat. They are now regarded as belonging to one species only, Kerr's *Felis bengalensis,* which has, however, been split up into at least ten subspecies. Most zoologists do not refer to it any longer under the generic designation *Felis,* but prefer to include it, together with several other Asiatic species, in the genus *Prionailurus.*

The skull is rather short, rounded, and has the orbits of the eye sockets open at the back. The anterior upper premolar is usually present.

Characteristics. The leopard cat is about the size of a domestic cat although it stands higher. The head is relatively small, with a short narrow muzzle. The ears are moderately long and rounded. The tail is rather less than half, sometimes not more than one-third, the length of the head and body. Colouration and markings differ to such an extent that Edward Blyth found himself writing, almost in despair, "The variations of this handsome little cat are endless." The ground colour is usually pale tawny above, but can range from rufous to greyish. The underparts are white. There are two whitish stripes running up from the internal corners of the eyes, and one or two white streaks across the cheeks. The dark spots extend over both the upper and underparts, and there are usually four longitudinal black bands running from the forehead to the hind neck, breaking up into short bands and rows of elongate spots on the shoulders. The Sumatran subspecies has fewer and smaller markings than the typical mainland form, while the leopard cats from Java and Bali can be distinguished by their rather dull colouration. Bornean specimens, on the other hand, are bright and quite rufous in tone. In China, the species is known as "chin-ch'ien mao," or the "money cat," as the numerous spots were likened to Chinese coins. The tail is spotted above and indistinctly ringed toward the tip. The soles of the

79

feet are dark brown, the backs of the ears black with conspicuous white marks which do not extend to the inner borders.

Measurements. The smallest specimens (subspecies *minuta*) are found on the Philippine Islands, the largest in the northernmost parts of the cat's area of distribution. Indian specimens have a head and body length of 61 to 66 cm (avg. 25 in) and a tail length of 28 to 30 cm (avg. 11 in). For the subspecies known as the Far Eastern forest cat (*Prionailurus bengalensis euptilura*), Novikov gives a head and body length of 75 to 90 cm (avg. 32 in) and a tail length of 35 to 37 cm (avg. 14 in).

Distribution. Baluchistan and Kashmir, south to about Coorg and the Palni Hills in peninsular India, eastward through Nepal, Assam, Burma, Malaya, Siam, Indochina, and eastern Tibet to China, where the species occurs in most parts of the country. North through Manchuria, Korea, and the Amur basin to the valley of the Ussuri and along the coast of the Sea of Japan to about 15° north latitude; found on the islands of Tsushima and Quelpart (now Saishu), on Formosa (Taiwan), Hainan, Philippines (Palawan, Panay, Calamianes, Negros, Cebu), Borneo, Java, Bali, and Sumatra.

Habits. The leopard cat is the most common wild cat of southern Asia, inhabiting forests and jungles both in low country and in hilly, even mountainous regions. In eastern Siberia it is often met with in stone pine forests of the Manchurian taiga type, particularly in somewhat more open stretches with plenty of fallen trunks. In winter, however, it tends to move into the scrub of the river valleys. It shows little aversion to the presence of man and often lives close to villages.

The leopard cat makes its den in hollow trees, under overhangs, in small caves, or under big roots. It hunts mostly at night, though it is by no means rare to see it on the move in broad daylight, and F. W. Champion once watched one hunting for mice among long grass. His flashlight camera, set up at night with a trip wire stretched across a jungle path, was occasionally triggered by leopard cats prowling along the man-made trail. Champion's experiences thus tend to contradict those authors who regard the leopard cat as a mainly arboreal animal, spending most of its time searching trees for birds, small squirrels, and tree shrews.

McMaster once saw one carry off a fowl nearly as large as itself, shaking it savagely and making a successful escape in spite of the abuse, uproar, and missiles which the theft produced. The Indian leopard cat must therefore be fully capable of preying on jungle fowl and other game-birds, hares, and perhaps also on mouse deer. In eastern Siberia it feeds mainly on rodents and birds, but is not adverse to catching fish and reptiles. It hunts squirrels, ground squirrels, and hares, and the explorer Nicholas Przewalski recorded it as attacking the fawns of roe-deer.

Stroganov describes the leopard cat as solitary in its habits, except at mating time, when several males may chase after one female. The gestation period lasts from sixty-five to seventy days. In Siberia the kittens, one to three (mostly two), are born around the second half of May. In India, too, births seem mainly to fall into May, but litters usually number three to four. Rudolf Mell, a German naturalist in southern China, twice had kittens brought to him in May. He records a litter of three, about two weeks old, found under a boulder in bush jungle. Clifford Pope of the American Museum of Natural History obtained three small kittens late in March at Nodoa on the island of Hainan. The leopard cat has often been said to be very fierce and absolutely untameable, but one kept by Pope was very friendly and followed him around like a puppy. Dr. Hans Petzsch, of the Halle Zoo, states that leopard cats can become quite as tame as domestic cats.

Rusty-Spotted Cat
Prionailurus rubiginosus
(GEOFFROY 1834)

The rusty-spotted cat is nearly as small as the black-footed cat of South Africa. Its relationship to the leopard cat is close enough to justify the inclusion of both species within the genus *Prionailurus,* but no interbreeding has ever been noticed in the areas where the two species overlap. The skull is short and rounded as in the leopard cat, but it has the nasal bones more distinctly narrowed, and the orbit of the eye completely encircled by bone. There are only two upper premolars in each jaw.

Characteristics. The rusty-spotted cat is smaller than a domestic cat and has small, rounded ears and a tail about half the length of head and body. Its fur is short and soft, grizzled grey with a rufous tinge and marked with lines of brown, elongate blotches. The belly and the insides of the limbs are white with large, dark spots. There are two dark face streaks, as well as two white superciliary streaks, which extend along the sides of the nose. Four dark streaks run from the top of the head to the nape. The tail is more rufous than the body, uniform in colour or only indistinctly spotted. The soles of the feet are black. The Ceylonese subspecies is described as much more brightly rufous than the continental form.

Measurements. Head and body are 40.6 to 45.7 cm (avg. 17 in); tail, 24 cm (9 in).

Distribution. Southern Ceylon and southern India. Has not been found on the Malabar Coast, but is not uncommon on the Carnatic. The species has been reported from the Central Provinces (Seonee) and from Gujerat.

Habits. The rusty-spotted cat of the Indian mainland does not enter dense jungles, but shows a preference for scrub and dry grass, for the dry beds of reservoirs, and for drains in open country and near villages. In Ceylon, however, it is a true forest dweller, occurring in the humid mountain regions of the south, but being absent from the dry northern parts of the island. It hunts at night and preys on birds and small mammals.

Jerdon wrote of this species: "I had a kitten brought to me when very young in 1846, and it became quite tame, and was the delight and admiration of all who saw it. Its activity was quite marvellous and it was very playful and elegant in its motions."

Robert A. Sterndale, too, was greatly taken in with the rusty-spotted cat as a pet, and gave a delightful account of the antics of two kittens a Gond tribesman had given him: "They became perfectly tame, so much so that, although for nine months of the year I was out in camp, they never left the tents, although allowed to roam about unconfined. The grace and agility of their motions was most striking. . . . At night the little cats were put into a basket, and went on with the spare tents to my next halting place; and on my arrival next morning I would find them frisking about the tent roof between the two canvasses, or scrambling up trees under which we were pitched. Whilst I was at work I usually had one on my lap and the other cuddled behind my back on the chair. One day one of them, which had been exploring the hollows of an old tree, close by, rushed into my tent and fell down in convulsions at my feet. I did everything in my power for the poor little creature, but in vain, it died in two or three minutes, having evidently been bitten by a snake. The survivor was inconsolate, refused food, and went mewing all over the place and kept rolling at my feet, rubbing itself against them as though to beg for the restoration of its brother. At last I sent into a village and procured a common kitten, which I put into the basket with the other. There was a great deal of spitting and growling at first, but in time they became great friends, but the villager was no match for the forester. It was amusing to see the wild one dart like a squirrel up the walls of the tent onto the roof, the other would try to follow, scramble up a few feet, and then, hanging by its claws, look round piteously before it dropped to the ground."

Fishing Cat
Prionailurus viverrinus
(BENNETT 1833)

The flashlight photographs F. W. Champion made of fishing cats trotting purposefully along a jungle path impress one with the outward resemblance of this feline to a viverrid, more particularly to the Asiatic civet cat, *Viverra zibetha*. Bennett, who described the species in the *Proceedings of Zoological Society of London,* referred to this striking similarity in naming it *Felis viverrina*. It was later included in the genus *Prionailurus,* and this necessitated the change of the specific designation from *viverrina* to *viverrinus*. The nasal region of the skull is remarkably narrow, and the socket of the eye generally surrounded by bone. The anterior upper premolar is present but very small.

Characteristics. The fishing cat is considerably bigger and heavier than the leopard cat, almost clumsy in build by comparison, with a big, broad head and a short, thick tail only one-third or one-quarter of the length of head and body. The fur is short and rather coarse, grizzled grey in colour and sometimes tinged with brown. The markings consist of elongate, dark brown spots arranged in longitudinal rows, and of six to eight dark lines running from the forehead over the crown and along the neck. The backs of the short, rounded ears are black with white central spots. The forefeet nave moderately well-developed webs between the toes, and the claw sheaths are not quite large enough to enclose completely the retractile claws, the ends of which are therefore left to project to a considerable degree.

Measurements. Shoulder height is 38 to 40.6 cm (avg. 15 in); head and body, 75 to 86 cm (avg. 32 in); tail, 25.5 to 33 cm (avg. 12 in); weight, 7.7 to 1⁴ kg (avg. 25 lb).

Distribution. Malabar Coast—between Cape Comorin and Mangalore—Sind, United Provinces, Orissa, Bengal, Oudh, Kumaon Terai, Nepal, Assam, Burma, Siam, Indochina, southern China, Formosa (Taiwan), Java, Sumatra, Ceylon, possibly Bali.

Habits. The fishing cat is partial to marshy thickets, reed jungles near water, coastal creeks, backwaters, and mangrove swamps.

84

It has been reported up to an altitude of about 1500 m (4900 ft) in the foothills of the Himalayas.

F. W. Champion found this species quite common in a forest of northern Oudh and secured his excellent photographs close to a stream which the cats seemed to visit in order to catch fish. Although the English name of the species is a literal translation of the Bengali "mach-bagral," doubts have been expressed with regard to its piscatorial habits, especially as, for some obscure reason, it has long been thought to have an aversion against entering water. W. G. Adams, who observed it in Ceylon, did, however, save its reputation as a fisherman, stating that it acted "exactly the same way as a tabby trying to get a goldfish out of a bowl." He described it as crouching on a rock in midstream or on a sand-bank, close to fairly deep water, and then using its paw to scoop out any fish that came within reach. We now know that the fishing cat often wades in shallows and does not hesitate to swim in deep water. There even are reports of its occasionally diving in pursuit of its prey. It is, of course, by no means entirely dependent on fish, and a large part of its food may, in fact, consist of crustaceans and aquatic molluscs, especially of ampullaria snails which abound in all Indian marshes. The fishing cat also takes snakes, frogs, small mammals, and birds. It is a powerful animal, able, on occasion, to rout a whole pack of dogs. A missionary living on the Malabar Coast claimed it entered huts to drag away small children. This story was met with a considerable amount of disbelief, but Sterndale once heard of a wild cat killed at Jeypore while in the act of carrying off a four-month-old infant. He thought that of all the felines smaller than a leopard only a fishing cat would have been capable of such a feat. The child, incidentally, was rescued alive.

Blyth once had a newly caught male of this species break through a partition into a neighbouring cage and kill a female leopard twice his size. Apart from this mishap, he found the fishing cat, of which he kept several in captivity at various times, to be a particularly tameable species.

Fishing cats have been bred in the Frankfurt Zoo, the litters consisting of two to three young. Petzsch states that the male takes part in the rearing of the young right from the time of birth, but it might be rash to regard this observation, made in captivity, as typical of the fishing cat's breeding behaviour in the wild. Prater reports a single kitten being taken in June at Canamore from a lair consisting of a beaten down patch among reeds, with tunnelled approaches from two sides. Near Chempera, Bihar, a female with two kittens was seen in April. Gestation lasts for sixty-three days.

Flat-Headed Cat
Prionailurus planiceps
(VIGORS and HORSFIELD 1827)

St. George Mivart, in his famous monograph *The Cat,* called this species a "very peculiar and exceptional cat." It is, in fact, even more aberrant than the fishing cat, having in its appearance features reminiscent not only of the viverrids, but also of the mustelids. Its skull is broadly flattened and pointed, with the nasal bones forming a ridge. The orbit of the eye is completely encircled by bone, and the anterior upper premolar has two roots and is larger and better developed than in any other cat.

Characteristics. Of about the size of a domestic cat, the flat-headed cat has an elongate body, short legs, and a short tail. The coat is thick, soft, and long, reddish brown on the top of the head, dark brown on the body, the white tips of the hairs giving it a silvery grey tinge. The underparts are white, generally more or less spotted and splashed with brown. The face below the eyes is light reddish, with two narrow dark lines running across each cheek. A yellow line runs up from each eye to near the ear. The insides of the limbs are rufous brown, the colour becoming lighter toward the feet. The tail is thickly furred, of reddish brown colour above, yellowish brown on the underside.

Measurements. Head and body are 53.3 to 60.9 cm (avg. 22 in); tail, 15.2 to 20.3 cm (avg. 7 in).

Distribution. Malaya, Borneo, Sumatra. In Sarawak, this species was found on the Barem River and up to 700 m (2300 ft) high on Mount Dulit.

Habits. Piecing together the scanty bits of information gathered from the jungle people of Sarawak, Charles Hose gave the following account of the flat-headed cat: "Common in low country and is often very destructive to gardens. It is very fond of fruit and has constantly been known to dig up and eat sweet potatoes which are grown by the natives." These lines were written in 1893, and for many years they were the sum total of what was known of the species. E. Banks has now published some additional notes, stating the species is nocturnal and hunts for frogs and fish along the river-banks. He heard of it being caught in fish traps occasionally and thought that it never raided hen houses. The only specimen, however, which B. E. Smythies, the well-known ornithologist, saw during some twenty years in Sarawak, was shot while after some chickens.

Practically nothing is known of the flat-headed cat's reproduction. In Sarawak, a single kitten was once picked up in January. A kitten from Selangor in Malaya lived for a year in captivity, changing the colour of its fur from grey to light brown. It became very tame and was at first fed on milk, eggs and dried prawns. Fish proved very acceptable later on. It consistently refused to touch rice.

It looks, in effect, as if the flat-headed cat were leading an at least partly piscatorial existence similar to that of its close cousin, the fishing cat, and one cannot help feeling highly sceptical of the predominantly vegetarian diet Charles Hose's informants described.

Iriomote Cat
Prionailurus (Mayailurus) iriomotensis
(IMAIZUMI 1967)

New insects, ticks, spiders, and other small creatures are constantly being described by devoted specialists, and every few years there is a mild flutter of zoological excitement when a hitherto unknown rat or bird turns up in some remote corner of the world. The discovery of a new species of cat in 1967, however, can be rated as something of a sensation. The animal was found on Iriomote, a small, mountainous island completely covered with rain forest and situated at the southern end of the Ryukyu group, 200 km (124 mi) east of Taiwan.

Yukio Tagawa, a Japanese writer and naturalist, first heard rumours of this feline at Naha, the capital of Okinawa. He forthwith set out to visit little-known Iriomote, where he found the cat to be well known to the natives. They occasionally caught it in wild boar traps and considered its flesh as a great delicacy. He was told that a skin and skull had recently been sent to the University of Okinawa. Returning to Naha, Tagawa managed to unearth the precious specimens and sent them on to Dr. Yoshimori Imaizumi of the National Science Museum in Tokyo. He then went back to Iriomote to capture one of these cats alive, but had to be satisfied with some further skulls. Tagawa did, however, impress upon the natives that a better use could be made of these animals than eating them, and a few live specimens were soon afterward sent to Imaizumi, who now had sufficient material for study. He noticed a close affinity to the leopard cat, the skull, however, showing juvenile rather than adult characteristics. The first upper premolar was absent.

While there can be no doubt with regard to the Iriomote cat being allied to the leopard cat, Imaizumi ventured on to much more uncertain ground when he postulated an equally close relationship to the kodkod or guiña of South America. Both felines are forest dwellers, and the striking resemblances, which cannot be denied, are much more likely to be due to parallel lines of evolution followed by two species living under similar ecological conditions than to any form of transpacific kinship.

Imaizumi felt justified in making his cat the sole representative of a new genus, for which he chose the designation *Mayailurus*. Hans Petzsch has since come to the conclusion that the Iriomote cat is more closely related to the leopard cat than Imaizumi assumed, and

88

should therefore be included within the genus *Prionailurus,* with *Mayailurus* having no more than a subgeneric status. Dr. Th. Haltenorth tells me that he fully agrees with this view. One can even wonder whether at some future date the Iriomote cat may not be relegated to the rank of a somewhat primitive subspecies of the leopard cat.

Characteristics. The Iriomote cat is of about the same size as a domestic cat, but has a relatively elongate body, a short tail, and short legs, thus displaying the characteristic low-slung build of a predator frequenting thick undergrowth. The ground color of the pelt is dark dusky brown. There are five to seven lines on the back of the neck, which come to an end in front of the shoulders. The spots are arranged in longitudinal rows and tend to merge into bands. The backs of the rounded ears are black with white central spots.

Measurements. Head and body are 60 cm (23 in); tail, 20 cm (8 in).

Distribution. So far only recorded from Iriomote Island.

Habits. A forest dweller of which practically nothing is yet known. As Iriomote has a surface of only 292 km² (113 mi²), the total cat population must be fairly low. The species has therefore been placed under full protection.

Ocelot
Leopardus pardalis
(LINNAEUS 1758)

Of the small- and medium-sized cats inhabiting tropical and subtropical America, the ocelot is certainly the best known. It was familiar to Linnaeus, who named it *Felis pardalis*. Gray, in his list of British Museum mammals, put it into a separate genus, *Leopardus,* which it now shares with the margay and several other species.

The ring of bone around the eye is incomplete at the back.

The ocelot is one of the most beautiful of felines, and it has suffered very badly from the stupid craze for fur coats made of the pelts of spotted cats, which recently swept through the world of so-called fashionable women.

Characteristics. The ocelot, like the leopard cat, taxes the zoologist's pen to the utmost. "No two animals are the same," wrote Hans Schmidt, and Richard Lydekker called it one of the most difficult members of the feline family to describe. The ground colour ranges from whitish or tawny yellow to reddish grey and grey. The dark markings run into chainlike streaks and blotches, generally forming oblique elongate spots bordered with black and enclosing an area darker than the ground colour. Head and limbs are marked with solid black spots. There are two black stripes on each cheek and one or two transverse bars on the insides of the forelegs. The backs of the rounded ears are black with yellowish central spots. The tail may be either ringed or marked with dark bars on its upper surface. Its under surface is whitish, as are the insides of the limbs. Individual and regional variations of the ocelot have at one time or another provided the basis for the description of a number of distinct species. Present-day taxonomists distinguish ten subspecies, of which some may be of rather doubtful validity.

Measurements. Within its extensive area of distribution, the ocelot varies not only in colour and markings, but also in size. E. Raymond Hall and Keith Kelson give a total length for males of 95 to 136.7 cm (avg. 45 in), for females of 92 to 120 cm (avg. 41 in), with respective tail lengths of 28 to 40 cm (avg. 13 in) and 27 to 37 cm (avg. 12 in). In Argentina, according to Schmidt, the head and body length varies from 80 to 100 cm (avg. 35 in), the tail length from 35 to 45 cm (avg. 16 in), and the shoulder height from 40 to 50 cm (avg. 18 in). Petzsch admits specimens with a total length of 150 cm

(59 in), but considers them as exceptional. Weight is 11.34 to 15.8 kg (avg. 29 lb).

Distribution. From Arizona and southwestern Texas to Paraguay and northern Argentina. Found in the mountain areas of Colombia, Equador, and northern Peru, but not on the high plateaus of southern Peru and Bolivia.

Habits. The ocelot is found in a great variety of habitats—in the humid jungles of Central America and the dense forests of Brazil, in mountain forests and in any type of thick bush, such as the thorny chaparral of the lower Rio Grande Valley of Texas. It feels at home in the very depth of vast forest tracts as well as in marshy areas and along river-banks, but never shows itself in completely open country. It can be said to be generally nocturnal, spending the day asleep on a branch, in a hollow tree, in a bunch of bromeliads shadowed by bushes, or in prickly opuntia scrub. While prowling around at night, it often follows a man-made path, and by setting up a flash-light apparatus with trip wires alongside a jungle trail on Barro Colorado Island in Gatun Lake, Panama, Frank M. Chapman succeeded in obtaining excellent photographs illustrating the predatory wanderings of this handsome cat. On examining his plates, Chapman noticed that the animals had for the most part been caught with the leading foot ten inches off the ground. As this would be most unusual on a perfectly open path, he thought that they had been able to sense the trip wire in the dark and made at least partial attempts to clear the flimsy obstruction.

The "chibi-guazu," or "big cat," as it is called in Paraguay, may, however, also be encountered in daytime. While collecting specimens for a mammalian study of Panama, Edward A. Goldman now and then caught glimpses of ocelots crossing small openings among trees, but strangely enough never encountered one when using a hunting lamp at night. On several occasions he spotted ocelots resting in trees during the day. When approached, they usually tried to escape by climbing slowly and steadily out of sight, but when discovery became certain, they ran down to earth and quickly disappeared in the forest. It is said that an ocelot pursued by dogs quite often does not immediately take to a tree, but first bounds away at great speed. All this seems to point to it being mainly terrestrial. It probably does most of its hunting on the ground, though occasionally it may possibly stalk monkeys or birds among the trees.

An excellent account of this species was given by Dr. J. R. Rengger, a Swiss naturalist who spent six years in Paraguay early in the nineteenth century. In thick forest he sometimes saw ocelots jump from one tree to another, but in doing so they displayed considerably less agility than, for instance, the puma. Rengger found that ocelots, even though they did not enter water without good reason, were strong swimmers and were fully capable of reaching safe land at times of excessive flooding. He did, in fact, see one swim across a part of the Rio Paraguay.

Rengger's observations in his book on the mammals of Paraguay are of great interest: "These cats live in couples within a well-defined territory. A hunter putting up one of a pair during the day, can be sure that the other will not be far away. A territory never contains more than one couple. It is rare for a male and female to roam about in company. Each of them hunts for itself, and they do not come to one another's assistance when killing a large animal or driving away an aggressor." This is, of course, a very early reference to territorial behaviour in a wild animal.

We know now that the inhabitants of an ocelote territory communicate with each other by means of mewing calls and by always depositing their droppings in one and the same place.

The mating season, according to Rengger, begins in October and continues until November. Mating takes place at night, and with yowls not unlike those of our domestic cat. The female conceals her kittens, usually two in number, sometimes up to four, in a hollow tree or in a thicket in the forest. As soon as they are able to eat, she brings them small animals. In Yucatán, ocelots are known to mate in October and breed in January, while in Texas kittens are born during autumn. Gestation lasts seventy days.

Rengger found that ocelots preyed upon birds and small mammals, such as young deer, young peccaries, monkeys, coatis, agoutis, pacas, rats, and mice. To this list, Edward W. Nelson adds rabbits and wood rats, as well as snakes and other reptiles. "Its reptile eating habit was revealed to me unexpectedly one day in the dense tropical forests of Chiapas," he wrote. "I was riding along a steep trail beside a shallow bush-grown ravine, when a tiger-cat suddenly rushed up the trunk of a tree close by. A lucky shot from my revolver brought it to the ground, and I found it lying in the ravine by the body of a recently killed boa about 6 to 7 feet long. It had eaten the boa's head and neck when my approach interrupted its feast."

Hen-houses are occasionally raided, but, as a whole, the ocelot shuns the vicinity of human habitations. Nelson considers it as much more quiet and less fierce in disposition than most other felines, and it has become popular as a pet, especially in the United States— much too popular, one might say, for the pet trade can be quite as harmful to a species as trapping for the sale of skins.

Margay, Long-Tailed Spotted Cat

Leopardus wiedi

(SCHINZ 1821)

The taxonomy of South American cats has long been in a state of great confusion. Not only were many colour variations given full specific distinction, but some of the species were mistaken for each other and wrongly named even in the most authoritative works. The margay, for instance, was frequently mistaken for both the ocelot and the oncilla, the little spotted cat. Schinz named it in honour of the Prince of Wied, whose expedition to South America contributed very materially to the knowledge of the Brazilian fauna.

Characteristics. The margay closely resembles the ocelot, and in many parts of South America it is referred to as the "little ocelot," while margay or marguey can be translated as "tiger cat." It is smaller than the ocelot, more slimly built, and stands relatively higher on its legs. It also has a longer tail. The coat is soft, yellowish brown, white on belly, chest, throat, chin, and on the insides of the limbs. On the upper part of the body, the markings, dark brown in colour, are arranged in longitudinal rows, with the centres of each spot slightly paler, but still darker than the ground colour of the pelt. The backs of the ears are black with white central spots. The tail is marked with broad transverse spots and rings. Kittens have uniformly black spots and dark grey paws. Taxonomists recognize ten subspecies of the margay.

Measurements. In males, the head and body length varies from 53.1 to 79 cm (avg. 26 in), in females from 46.3 to 58.9 cm (avg. 20 in); the tail length from 33.1 to 51 (avg. 16 in) and from 34.2 to 44 cm (avg. 15 in) respectively. For the subspecies occurring in Panama (*pirrensis*), Goldman reports the tail to be 10 cm (4 in) longer than is usual in the local subspecies of the ocelot.

Distribution. The status of the margay as a member of the fauna of the United States rests on a single specimen taken in Texas at Eagle Pass on the Rio Grande. The species is rare in Mexico, and only two specimens figure in a collection of fifteen thousand Mex-

93

ican mammals brought together by Goldman and Nelson. From Panama, northern Colombia, and Peru, the margay ranges south to northern and eastern Paraguay, northern Uruguay, and to Misiones and Tucumán in northern Argentina.

Habits.   Being much more arboreal than the ocelot, the margay is mainly—if not exclusively—a forest dweller. It climbs with great agility and is thought to forage almost entirely in trees, catching birds, small- and medium-sized mammals, and possibly lizards and tree frogs. In northern Paraguay, where Rengger obtained one single specimen only, he found the Guarani Indians regarding this species as being much less common and more diurnal than the ocelot. He was told that it preyed mainly on birds.

Geoffroy's Cat

Leopardus geoffroyi

(d'ORBIGNY and GERVAIS 1843)

Geoffroy's cat, named after Geoffroy St. Hilaire, the French naturalist, and the kodkod of Chile were originally thought to be races of
one and the same species, but zoologists later accorded them separate specific status. Both have the anterior premolar minute, the
skull remarkably short, wide, and convex. This also applies to the
oncilla, and the three species were for a while considered as representatives of a separate genus, *Oncifelis*. They are now regarded as
members of the genus *Leopardus*, which also includes the ocelot and
the margay.

Characteristics.   The "gato montes" or "mountain cat," as Geoffroy's cat is called in Argentina, is of robust build and has a relatively
large head. It is another very variable species, brilliant ochre in the
northern parts of its area of distribution, silvery-grey in the south,
with every intermediate shade between those two extremes occurring in some place or another. Body and limbs are covered with
numerous small black spots of nearly equal size, and placed at equal
distances from one another. In some individuals the markings on
shoulders and flanks tend to form rosettes and wavy lines. There are
several black streaks on the crown, two on each cheek, and one between the shoulders. The backs of the rounded ears are black with
large white central spots. The tail is spotted at the base and ringed
toward the tip. Specimens from the Gran Chaco are small and short-
haired. The largest individuals are found in Patagonia.

Measurements.   Head and body are 55 to 65 cm (avg. 23 in);
tail, 35 cm (14 in). Petzsch gives a total length of 70 to 110 cm (avg.
35 in), with three-eighths going to the tail.

Distribution.   From the Bolivian Andes (Cochabamba, 3500 m
[11,500 ft]) and the mountains of northwestern Argentina (Jujuy,
Salta) through the Gran Chaco to Uruguay and southernmost Rio
Grande do Sul in Brazil, south through the length of Argentina to
the Rio Gallegos in Patagonia.

Habits. Geoffroy's cat is an inhabitant of scrubby woodlands and open bush country in both plains and foothill areas. It is mainly terrestrial and preys upon small mammals and birds. The litter consists of two to three young. Captive individuals are said to become tame. A male that had come to the Halle Zoo as an adult animal attacked and killed all the female domestic cats which were introduced into its cage for cross-breeding purposes.

Kodkod, Guiña
Leopardus guigna
(MOLINA 1782)

The kodkod was first mentioned and named by Juan Ignacio Molina, the Chilean-born librarian of the Jesuit College in Santiago. He left Chile in 1767 and went to Bologna, where he wrote a book on the fauna and flora of Chile which is still of great value, even though Molina was rather credulous and let himself be convinced of the existence of a membraneous-winged quadruped with stout lizard's legs and a fish tail, and of a "hippopotamus" with palmated feet and sleek fur. The kodkod, which he named *Felis guigna,* remained almost unknown until a German naturalist, Philippi, found it to be common around Valdivia and not only published a detailed description, but also a reasonably good picture as well.

Even though it was at one time regarded as conspecific with Geoffroy's cat, the kodkod was later considered as sufficiently different to be put, together with the oncilla, into a subgenus, *Noctifelis,* of the genus *Oncifelis.* It is now included within the genus *Leopardus.*

Characteristics. The kodkod is a small feline; one subspecies is about the size of the black-footed cat. It is thus probably the smallest cat of the Western Hemisphere. Buff or grey brown in colour, the kodkod is heavily marked with rounded, blackish spots on both upper and lower parts, with a slight tendency to streaking on head and shoulders. The tail is narrowly ringed with blackish. The backs of the ears are black with white central spots. There are two subspecies: one, large, pale in colour, with unspotted feet, occurs in central Chile (*tigrillo*), the other, smaller, more brightly coloured, and with spotted feet, in southern Chile (*guigna*). Melanistic specimens are not uncommon.

Measurements. Subspecies *guigna:* head and body are 39 to 45 cm (avg. 16 in); tail, 19.5 to 23 cm (avg. 8 in). Subspecies *tigrillo:* head and body are 49.3 cm (19 in); tail, 22.9 cm (9 in).

Distribution. Central and southern Chile, from about Coquimbo to the Chiloé and Guaitecas Islands; also found in the Andean lakes district of Argentina (Chubut and Santa Cruz).

Habits. All authors seem to agree on the kodkod being a forest dweller with nocturnal habits. At this point, however, their unanimity ends, with some making it out to be an expert climber, living mostly in trees, while others regard it as terrestrial, taking to trees only in an emergency. It most probably preys mainly on small mammals. Philippi gave an extraordinary account of whole parties of kodkods raiding the chicken-houses of Valdivia, and this may have induced H. L. Blonk to postulate a fairly high degree of social behaviour for this species. He thought that it might actually live in packs, but no proof for this assumption has yet been forthcoming.

Oncilla, Little Spotted Cat

Leopardus tigrinus

(SCHREBER 1775)

Elliot, in his *Monograph of the Felidae* regarded the oncilla as identical with Geoffroy's cat, while Mivart treated it as a distinct species. For a long time it went under the designation *Felis tigrina*. Taxonomists then placed it in the subgenus *Noctifelis* of the genus *Oncifelis,* naming it *Oncifelis pardinoides* (Grey 1869). A few years ago, Leyhausen suggested that it might be fairly closely related to the margay, with which, incidentally, it has been confused on many occasions. Comparison of its chromosomes with those of members of the genus *Leopardus* has since confirmed this view, and it is now known as *Leopardus tigrinus.*

Characteristics. The oncilla's pelt varies from light to rich ochre and is marked with rows of large dark spots which take the form of black, bordered blotches on the upper parts. The underparts are lighter in colour, often whitish, and less spotted. The limbs are much spotted externally. The black-tipped tail has ten or eleven rings. One-fifth of all oncillas are said to be melanistic. Taxonomists distinguish four subspecies.

Measurements. The oncilla varies considerably in size. The head and body length is generally given as 50 to 55 cm (avg. 21 in); tail length, 25 to 42 cm (avg. 13 in). Leyhausen had a pair of very small oncillas, which were hardly bigger than black-footed cats. The male weighed 2.75 kg (6 lb), the female between 1.75 and 1.5 kg (avg. 4 lb).

Distribution. From Costa Rica to the Andean zone of western Venezuela, Colombia, and Equador, possibly northern Peru, and through eastern Venezuela, Guinea, and Brazil to Paraguay and northern Argentina, where it ranges from Misiones to the Chaco of the Salta Province.

Habits. The oncilla lives in forests, and very little is known of its habits in the wild. Leyhausen has, however, published some notes on its breeding in captivity. Female heat lasts for several days, and the gestation period was established as having a duration of seventy-four to seventy-six days. Litters numbered one to two young. The kittens observed by Leyhausen developed slowly, opening their eyes at seventeen days and beginning to nibble solid food within fifty-five days, at an age when domestic kittens have already turned into expert hunters. The male was seen to exhibit very marked aggressivity toward the female oncilla and also toward female domestic cats, of which he killed one of a size much larger than himself. Matings with domestic cats did take place, but of seven kittens no less than three were born dead.

Pampas Cat

Lynchailurus colocolo

(MOLINA 1782)

Taxonomically, the pampas cat has had as checkered a career as that of the oncilla. Even though it had long been known in Argentina as the "gato pajero," the grass cat, it was first described from Chilean specimens by Molina, who recognized it as a species distinct from the kodkod. He gave the following account of the two felines: "The guigna (*Felis guigna*) and the colocolo (*Felis colocolo*) are two beautifully marked wild cats which inhabit the forests of Chile. They resemble the domestic cat, but are a little larger, the head and tail a little longer. The guigna is of a fulvous colour, varied with rounded black spots, four or five lines [8–10 mm (avg. 0.4 in)] in diameter, extending to the end of the tail. The colocolo is white, irregularly spotted with black and yellowish. Its tail is annulated with black to the tip."

In Molina's time, the Araucanian name for the pampas cat was "kudumu," and this may have been corrupted to "colocolo" by the Spanish settlers. It is, however, possible that Molina chose the name in honour of Colocolo, a renowned Araucanian warrior chief.

In 1816, Desmarest gave the name *Felis pajeros* to a pampas cat obtained south of Buenos Aires, and for a long time the species was generally known under this designation, with Molina's *colocolo* used only to distinguish the Chilean subspecies. Angel Cabrera, in his list of South American mammals, uses *colocolo* in place of *pajeros*.

In its appearance, the pampas cat shows a marked outward resemblance to the Asiatic steppe cat, especially with the subspecies known as the Gobi cat. Its skull is short and convex, with the nasal region much compressed and the nasal bones very narrow, superiorly. The anterior upper premolar is absent.

Characteristics. The pampas cat is of about the same size as the European wildcat, but rather more robust in build, with a smaller head and shorter tail. The face is broad, the ears are more pointed than in other South American felines. The backs of the ears are black with greyish white central spots in specimens from the northern areas, grey and unmarked in southern animals.

The coat is long, with the hairs on the back attaining 7 cm (3 in) in length and forming a kind of mane. The colour is very variable,

101

ranging from yellowish white and greyish yellow to brown, greyish brown, silvery grey, and light grey, with transverse bands of yellow or brown running obliquely from the back to the flanks. Two bars run from the eyes across the cheeks, meeting beneath the throat. The legs and the thick bushy tail are marked with more or less visible brown bands. The colocolo of Chile is somewhat more distinctly marked than the gato pajero of Argentina. Cabrera distinguishes seven subspecies.

Measurements. Argentinian specimens: shoulder height is 30 to 35 cm (avg. 13 in); head and body length, 60 to 70 cm (avg. 25 in); tail, 30 cm (12 in). Chilean specimens: head and body length is 56.7 to 64.2 cm (avg. 23 in); tail, 29.5 to 32.2 cm (avg. 12 in).

Distribution. Mountain areas of Equador and northern Peru, inland regions of Brazil, at least as far north as the Mato Grosso plateau, southern Peru, parts of Bolivia, central Chile from Coquimbo to Concepción, Paraguay, and Uruguay. Argentina from Jujuy, Salta, and the Chaco to southern Patagonia. Old reports of its occurrence in Guiana may have originated through confusion with some other species.

Habits. In most parts of Argentina this cat inhabits open grass lands, hiding in the high pampas or "pajero" grass, from which its Spanish name "gato pajero" is derived. In the northern regions, between Tucumán and Salta, it enters humid forests. In Chile, Wilfred H. Osgood found it common and generally distributed even in the most populous parts of the country.

The pampas cat is mainly terrestrial, though it may run up a tree to escape pursuit if one happens to be within reach. It hunts at night, killing small mammals, especially guinea pigs, as well as ground-inhabiting birds. It is said to be very partial to tinamous, which in South America take the place of the Old World partridges and francolins, and to make a nuisance of itself by frequently raiding hen-houses. Azara, who was the first to give some account of its habits, wrote: "On one occasion in April I took from the uterus of a female paja-cat a single young one, with hair just commencing to grow; it is said, notwithstanding, that they bring forth two, or even three at birth."

The gato pajero has the reputation of being very difficult to tame and is therefore rarely seen in zoological gardens.

Mountain Cat, Andean Highland Cat

Oreailurus jacobita

(CORNALIA 1865)

The mountain cat, perhaps the least known of all the South American cats, is represented in museum collections by only a very few specimens. Its skull differs from all other feline skulls by having very peculiar double-chambered bullae, and this certainly justifies the placing of this species into a genus of its own.

Characteristics. The mountain cat is larger than both the colo-colo and the kodkod. It has a remarkably soft and fine coat, the hairs being about 4 cm (2 in) long on the back, and 3.5 cm (1 in) on the uniformly bushy tail. The colour is pale silvery grey, more ashy on the back, spotted and transversely striped with irregular brown or orange yellow markings, which turn to blackish on the whitish underparts and on the limbs. The light-tipped tail has about nine blackish or brownish rings. The backs of the ears are dark grey. In the consistency of its fur, as well as in colouration and markings, the mountain cat resembles the snow leopard and Pallas's cat, which both occur in similar habitats.

Measurements. Head and body are 60 cm (23 in); tail, 35 cm (14 in).

Distribution. The high Andes of northeastern Chile, southern Peru, southern Bolivia, and northern Argentina. The type specimen was collected in Bolivia, between Potosí and Huanchaca.

Habits. The mountain cat inhabits the arid and semi-arid zone of the Andes and is said to enter the snow region occasionally. It kills small mammals, particularly chinchillas and viscachas.

Jaguarundi

Herpailurus yagouarundi

(GEOFFROY 1803)

The jaguarundi is even less feline in appearance than the flat-headed cat of Borneo, so much like a mustelid that German zoologists call it the weasel cat. Otter cat might be an even better name, for this species shows the greatest outward resemblance to the otter. The skull is very elongate and flattened, with the nasal region compressed laterally. The anterior upper premolar is present. Some taxonomists regard the jaguarundi as related to the mountain cat, while others prefer to place it in the vicinity of the puma.

Characteristics. The jaguarundi is a small cat with short legs, a small, flattened head, a slender, elongate body and a very long tail. The ears are short and rounded, the coat is uniform in colour, varying from blackish to brownish grey and from foxy red to chestnut. The two colour phases were once thought to represent two distinct species, the grey one being generally called jaguarundi, the red one, eyra. We now know that they occur side by side and will mate with each other. Red and grey kittens can be found in the same litter. They are spotted at birth, but lose these markings as they grow up.

Measurements. Shoulder height is 35 cm (14 in); length of head and body, 55 to 77 cm (avg. 26 in); tail, 33 to 60 cm (avg. 18 in); weight, 4.5 to 9 kg (avg. 16 lb).

Distribution. From Arizona and the lower Rio Grande Valley of southern Texas to southern Brazil, Paraguay and the Misiones and Chaco regions of northern Argentina. The jaguarundi penetrates the inter-Andean valleys of Peru and the sub-Andean districts of northwestern Argentina, from Jujuy to Mendoza.

Habits. The jaguarundi is a lowland species, inhabiting forest and bush. In southern Texas it is partial to the dense, thorny thickets of mesquite and stunted acacias known as chaparral. Rengger, who studied it in Paraguay, mostly encountered the jaguarundi along forest edges, in thickets and hedgelike strips of scrub, intermingled with spiny bromeliads, but never in open country. He described it as agile, moving along with the gait of a domestic

104

cat, tail lowered, obliquely pointing toward the ground. It hunts in the evening and morning. Even though it generally spends the noon hours asleep in its den, the jaguarundi is much less nocturnal than most other cats and can often be seen prowling about in broad daylight. Being sinuous in build and very low on its legs, it must find it easy to make its way through the most viciously tangled undergrowth and probably does most of its foraging on the ground. It is, however, an agile climber, and mammalogist Vernon Bailey records shooting jaguarundis out of trees while hunting deer at night.

According to Rengger, the jaguarundi preys mainly on birds, but also takes small mammals, such as guinea pigs, mice, agoutis, rabbits, and very young deer. The Swiss naturalist gave an excellent account of the animal's way of hunting:

> As jaguarundis only too often approach human dwellings in order to steal chickens and ducks, I often had opportunities to observe it on its forays, or to create those opportunities myself by tying a hen to a long piece of string near a hedge I knew to be inhabited by one of these predators. After a short while, the jaguarundi's head poked out from among the bromeliads, now here, now there, the animal peering around attentively in order to make sure that the coast was clear. It then tried to approach the hen unseen, keeping its body close to the ground and hardly disturbing the blades of grass in its stalk. Having got to within six or eight feet of its prospective victim, the jaguarundi slightly contracted its body and darted at the bird in a well-aimed spring, grabbing it by the head or neck with its teeth and immediately attempting to drag it into cover. In stalking, it did not twitch its tail as much as other cats I have observed. It is often seen near houses, watching the poultry from the cover of some shrubbery. I never found it on trees, except when chased by dogs, in which case it passes from one tree to another with great agility. I have, however, been told that at night it quite often takes sleeping hens out of trees. It does not kill more than one animal at a time. Should its prey be too small to satisfy its hunger, it will immediately hunt again. . . . On its hunting trips it does not roam very far. It swims well, but does not enter the water without necessity.

On a collecting trip to Guerrero on the Pacific coast of Mexico, Edward Nelson was told by the natives that the jaguarundis of that region showed a preference for the vicinity of streams and entered the water freely.

Of the jaguarundi's breeding habits Rengger was able to give the following information:

> It is generally met with in couples which live within well-defined territories. These territories are quite frequently shared with other pairs, the

jaguarundi differing in this respect from all other species of cats. My dog once chased six adult jaguarundis out of one hedge. Mating takes place from September to November. The animals can then be heard fighting among the bromeliads, uttering screeching noises. The female seems to have a gestation period of nine to ten weeks. The two or three young are born in a thicket or in a hollow tree, sometimes in a ditch overgrown with scrub. The mother never leaves her offsprings alone for any length of time, and as they grow up, she brings them birds and guinea pigs. After some time she takes them out hunting. She does, however, not defend them against humans or dogs and runs away from her den as soon as it has been discovered by a hunter.

In Mexico, jaguarundis are said to be solitary, except during the mating season, which falls into the months of November and December. Kittens have, however, been reported not only in March, but also in August, and there may possibly be two litters per year.

Rengger found captive jaguarundis to become tame and affectionate, but whenever they were given their freedom for only one moment, they immediately streaked away to the court-yard in order to catch a hen or a duck. Even when put on a leash they did their utmost to get at the birds. A jaguarundi that had just seized a duckling let itself be picked up by its collar and swung through the air without relinquishing its hold on the bird. If the victim was torn away from it by force, the cat snapped its jaws in great fury and tried to bite the hand that had robbed it of its prey.

Jaguarundis chirp like birds and purr when in a friendly and playful mood. In pre-Columbian times, the inhabitants of some parts of South America apparently kept them as domestic and semi-domestic animals in order to keep rats and mice in check.

Forest wildcat, *Felis silvestris silvestris*

African wildcat,
Felis silvestris lybica

A young sand-dune cat,
Felis margarita

TIERBILDER OKAPIA

Jungle cat, *Felis (Chaus) chaus*

TIERBILDER OKAPIA

DR. BERNHARD GRZIMEK, FROM TIERBILDER OKAPIA

Pallas's cat, *Felis (Otocolobus) manul*

Lynx, *Lynx lynx*

THE WORLD WILDLIFE FUND

Bobcat, *Lynx rufus*

Caracal,
Caracal caracal

Serval, *Leptailurus serval*

Golden cat, *Profelis aurata*

B. A. TONKIN, FROM MAX-PLANCK-INSTITU

Temminck's cat, *Profelis temmincki*

Leopard cat, *Prionailurus bengalensis*

Fishing cat, *Prionailurus viverrinus*

Flat-headed cat, *Prionailurus planiceps*

Iriomote cat, *Prionailurus (Mayailurus) iriomotensis*

Ocelot, *Leopardus pardalis*

Margay, *Leopardus wiedi*

Geoffroy's cat,
Leopardus geoffroyi
DR. PAUL LEYHAUSEN,
FROM MAX-PLANCK-INSTITUT

Oncilla, *Leopardus tigrinus*

DR. PAUL LEYHAUSEN, FROM MAX-PLANCK-INSTITUT

E. KOHLER, FROM MAX-PLANCK-INSTITUT

Pampas cat, *Lynchailurus colocolo*

A young jaguarundi,
Herpailurus yagouarundi

P. SCHAUENBERG, FROM THE WORLD WILDLIFE FUND

Puma, *Puma concolor*

Clouded leopard, *Neofelis nebulosa*

Snow leopard, *Uncia uncia*

Lioness and lion, *Panthera leo*

C. A. W. GUGGISBERG

White tigers, *Panthera tigris*

Leopard, *Panthera pardus*

Jaguar, *Panthera onca*

A cheetah mother and her juvenile cub, *Acinonyx jubatus*

Puma, Cougar

Puma concolor

(LINNAEUS 1771)

The early North American settlers were exceedingly lavish in be-
stowing names upon the big cat that figures as "puma" in most natural history books. They called it cougar, panther, painter, catamount, lion, Mexican lion, silver lion, mountain lion, mountain
demon, mountain devil, mountain screamer, brown tiger, red tiger,
deer tiger, deer killer, Indian devil, purple feather, king cat, sneak
cat—or simply varmint. The word "puma" comes from the Quechua
language of Peru, while "cougar," which is also widely used, may be
a derivation from the "sussuarana" of the Tupi Indians. The Span-
iards of Argentina and Central America referred to the animal as
leon or leon americana, the Portuguese in Brazil as onça vermilha—
red jaguar—and leao. It is thus evident that to a majority of Europeans it immediately brought to mind the lion of the Old World.

The first European explorer to mention the puma must have
been Amerigo Vespucci, who, in 1500, referred to "lions" among the
animals encountered on an expedition to Venezuela. A couple of
years later, Christopher Columbus saw "lions," along the coasts of
Honduras and Nicaragua. As far as North America is concerned, Sir
John Hawkins suggested in 1565 that there were "lions and tigers"
in Florida. Writing about the same area in 1598, René Laudonnière
reported having observed "a certain kinde of beast that differeth
little from the lyon of Africa."

Captain John Smith recorded the puma for Virginia when he
wrote in 1610, "There be in this country lions, beares, woulves,
foxes, muske catts, hares, fleinge (flying) squirrels and other squirrels." The Dutch settlers of New Amsterdam regarded the puma as
identical with the African lion, but they could not help wondering
why all the skins brought in for sale by the Indians were of maneless
lionesses only. When questioned on this point, the Indians had an
answer: The males, they said, lived among mountains many day's
travel away, and were so terribly fierce that nobody in his right mind
would dare to go after them.

Zoologically, the puma has very little in common with the lion or
with the other big cats—tiger, leopard, and jaguar. The ossified
hyoid gives it the ability to purr like a huge tabby. It has a catlike
scream, but does not roar and must probably be regarded as having

107

descended from some small cat, going through an evolution more or less parallel to that of the so-called big cats without being in any way closely allied to them. While the pupils of most small cats contract to a slit, those of the puma remain round, as, for instance, those of the jaguarundi. There are taxonomists who postulate a distant relationship with that species.

The puma was named *Felis concolor* by Linnaeus, but its isolated position, without any near living relatives, was recognized by Sir William Jardine as early as 1834, when he proposed to change the generic designation from *Felis* to *Puma*. The skull appears remarkably short and rounded. The first upper premolar is present.

Characteristics. The puma's head is small, almost bullet-shaped, with the facial part short and rounded. The ears are small, short, and rounded, without terminal tufts. The neck is comparatively long, the body very elongate, lithe, and narrow. The limbs are strong and muscular, with the hind legs considerably higher than the forelegs, giving a greater elevation to the rump than to the shoulders.

The tail is long, cylindrical, and well haired. The pelage in tropical regions is short and rather bristly, longer and softer in northern and southern areas. Its colouration varies enormously. As in many other cats, there are red and grey colour phases, the first ranging from buff, cinnamon, and tawny to cinnamon-rufous and ferruginous, the second from silvery grey to bluish and slaty grey. Red forms generally dominate in tropical countries, brown and grey ones in dry habitats, while the pumas inhabiting the humid forests of the northern Pacific Coast tend to be of a sombre colouration. A striking variability can, however, be encountered within one and the same locality, and Theodore Roosevelt, hunting in Colorado, records shooting both red and slaty grey pumas.

The colouration becomes abruptly lighter on shoulders and flanks and usually turns to dull whitish on the underparts. The sides of the muzzle are black, upper lips, chin, and throat almost pure white, the backs of the ears, black with or without greyish or reddish median patches. The tail is of the same colour as the back on its upper side, lighter below, and dark brown or blackish for the last 5 to 10 cm (avg. 3 in) of its length.

Young pumas are yellowish brown, but differ from their parents by having a striking pattern consisting of irregular rows of large black spots. Three to five more or less interrupted longitudinal lines run backward from the nape and curve inward at the shoulders to form a median row of narrow, elongated spots, which, in some specimens, can run into a black line on the rump. The tail is ringed. These markings fade out gradually and for the most part disappear when the animal is about half grown. However, traces of the juvenile pattern can occasionally be seen on the skins of adult tropical specimens.

Black pumas have occasionally been obtained in South and Central America, but never in the United States or Canada. Cases of albinism seem to be very rare.

The numbers of subspecies enumerated by various authors range from twenty-six to thirty.

Measurements. The puma varies almost as much in size as it does in colour, with the largest specimens being found in the extreme northern and southern parts of its area of distribution. Shoulder height is 60 to 76 cm (avg. 27 in). Male: head and body length is 105 to 195.9 cm (avg. 59 in); tail, 66 to 78.4 cm (avg. 28 in). Female: head and body length is 96.6 to 151.7 cm (avg. 47 in); tail, 53.4 to 81.5 cm (avg. 26 in). Weight of male is 67 to 103 kg (avg. 191 lb); of female, 36 to 60 kg (avg. 108 lb). According to Petzsch, weights may differ even more, from 25 kg (56 lb)—southern Mexico, Guatemala, Honduras—to 110 kg (248 lb). In Idaho, males were found to vary in weight from about 59 kg (133 lb) to 82 kg (185 lb), averaging 68 kg (153 lb). There was less divergence in female weight and the average is around 45.3 kg (102 lb). The biggest Colorado puma—a male—measured by Theodore Roosevelt, had a total length of 2.43 m (8 ft) and a weight of 102.94 kg (232 lb).

Distribution. The puma is the most widely distributed of American cats. It originally ranged from Vancouver Island, the Peace River and Cassiar districts of British Columbia, central Alberta, western Saskatchewan, southern Ontario, southern Quebec, New Brunswick, Nova Scotia, and Maine to the Straits of Magellan.

The species has become rare in many parts of northern America, and not so long ago it was thought to be extinct in eastern Canada and in the central and eastern United States, with the exception of a few hanging on precariously in the Florida Everglades, the Okefinokee Swamp of Georgia, and possibly in New Brunswick and Nova Scotia. We now know that it still occurs in some numbers in eastern Canada, and there have been recent—though not very well substantiated—reports of its continued existence in Maine, northern New York, New Jersey, and in the remoter parts of the southern Appalachians. Within the United States, cougars can be found in many of the wilderness areas in the west of the 100th meridian, and are most numerous in the Rocky Mountain states, Texas, and New Mexico, and in the coastal ranges of California, Oregon, and Washington. The New York Zoological Society has estimated the number of pumas surviving in the West at about 4000 to 6500. It is still present in Alberta and British Columbia in Canada.

H. Hesketh Prichard could still say after he explored the southernmost part of the puma's range in 1900: "The number of pumas in Patagonia is very great, more so than any zoologist has yet given an idea of." He had to add, however: "During one winter, two pioneers killed 73 near Lake Argentina. Near San Julian, immense numbers are yearly destroyed, but lately, owing to the advent of settlers, they are becoming less numerous."

The puma, eradicated from the more densely settled areas of South America, has nevertheless managed to hold out amazingly well. As recently as 1940, Cabrera referred to it as abundant in the interior of Argentina and especially in Patagonia, and he was, at that time, able to record its presence in the mountain areas of the southern part of the Buenos Aires Province. During the last thirty years, its range is sure to have been further restricted, its numbers drastically reduced, but it must be widely distributed even today.

Habits. In order to occupy an area of distribution extending over about 100 degrees of latitude, from the bleak shores opposite Tierra del Fuego through the Tropics to a point not more than 800 km (495 mi) from the Arctic Circle, an animal has to be highly adaptable. And the cougar can, in fact, exist in almost any place which offers it a sufficiency of prey and adequate cover. It feels equally at home in coniferous forests, swampy jungles, and tropical forests, in open grass lands, dry bush, and semi-deserts. Pumas can be encountered in the higher regions of the Olympic and Cascade mountains, at the very bottom of the Colorado Valley, and up to 3350 m (11,000 ft) on Mount Whitney. In many parts of South America it occurs at sea level, but Edward Whymper also recorded it at 4500 m (14,800 ft) near Mount Pichincha in the Equadorian Andes.

The adjectives most often applied to the animal which Stanley P. Young, a senior biologist of the United States Biological Survey, and Edward A. Goldman called the "Mysterious American Cat" in their excellent monograph, are "secretive, elusive and wary." Just how secretive the puma can be is well illustrated by the fact that a famous Montana hunter who killed about seventy, had to admit he had never seen one of his victims before the dogs had driven it up a tree.

The cougar, naturally shy and skulking, is also predominantly nocturnal. Where it does not have to fear human persecution, it can occasionally be encountered between sunrise and sunset. And a scarcity of prey may even force it to hunt in broad daylight. During winter in Idaho, Hornocker found it hunting as much by day as by night, if not more. Observed on its forays, the puma is seen to walk rather sedately, with head down and ears back, the muscular legs creating an impression of considerable strength. The big cat does, however, also give displays of great agility. It can bound along at high speed and feels perfectly at home in trees. The relatively long hind legs give it tremendous leaping powers, and when pursued by dogs, it usually does not climb a tree, but leaps onto it, covering in its first jump a distance of from 3 to 5.5 m (avg. 14 ft). Leaving a tree, it will jump from high up, hit the ground with its feet ready to bound away immediately. Young had evidence of a puma, alarmed by a magnesium flare, jumping 4 m (13 ft) on a slight downhill slope from a normal walking stance. Other naturalists have recorded springs of 6 (20 ft) and up to nearly 12 m (39 ft).

It swims well but shows a definite aversion to water and only enters it when forced to do so out of utmost necessity. In preference to swimming a swollen stream, a puma pursued by Rengger's dogs ran up a trunk to a branch overhanging the water and leaped across to a tree on the other bank.

Solitary for most of the year, each individual inhabits a territory of possibly about 30 km² (12 mi²), though in some cases the home range may have a radius of as much as 50 to 65 km (avg. 36 mi). Maurice G. Hornocker, during five winters spent in studying a puma population of ten adults within a 518-km² (200 mi²) area of Idaho, collected data which made him estimate the winter home ranges of males to vary from 39 to 77 km² (avg. 22 mi²), those of females from 13 to 64 km² (avg. 15 mi²).

As they are great wanderers, pumas apparently do not usually have fixed dens, except during the breeding season. They spend the day in some thick cover, in mountain areas perhaps in a cave or under an overhang or in a rock fissure and then move on to some other place. In course of their wanderings they often travel large distances. A professional hunter followed a puma track for two days in the Manzano Mountains of New Mexico and reported that the cat had covered thirty miles without making a kill or stopping for any appreciable length of time. Vernon Bailey, of the United States Biological Survey, had a similar experience at 3000 m (9800 ft) in the Mogollon Mountains of New Mexico. He struck very fresh tracks one October morning and followed them as rapidly as possible—but he had to give up after several miles without having caught even a glimpse of the animal. He did, however, notice three places where it had scratched up little heaps of earth and spruce needles from beneath the snow. At least two of these were quite obviously sites which the cougar in its wanderings visited regularly in order to place territorial scent marks.

Each winter, about half a dozen vagrant pumas passed through Hornocker's study area:

> Wandering lions of both sexes appear to know when they are in another lion's home ground. The resident scrapes together leaves, twigs, or pine needles into mounds from four to six inches high, then urinates on them, to make sight and scent markers delineating its territory. We found such "scrapes" under trees, on ridges, and at lion crossings, where the markers act as traffic lights on regularly traveled paths. Whenever we traced a newcomer to one of the scrapes, the trail showed that the lion had abruptly changed its course, knowing that another lion or family was in the vicinity, and retraced its route for two or three miles before trying a different area.

For this type of behaviour, Hornocker coined the term "mutual avoidance."

Sight is the cougar's most acute sense, and it undoubtedly plays a major part in locating prey. While hearing is certainly very good, the sense of smell is considered as poorly developed by the majority of authors. Stanley P. Young, who has a very good knowledge of pumas in the field, does not agree with this and regards it as keener than that of the bobcat, although less so than that of either the wolf or the coyote. He thinks that much of the stalking is done by scent alone.

The cougar's prey naturally varies greatly according to habitat, season, and geographical region. For North America, the list of victims includes white-tailed deer, black-tailed or mule deer, elk, moose, pronghorn antelope, mountain sheep, Rocky Mountain goat, peccary, beaver, mice of various kinds, mountain beaver, hares, porcupine, coyote, marten, skunk, wild turkey, fish, slugs, and grasshoppers.

A laboratory analysis, performed by the U.S. Fish and Wildlife Service on 113 stomachs collected in nine Western states gave the following percentage of food items according to volume and frequency: In spring: deer, 56/58; porcupines, 14.7/19; sheep and goats, 6.4/6; horses and cows, 9.7/10; other mammals, 10/13. In summer: deer, 56.3/56; porcupines, 25/25; horses and cows, 6.2/6; other mammals, 12.5/13. In autumn: deer, 42.5/45; porcupines, 30/35; sheep and goats, 7.5/10; horses and cows, 10/10; other mammals, 5/5; carrion, 5/5; grass trace, 5. In winter: deer, 72.6/74; porcupines,

16.4/17; sheep and goats, 5.4/9; horses and cows, 2.2/2; other mammals, 10.1/4; carrion, 1.1/2; grass, 2.2/2.

The examination of forty-three Californian stomachs showed that only two out of the total number, less than 5%, contained domestic stock, while thirty-four, or 80%, contained deer.

Twenty-eight puma droppings picked up on the Olympic Peninsula of Washington State, home of Roosevelt's wapiti, contained remains of eleven varying hares (32.25%), eight black-tailed deer (23.55%), three wapiti (8.82%), two pine squirrels (5.88%), two mountain beavers (5.88%), two white-footed mice (5.88%), two wood-rats (5.88%), one meadow mouse (2.94%), one flying squirrel (2.94%), and small quantities of unidentifiable bones and hair.

John F. Schwartz, who examined the droppings, stressed the cougar's obvious reliance on a rather large variety of so-called "economically neutral" species.

In Idaho, Hornocker found pumas to prey mainly on the herds of wapitis and mule deer, which were nevertheless steadily increasing in numbers. Grazers do, of course, tend to multiply up to the point of eating themselves out of food. When this happens, the resulting winter mortality is enormously heavy, and it will take years for the vegetation and for the animal populations to recover from such a catastrophe. Hornocker therefore came to the conclusion that, under conditions as they existed in Idaho, puma predation was beneficial to the game animals. His researches showed that to a considerable extent there was a culling of the poorest specimens, for not only were a high proportion of the animals killed either young or very old—three-quarters of the wapiti, for instance, were under one and a half or over nine and a half years—but half the victims could be proved to have suffered from malnutrition.

Besides elk and mule deer, Hornocker's pumas also took snowshoe rabbits, wood rats, mice, squirrels, raccoons, and coyotes. He tells of one having made a full meal of nothing but grasshoppers.

Young records a few rare cases of cannibalism, especially of dead or trapped pumas devoured by individuals of their own species. Males have been known to kill and eat cubs when the mother was not present to protect them.

Huemul or Andean deer and guanacos seem to form the major part of the cougar's prey in Patagonia. Darwin mentioned them as killing rheas and viscachas in La Plata, while Rengger lists agoutis, pacas, red and grey brocket deer, peccaries, monkeys, rheas, sheep, calves, and colts for Paraguay. In the Mato Grosso region of Brazil the victims are said to consist mainly of pampas deer, brocket deer, ant-eaters, and rheas.

In Guiana the puma often follows the herds of peccaries, but the Indians regard it as first and foremost an enemy of deer and call it by a name which, in translation, corresponds to the designation "deer tiger." formerly in use among the North American settlers.

As Young points out: "Although the puma takes a wide range of food, both wild and domestic, nevertheless its favorite food, when available, is unquestionably the deer. Its extensive range attends to this fact, and in general it may be said that the puma goes with the deer." Throughout its area of distribution it must once have been one of the main factors regulating populations of cervidae, and it should never have been eradicated from the Yellowstone and Jackson Hole areas, which are now disastrously over-populated with wapiti.

The moose figures among the cougar's victims on the basis of hearsay evidence picked up among the Indians of the southern Mackenzie region. This has never been confirmed, but one could certainly visualize a puma taking a young or half-grown moose. It has, after all, been found quite capable of bringing down full-grown and perfectly healthy wapitis.

In Argentina, the puma has long had the reputation of an animal not only absolutely harmless to man, but actually harbouring mysteriously gentle instincts toward humans, which were said, on occasion, to make it act in a friendly and even protective way. The gauchos called it *amigo del christiano* (the Christian's friend), probably on recollection of an event supposed to have taken place in 1536, at a time when an Indian siege had reduced the Spanish inhabitants of Buenos Aires to near starvation. A girl named Maldonada slipped out of the town to search for edible roots, but lost her way. She probably lived for a time in an Indian village, but according to one version she found shelter in a cave inhabited by a female puma and her cubs, the animals accepting her as the wolves accepted Rudyard Kipling's Mowgli. After peace had been restored, she was found by a party of soldiers and brought back to Buenos Aires, where the governor accused her of having sided with the Indians. She was taken to a forest about a league from town and chained to a tree so she would be devoured by wild beasts. When some people went out two nights and a day later to collect her remains for burial, they found Maldonada alive and unharmed, a great female puma keeping sentry before her and "guarding her from a host of other pumas and jaguars that chafed and mouthed on every side." Not wishing to appear more heartless than a puma, the governor thereupon pardoned her. According to W. H. Hudson, the legend of Maldonada was, in his time, as familiar to Buenos Aireans as the story of Lady Godiva's ride to the inhabitants of Coventry, and it may well have helped to colour the way Argentinians tended to view the "leon." The animal, however, did not benefit from this to any great degree, for the gauchos were not prepared to tolerate the "amigo del christiano's" depredations among their livestock and hunted it mercilessly with lassos and bolas.

Out of North America there has come a goodly crop of horror stories giving gory details of unprovoked attacks by cougars. Those dating back to pioneer times cannot be checked anymore, but of the more recent ones, the majority have tended to melt away under close scrutiny. Of the many reports investigated by A. Bryan Williams, for thirteen years chief game warden of British Columbia, only one could be verified. It referred to an attack on two children, who, acting with great presence of mind, managed to beat off the cat, escaping with sundry bites and lacerations. When the cougar was killed a short time later, close to the spot where it had attacked the children, it was found to be of small size, probably not more than three or four years old, with a cataract in the left eye and the other possibly affected as well. It was thus greaatly hampered in obtaining its normal food.

"Apart from the above case," Williams added, "out of all reports that have come in, not one of an attack on a human being has been verified."

A number of maulings of a similar nature, mostly of children, have had their authenticity proved through the researches of Stanley P. Young, Bruce Wright, Roger A. Caras, and others: There was, for instance, a news item, published in March 1962, which told of a six-year-old boy of Hinton, Alberta, being attacked only three hundred yards from his home. A housewife rushed to his rescue, grabbed the puma by its ears, and pulled it off the frightened child. Bruce Wright found the aggressor to have been a half-grown cub in poor condition, which had apparently been abandoned by its mother and was starving, frightened, and quite capable of acting in an abnormal manner. The boy escaped with a few scratches. Young quotes the well-authenticated case of a boy at Malott, Washington, being attacked and killed, probably because he started to run at the sight of a puma following him out of curiosity.

A man in New Brunswick had a puma jump on his back while lying flat on his face, drinking from a stream. The animal probably mistook him for a deer quenching its thirst. A puma that sprang from a ten-foot-high ledge and injured a friend of Theodore Roosevelt's by knocking him out of the saddle may also have taken the horse and its rider for a game animal.

Rabies, from which pumas are known to suffer occasionally, is sure to have been the cause of some attacks on humans. When a female charged and wounded two boys near Morgan Hill, California, a woman came to their aid and was badly torn herself. Seven weeks later two of the persons involved in the incident developed rabies and died of it.

Hans Schmidt, in his book on the mammals of Argentina, declares the puma as "not dangerous to man." Roger A. Caras, however, gives a somewhat more qualified judgement: "The great cat is listed as 'harmless' and as an animal that can be dealt with with complete impunity. This bravado is foolish and dangerous. The mountain lion is a large predatory animal equipped, as are all cats of its size, to kill fast, strong prey often many times its own weight and size. It moves swiftly from ambush and kills with great efficiency. Such an animal is not to be toyed with. It apparently attacks man only on very rare occasions. When it does so it can be considered as acting in an abnormal manner."

Having spotted a prospective victim, the puma stalks it silently, with great stealth, making excellent use of whatever cover it can find. After having manoeuvred itself into a position from which an attack can be launched, it makes use of its phenomenal jumping powers. A Canadian geologist who was lucky enough to see a puma bring down a Rocky Mountain goat, described it as having made the most beautiful leap he had ever seen, curving through the air and landing squarely on the goat's back. The victim gave one cry, and the two animals rolled out of sight, thus making it impossible for the observer to ascertain the way in which the goat was killed.

Dan McCowan describes an actual killing as follows: "The neck of the luckless captive is broken by a violent blow or a powerful wrench with the paw." Many authors agree with him, but Rengger stated long ago that the puma immediately "tears open" its victim's throat to lick the fresh blood. He may possibly have seen cougars grab animals by the throat in order to kill them through strangulation as other big cats generally do.

Animals killed by pumas have often been found with the neck broken, but this could have been caused more or less accidentally, through the impact of the attack, which must be quite formidable. Coming upon a deer killed only a short time before, Edward W. Nelson made a careful study of the tracks and discovered that from a knoll at the edge of a little glade the puma had leaped on its victim's back and hit it with such force that it had slid 3 (10 ft) to 3.5 m (12 ft) across the sloping ground, apparently having been killed on the instant. A puma trail followed by the same naturalist on a snow-covered New Mexico mountain, led to the top of a projecting ledge, from which the cat had leaped 6 m (20 ft) out and down, landing on the back of a deer and sliding with it 15 m (49 ft) down the snowy slope.

While stalking can be considered as their most usual way of hunting, cougars will also make use of any opportunity that allows them to ambush their prey. A. Bryan Williams knew a salt lick at which one or two mule deer were killed every week. Whenever he visited the place, there were fresh signs of puma, and he found numerous remains of kills in the vicinity. Some of them were hidden in the thickets of neighbouring gulches, others had been carried off a certain distance and left in the open. Some were partly eaten, a few almost entirely so, and an occasional one not even opened up. The deer, strangely enough, kept coming to the lick despite the amount of slaughter that went on in the vicinity, and Williams, sometimes on the edge of a ravine, occasionally on one of the trees nearest to the lick, sat up for many a night, hoping to observe a puma in action.

He failed to see a kill actually being made, but on one occasion there was ample evidence to show that a cougar had jumped down upon a deer from one of the lower branches of the very tree Williams himself was in the habit of climbing. The tracks showed that the victim collapsed without a struggle, the cat remaining on top of the animal until it was ready to carry the carcass away.

When Williams found the kill, the puma had covered it up with leaves, moss, sticks, and dirt, and all that could be seen was one hind leg sticking out. The carcass had not been opened yet and there was no wound visible. "Not a scratch could I find, until I had skinned it. Up where the neck joined the skull there was a mass of congealed blood. The neck was broken, but the body was hardly marked, just a few bruises and claw marks high up on the shoulders. The deer was a very old doe that had not had any fawns that year, and she was fat and heavy and must have weighed more than the cougar, which, judging from his tracks, was only a small one."

The North American porcupine, which must be considered as a fairly important food item for the cougar, is mainly arboreal, and we can assume that many of these sluggish animals are caught up among the trees. In South America, pumas have certainly been seen to pursue much more agile prey through the branches, and Rengger has given a graphic account of such a chase:

> As I waited for my hunting companion, leaning against a tree and facing the setting sun, I heard the flute-like calls of some capucine monkeys which had assembled in a fruit-bearing tree not far away. I grabbed my gun, intending to stalk them, when the whole band suddenly took flight

in my direction. They approached from tree to tree, swinging from branch to branch with characteristic agility, their plaintive cries and the incessant fall of excrements betraying their mortal fear. They were escaping from a cougar, which bounded after them from tree to tree in fifteen to twenty foot leaps. With quite incredible dexterity it slipped through the tangle of liana-festooned branches, ran audaciously along the boughs until they bent down, and then jumped with perfect confidence on to the branches of another tree."

Having successfully brought down an animal, the cougar may take its kill to some sheltered spot, perhaps 100 m (325 ft) to 400 m (1300 ft) away. Being an extremely powerful animal for its size, it is well able to drag a victim five times its own weight. One puma, for instance, lifted a 250-kg (560 lb) heifer out of a narrow water-hole and then moved it up the side of a mountain.

The meal is begun upon a thigh, close to the groin, or by opening the belly and devouring the entrails, the puma squatting over its kill like one of the small cats; the fore-feet are placed on the ground and the animal makes almost no use of them while feeding. When it has consumed enough meat for the time being, it generally hides the carcass under a low mound of sticks, leaves, and other materials which it scrapes together with its paws. This seems to be a fairly constant and certainly very widespread habit. Félix de Azara referred to it long ago in his work on the quadrupeds of La Plata and Paraguay, and Hesketh Prichard mentions it for Patagonia, where, however, the vegetation may be so scarce that the puma has to be content with making a mere pretence at burying the kill, sometimes throwing upon it just one small bunch of thorns.

The puma now retires to a lair, sometimes situated at a considerable distance from the kill, for a digestive siesta, but it will probably come back for another meal after a day or two and may even visit the carcass quite a number of times in course of the next week or ten days. Should an opportunity present itself for making a fresh kill, the old one will at once be forgotten. If nothing of this kind happens, the carcass is sure to be abandoned for good just as soon as the meat goes putrid. Several pumas feeding on one and the same kill usually belong to a family group.

Most authorities are of the opinion that about fifty white-tailed or black-tailed deer might make up a cougar's annual bag, but Vernon Bailey thinks that a hundred would be nearer the mark. A hunter followed a puma's track for eleven days and found that during this period it killed two Rocky Mountain rams and a five-point deer. The sheep were almost entirely consumed, and the cougar rested for two days after the killing of each. Heavy snowfalls made the pursuer lose the spoor, but he came up with the puma again after it had killed the deer.

If a cougar fails in its attack upon a deer, wild sheep, or mountain goat, it may make a few bounds in pursuit, but will, as a rule, soon give up. Swift as it is over a short distance, it has not got the stamina to run down the ungulates which form its principal quarry. According to Hesketh Prichard it can easily be galloped down, rarely running more than three hundred yards or a quarter of a mile when hunted on horseback. There have been reports of three pumas, probably a mother and her cubs or youngsters having become independent a short time ago, chasing a deer, one at each side and the other at the rear. As a rule, however, the puma is a lone hunter, and cooperation outside family groups would certainly be most unusual.

There have been many accounts of one puma killing 30, 40, or even up to 192 sheep in one night. Such mass slaughter, usually put down as performed in an access of "blood lust," results from the fact that the cat's urge to pounce upon a victim is constantly being reactivated by the penned-in animals helplessly milling around it. The situation it finds itself in is quite abnormal, and so, of course, is the puma's reaction. It would never be able to perform a massacre of this kind among the wild animals which form its natural prey, for they take flight the moment one of a herd has been struck down.

The puma has been in many ways one of the most controversial of the large-sized cats, and an especially heated dispute has for a long time been raging on the subject of the high-pitched yell which induced some old-timers to call it the "mountain screamer." In pioneer days, when cougars were still common, this vocal eccentricity seems to have been well known, and there are some classic stories of backwoodsmen mistaking the steam whistle of the first river steamer or railway engine in their experience for the scream of a "catamount." Some professional cougar hunters—whose acquaintance with the species was, after all, restricted to the behaviour of frightened individuals up a tree and surrounded by a pack of ferocious cougar hounds—declared they had never heard it and provided the debunkers of more recent times with a welcome opportunity to consign the puma's scream into the realm of pure myth. A debunker worth his salt will, of course, make as famous a personality as possible the target of his scorn, and in connection with the puma's vocalization, the choice fell upon that great outdoorsman, naturalist, and conservationist, Theodore Roosevelt. The way the debunkers put it, one would think that in stating to have once heard it, Roosevelt practically launched the story of the cougar's "woman-in-agony" scream—and to this is generally added the suggestion that he was most probably deceived by the voice of the great horned owl. What Roosevelt really wrote was this:

> I am not sure that I ever heard one; but one night, while camped in a heavily timbered coulie near the Killdeer Mountains, where, as footsteps showed, the beasts were plentiful, I twice heard a loud, wailing scream ringing through the impenetrable gloom which surrounded the hills around us. My companion, an old plainsman, said this was the cry of the cougar prowling for its prey. Certainly no man could well listen to a stranger and wilder sound.

And nobody could have expressed himself more factually or with greater caution!

Even if some people living or travelling in cougar country have never heard the scream, others have, and among them are such highly respected naturalists as, for instance, Edward W. Nelson who wrote:

> It has a wild screaming cry which is thrillingly impressive when the shades of evening are throwing a mysterious gloom over the forests. In the mountains of Arizona one summer a mountain lion repeatedly passed along a series of ledges high above my cabin at dusk, uttering this loud weird cry popularly supposed to resemble the screech of a terrified woman.

Another well-known zoologist, N. Hollis, jotted down the following notes while doing field-work in Louisiana:

> Feb. 23, 1904. Heard panthers crying about nine o'clock last night. There were probably two of them, as the calls were sounded at short intervals, sometimes only about a minute apart, and one seemed a little farther away. The animals were evidently moving along to the north. The cry is a long drawn out, shrill trill, weird and startling. It commences low on the scale, gradually ascends, increasing in volume, and then lowers at the end.

Could these experienced naturalists, and many others, all have been taken in by the great horned owl? In his delightful book *A Naturalist's Life of New York,* William Beebe recalls the abundance of cougars around the old Dutch settlement of New Amsterdam, and then goes on to say:

> I once stood in front of a cage in the Bronx Zoo close on midnight and watched the tawny inmate as it gave utterance to a loud, long drawn out quavering cry which seemed as if it would never stop, and epitomized the essence of wild nature. To imagine it, multiply the most awesome yowl of a backfence tommy by several times its amount of ominous, menacing, portentous, terrifying, appalling character, and you will rea-

lise what must now and then have frightened little Dutch babies fairly out of their cradles as they lay shivering in their fathers' log cabins in the wilds of Westchester many, many years ago."

A director of the Cincinnati Zoo once admitted having doubted the scream, until one of his captive pumas gave an eerie and adequate demonstration. From the files of the U.S. Fish and Wildlife Service, Stanley P. Young extracted the following matter-of-fact statement made by Robert Bean of the Chicago Zoological Park: "We have never yet had a female mountain lion which did not scream, and in various collections would probably have had twenty to twenty-five females. I never heard a male puma scream, however, but they frequently whistle. Their voice is much like a man whistling on his fingers." Young himself only heard the scream once, in the Zoological Park of Denver, Colorado, in this case, however, coming from a male.

Darwin was probably the first to link the cry with the breeding season. Hesketh Prichard, in Patagonia, had two individuals walking round and round his camp, calling to each other—most probably a courting couple. It was the only time during his Patagonian expedition that he heard pumas break silence.

Just as the famous scream can be described as the enormously amplified screech of an ordinary cat, all the other vocal utterances—low growls, mews, hisses, spits, and caterwaulings—are definitely catlike in character, though intensified in proportion to the respective sizes of cat and puma. The purr, too, is generally louder.

The puma does not have a definite breeding season, and mating can take place at any time of the year. In North America, there are records of young cubs for every month, even though the majority are born in late winter and early spring. For Oregon, Bailey reports births irregularly from April to August. In central Idaho, breeding is largely limited to winter and early spring.

The female is in heat for approximately nine days, and she may be followed by up to four or five males who fight each other noisily. She, in turn, is quite ready to use her claws when pressed too hard by her suitors, and the victorious male approaches her with a certain amount of caution. He bites her neck during the act of mating and then quickly jumps aside in order to escape from her irate retaliation.

There is, however, evidence of a certain amount of gamboling and cavorting also forming a part of the mating behaviour. Young, coming to a place where pumas had apparently been indulging in amorous games, found numerous traces of fresh urine and dung scratches about twelve feet from a tree against which the cats had been jumping. The association between the two marital partners is a short one—about two weeks according to Hornocker—and the female may afterward mate with other males. The evidence so far available points to her completely isolating herself before she gives birth, with the male assuming no family duties or responsibilities of any kind.

After a gestation period of about ninety to ninety-six days, the cubs—one to five, exceptionally six, with three or four as the most common numbers—are dropped in a cave, under an uprooted tree or in a thicket. They are 20 to 30 cm (avg. 10 in) long at birth and weigh 226 to 453 g (avg. 12 oz). Their eyes are tightly closed for a week or ten days, but always fully open at the end of the second week. The furry, ring-tailed kittens are extremely playful and soon begin to romp about outside the den. Lactation lasts for three months, but can go on until they are almost half grown. The cubs eat meat when about six weeks old, and young pumas kept in captivity have been known to devour up to 113 g (4 oz) of raw liver at a sitting. Their weight increases to about 4.5 kg (10 lb) during the first eight weeks, and attains 13.6 to 20.4 kg (avg. 38 lb) when they are six months old.

The mother purrs contentedly whenever she tends her offspring. She soon begins to bring them bones and meat to chew upon, and will later fetch them from the den and take them out to a deer she had killed, leading them back after they have eaten their fill. Hornocker thinks that the family leaves the den when the cubs are about two months old, resorting from then on to temporary dens and caves.

By autumn, pumas born in spring will accompany their mother on her hunting expeditions, and at the end of the winter they are able to kill game by themselves. They could, under favourable circumstances, get along on their own, but they usually stay with the mother for several months more, sometimes for another year. The family then disperses, the youngsters probably beginning to breed when they are about three years old.

In many parts of its area of distribution, the puma must encounter serious ecological competition from the jaguar, and it is more than likely that whenever the two species share the same habitat, this competition will lead to a certain amount of friction. In some South American countries the puma is thought to be the dominant species, in W. H. Hudson's words "the persistent persecutor of the jaguar, following it and harassing it as a tyrant-bird harasses an eagle or hawk, moving about it with such rapidity as to confuse it, and when an opportunity occurs, springing upon its back and inflicting terrible wounds with teeth and claws." Neither Azara nor Rengger could find any proof for this story, and we are safe to assume that it is the puma that will give way to the bigger and stronger jaguar, just as the leopard gives way to the lion. A similar legend at one time sprang up concerning the puma's relationship with the grizzly bear, and one author even stated that carcasses of bears killed by cougars had been found in northern California. Young, however, points out that all accounts of puma-grizzly clashes coming from hunters and trappers tend to show that the puma gave the grizzly a wide berth. This is all the more easy to believe, as a cougar has on one occasion been known to get the worst of it in an encounter with a wolverine, an animal reputed for its strength and fighting pluck, but considerably smaller in size than the cat it defeated.

As a whole, however, the puma has few enemies apart from man, and it can even be considered as remarkably free of parasites and harmful diseases. It probably suffers rather more from ticks than from fleas, and a few round-worms and tapeworms have been found in its stomach, the immature stages of some of the latter occurring in the deer which form the puma's favourite prey. Rabies seems to be about the only disease affecting it at all seriously.

Like all other hunters, human or animal, the puma is by no means infallible, and it may occasionally bungle things badly enough to come to serious harm. One was injured at Hell Creek, Montana, when a mule deer it tried to kill, leaped or fell off the edge of a perpendicular bank and landed on its back with the aggressor underneath. W. H. Hudson tells the story of a man of El Carmen in Patagonia who, while riding near the Rio Nero, had his curiosity aroused by the behaviour of a cow standing alone in the grass, her head raised and watching his approach with every sign of dangerous excitement. Knowing that she had recently dropped her calf, he began to search for it, and while he was doing so, the cow repeatedly charged him with great fury. Eventually he found it lying dead in the long grass—and by its side a full-grown puma, also dead and with a large wound behind the shoulder. The tooth-marks on the calf's throat gave proof that it had been killed by the puma, which, in turn had been attacked and gored to death by the cow.

If a puma manages to survive human persecution as well as the hazards of its predatory existence, death will eventually catch up with it in the form of slow starvation due to the effects of age—worn or broken teeth and gradual bodily deterioration which reduces the animal's strength and agility. Old pumas have been shot which, as Young puts it, were shadows of their former selves. Longevity has been estimated at about twelve, possibly up to fifteen or even twenty years.

Pumas are mostly hunted with dogs, and they generally show an amazing lack of fighting spirit when cornered. Bryan Williams said:

> They do not show much inclination to make a fight of it, but will slink under a log if they can or hide in some thicket, and though they may snarl and spit at you, they never charge out. Under very favourable circumstances cougars will summon up enough courage to jump on a small dog, and once in a while even a fair sized one; even collies have fallen victims to them; but it always happened when the dog had been taken unawares, as even a foxterrier will send them flying away if he goes at them in earnest.

Puma meat was eaten in early Virginia, and Azara's peons in Paraguay at times gave it preference over beef. Darwin's experience at an Argentinian outpost on the Rio Tapalquén is worth quoting: "At supper, from something which was said, I was suddenly struck with horror at thinking that I was eating one of the favourite dishes of the country, namely a half formed calf, long before its proper time of birth. It turned out to be puma. The meat is very white and remarkably like veal in taste." When questioned by Darwin the gauchos differed in their opinion whether jaguar was good eating or not, but they were unanimous in saying that puma was excellent.

Pumas do well in captivity and have been bred successfully in many zoological gardens. They tame down easily, and some have been trained to perform in moving pictures and circus arenas.

Clouded Leopard
Neofelis nebulosa
(GRIFFITH 1821)

While many zoologists regard the clouded leopard as allied to the big cats of the genus *Panthera,* others see it as an Old World parallel to the puma, as the giant descendant of a small cat, without any close association with lion, tiger, leopard, and jaguar. They link it with the marbled cat—which, in actual fact, looks exactly like a miniature edition of the clouded leopard—in the same way as the puma is sometimes linked with the jaguarundi. It can be said that in this species the characteristics of the big and small cats are blended to almost equal parts. The hyoid is ossified, making it possible for the clouded leopard to purr. The pupils, neither round nor linear when contracted, have vertically oblong apertures.

The skull, is long, low, and narrow, with the orbits widely open behind. The upper canines are relatively longer than in any other living feline, almost tusklike and with a very sharp edge posteriorly, coming in this respect, as Sterndale remarked a long time ago, nearest to the extinct sabre-toothed tiger. The gap between canines and premolars is very broad, with the first upper premolar frequently wanting.

The clouded leopard was first brought to the notice of the scientific world by Sir Stamford Raffles, who mentioned it in his *Descriptive Catalogue of a Collection Made in Sumatra,* without, however, giving it a scientific name. The specimen on which Griffith based his *Felis nebulosa* is thought to have come from China. Little attention seems to have been paid to his description, for in 1823 the clouded leopard was named *Felis diardii* by Cuvier, in honour of Pierre-Medard Diard, the French naturalist, and two years later Horsfield, in collaboration with Temminck, came up with still another name, *Felix macrocelis.* Desmoulins popularized Cuvier's *diardii* in his *Dictionnaire classique d'Histoire Naturelle,* and the name was subsequently used by Blyth, Jerdon, and Sterndale. Horsfield's *macrocelis* became just as well established, partly through the writings of Robert Swinhoe, who was the first to report the clouded leopard from Hainan and Formosa. In accordance with the rules of priority, both *diardii* and *macrocelis* eventually had to give way to *nebulosa,* while the generic designation *Neofelis* was proposed by Gray in 1867.

Raffles referred to the animal by its Malay name, "rimauda-

125

han," which is usually translated as "tree tiger." Swinhoe pointed out that the Chinese, on account of the markings recalling the shape of mint leaves, call it "mint leopard," in distinction from the common leopard, whose spots, shaped like coins, earned it the name of "golden cash leopard." Swinhoe described the clouded leopard of Formosa as a distinct species, naming it *Leopardus brachyurus*. It is now recognized as a somewhat smaller, more brightly coloured subspecies with a relatively shorter tail.

Characteristics. The clouded leopard is of about the size of a small leopard. It has a long body, short limbs, and a tail that can be almost equal in length to head and body. The coat varies from earthy brown to pale or rich yellowish brown. On the cheeks and sides of the head there are two black bands, one extending from the eye to beneath the ear, the other, more or less parallel, passing backward from the angle of the mouth. The backs of the relatively short, rounded ears are black with greyish central patches. Two broad bands, with narrow lines or rows of elongate spots between them, run from the ears to the shoulders, and continue along the back in the form of oval or elongate patches. The flanks are most handsomely marked with large, irregularly disposed cloudy blotches of a darker shade of colour than the background and partially edged with black. The underparts are white or pale tawny, marked, as are the limbs, with big black spots. The tail, well furred and of nearly the same thickness throughout, is encircled by black rings, some of which may be interrupted at the sides.

Measurements. A male from near Darjeeling stood 53.3 cm (21 in) at the shoulder, had a head and body length of 93.9 cm (37 in), a tail length of 76.1 cm (30 in), and a weight of 21.9 kg (49 lb). Canines of 3.81 (1 in) and 4.44 cm (2 in) have been measured.

Distribution. From Nepal, Sikkim, Bhutan, and the Assam Hills to Burma, Malaya, lower Siam, Indochina, and southern China, where it has been recorded as far north as Fukien; also Hainan, Formosa, Borneo, Sumatra. While searching for the Iriomote cat, Tagawa heard the natives of Iriomote Island speak of a tiger-like cat which they called "Yamayama" and described as of about the size of a sheep-dog. This might possibly refer to the clouded leopard.

Habits. The "rimau-dahan" is a forest dweller, secretive, retiring, and seldom seen. Raffles obtained two cubs when visiting Ben-

coolen on the west coast of Sumatra, and he described them as remarkable for good temper and playfulness:

> The natives assert that when wild they live principally on poultry, birds
> and smaller kinds of deer. They are not found in numbers, and may be
> considered rather a rare animal even in the southern part of Sumatra.
> Both specimens were procured from the interior of Bencoolen, on the
> banks of the Bencoolen River. They are generally found in the vicinity
> of villages, and are not dreaded by the natives, except as far as they may
> destroy their poultry. The natives assert that they sleep and often lay in
> wait for their prey on trees; and from this circumstance they derive the
> name of "dahan," which signifies the fork formed by the branch of a
> tree, across which they are said to rest, and occasionally stretch them-
> selves.

Jerdon had a cub from the vicinity of Darjeeling and found it
just as tame and playful as the ones Raffles had written about. He
was not able to add much to the scanty knowledge of the species, except for stating that the Lepchas of Sikkim declared it to be destructive to sheep, goats, pigs, and dogs.

In course of the last century, a few specimens reached the London Zoo, and Sterndale quotes the account given of one of them by
a Professor Parker:

> As soon as the iron door of its cell was raised, it would come out into the
> large cage with a peculiar sailor-like slouch, for owing to the shortness of
> its legs, its gait was quite different to that of an ordinary cat, and al-
> together less elegant. The expression of the face, too, was neither savage,
> nor majestic nor intelligent, but rather dull and stupid. It was fond of as-
> suming all kinds of queer attitudes. [The naturalist, Alfred Edmund]
> Brehm describes one as lying prone on a thick branch placed in its cage,
> with all four legs hanging down straight, two on each side of the
> branch—certainly a remarkable position for an animal to assume of its
> own free will.

The position which so much puzzled the professor we now know to
be very frequently assumed by leopards and tree-climbing lions.

Zoological manuals took to presenting the clouded leopard as a
nocturnal animal that hardly ever left the green world of the trees.
Several modern authors have described it as more arboreal than
most other cats, preying almost exclusively upon large birds. One of
them, H. L. Blonk, even explained the peculiarities of its dentition—
the long canines and the broad gap between canines and premolars—as an adaptation to this highly specialized way of life. Nobody
remembered what Raffles and Jerdon had written.

Some doubts as to the strictly arboreal existence of the clouded leopard should, however, have arisen from the fact that most of the specimens bagged by European sportsmen were shot on the ground, as they left cover while a stretch of forest was being beaten for other game. Stebbing, for instance, saw one shot on a hillside in course of a beat for pheasants and barking deer. W. H. Matthews, a long-time resident in the Darjeeling District, where clouded leopards do not seem to be uncommon, shot three in beats, one over a goat and one up a tree. He once came upon a very old female just about expiring after having been caught by dogs. On another occasion, Matthews picked up a male that had died after an all-night battle with another cat, either a clouded leopard or a common leopard.

Some interesting information has come from Sarawak, where E. M. Selous and E. Banks who, when out after wild pigs, twice had their dogs bring to bay a clouded leopard on the ground. They also found two cubs, about five to six weeks old, not in a hollow tree, as is usually assumed, but on the ground in the jungle.

A young male, which Selous and Banks kept in captivity, was often active by day and behaved rather clumsily when balancing on a branch. In his movements he gave a somewhat sluggish impression, slinking along in a slouching gait—the "peculiar sailor-like slouch" of Professor Parker—with his head held low and the long tail curled sideways. He also had an upright walk, a doglike trot, and a gallop. He would not take dead meat and therefore had to be fed with live monkeys, chickens, and rats which he attacked with a sudden rush, bowling them over with a blow of one of his large forepaws before killing them with a single bite. Chickens, of which he was able to consume two a day, were carefully plucked before being eaten, while the rough, rasping tongue was used to lick the fur of a monkey off the skin. The animal was heard to chuckle when pleased or excited and to growl when annoyed. He also uttered a moaning roar, comparable to the sound caused by wind blowing over the mouth of an open jar.

Analysing their observations both in captivity and in the wild, Selous and Banks came to the conclusion that the clouded leopard is much more diurnal and terrestrial than it has been assumed to be. Wild pigs probably are its favourite food, at least in Sarawak, and there is evidence of its repeatedly returning to a kill. S. H. Prater was thus undoubtedly correct when he wrote, in direct contradiction to many other authors, "Its powerful jaws and great canine teeth and sturdy build adapt it to the killing of deer and equally large animals."

Couples may possibly remain together for some time, for there are accounts of two clouded leopards coming out of cover together. Some natives of Sarawak even watched a pair dragging a proboscis monkey out of a tree and killing it. When they tried to approach the cats, the female went for them, and they had to beat a hasty retreat to the boat in which they had left their arms. The female was shot, but when the men landed again, in order to pick her up, they were immediately attacked by the male. Such aggressive behaviour toward humans must be very rare, though Prater does mention a clouded leopard advancing to attack a herd boy, who killed it by splitting its skull with an Indian bush knife.

Dense, evergreen forests are usually said to form the "rimau-dahan's" habitat. In Sarawak, however, it is quite frequently met with in secondary forests. Charles Hose found it not only in low country, for instance on the Barum River, but also at 1500 m (4900 ft) on Mount Dulit. Stebbing thinks that in the Himalayan foothills it may occasionally go up to 2000 (6500 ft) or 2400 m (7800 ft). The sightings recorded by Matthews extend from 300 m (980 ft) in the valley of the Runjeet River—a favourite haunt of jungle fowl—to Kirseong at 900 m (2950 ft).

Until very recently practically nothing was known of the clouded leopard's breeding habits. In December 1962, however, the Frankfurt Zoo acquired a pair of these animals, and the female produced a first litter the following spring. In the course of four years, she presented the zoo with no less than twelve cubs, while another female, also imported in 1962, had a litter in 1966. The gestation period was found to have a duration of eighty-six to ninety-two days, and litters numbered from one to five cubs.

Karl Fellner, who made a meticulous study of the first Frankfurt litter, reports that, after having given birth to a male and two females, the mother remained invisible inside the breeding box for five consecutive days. For some time afterward she then came out for food at night only, and for a considerable period she never left her litter for more than a short spell. The cubs were four weeks old when for the first time she spent a few hours away from them. Six weeks later she took to sleeping outside the box.

Lactation lasted for five months, and the male cub was soon noticed to develop much more quickly than his two sisters. At an age of six months, he had attained a weight of 1155 g (40.7 oz), as compared with 1060 (37.1 oz) and 1050 g (36.8 oz) of the females. At thirty-two and a half weeks, the cubs weighed 12 (27 lb), 7.5 and 7.5 kg (16.9 lb) respectively. The cubs began to open their eyes on the twelfth day, and on the nineteenth day for the first time came crawling out of the box, which was standing on the ground.

The two cubs of the second litter, born in a box placed on a shelf about 29 inches above ground, were not allowed out for over five weeks. One that walked around the cage on the thirty-fifth day—possibly having fallen out of the box—was immediately fetched back. On the thirty-ninth day, however, the female stretched out on a tree trunk that was leaning obliquely against the box and began calling to the cubs. She then slowly backed down the trunk, thus inducing the cubs to follow her down to the ground, where they played about for twenty minutes before returning to their "den" all by themselves. This observation certainly gives a good indication of how flexible animal behaviour can be in adaptation to prevailing circumstances.

At the age of three weeks, the cubs of the first litter wrestled with each other inside the box and began to run after their mother. A week later, they played with her, and from then on they rapidly became more and more lively. At six weeks, when they romped and played in spurts lasting from fifteen to forty-five minutes, they jumped up high in the air and also made first attempts at climbing the tree standing in the enclosure. It was about then that they began to show a certain interest in solid food, but for some time to come, dead animals were mainly regarded as toys. At ten and a half weeks the cubs ate pigeons, feathers and all.

Whenever live chicks were placed within the cage, the female picked them up and carried them, still alive, to the cubs, so that they themselves could kill them. This took place for the first time when the youngsters were eleven and a half weeks old. They never tried to catch hold of the birds with their paws, but invariably grabbed them with the mouth, directing their bites toward the heads and necks of the victims. At four and a half months they managed to kill full-grown hens, but found the big, tough birds too much of a mouthful and left them uneaten. When her offspring had reached an age of five and a half months, the mother again took over the job of killing the hens which the cubs now were able to devour without any help. Calling out to the cubs, the female uttered a sound somewhat like "ma-ma." This was answered with a low and very soft "me-me."

When the cubs were five months old, the female displayed unmistakable signs of being in heat again, but remained patient and tolerant toward her litter and never tried to snatch food away from the youngsters. One of these was taken away from her at the age of seven, the other two at seven and three-quarters months. She was then reunited with the male and mating took place forthwith.

Clouded leopards have been recorded to attain an age of sixteen years in captivity.

Snow Leopard, Ounce

Uncia uncia

(SCHREBER 1775)

The snow leopard was first brought to the notice of the European public in 1761, when Buffon produced a recognizable figure of this beautiful cat, but slipped up in stating that it occurred in Persia and was trained for hunting, presumably getting it mixed up with the cheetah. The French naturalist called it "once," a name derived from the "lyncaea" that had long been applied to lynxes and various other felines. In French and English, "once" and "ounce" are still used for the snow leopard, while the Spanish "onza," the Portuguese "onça" and the German "Unze" all refer to the jaguar. Schreber Latinized Buffon's "once" when giving the species its scientific name of *Felis uncia.* He assumed it to occur in "Barbary, Persia, East India and China," and we can hardly blame him for this, considering that the few skins so far seen by Europeans had probably gone from hand to hand in the fur trade, ending up far from their places of origin in the palaces of Oriental potentates or Chinese mandarins. It was only when naturalists such as Peter Simon Pallas and Samuel Gmelin set out to explore the more remote parts of Russia's Asiatic empire that information regarding the snow leopard's true home began to come in.

In a *List of Quadrupeds of Russia and Siberia,* which he sent to Thomas Pennant in April 1779, Pallas wrote of the "ounce:"

> Is pretty frequent in the Bucharian and Altaic mountains, and sometimes seen on the chain that borders upon Siberia. When I was in Siberia, one of a very whitish hue had been kill'd near Tumkinskoi Ostrog on the west side of Lake Baikal, the skin of which is in the Cabinet at Petersburgh. In general this is well known to the Tungusian hunters that live about that lake, and skins of it, as also of the leopard, are frequently brought to us by the Bucharian traders.

Griffith published an illustration taken from a specimen that had somehow found its way to the Tower Menagerie via the Persian Gulf, but Cuvier and Temminck ignored the species, probably suspecting it to be nothing but a long-haired race of the common leopard. Sir William Jardine, in 1834, was not too sure about this either. Introducing the ounce as an animal "which is yet almost unknown," he published an improved version of Buffon's figure and wrote:

131

"We think that naturalists who have the opportunity of seeing or receiving specimens from northern and western Asia should keep this species or variety (whichever it may prove) in recollection."

When British sportsmen began to penetrate the Himalayan valleys in search of ibex and other game, they encountered the snow leopard in the southernmost parts of its range, and zoologists soon had plenty of opportunities to study it from skins, skulls, and, in due course, also from live specimens. The first snow leopard of the London Zoo, a young animal obtained from Bhutan in 1891, did not survive long. Of the second, which arrived in 1894, it is said that on the voyage to England it became a great pet of the ship's cook who taught it to drink tea and milk in addition to the mutton broth which it apparently favoured.

The generic designation *Uncia* in place of Schreber's *Felis* was proposed by Gray in 1854.

Like the clouded leopard, the snow leopard takes up an intermediate position between the small cats and the members of the genus *Panthera,* but it is thought by most taxonomists to stand much closer to the latter, so close, in fact, that J. Ellerman and T. C. S. Morrison-Scott, in their *Checklist of Palaearctic and Indian Mammals,* refer to *Uncia* as a subgenus of *Panthera.* It seems preferable, however, to follow Hemmer and Petzsch in giving it separate generic status. It certainly has many of the attributes of the big cats. The hyoid, for instance, is only partially ossified, but the ounce is nevertheless able to purr. It does not roar, like the members of the genus *Panthera,* and has some behavioural peculiarities, such as its way of feeding, which are reminiscent of the small cats. The cubs display a striking resemblance to those of the puma. The pupils are round in contraction.

The ounce's skull is relatively large, very much shortened and broadened in the region of the brain-case. It differs considerably from that of the leopard, being much higher and more convex when viewed from the side, with a depression at the hind end of the nasal bones which are short and broad. The anterior upper premolar is present.

Characteristics. The ounce is somewhat smaller than a leopard, but has a relatively long tail. The muzzle is short, the forehead high, the chin vertical. The body is elongate, the limbs are powerful and of moderate length. The fur is long, dense, and rather woolly, the hairs attaining a length of 3 cm (1 in) on the mid-back, 6.5 cm (2.5 in) on the belly, and 5 cm (2 in) on the tail. The background colour is smoky greyish, with a light yellowish tinge, especially on the flanks, and turning whitish on the belly. The head is dotted with round black spots. The backs of the short, bluntly rounded ears are black at tips and bases, with the median parts brownish smoky grey. The body is marked with large, somewhat blurred rosettes among which small, compact spots can be seen. The well-furred tail appears very thick and is marked with rosettes which form a pattern of transverse rings. The markings are most intense and conspicuous in young individuals but tend to fade and become diffuse with age.

Measurements. Two Kashmir specimens measured by Colonel A. E. Ward had the following dimensions: Male, head and body length, 111.7 cm (43.6 in), tail, 91.4 cm (35.6 in); female, head and body length, 99 cm (38.6 in), tail, 83 cm (32.4 in). Prater gives a head and body length of 100 to 110 cm (avg. 41 in) and a tail length of 90 cm (35 in). The measurements published by Ognev—head and body length 1.30 m (4 ft), tail, 90 cm (35 in)—must be near the upper limit. The shoulder height is about 60 cm (23 in); the weight, 65 to 75 kg (avg. 158 lb).

Distribution. From the Hindu Kush Mountains, Chitral, Gilgit, Hunza, and the Karakoram Range eastward along the Himalayas and across the Tibetan Plateau to the Kunlun Mountains and Szechwan, north from the Pamirs through the Tien Shan and Altai ranges to the Sayan Mountains on the Russo-Mongolian border southwest of Lake Baikal.

Snow leopards are not nearly so common on the southern slopes of the Great Himalayan Range as on its northern side, but they do extend a short distance along the Dhauladar and Pir Panjal ranges. Major G. Burrard found them especially numerous in the Zaskar Range of southern Ladak. Rumours of its occurrence in the Kopet Dagh Range on the Iranian-Turkmenistan border and in various areas east of Lake Baikal have never been confirmed and may have originated from confusion with long-haired forms of the common leopard.

Habits. The ounce is an inhabitant of high mountain regions, where in summer it can most often be encountered on alpine meadows above the timber-line. It also enters rocky wildernesses and visits the world of snow fields and glaciers, ranging up to at least 5400 m (17,700 ft) in the Ladak Range. As Colonel Ward put it, the only limit at high elevation for the ounce is where game cannot dwell. In winter the snow leopard follows the general migration of game and domestic stock to lower levels, down to 2100 (6900 ft) and even 1800 m (5900 ft) in Kashmir. It may then take up temporary residence among evergreen oaks, in coniferous forests or among rhododendron scrub, occasionally extending its forays to the outskirts of villages. There are places in central Asia where snow leopards are said to remain in the tree and scrub zone all the year round.

Most parts of the snow leopard's homelands are thus remote and difficult of access. Until quite recently, long and arduous journeys were necessary to reach even the fringes of its area of distribution, and the traveller could count himself lucky if he caught just one fleeting glimpse of this beautiful but exceedingly shy and secretive cat.

Under these circumstances it is hardly surprising that even until a short time ago there were no photographs showing the snow leopard in its rugged habitat. George Schaller was the first to photograph them. He was spending a winter in the Chitral Gol Reserve to study the habits of that magnificent wild goat, the markhor. Coming upon snow leopard spoor at about 3350 m (11,000 ft), Schaller decided that in addition to watching markhor, he would do everything possible to see one of these cats.

A week's study of tracks revealed the presence of three ounces within the reserve, a female with a cub and a small, probably subadult individual. Realizing that the chances of catching sight of one while roaming around the mountains was very slim indeed, Schaller staked out domestic goats at five different places. After two weeks his patience and perseverance were rewarded: the mother ounce had killed a goat, and this gave Schaller a unique opportunity for observation and photographs.

When the first goat had been eaten, two more were provided in succession, and Schaller was lucky enough to be present late one afternoon when the female killed the second of these.

In the New York Zoological Society's magazine, *Animal Kingdom,* Schaller gave the following account of what he saw:

> She advanced slowly down the slope, body pressed to the ground, carefully placing each paw until she reached a boulder above the goat. There she hesitated briefly, then leaped to the ground. Whirling around, the startled goat faced her with lowered horns. Surprised, she reared back and swiped once ineffectually with a paw. When the goat turned to flee, she lunged in and with a snap clamped her teeth on its throat. At the same time she grabbed the goat's shoulders with her massive paws. Slowly it sank to its knees, and when she tapped it lightly with a paw, it toppled on its side. Crouching or sitting, she held its throat until, after eight minutes, all movements ceased. Judging by tooth marks on the throat, she had also killed the two previous goats by strangulation.

The snow leopard is both powerful and agile. Ionov, a Russian observer quoted by Ognev, saw one leap not less than 15 m (49 ft) uphill over a ditch. It is quite often active in daytime, especially in the early morning and late afternoon. Prospective victims are stalked or ambushed, and in their search for prey, ounces like to patrol the ridge-tops. Stockley twice found places where, in the soil softened by the melting snow on top of a crest, there was a regular puddled path of snow leopard tracks.

One of the best descriptions of a hunting snow leopard was given by C. A. Stockley:

> I was watching a herd of ibex through a powerful telescope, and a snow leopard suddenly raced across the hollow in which they were feeding and made an attempt on a buck, which started away just in time. The leopard's outstretched claws raked a great lump of hair from the ibex's coat as it wheeled away, and the whole herd bolted to the edge of the hollow, halting on a small ridge, 100 yards away, and staring back at the leopard, which stood waving its great tail in the middle of the hollow. After a minute or so both the parties departed in opposite directions.

The ounce's choice of prey varies according to the species of game available. Ibexes seem to be its preferred victims in some areas, wild sheep, such as shapoo and bharal or blue sheep in others. In the Sutley Valley, for instance, it is known as the "bharal-hay"— the blue sheep killer—due to its predilection for that species. It takes tahr, goats, musk-deer, marmots, snow-cocks, monal pheasants, and red-legged partridges. Russian observers have listed Persian gazelles in the Ala-Tau Mountains, and wild boar in the Trans-Ili Altai. Domestic animals—sheep, goats, and dogs, even the occasional horse, cow, or yak—are taken as well, especially in winter when the cats establish themselves in the vicinity of villages. Of sixteen droppings picked up by Schaller in Chitral Gol Reserve, five contained hair of markhor, eight the remains of domestic sheep and goats, two a large-leafed herb, and one just earth.

Snow leopards have vast territories, within which they move about a great deal, often covering long distances in the process. While following their tracks, Schaller came to places where pungent scent marks had been left on tree trunks or rocks. He also found scrapes, with or without droppings.

Within its home range, an ounce finds plenty of rock crevices and clefts to hide in, and there have been reports of one and the same den having been used for several years in succession. In the Kirghiz Ala-Tau, snow leopards often rest on the huge nests black vultures build in low juniper trees. African leopards have occasionally been seen to lie down on top of a vulture's nest, but large quantities of moulted fur seem to indicate that with the Ala-Tau ounces this is quite a regular habit.

In zoological gardens the gestation period has been found to last for 98 to 103 days. According to Russian authors, mating takes place in late winter and early spring, the two, three, and more rarely four or five cubs are born in April and May. By the middle of summer the young are said to be able to accompany their mother on her hunting trips, and the litter apparently stays together during the next winter.

The cub seen by Schaller was about four months old, a "black and white puff of fur," which meant that it would have been born in August. Game guards stated positively that the female had first been seen with two cubs, and it thus looked as if one might have succumbed to the hardships of winter. The surviving cub kept out of sight most of the time, while the female guarded the kills and drove off thieving crows. Whenever it came out of hiding, it greeted its mother by rubbing its cheek against hers.

In the Chin-meng Mountains of Szechwan a solitary cub was found in a cave about four feet square, which must have been in use as a den for a very long time, for it was carpeted with moulted fur to a depth of about 1.27 cm (0.50 in).

Ward saw two cubs in the Liddar Valley, at an altitude of less than 3000 m (9800 ft) and later obtained possession of them after they had been caught by goat-herds. They became quite tame, and when a big shelf was put up on the veranda for them to sleep on, they would jump up and down, time after time, with extraordinary ease. Directly they touched the veranda floor, they twisted round and bounded back onto the shelf. Nothing would, however, induce them to climb a tree, and even if their food was placed on a bough, they jumped and tried to reach it, but never climbed up the trunk.

Accounts of the ounce generally leave one with the impression of an animal going its own solitary way, except, of course, for a mother and her cubs or for a courting couple. Ionov once watched a playful encounter between two ounces. The first one, running along a mountain stream, suddenly crouched as if preparing to attack. That moment the other snow leopard appeared. The two reared up on their hind legs and exchanged blows with their forepaws. One ran away, the second followed and overtook it in an enormous bound. They rolled about in the grass for a while and then jumped up, arched their backs at each other and went off in different directions.

It has been suggested that pairs might possibly occupy joint territories and co-operate in hunting, one chasing the prey from one part of the valley to where the partner lies in ambush. In 1884, a mission station in Lahaul, did, in fact, suffer from the depredations of two snow leopards. A British officer hunting in the area bagged one of them, a male, late one evening. Next day he shot an ibex and dragged the carcass to the spot where the ounce had fallen. The female came at dusk and was also shot. In this case the two ounces had certainly been hunting together—but were they a couple, or a mother with an almost full-grown youngster? A male in the Dresden Zoo displayed a fatherly interest in his progeny and took part in rearing the cubs. No male, however, showed up in the vicinity of the mother and cub observed by Schaller.

There seems to be no record of a snow leopard ever having made an unprovoked attack upon a human being. The species has, however, suffered very badly from the hand of man, not so much because of its occasional depredations on domestic stock, as for the sake of its magnificent fur. Snow leopards may be wary and secretive, but they are quite easily caught in traps, snares, pitfalls, and even nets. Some years ago, Stroganov assessed the total world catch as "no more than a thousand," but even this was far too much. There seems to have been a sharp decline in numbers since Stroganov's time, for two more recent Russian authors estimated the total of snow leopards taken annually within the Soviet Union at from twenty-four to sixty. The species is now fully protected in all Russian-controlled areas.

The ounce has fared especially badly in Kashmir. Fur traders in both Pakistan and India pay up to 600 rupees for raw skins. With such an inducement to ruthless killing, it might be very difficult to protect the snow leopards of the Chitral Gol, Nanda Devi, and Tons sanctuaries from being wiped out by poachers.

There is one ray of hope, however: The International Fur Trade Federation has agreed to impose among its members a total ban on trade in snow leopard skins. It is now up to the authorities in Europe and America to put a complete ban on their importation, in order to prevent a certain type of status-symbol-mongering tourist from bringing back skins acquired in India and Pakistan. When the demand for its fur is gone, the snow leopard would have a fair chance of survival.

Lion
Panthera leo
(LINNAEUS 1758)

Of the lion it can be safely said that it has made a deeper and more lasting impact on human imagination than any other animal. At an early time in history it attained a prominent place in myth, fable, and folklore. It was made a symbol of bravery and magnanimity and even found itself elevated to the exalted status of "King of Beasts." Its name has become firmly established in the everyday colloquialisms. Expressions such as "the lion's share," "lion-hearted," "as strong as a lion," and "entering the lion's den" are used constantly.

Egyptian pharaohs were sometimes represented as lion-bodied sphinxes, while the Assyrians liked to show their bearded kings as huge, winged lions with human heads. Stone lions have long been mounting guard outside Hittite fortresses, Mycaenean strongholds, and Gothic cathedrals, and they can still be seen as symbolic sentinels in front of palaces and public buildings all over the world. A huge lion overlooks the battle-field of Chaeronea in Boeotia, where Philip of Macedonia and his son Alexander defeated a Greek army. Of a much more recent date is the "Lion of Lucerne," cut into a cliff in remembrance of the heroic last stand of the Swiss guards defending the Tuileries. Ever since 1144, when Henry the Lion, Duke of Saxony, included it in his coat of arms, the lion has played an important part in heraldry. Today, as could hardly have been expected otherwise, it has gone into advertising.

There is, of course, no such thing as a "King of Beasts." This title is a purely human concept not applicable to animal life as it really is. The lion cannot be called "brave" in the way a medieval knight, displaying a lion "rampant" on his shield, would have understood the word. It certainly is not "magnanimous," nor is it "cowardly," as modern authors have often maintained. As a predatory animal it has to kill in order to survive, and in doing so it plays an important part in the ecology of areas swarming with ungulates. Being of a considerable size, as well as enormously strong, it is quite able to defend itself when disturbed, cornered, or wounded, but as a rule it much prefers, in case of danger, to slip away as long as the going is good, and to keep out of sight until the coast is clear again. Its instincts—as those of all other animals—are geared to keeping alive as long as possible in order to propagate the species, and in this scheme of things there simply is no room for heroics or magnanimity.

All these rationalizations will, however, blow away like straws in the wind the very moment you catch sight of a big, well-maned lion standing with its head erect, surveying the vast, rolling plains that is its home. It is then easy to understand the powerful fascination this big cat has exercised over the human mind for thousands of years. Even though the lion may not really be the "King of Beasts," even though we know it to be neither regal nor brave—there are the times when to the eyes of most of us it truly looks every inch a king.

The lion was familiar to the Ice Age hunters of Europe, who depicted it on the walls of their caves. It made its first appearance during the Cromer Interglacial, the warm interval between the first and second—or Günz and Mindel—glaciations. It was then a cat of enormous size, one of the largest felines the world has ever seen. Numerous finds in France, England, and Germany testify to its having been a common animal of the Holstein and Ilford interglacials. It gradually became smaller in size, but the lions of the last—or Würm—glaciation were still larger than our present-day African lions.

The big Pleistocene lions were at one time regarded as belonging to a separate species, known as the cave lion, *Felis spelaeus* Goldfuss. When the skeletons of somewhat smaller lions came to light, some authors suggested that the "cave lion" might really have been a tiger. Pleistocene tigers have, however, been found in China, and their remains differ from those of the European cave lions. Apart from their size, the latter resemble the present-day lions too closely to justify a separation of the species, and the cave lion is now given subspecific status only.

The lion as an inhabitant of mainly open country withdrew when post-glacial Europe became densely forested, probably disappearing from most regions during the Azilian period of the Neolithic. There is no doubt, however, that in classic times it still existed in the Balkans. Herodotus (484–430 B.C.) mentioned it as occurring in considerable numbers between the rivers Achelous in Acarnania and Nechus in Thrace. When Xerxes advanced through Macedonia in 480 B.C., several of his camels were killed by lions. Aristotle agreed with Herodotus as far as distribution was concerned, but considered the lion as a rare animal. George Jennison thinks that there probably were no lions left in Europe in the first century B.C. Other authors, however, assume the species to have vanished from Greece between the years A.D. 80 and 100. The lion, named *Felis leo* by Linnaeus, has all the characteristics of the genus *Panthera*. The pupils are round when contracted, and instead of screaming like an overgrown tom-cat, it roars in a most impressive manner. It is unable to purr, the hyoid being incompletely ossified, with its lower part consisting of an extensible ligament measuring 15 cm (6 in) when relaxed and 22.5 cm (9 in) when stretched. The lion differs, however, from tiger, leopard, and jaguar by its sociable habits, a pronounced sexual di-morphism, and by having a tuft at the end of the tail, within which there is normally hidden a horny spur separated from the last cau-dal vertebra. Some taxonomists have therefore allocated it a special position among big cats, placing it into either a subgenus or genus for which the name *Leo* has been proposed. If this view is accepted, the species would have to be named *Panthera (Leo) leo* or *Leo leo*.

Lions have, on the other hand, often been crossed with tigers. The resulting hybrids, known as "ligers" or "tigons," according to whether they descend from a male lion and female tiger, or a male tiger and a lioness, were long thought to be invariably sterile. In 1943, however, a fifteen-year-old hybrid between a lion and an "Is-land" tiger was successfully mated with a lion at the Munich-Hellabrunn Zoo. The female cub, even though very delicate, was raised to adulthood.

The Koshien Zoo in Japan has had great success in cross-breed-ing "leopons," obtained through mating a male leopard with a lion-ess. Around the turn of the century, three cubs were born in the Chicago Zoo from a male jaguar and a female leopard. They were sold to a travelling menagerie, and the male was killed by a lion, while the females grew to jaguar size. They were mated with a lion—which they seemed to prefer to a leopard—and produced several lit-ters. One of these jaguar-leopard-lions came to the London Zoo. The animal looked like a young, slim lioness but was marked with brown spots of a jaguar- or leopard-like pattern.

The lion's skull is massive, thick, and heavy, remarkably flat on its upper surface, but with well-developed sagittal and occipital crests. The base-line of the lower jaw is slightly convex. The first upper molar is present.

Characteristics. The lion has a broad face, rounded ears, a rel-atively short neck, and a well-proportioned, muscular body rather more drawn in at the belly than that of the tiger. The coat varies considerably in colour, running through the whole scale from light buff and ochre-tinted silvery grey to yellowish red and dark ochre brown. Underparts and insides of the limbs are always lighter, buffy in males, and whitish in females. The outside of the ear is marked on its basal part with a conspicuous black patch. The tuft at the end of the tail is always black, and there may be some blackish hairs on the backs of the hind legs. Lion cubs are marked with spots, which often persist, especially on belly and legs, until the animal is fully adult and may even remain visible all through life.

The mane carried by the male is mostly yellow, brown, or reddish brown in young specimens, but tends to darken with advancing age and may eventually be wholly black, or black with a yellow ruff framing the face. There are lions of three to three and a half years with small, but already darkening manes, as well as considerably older ones with well-developed yellow, brown, or reddish brown manes. All the really fine, cloaklike manes I have seen, however, have been very dark. In Nairobi National Park I obtained a series of colour slides of a lion which, in July 1962, was about four years old and had a scraggy, yellow mane. A photograph taken in October of the same year shows the mane still yellow, but considerably fuller. It then began to darken, and by 1964 it had become very big, yellow and dark brown in colour. In 1965, the lion in question was a truly superb specimen, its mane long and flowing, blackish brown except for a broad yellow ruff.

Within the same geographical region there is so much individual variation that one cannot escape a feeling of considerable scepticism with regard to the ten to thirteen subspecies named by taxonomists, mainly on the basis of size, colouration of the coat, and colouration and development of the mane. The Masai lion, *Panthera leo massaicus,* is supposed to have a medium-sized mane which gives the appearance of having been brushed back from the forehead; yet within the area of distribution allocated to this subspecies, I have seen lions with enormous manes, and while some did look as if they had been brushed back, others could have been brushed upward or even forward in a windswept style. Lions inhabiting cool, open highlands may, on the average, have fuller manes than those living in hot, semi-desert areas or in dense thorn-bush, but the "maneless" lions that have been described from India and reported from various parts of Africa must all have been young males. Some years ago, a male in Nairobi National Park took to killing lionesses. As he was at that moment the best-maned lion in the park, the authorities felt rather hesitant about killing him, and it was finally decided to castrate him in the hope that this might improve his ways. Within three months he had completely lost his hirsute adornment and turned into a truly "maneless" lion, which many visitors mistook for a lioness. The experiment was a failure, insofar as the lion later resumed his murderous attacks on lionesses and had to be shot after all, but it did at least provide an interesting demonstration of the connection between mane growth and hormonal activities. Elderly females sometimes tend to develop side-whiskers, which on rare occasions may assume the appearance of a very small mane.

The now extinct Barbary and Cape lions not only had very full manes, but also a fringe of hair running along the belly. Many Barbary lions were brought to Europe during the last century, and the belly manes that can often be seen in zoo- or menagerie-born specimens give proof of their blood being present even today. I have never seen a lion with a belly mane in East Africa and do not know of anybody who has, but really big-maned lions often sport black tufts at the elbows. Apart from the absence of a belly mane, the most magnificent lion I have ever seen looked very much like the Cape lions painted by William Cornwallis Harris in South Africa during the 1830s. It was a Serengeti National Park lion of exceptionally large size and carried a pitch-black mane that covered part of the back and hung down in front to well between the legs.

In 1960, two albino cubs were reported from the Kruger National Park. Sir Henry Layard, the archaeologist, once saw a very big Persian lion that was very dark brown in colour, in parts almost black.

Measurements. I once measured and weighed two lions, a male and a female, which had been brought to the Kenya Medical Research Laboratory for parasitological examination. All the measurements were taken in a straight line between two pegs. The lion, which may have been between eight and nine years old, had a total length of 2.66 m (9 ft) (head and body, 1.75 m [6 ft]; tail, 0.91 m [3 ft]), a shoulder height of 0.94 m (3 ft), and a weight of 167.5 kg (377 lb). He had lost a considerable amount of blood, and on dissection proved to have practically no fat at all. The lioness had a total length of 2.23 m (7 ft) (head and body, 1.47 m [5 ft]; tail, 0.76 m [2 ft]), a shoulder height of 0.78 m (3 ft), and a weight of 133.35 kg (300 lb).

Colonel R. Meinertzhagen recorded the weights and measurements of all the lions he shot in Kenya. Fourteen males varied in weight from 148.23 to 190.96 kg (avg. 383 lb); in total length from 2.47 to 2.84 m (avg. 9 ft); in shoulder height from 81 to 106 cm (avg. 37 in). The corresponding figures for five lionesses were 121.2 to 184.5 kg (avg. 344 lb); 2.41 to 2.73 m (avg. 8 ft); 0.86 to 1.02 m (avg. 3 ft). One of the biggest Kenya lions ever obtained measured 3.33 m (11 ft). In former British Somaliland, where according to the textbooks lions should be exceptionally small, Lord Wolverton shot a small-maned giant of 3.30 m (10.8 ft) and a fine, black-maned specimen of 3.23 m (10.6 ft).

F. C. Selous shot a large lion close to the Rhodesian settlement of Hartley Hill. The animal was in splendid condition, the belly being covered by a half-inch layer of fat. It had to be cut up for weighing, as the only scale available did not register more than about 100 kg (225 lb). The overall weight of the various parts amounted to 184 kg (414 lb), and, since plenty of blood had been lost, Selous felt justified in adding about another kilogram. The skull alone weighed 2.04 kg (5 lb). The total length was 3.02 m (10 ft), the shoulder height, 1.12 m (4 ft). Selous came to the conclusion that a wild lion weighing more than 181 kg (407 lb) must be considered as exceptional.

The Cape and Barbary lions are assumed to have been considerably larger than the lions of tropical Africa, but it is very difficult now to obtain reliable data. Of two stuffed Cape lions in the Stuttgart Museum, the male has a length of 2.90 m (9.5 ft), and a shoulder height of 1.10 m (3.6 ft), while the lioness is 2.58 m (8.5 ft) long and 0.89 (2.9 ft) high. A male Cape lion in the Wiesbaden Museum has a total length of 2.76 m (9.1 ft), a head and body length of 1.94 m (6.4 ft), and a shoulder height of 1.06 m (3.5 ft). One cannot help wondering whether Cape lions really were any larger than their cousins farther north. Brehm—without quoting his sources—gave the shoulder height of the Barbary lion as 0.80 to 1.0 m (avg. 3 ft), the total length as from 2.35 to 2.80 m (avg. 8 ft). Sir Alfred Pease heard of an Algerian lion that was said to have had a total length of 3.25 m (11 ft), a head and body length of 2.50 m (8 ft), and a shoulder height of 0.95 m (3 ft). Dimensions like these have, however, been reported from other parts of Africa.

Distribution. A few hundred years ago, the lion's area of distribution extended from the Cape of Good Hope to the Mediterranean, and eastward through Palestine, parts of the Arab Peninsula, Asia Minor, Mesopotamia, and Iran to northern India. As far as we know, lions never occurred east of the Gulf of Bengal, either in historic or prehistoric times. In 1810, the species was exterminated in Sind, in 1842 in Punjab. In central India lions were still common in the late 1850s, but in 1891, W. T. Blanford wrote, "In India, the lion is verging on extinction. There are probably a very few still living in the wild tracts known as the Gir of Kathiawar, and a few more in the wildest parts of Rajputana, especially in southern Jodhpur, in Oodaypur, and round Mount Abu. About 20 years ago, lions were common near Gweilor, Goona and Kota, and a few still existed near Lalitpur, between Saugor and Ihansi." About 175 survivors in the Gir Forest are all that is left of India's lions.

As far as Iran is concerned, a lion was killed south of Shiraz in

1923, and sightings have been reported in 1928 and 1929. Some authors think it possible that there may be a few Persian lions even today. In Mesopotamia, lions were last seen during the First World War. In former times, the species was widely distributed in Asia Minor, and it certainly still existed on the upper reaches of the Euphrates during the 1870s. From Palestine it is thought to have disappeared at the time of the Crusades. In course of a zoological exploration of Yemen, Hugh Scott, the English entomologist, came to the conclusion that lions must have occurred in that country at a comparatively recent date. In Egypt it had become extremely rare by the second half of the eighteenth century.

In 1880, there were still lions in Tunisia, close to the Algerian border, but they disappeared soon afterward, the last one being killed in 1891. In Algeria, where lions were common at the time of the French conquest, the last specimens were shot in 1891 and 1893, at Souk Ahras and Batna respectively. It seems certain that by 1880, there were no lions left in the parts of Morocco situated to the north of the passes of Bu Regreg and Taza, but in 1901 they could still be encountered quite frequently in the forests of Buda. In 1911, a few survivors roamed through the forests of Zaian and Beni Mgild. According to Cabrera they became extinct between 1920 and 1925. In 1930, however, a forester at Ouiouane rang up the nearest military post and reported a lion wandering around his house. Tracks thought to be larger than those of a leopard were found the following day—but nothing further was seen or heard of the animal, whatever it may have been.

Several lion encounters are mentioned in the diaries of Jan van Riebeeck, the founder of Cape Town. When he went for a walk in his garden on June 16, 1659, one jumped up in front of him and ran away. In 1707, Peter Kolb reported lions close to Cape Town. The great eighteenth-century travellers—Sparrman, Paterson, Carl Peter Thunberg, François Levaillant—began coming across them as soon as they left the immediate vicinity of the town. In the northern and northwestern parts of what is now the Cape Province, the big cats held out far into the nineteenth century, and one was killed near Bathurst, about half-way between Port Alfred and Grahamstown, in 1850. No lions can today be found south of the Orange River, but about a hundred are protected in the Kalahari Gemsbok National Park, situated in the northern part of the Cape Province.

The second half of the nineteenth century brought about the lion's extinction on the High Veld north of the Orange River, and the shooting of one near the Johannesburg suburb of Springs in 1898 was rated as a major sensation. The big cats survived, however, in the Low Veld, especially in the area which was to become the Kruger National Park.

A lion shot by General Bisset in 1865 was long considered as the last recorded for Natal. During the 1930s, however, a solitary individual established itself in the Mkuzi Reserve, and another appeared in the Umfolozi Reserve at the beginning of the 1960s. I saw its tracks and one of its victims, a very old kudu bull, in 1961. It has probably wandered south from Mozambique, and I have heard that it acquired a mate a few years after my visit. At present, good numbers of lions are found in the Kruger National Park, in southern Mozambique, in the Wankie National Park of Rhodesia, in Botswana, and in the northern parts of South-West Africa, especially in the Etosha Pan.

North of the Zambezi, the lion ranges through Angola, the southern parts of the Congo basin, Zambia, and the whole of eastern Africa to Somalia, the low-lying southern and western parts of Abyssinia and the Sudan. It is not found in the equatorial forest belt. From the Sudan it extends westward through Chad, the Central African Republic, northern Cameroon, northern Nigeria, Upper Volta, and Mali to Senegal and southern Mauretania, the northern limit of its area of distribution being formed by a line running from 16° to 17° north latitude in Darfur and Ennedi south to about 14° and then north again to 18° in Mauretania. Not so long ago, lions occurred a good bit farther north, in the mountain area of Air, but the last ones were killed in 1915 and 1918.

Within tropical Africa, the main stronghold of the species is now in Kenya, Tanzania, and Uganda, where lions can be observed and photographed in many national parks and game reserves. The lions of Nairobi National Park, the Masai Mara Reserve, and the Serengeti National Park are world famous, but visitors also get excellent views in the Tsavo National Park, in the Samburu Reserve, and at Amboseli, in Ngorongoro Crater, in Terengiri and Manyara National parks, as well as in the Kidepo, Queen Elizabeth, and Murchison Falls National parks of Uganda. The Kafue and Luangwa Valley National parks of Zambia must also be mentioned as good places for seeing lions.

Habits. In literature, the lion has often been referred to poetically as the "King of the Desert," and painters have frequently shown it against a background of arid sand dunes. It would, of course, be impossible for a lion to exist for long in absolutely waterless desert tracts, but the species quite often roams through semidesert areas. Its favourite habitats, however, are grassy plains, savannahs, open woodlands, bush, and dry scrub. It frequents the belts of acacia tree and bush bordering rivers, but rarely enters closed-canopy forest. Lions have always been absent from the rain-forest belt, but in Uganda, they have been reported as penetrating forests after the wet season, possibly in search of giant forest hogs, and they are found quite regularly in the bamboo zone of the Virunga Volcanoes. On Mount Elgon, they go to a height of 3600 m (11,800 ft), and solitary individuals can often be found roaming through the tussock grass zone of the Aberdare Mountains. On Mount Kenya, lion tracks have been seen close to the snow-line.

The outward appearance of the lion creates a definite impression of power. Even when it is quietly walking across the veld, the play of the muscles under the sleek, tawny coat leaves no doubt in the observer's mind that he is looking at an animal that, in relation to its size, is capable of formidable feats of strength. When skinning an adult male that had been brought to the Kenya Medical Research Laboratory, I was deeply impressed by the tremendous development of his muscular system, especially on shoulders, neck, and anterior limbs. The tendons of the forelegs were cordlike, thick and tough, noticeably better developed than those of the hind legs.

The lion's normal gait is quite slow, the animal walking along with its head held in line with the back or sometimes lower. The belly swings from side to side, especially when the animal has gorged itself to repletion. At a walk it covers about 4 km (2 mi) an hour. At times it changes over to a trot which is much faster and can be kept up for a considerable time. In high grass it occasionally moves in high, doglike bounds. Stalking its prey, the lion makes itself very flat and glides along close to the ground until it is in position for the last deadly rush.

The lion cannot be considered as a true "jumping cat" like the lynx and the puma, for if we take the length of its legs in proportion to the spine, we get 88% for the forelegs and 106% for the hind legs, as compared with 91 and 120% in the case of the lynx. It is nevertheless capable of remarkable performances, bounds of 6.10 (20 ft), 8 (26 ft), and even 12 m (39 ft) having been reliably reported. Vaughan Kirby saw a lioness jump with ease to the top of a 3.5-m-high (11.5 ft) embankment.

Young lions often play about on trees, and they occasionally take to the branches when chased by dogs. There are places, such as the Manyara National Park and the southernmost sector of the Queen Elizabeth Park in Uganda where adults quite regularly climb trees in order to rest on thick branches, sometimes at a considerable height above ground. They possibly do this to escape the unwelcome attentions of biting insects, such as stable flies (*Stomoxys*) and tsetse flies, which swarm among the bushes but do not go up into the trees. In the Manyara area, tree climbing certainly is a long-established habit, for I have heard of it being observed some time before the Second World War. In the Seronera area of the Serengeti National Park, I recently saw an adult and fully fed lioness extended on a horizontal branch about 4 m (13 ft) from the ground.

A watercourse is no obstacle to a lion. It is known that lions swim quite well, and they regularly cross the Okavango River, as well as the Kunene which is 25 to 30 m (avg. 90 ft) wide. Lions have on several occasions appeared on Ukerewe Island in Lake Victoria, which is separated from the mainland by about 200 m (650 ft) of water.

If you study lions in their native habitat, you will soon realize to what an extent they rely on their sense of sight. With concentrated attention, they watch game animals moving about hundreds of metres away in a down-wind direction, and when stalking in open country, they keep their eyes firmly fixed on their quarry. They glance up at vultures circling overhead, and in Nairobi National Park they can often be seen following the course of an aircraft with their eyes. As far as moving objects are concerned, their sight is excellent—there can be no doubt about that.

Hearing is well developed, too. The distant grunt of another lion or the call of a jackal coming from far away across the plain, barely audible to the human ear, will cause immediate reaction. The ears are in constant movement, turning this way and that in order not to miss anything, and more than once have I seen a lion, lying next to my car, lift its head and turn its ears to listen intently to some sound which I was quite unable to hear.

Many experienced observers have declared themselves convinced that a hunting lion also makes use of its nose. Selous, always very careful in his statements, maintained that lions found their prey with the help of their sense of smell, either by winding animals directly or by following a scent trail. W. B. Cotton, after having hunted lions in the Sudan, gave it as his opinion that, although less acute than in dogs and hyenas, the lion's sense of smell was nevertheless keen enough to enable it to follow a scent track with the nose.

On the open plains, it is difficult to ascertain to what degree scent really does come into use. Able to overlook miles of country in every direction, lions can easily spot prey by eye and keep it in sight during most of the stalk, especially when hunting in daytime. I have, however, seen many a lion lift its nose into the air, quite obviously testing the wind. On one occasion I spent several hours near some lions resting close to a river-bed. Going back on the following day, I found them gone, but when I was about to leave the place, there appeared a solitary lioness which I definitely knew not to be a member of the pride I had been watching. When she passed the exact spot where the lions had lain, she stopped abruptly and then ran to and fro for several minutes, busily sniffing the ground and the nearby bushes. She behaved exactly like a dog that has come across an intriguing scent, and there could be no doubt about her attention having been aroused by the almost day-old smell of the other lions. In order to judge the part scent may, on occasion, play in finding prey, one would have to observe lions in dense bush, where a network of branches makes the most acute pair of eyes practically useless for distances of over a dozen yards or so.

During the many years he spent in the Kruger National Park, J. Stevenson-Hamilton has been able to do just this, and he wrote:

> I have sometimes seen it stated that lions have no power of scent and hunt entirely by sight. I am sure nothing could be farther from the truth. Putting aside the fact that, for instance, in parts of the Kruger Park, visibility is limited to a few paces, and that a lion, like all other wild animals, except the primates, is unable to distinguish a perfectly stationary object even at a comparatively short distance, I have again and again seen them testing the wind and following up a tainted breeze, while less experienced ones always get to the leeward of a strange object, such as a motor car, and sniff the scent quite audibly. I have seen a single lion who thought itself unobserved, working out a spoor methodically like a hound.

The lion does not possess the monkey's deft fingers or the elephant's highly versatile trunk and is therefore unable to do many of the things which make monkeys and elephants appear so highly intelligent to human eyes. On the other hand, the members of a pride of lions are, as shall be shown, able to co-operate when hunting, and if we judge an animal's mental faculties by the way it can adapt itself to changing conditions, the lion does not do at all badly. It is by nature a more diurnal animal than the other big cats, but wherever it is persecuted and harassed by man, it speedily goes over to an almost completely nocturnal existence. In East Africa up to the beginning of this century, lions could often be seen hunting in broad daylight, but a rapidly increasing number of European settlers and visiting sportsmen then made them realize that it was not safe to be found out in the open after sunrise. They also seemed to appreciate the danger of betraying their whereabouts by roaring, and a few low and grating grunts at long intervals were practically all that could be heard of them in regions where hunting pressure was especially high.

During the Boer War, great numbers of ungulates were shot in the Sabi Game Reserve, now the Kruger National Park, for the provisioning of the troops. Later, after the reserve had been re-established, the carnivores were systematically decimated in order to give the badly shot-up game herds a chance to recover. For many years, the lions led almost entirely nocturnal lives, just like their equally hard-pressed East African cousins. The change-over from game reserve to national park brought complete protection to the carnivores, and the lions, hitherto so secretive and retiring, soon began to show themselves in daytime. Instead of hiding in dense bush or among the boulders of rock kopjes, they remained in the open, resting in the shade of trees or bushes, and even settling in the middle of roads when it rained or when the grass was wet with dew. They hunted less and less exclusively by night, and today, in the Pretoriuskop sector, they chase the numerous impalas at any time of the day.

The same development took place in East Africa. Although the lions of the various parks and reserves frequently hunt at night, they can also be seen stalking game in broad daylight. I have come across fresh kills even at high noon.

In Nairobi National Park, as well as in the Mara Reserve and in the Serengeti National Park, the lions were the first animals to get used to motor cars. They soon realized that those noisy, smelly monsters could not be preyed upon, nor were they in any way dangerous. So they simply ignored them. It can, of course, happen that a lion, in the excitement of mating or when in a bad humour due to a festering wound, growls at a car or even rushes toward it in a threatening manner, but it would probably show the same resentment toward any other intruder, including members of its own species.

The human scent is certainly covered by the smells of oil, petrol and hot rubber. The lions can see the passengers in the car, but obviously do not recognize them as human beings. Many years ago, when there was yet no code of regulations on what you could and could not do in national parks, I made the experiment of getting out of a car, about 70 m (230 ft) from two fully fed Serengeti lions resting under a tree. While they had paid not the slightest attention to the vehicle—an open-sided safari car with all of us plainly visible—the two big-maned males now made off in great haste, running for the nearest cover.

One morning, when my wife and I were strolling along the Hippo Pools of the Athi River, we suddenly discovered three lions—two lionesses and a male—walking through the yellow grass on the other side of the narrow watercourse, which at that time consisted of just a series of pools. We stopped dead, but one of the lionesses had already spotted us. She turned round and trotted back the way she had come. The lion halted under a bush, eyeing us suspiciously, while the other lioness approached the river-bank and crouched down, switching her tail and growling. At that moment, the lion turned and went up the hillside. The lioness watched him go, growled once more, and then retreated as well.

Lions tend to avoid unnecessary risks, and most encounters with humans take more or less the same course as the one just described, provided nobody panics and runs away. That, of course, would invite immediate pursuit, while a hasty shot, wounding one of the animals, might result in a swift and ferocious charge. The responsibility for any damage done would in both cases not be entirely on the side of the lion.

This does not mean that there are no unprovoked attacks. Quite apart from "man-eaters," which kill human beings for food, there is the possibility of inadvertently getting too close to a lion, thus overstepping the so-called "critical distance," where the reaction to man switches from flight to attack. An unprovoked charge of this kind will, however, not always be carried through and may turn out to be a mere attempt at intimidation. After a threatening rush the animal quite often slows down, stops half-way, and then withdraws discreetly.

It is well, however, to remember a remark made by Eric F. V. Wells, who made a study of lions both in the wild and in captivity: "The lion is a creature without rules and without exceptions." Lions can, in fact, be downright lazy and highly active, brashly bold and coyly retiring, inordinately curious and most amazingly timid.

Camping on the edge of the Mara Reserve, my wife and I woke up in the middle of the night because our tent was wobbling as if shaken by a sudden storm. There was a tearing sound, and I fully expected the flimsy shelter to be run over by a rhinoceros. Nothing further happened, however, and we soon fell asleep again.

When I stepped outside in the first light of morning, I discovered the spoor of a lion coming right up to the tent. I am sure that it had approached the strange object out of sheer curiosity. It then stood with its forepaws partly on the cloth, probably sniffing at the closed mosquito curtain. Something must suddenly have frightened it—I may have coughed or snored, or possibly it did not like our scent—whatever it was, our visitor hastily bounded away. As it did so, one of its claws got hooked in the tent cloth, and this very nearly brought the whole structure down. We still point out the long tear, neatly mended, when we are out camping with friends.

Lions are stimulated by wet weather, and they then appear live-lier, more agile, perhaps to a certain degree even more unpredict-able than at other times. I have watched full-grown lionesses playing about like kittens in pouring rain, and some authors are of the opin-ion that the big cats are most dangerous on dark, rainy nights.

The lion's features are very expressive, and it is possible to read the animal's feelings and moods—curiosity, fear, interest, vexation, anger—on its face. If it is in a bad humour, it wrinkles nose and forehead and bares its fangs at short intervals. When it gets really angry, it puts back its ears, the amber-coloured eyes, so serene at other times, begin to glitter, it opens its mouth and deep growls emerge from the chest. The tail switches from side to side. If it sud-denly becomes rigid and jerks upward two or three times in quick succession, an attack can be expected. A lion may charge without first giving this danger signal, but it hardly ever jerks its tail without attacking afterward.

The lion is more gregarious than most other cats, being frequently encountered in family groups or "prides," which origi-nate primarily through the teaming up of lionesses with cubs, all probably related to each other. They can be joined by childless fe-males and by one or more males who either stay with the pride for a short while or accompany it during more lengthy periods. Local and seasonal factors account for considerable diversity and no hard-and-fast rules can be set up as to the composition and size of prides. A large pride in the Serengeti National Park consisted of three big males, six lionesses, and thirteen youngsters of about ten to fourteen months. In Ngorongoro Crater there was at one time a pride of no less than twenty-one lionesses and cubs. Two splendid males joined the big family whenever they felt like it. The largest prides I have so far seen numbered up to thirty animals, but prides of thirty-five have been reported from the Kruger National Park. In the Sudan, however, lions are mostly met with in twos and threes. Prides of more than four or five are definitely rare. A. L. Butler, for many years chief game warden of the Sudan, only once heard of a pride of seven. The same applies to Chad and the Central African Republic.

Prides generally tend to be considerably larger in open country than in thick bush. The largest prides are naturally formed in regions with an abundance of game. Each pride has a fairly well-defined hunting ground, the extent of which is determined by type of habitat, availability of game, and especially by the number of lions involved. Big prides obviously need a larger territory than small families. A pride of two lionesses and eight cubs, observed for about two years in Nairobi National Park, roamed over an area of approximately 33 km² (13 mi²). A lioness with three cubs held an adjoining territory covering not more than 20 km² (8 mi²).

Migratory movements of a limited extent do occur among the ungulates of Nairobi National Park, affecting particularly the wildebeest and zebra, but there are enough sedentary animals for the lions to have a sufficiency of prey all the year round. In the Serengeti region, the great masses of wildebeest, zebra, and gazelle, following the dictates of the seasons, migrate to and fro between the treeless eastern grasslands and the western savannahs, and while in a certain area there will, at a given moment, be a superabundance of prey, ungulates can be quite scarce at other times. I long ago came to the conclusion that many Serengeti lions did not stick to territories, but followed the migrating herds. This has now been confirmed by George Schaller, who found these "nomads" to roam over as much as 3885 km² (1500 mi²). The majority of Serengeti lions, however, are sedentary, their hunting grounds extending over from 20 (8 mi²) to 380 km² (147 mi²).

The Serengeti prides seem to be fairly jealous of their territories, threat displays and actual fights being by no means uncommon in cases of trespassing. Hostile demonstrations and outright battles do occur in Nairobi National Park, but they are comparatively rare, and family groups have been known to live in amicable neighbourliness, with their territories overlapping to a not inconsiderable degree.

Between the territoriality of males and females there is a fundamental difference. As far as the lionesses are concerned, the territory is first and foremost a hunting ground; for the lions, however, it is an area containing a certain number of lionesses. Two, three, or more lions frequently join forces in order to dominate a territory, defending it against any strange male that tries to intrude and chasing away the young males born within the area soon after they have become independent of their mothers. The territory held by two Nairobi Park males which I observed for about six years covered an area of roughly 140 km² (54 mi²). It extended from the park to the adjoining game reserve and contained the hunting grounds of several prides and single lionesses. Although the two males wandered from family to family, claiming their share of the kills made by the lionesses, they could quite often be found keeping each other company away from the prides. When a lioness came in heat, one or the other—or both—went after her. There were occasional clashes over the favours of a lady, but these disagreements never lasted long, and after a separation of perhaps a week or so, the two males—possibly father and son, for there was a noticeable difference in age—resumed their companionship. They were eventually driven out by younger and more vigorous males, and in course of the succeeding years, more or less the same pattern was established over and over again.

The attachment between the sexes is thus of a much looser nature than was formerly assumed. Even in the Serengeti region, where males seem to attach themselves to prides more firmly and for longer periods than in Nairobi National Park, Schaller found that of twelve prides only three had the same males at the end of three years. The other males had either left the pride or were forced out by nomadic males which took over the territory.

Under conditions as they exist in the Serengeti, the integrity and success of a pride apparently depends to a certain degree on the presence of males. Schaller had evidence of this when of the two males accompanying the "Seronera Pride," one was killed and the other driven away by intruding males. "The lionesses remained," he reported, "but their success in keeping cubs alive was much lower (19%) than that of a neighbouring pride (46%) that was under the jurisdiction of vigorous males. It was two years before the pride settled down to a normal social life."

In Nairobi National Park, where conditions are much more stable, females get along very well without having any males in constant attendance, and they are in no way affected by changes in the overlordship of their area. The same probably applies to the Amboseli Reserve.

A male lion places scent marks in various parts of his territory. He throws up his tail, backs against a bush and sprays it, the rear part of his body quivering in a way characteristic of all felines. Strangely enough, I never observed any marking on the part of the two big males holding a 140-km^2 (54-mi^2) territory for about six years. They may have felt so well established and secure that they only sprayed on comparatively rare occasions. Their many successors, however, have all marked frequently, especially during the early periods of their respective tenures.

Both males and females can be seen scratching tree trunks, but it is doubtful whether this has any territorial significance. It happens very casually and looks more like a stretching exercise. There do not seem to exist any proper scratching trees as have been reported in connection with other felines.

The sociable habits of the lion could account for its being considerably more vocal than the other big cats. The air of strength so apparent in the lion's deportment is underlined by the spectacular roar that is, of course, its best known form of vocalization.

"Auah-auah-auah-huh-huh-huh-huh"—the mighty sounds roll

through the African night like thunder, making the air vibrate with their volume. The animal may be a mile or two away, but the successive bursts reach you with a forceful impact. No animal sound I know of can be compared with it, except the roar of a rutting stag, but the roar of a male lion is more impressive, more powerful, and more deeply stirring—a sound that really belongs to the times when the earth was still young.

It is true that Dr. Livingstone dismissed the lion's roar with a few contemptuous sentences: "The silly ostrich makes a noise just as loud, yet he never was feared by man. To talk of the majestic roar of the lion is mere majestic twaddle— In general, the lion's voice seems to come deeper from the chest than that of the ostrich; but to this day I can distinguish between them with certainty only by knowing the ostrich roars by day and the lion by night."

The voice of the lion and the voice of the ostrich are worlds apart, and it is hard to imagine how Livingstone, otherwise a keen and sympathetic observer of nature, could ever have mistaken one for the other.

A. W. Hodson, for instance, must have been thinking of Livingstone's deprecating remarks when he wrote: "Authors who describe the roar of the lion as an insignificant sound can have no experience of real lion country. The roar—or perhaps it would be better to describe it as the booming thunder it makes—is without exception one of the most magnificent and awe-inspiring sounds ever heard in nature."

Sir Samuel Baker, who discovered Lake Albert and who knew the jungles of India and the forests of North America, admitted that there was nothing so beautiful or enjoyable to his ears as the roar of the lion upon the still night. Another explorer, Thomas Baines, compared the deep-toned roar with the bass of a cathedral organ. Dr. Ad. David, a Swiss big-game hunter, wrote, "It penetrates to the very marrow and causes a prickly feeling of well being."

The roaring lion usually lowers its head and arches its back at the same time. The muscles of its throat swell up, the flanks are drawn in, and the chest widens like a bellows. The air is expelled with such force that puffs of dust can sometimes be seen raising from the ground a few feet in front of the animal. When roaring while lying down, the lion puts its head up like a barking dog.

Under favourable conditions, the sound may carry more than five miles. It is, however, very difficult to judge the distance from the roaring animal, and one can even be mistaken with regard to the exact direction from which the sound comes. The voice of the male is deeper and fuller than that of the female.

As a rule, lions begin to roar shortly after the sun has gone down, and they go on, at intervals, for about an hour. Silence then descends upon the veld, broken only by the occasional low grunts lions utter to keep in touch with each other, by the thunder of herds trying to circumvent the hunters, and finally by the outcry of an animal successfully brought down. Once a kill has been made, a triumphant roar may be heard, which soon gives way to the growling and snarling without which a lion feast is unthinkable. When the lions, after having gorged themselves, are on the way to the nearest water-hole, an hour or so before sunrise, they roar once more, singly and in chorus, and it is frequently at that time that the best concerts can be enjoyed. Lions sometimes roar shortly after 4 P.M., as well as for quite a time after daybreak, and there are occasions when they can be heard in the middle of the day. They may occasionally roar out of sheer excitement, and a certain amount of this extraordinary expenditure of force may also serve as a psychological outlet for surplus energy, very necessary in an animal that, like the lion, has long periods of inactivity. Roaring is undoubtedly also of considerable importance as a way of acoustically demarcating the territories held by individuals and prides.

Many years ago, before I knew the lions of Nairobi National Park individually, I was taking photographs of three males, when suddenly a deep-throated roar came from somewhere nearby. My three lions literally "jumped out of their shoes" and went bounding away. I never saw the lion responsible for that hasty departure, but judging from the volume of his voice, he must have been a big fellow. On another occasion, my wife and I were watching two males strolling along the Rutshuru River in the Albert National Park. They finally lay down under some bushes, and it looked as if they had settled for the day. A third lion, invisible to us, then roared quite close to where we stood. He did this just once, but the warning was sufficient. The two males were up and across the river in no time. Without stopping even once they trotted up a hillside and vanished for good.

One morning, in Nairobi National Park, we were able to watch a lion set about to "conquer" a territory that had for some time been held by two males. The intruder, whom we had never seen before, trotted around in wide circles, half a mile or more in diameter. While doing so, he frequently sniffed the ground, probably in order to make an "inventory" of all the lions present within the area, left scent marks in many places, and roared at short intervals. Whenever he caught sight of other lions—male or female—he went for them and chased them around. A few days later he had firmly established himself, and I never saw the former owners of the territory again.

Territorial marking by acoustical means appears to play a more important part with lions than with most other felines, and this may, of course, account for the little use—if any—that is made of scratching trees.

Apart from its roar, the lion is able to produce a wide range of other sounds. There is a low grunt, uttered to keep in touch with companions, a purring rumble, often heard from playing animals, a growl of warning, deep, rumbling sounds, interrupted by muted roars, that indicate anger, and the ominous cough that precedes an attack. One occasionally hears a sound closely resembling a "miaow," and there is a low moan which the lioness uses to call her cubs.

Hunting is largely done by the females, the males being only too pleased to invite themselves to free meals whenever possible. In the Amboseli Reserve, my wife and I once came across a number of lionesses and youngsters feeding on a three-quarter-grown giraffe. We watched them for some time, but suddenly they all stopped chewing at the carcass, jumped up, and looked across the plain, displaying signs of considerable agitation. Using our field-glasses, we spotted a male that was coming in our direction, making a bee-line for the kill. As he got nearer, we recognized him as a lion we knew as "Kichule." He was easy to know, because he had lost one ear in some ancient brawl. We had seen him on various occasions, always singly and usually at quite a distance from where the giraffe had been killed.

When he was about 50 m (164 ft) away, Kichule began to run. Bounding along at full speed, he charged into the midst of the pride, scattering lionesses and youngsters in all directions. For a while they watched him from a distance, as he greedily tore at the carcass. The majority of them then slowly came back, gathered at the end of the kill opposite to that claimed by Kichule, and continued their interrupted meal. The male was too busy to pay much attention, but when some of the youngsters began to crowd in on him, he growled an unmistakable warning. They immediately retreated, but after a time, one moved even closer. Roaring loudly the lion suddenly jumped across the kill, and, with big paws flailing right and left, he gave the lionesses and cubs a tremendous thrashing. One lioness, trying to get out of reach, turned a complete somersault and another threw herself on her back and raised her paws in an attempt to fend off the blows. The commotion lasted for perhaps two minutes, and stopped abruptly when the members of the pride had flattened themselves on the ground, everyone adopting an attitude of "submission." For a while Kichule stood over them, growling, and then retired to his end of the kill. The lionesses and youngsters began feeding again—but in course of the next few hours, the same scene was repeated at least half a dozen times.

I have notes on many similar incidents. Once a male stretched out lengthwise on top of a wildebeest carcass, allowing a lioness—who most probably had made the kill—to touch only just the nose of the dead animal and nothing else. He finally got up, seized the wildebeest and dragged it away from the female. At such time one begins to understand the meaning of the expression "the Lion's Share."

It would, however, be quite incorrect to state that males never hunt, and when it comes to killing buffaloes, their superior weight and strength often play a decisive part. I have known three males in the Amboseli Reserve who regularly hunted on their own and made a specialty out of bringing down big bull buffaloes. They developed an amazingly efficient technique in dealing with these formidable animals. In the very same game reserve, however, I have seen a buffalo go for two lionesses and put them to flight.

Except when fully gorged, lions are always on the alert, always ready to seize a sudden and unexpected opportunity for making a kill. On a recent safari to the Mara Reserve, I came across a lioness quite obviously on the look-out for a suitable quarry. She displayed some interest in a big herd of wildebeest, but they were quite far away at the bottom of a shallow valley, and I did not expect her to make a kill before several hours had gone by. The situation was completely changed, however, when the wildebeests were stampeded up the side of the valley by some motor-cars. They galloped in the direction of the lioness, who was not slow in making full use of the occasion. As the wildebeests rumbled past, she raced forward, bowled over a somewhat more than half-grown animal that was running on the outside of the herd, and grabbed it by the throat. I was able to get close to her within a couple of minutes and to photograph her while she killed her victim by strangulation. She held its throat for about six minutes.

Had the wildebeests not stampeded in her direction, she would slowly have worked her way toward the herd and tried to stalk an animal grazing at some distance from the others. To watch a lioness perform a long-range stalk of this kind is a thrilling and highly fascinating experience. She moves slowly, with utmost care, freezing into immobility whenever the quarry turns her way, and, if necessary, remaining absolutely motionless for long periods, even though she may be literally dribbling with greed. The way she can make herself invisible is truly amazing. Old-time white hunters used to tell their clients that a lion can hide behind a matchbox on a billard table, and even though this may be something of an exaggeration, the fact remains that the tawny cats know how to make use of the most scanty bit of cover and are able to flatten themselves to a most astonishing degree. Should the stalker be a male, a yellowish brown mane may appear like a bunch of grass, a dark one like a bush. I have had plenty of opportunities to fully appreciate the concealing effect of a lion's colouration, and there can be no doubt about it playing an important part in the big predator's struggle for survival.

The stalking lioness tries to edge behind her quarry as she wants to be sure of a surprise attack. And even having reached a point so near that one would think it impossible for her to miss, she will not rush at an animal as long as it looks her way. The final rush at a quarry is most impressive, both with regard to speed and harmony of movement. I remember a lioness, whose presence I had not even suspected, suddenly getting up close to my car in order to chase a Thomson's gazelle. Her gait was resilient and elegant, almost like a cheetah's, and for a short time it looked as if she might catch the animal before he really could get into his full stride. The buck had to make a supreme effort to outdistance her, but he did manage to escape, and the lioness stopped after having run about 60 (195 ft) to 70 m (230 ft).

A Thomson's gazelle can easily do 60 km (37 mi) per hour, perhaps up to 80 km (50 mi) for a limited period, while cheetahs have been reliably clocked at 70 to 82 km (avg. 47 mi) per hour. Having seen lions chase both thomies and cheetahs, I think that over a short distance they can attain a speed of between 50 and 60 km (avg. 34 mi) per hour. To make a kill, the lion thus needs the full advantage of surprise. The closer it can get to its prey, the better, and the final rush has to be timed extremely well. If the quarry is not caught at once, pursuit is usually given up after some 50 (31 ft) to 100 m (62 ft). Here again, there is no hard-and-fast rule, and Selous, for instance, saw a full-grown male chase after four greater kudus, tearing along close to the ground as fast as his legs would carry him, and looking exactly like a big mastiff.

One morning, in Ngorongoro Crater, I watched a lioness come out of an acacia forest and stalk toward some gazelles, zebras, and hartebeests grazing not far from the wood. The hartebeests soon spotted her and made off, whereupon she stopped, sat down, and looked at the gazelles and zebras. After a while she resumed her stalk, showing special interest in a herd of Grant's gazelle consisting mainly of males, but with a few females and fawns among them. Even though they had not joined the hartebeests in flight, the gazelles were thoroughly alerted. In addition, they stood in short grass that offered absolutely no cover. The chances for making a kill seemed very poor indeed. To my amazement, the lioness, on leaving the high grass, fell into a gallop and raced straight at the gazelles. They fled immediately, but she kept up the pursuit and it became apparent that she was after one of the fawns. The chase covered a distance of some 400 (1300 ft) to 500 m (1600 ft), the largest stretch I have ever seen a lion run full out, and the distance between the predator and quarry gradually narrowed. At the very last moment, the young gazelle swerved sharply, but the lioness was not taken by surprise. Swinging round just as fast, she caught up with the fawn after some 20 (65 ft) or 30 m (98 ft), knocked it over, and grabbed it by the throat.

Generally speaking, it can be said that solitary lions do not usually run down a quarry, but stalk it cat-fashion and catch it in a surprise rush. Lions sometimes hunt from ambush, lying in wait near a water-hole and letting the game come to them. Two lionesses hunting together often separate on having spotted an animal and go off on more or less divergent lines, but each of them will finally turn inward, and, having performed this pincer movement, they stalk up to the quarry from opposite directions. Should one of them be spotted prematurely or miss her attack through rushing forward too early, there is a good chance that the quarry will, in its flight, pass close to the other lioness which may then be able to bring it down. This technique is frequently used by Nairobi Park lions, and I have also observed it in the Amboseli Reserve.

It should be easy to see how, out of this pincer movement, must have developed the famous communal hunts which have been well described by observant sportsmen such as Colonel Meinertzhagen, Hugh Copley, and others. I must admit that when I came to East Africa nearly thirty years ago, I felt rather sceptical with regard to these performances, but I soon became fully convinced. The first communal hunters I was able to observe were a group of youngish animals which had just become independent of their mothers. Beginning to hunt sometime before sunset, they spread out on spotting a solitary hartebeest. One lioness went far ahead of the others, not in a straight line toward the quarry, but keeping very much to the right and in a very obvious effort to outflank the hartebeest. Her companions—among which there were both males and females—moved forward in a skirmishing line, stopping from time to time, making themselves flat so that not much more than the tips of their ears could be seen, and then advancing again. The hartebeest soon became aware of their approach. It watched them attentively, but did not notice the leading lioness which, moving ever so slowly,

nearly managed to by-pass the antelope. Then, suddenly, the hartebeest fled, galloping just so far that it could still see the lions. The
hunters immediately lost interest, their bodies relaxed, they began to
look around, and one rolled in the sand. After a few minutes they
reunited and went off in single file.

Since that time, I have observed similar performances on various
occasions. Once I was able to look down into a valley where half a
dozen lions—males and females—were moving in on a buck impala
standing in a clump of bush. They managed to surround it completely, but it nevertheless got away at the very last moment, lack of
visibility probably having hampered the lions' co-ordination. In
Ngorongoro Crater I saw a large pride "driving" a herd of zebra
toward some lionesses which had performed a flanking manoeuvre.

Some behaviourists seem to find it difficult to accept the fact of
actual co-operation, and a few years ago H. Kruuk and M. Turner
expressed their doubts in the following words:

> We do not have any indication that when a pride of lions is hunting
> together, anything more than "accidental" co-operation occurs between
> them, and the references to organized co-operation between two parties,
> viz. one or more lions deliberately stampeding a herd of game in the di-
> rection of other members of the pride lying in ambush are not based on
> sufficient data to rule out coincidences. Of course this does not imply
> that a system like this cannot exist, but more systematic observations
> would be required to prove that lions hunting together behave dif-
> ferently from lions hunting alone. So far it would seem most likely that
> each lion goes his own way to catch and kill a victim, if one member of
> the pride stampedes a herd, other lions may make use of this as they also
> do when cars cause a herd to run away.

The paper quoted above refers specifically to the lions of the
Serengeti area, and it got me wondering whether for some reason or
other the Serengeti lions might have less of a tendency toward communal hunting than those of Nairobi National Park, Ngorongoro,
and other places. George Schaller, however, who has since studied
the Serengeti lions, accepts communal hunting and writes:

> When several lions spot potential quarry, they characteristically fan out
> and approach on a broad front, sometimes spread out over 200 yards of
> terrain. By spreading out widely, lions increase their chance of coming
> in contact with prey. . . . Co-operation, while clearly evident, is rela-
> tively simple in nature. On 29 occasions during my study, one or more
> lionesses encircled the prey, sometimes by detouring far to one side. The
> other lions waited during the flanking movement as if in anticipation of
> prey fleeing in their direction.

As can be gathered from what has so far been said, lions are by no means infallible hunters. I have witnessed a lot more failures than success, and Schaller, too, puts the rate of failures very high. Of the success rate as determined by the different ways of hunting, he has this to say:

Unexpected hunts are highly productive (61 percent success), as are such minor ways of obtaining food as digging for warthogs. Stalking by single lions, driving and ambushing are equally successful, but running by single lions show a low return (8 percent). When two or more lions hunt together, their success is 30 percent, an important figure not only because it is sizeable, but also because this method of hunting is responsible for nearly half the attempts. Large lion groups do not catch prey more successfully than small ones, but there is an increase in the actual number of animals captured.

Small prey is knocked down by a quick swipe of a paw. An adult wildebeest or zebra is usually rushed from the rear, the approach being on a more or less oblique line from one side or the other. It is then caught hold of with one paw on the back, with the other on chest or muzzle, and grabbed firmly with the fangs at the back of the neck. The victim may, of course, be bowled over by the sheer impact of the attack, otherwise it is dragged down, seized by the throat, and killed by strangulation. If, in course of the struggle, it turns a somersault, the neck can easily be dislocated. I have, in fact, seen several wildebeests with broken necks, but I do not think that lions actually aim at killing their victims in this way, as was assumed by some of the earlier authors.

Young lions that have only recently become independent of their mothers are not able, yet, to kill as quickly and efficiently as their elders usually—though by no means always—do. In Nairobi National Park three two-year-old cubs killed a wildebeest entirely on their own. R. Hutton of the *East African Standard,* who witnessed the incident, gave me the following account of what happened:

The young lions emerged from some scrub where they had been sleeping, and one of the females immediately began to stalk a wildebeest grazing about 200 metres away. She approached it at a fairly rapid trot, but each time the wildebeest moved as though it might face her, she dropped flat on her belly and remained motionless for several minutes. The other two lions did not seem to take any interest in the proceedings. The lioness made her rush from a distance of about ten yards and went straight for the wildebeest's head. The animal, only noticing her when she was almost on top of it, reared up violently, but could not prevent her from obtaining a firm grip on the muzzle. The other two lions now came trotting up, and while the first lioness retained her hold, the second began clawing at the wildebeest's body in what looked like a clumsy attempt at rolling it over. The male seemed to have no very definite idea of what it was all about and at first did little more than make one or two tentative passes at the wildebeest with his paws. Only towards the end of the struggle did he eventually stand up against the victim in an effort to bring it down by the force of his weight. The wildebeest uttered puffing grunts, as though passing air through constricted nostrils.

After about ten minutes of this, the animal was thrown off its feet, but it was far from dead. Instead of now shifting her grip to the throat and finishing the victim off quickly, the lioness which had led the attack still held on to the muzzle, preventing the animal from regaining its feet by forcing the head backwards and to one side. The other two lions meanwhile proceeded to bite into its vitals. The unfortunate creature did not die until a good twenty minutes after having been thrown down.

It was a cruel and messy business—but over thousands of years, humans have treated animals no less cruelly, and a considerable part of humanity does so even today. An animal dying in a wire snare or from a badly aimed charge of shot suffers as much—if not more—as the wildebeest killed by those young lions.

Stevenson-Hamilton mentions a fight between two lions and a buffalo that lasted for two hours. One of the cats attracted the buffalo's attention, while the other eventually managed to bite through the tendons of the hind legs. In dealing with large game, this method of incapacitating a quarry seems to be used fairly frequently, and that very gifted artist, John Guille Millais, drew such a scene from the description given him by a Boer hunter, Roelf van Staden. Two of the lions, a male and a female, had got hold of the buffalo's hind legs, van Staden said, another hung on to its shoulders, while a fourth tried to grab a foreleg.

During the 1950s, the prey of the Nairobi Park lions consisted mainly of wildebeests, a good dozen of these animals killed to every zebra brought down. Toward the end of the decade, they took rather more zebras than before and also killed an occasional hartebeest, but retained their very marked preference for wildebeests. The sixties brought a lot more rain than had fallen during the fities, and when in 1964 most of the wildebeests migrated to the plains south of the park—as they always had done during the wet season— a large part of them did not return. The hartebeests began to increase in numbers, but the lions went on preying chiefly on the reduced wildebeest population and several years went by before the now very numerous heartebeests for the first time topped the list of lion kills. The hartebeests of Nairobi National Park are fairly sedentary, and therefore available to lions at all times of the year.

Kruuk and Turner reported from the Serengeti that from 1957 to 1965, wildebeests accounted for half of the lion kills and zebras for another quarter. Schaller, on the basis of data collected from 1966 to 1969, found that among lion kills the proportion of zebra—which make up about 25% of the total migratory game population—was amazingly high in comparison with that of the much more numerous wildebeests, probably due to their greater availability throughout the whole of the Serengeti area.

In the Kruger National Park, wildebeests for a long time topped the list of lion kills. Water-buck came next, zebra third, and then followed impala, kudu, and sable. Impala have now become so numerous that in certain parts of the park they have moved to first place as lion victims. On the Bahr-el-Ghazal and Bahr-el-Zeraf, lions kill mainly white-eared kobs, old males by preference, it is said. On the Athara and Setit rivers, Soemering's gazelles and reed-buck head the list of prey, followed by buffaloes, roan, water-buck, wart-hog, and giraffes.

In certain savannah woodlands, where buffaloes are more numerous than zebra, wildebeest, and hartebeest, lions are said to prey almost exclusively on the big black bovines, keeping close to the enormous herds and killing calves, cows, and even bulls. When Wilhelm Kuhnert, the animal painter, was after lions in what was then German East Africa, the locals told him: "If you want to shoot lions, follow the herds of buffalo."

Lions kill a lot more giraffes than was formerly assumed. In Nairobi National Park, for instance, no less than ten were brought down from January 1965 to May 1967, nine of them adults and one very young. A good number of victims have been recorded since then, and I have also seen giraffe kills on Mount Marsabit and in the Samburu and Amboseli reserves. With the element of surprise on its side, a lion does not seem to have any great difficulty in toppling over even the biggest giraffe. Audrey Moore, wife of former Serengeti game warden Monty Moore, reports that males, who like to do things the easy way, quite often attack giraffes because they are such easy prey. Alerted in time, however, the huge ungulates are capable of putting up an effective defence, hitting at the attackers with chopping downward blows of their forelegs. I have seen giraffes look down on lions only 15 (50 ft) to 20 m (66 ft) away, obviously quite confident that they would be capable of dealing with any hostile intentions.

In parts of Africa where game is scarce, lions occasionally turn into real pig eaters. In the grass lands of Cameroon, the wart-hog is said to be their favourite prey, while in certain districts of Tanzania, they mainly kill bush pigs, which do great harm to cultivations. Lieutenant Hans Paasche, a German naval officer who served in East Africa before the First World War, often heard European planters say "Please do not shoot my lions!" He was told over and over again that undue decimation of lions would bring about an immediate increase in the pig population. C. J. P. Ionides, the famous East African hunter-naturalist, found the lions inhabiting the coastal areas near Kilwa and Lindi to prey mainly on bush pigs and wart-hogs. He saw them dig up wart-hog burrows and once shot a lion that was holding a half-grown pig caught in this way with its fangs, shaking it violently. When the bullet hit the lion, the wart-hog quickly ran back into its hole.

In 1949, several lions attacked two fully grown hippos near the Mzima Springs of Tsavo National Park. They threw the big animals on their backs and bit their chests and throats. In Uganda, where hippos are very numerous, such incidents are of frequent occurrence. Hippos leave the water at night in order to graze on land, and calves that stray from their mothers fall an easy prey to lions. In the Albert National Park, young hippos have been found to be among the lions' favourite victims.

Selous once came across a young elephant which lions had killed by deeply biting into its throat. In the Luangwa Valley of Zambia, an elephant about 1.80 m (6 ft) high and with tusks almost 23 cm (9 in) long, became the victim of a pride, the lions first hamstringing it by severing the main tendons of the left hind leg. They then killed it by biting the lower parts of the throat. One of the young elephants brought up by David Sheldrick, game warden of Tsavo-East, was on one occasion attacked and thrown down by a lioness. She clawed its back and tried to bite its throat, but was fortunately driven off by a game scout before she could do too much damage. From Uganda, C. R. S. Pitman reported that young elephants are not infrequently killed by lions. Attacks on fairly big cow elephants have been reported, and Selous considered such accounts as within the range of possibility.

I have seen male elephants pass fairly close to lions, without either party paying much attention to the other. On one occasion, however, eleven bulls drinking at night suddenly bunched together in protective formation and walked away quickly and silently when five lionesses appeared at the same water-hole. Cow elephants have, on the other hand, been known to attack and chase away lions.

Twice I have seen the rather ludicrous spectacle of a rhinoceros blundering right through the middle of a pride, with lions bounding away in all directions. Young rhinos, which could easily be killed, have a habit of sticking as close to their mothers as possible, and cow rhinos are well able to look after the safety of their offspring. Major N. H. M. Taberer, a former game warden of Amboseli Reserve, has, however, reported two male lions attacking and bringing down an almost full-grown rhino. Taberer heard the commotion, and the rhino was not dead yet when he reached the spot. One of its forelegs was broken, and it had to be shot.

The lion is the dominant predator of the African veld, with leopard and cheetah as its ecological inferiors. In Nairobi National Park I have seen them chase cheetahs off their hunting grounds, and a pride once surprirised a very old cheetah while asleep and killed it. In the Kagera National Park, according to S. Frechkop, a leopard was killed by a lion.

There can hardly be an animal within the lion's habitat that does not fall prey to it at one time or another. With a quick blow of a paw, it catches the hare that jumps up at its feet. It likes to kill porcupines and sometimes receives nasty wounds in doing so. During lean times it does not disdain to eat grass-rats, cane-rats, and gerbils. At Seronera I once saw a lioness flush a quail and catch it in mid air. I have come across lions at ostrich kills in Nairobi National Park and know of a whole brood of young ostriches being gobbled up shortly after hatching. From Uganda and Lake Rudolf come reports of crocodiles being killed and eaten. The lion is also known occasionally to crack open a tortoise. In the Kruger Park, a lion was seen approaching a python, cleverly avoiding the snake's immediate attack. When the python went for him a second time, the lion jumped forward and practically bit it in two. He then ate part of the big snake and finally settled down to rest beside the kill. Fish, especially cat-fish, living in shallow, muddy pools, are thrown out of the water with a swipe of the paw. Lions also feed on locusts and termites.

Carrion is eaten avidly, even through it may already stink to high heaven. A game scout once showed me a dead rhino near Mzima Springs, which had been killed by an ill-tempered hippo. It was crawling with maggots, but several lions had fed on it the night before. The skinned carcasses of lions shot by hunters are occasionally eaten by other lions, and there have been cases of real cannibalism, of lions killing and eating member of their own species. Let us add, that lions will occasionally not only eat fruit, peanuts, rotten wood, and grass, but even pick up all sorts of garbage around African villages.

Lack of game induces them to depend to a considerable degree on domestic stock. In North Africa they used to prowl around the "douars," the Arab camps, where they had the best chance of making a kill. The nomads inhabiting the countries between the White and Blue Nile told Brehm: "The lion is our king, he asks for more tribute than the Turkish Pasha."

A. Blainey Percival had striking proof of how much these attacks on domestic animals depend on local conditions. Camping near Kiu at the beginning of a safari, he had seven donkeys and two camels killed by lions breaking into a boma, an enclosure made of thorn-bushes. When, a couple of days later, he sent some men with donkeys ahead to a camp-site in the game reserve where lions were liter-ally swarming, he warned them to be sure and build a good strong enclosure, but got the rather startling answer: "Oh, we don't need much of a boma there, the lions won't trouble us, for there is plenty of game."

Man himself has quite often figured on the lion's bill of fare. An Assyrian ivory panel from Nimrud, dating back to the eighth cen-tury B.C. and now in the British Museum, shows a lion grabbing a human being by the throat and may well be one of the very earliest representations of a man-eater. At the beginning of the eighteenth century, Peter Kolb heard of a sentry standing guard in front of an officer's tent on the outskirts of Cape Town being knocked down and carried away by a lion. Stories of man-eaters have, in course of time, come from all over Africa, from the Cape Province, Transvaal, Rhodesia, Botswana, Mozambique, Zambia, Angola, Tanzania, Kenya, Uganda, and Somalia, from the Sudan, the Central African Republic, Ashanti, Nigeria, and from several of the countries that used to form French West Africa. Some authors have tried to make a man-eating lion appear as an abnormal beast, likening it to a homi-cidal maniac. It is difficult to follow their reasoning, for the equiva-lent of a homicidal maniac would surely be a lion that kills and eats members of its own species. A man-eater is an animal that, instead of more or less specializing in killing wildebeest, zebra, buffalo, or young hippo, has chosen to prey upon the mammalian species for which the name "Naked Ape" has recently been coined. This prefer-ence can be due to quite a variety of reasons. It is perfectly true that a considerable number of man-eaters have proved to be old or dis-abled individuals, which had accidentally discovered that humans can be caught and killed with much greater ease than antelopes, ze-bras, and wart-hogs. Where game has been completely eradicated, lions come in close contact with man through killing domestic stock, and, although conservative in their predatory habits, some of them may eventually switch from cattle to herdsmen and to humans in general. A lioness that has made the killing of humans something of a specialty will naturally teach her cubs how to hunt people, and

there may eventually be a real outbreak of man-eating. Let us re-
peat, however, that such incidents are most likely to occur in regions
where man has shot out the game animals which used to form the
lions' traditional prey.

Of all the man-eating lions, none have become more famous
than the "Man-eaters of Tsavo," which, at the time of building the
railway line from Mombasa to Lake Victoria, raided the coolie camps
near present-day Tsavo station. Colonel J. H. Patterson's book on
how he finally managed to shoot the two man-eaters has remained a
best-seller for almost seventy years. At the end of 1898, when the
events described by Patterson took place, the surroundings of Tsavo
looked very different from what they are now. On leaving the gallery forests fringing the Tsavo and Galana (Sabaki) rivers, the
hunter or traveller found himself in a parched, thorny wilderness of
stunted trees, through which progress was only possible on rhino
tracks and on a narrow, tortuous Masai war-path. Game was remarkably scarce, Patterson recording water-buck along the rivers, dikdik,
lesser kudu, and rhino in the bush. The lions must have greeted the
sudden appearance of large crowds of railway workers with considerable enthusiasm. Here, at long last, was a rich supply of food, of
easily obtainable food at that. Of elephants Patterson never saw a
sign, for they came later, first paying seasonal visits to the Tsavo
region and then establishing themselves for good. They have cleared
away much of the bush and destroyed enormous numbers of trees.
Areas which I knew as fairly dense, bushy savannah twenty years ago
are now open grass land with an occasional tree here and there.
Game animals of many species have become plentiful, and the
present generations of Tsavo lions must find hunting very much easier than their ancestors seventy years ago. No need for them to make
the same use of today's crowds of tourists as had been made of the
unfortunate railway workers.

The number of animals killed by lions has often been greatly exaggerated, with published estimates varying from sixty to three
hundred victims per lion per year. In Nairobi National Park, a pride
consisting of two lionesses and eight small cubs accounted for twenty
head of game in the course of twelve weeks—one head per lion every
six weeks. A year later, when the cubs were being taught to hunt,
the kills amounted to one animal a fortnight for each member of the
pride. Taking these figures as a minimum and maximum, we get an
average of one animal per lion every four weeks, or thirteen animals
per lion per year. Assuming that solitary individuals kill more
often—leaving considerable portions of their kills to scavengers—and that a certain number of kills, especially of impala, ga-

zelles, and wart-hogs, escape our attention, we should still be safe to assume the number of animals killed in one year at about twenty head per lion.

Stevenson-Hamilton estimated the average annual number of animals killed in the Kruger Park at ten to twelve per lion, while Eric F. V. Wells's calculations for the same area worked out at nineteen animals per lion. In the Albert National Park, where apart from an occasional buffalo, lions prey mainly on young hippos, topi and Uganda kob, E. Hubert arrived at twenty head of game per year.

Having killed a wildebeest or a zebra, lions first of all lick up whatever blood may be flowing from various wounds. I once saw a lioness lick the legs of a freshly killed wildebeest with such energy that the hair was rubbed off in patches. I don't know what made her do this, for there was no blood visible, but other observers have noted the same type of behaviour.

The carcass is then opened in a place where the skin is particularly thin, for instance at the flanks, especially where the thigh joins the belly. The intestines are neatly pulled out, and liver, kidney, heart, lights, and sometimes also the guts eaten. The paunch is sometimes drawn several yards away from the kill. Grass, leaves, or sand may be scraped over it, but where the ground is hard and almost bare, it is left uncovered. I once saw a lioness perform a few scraping movements of a more or less symbolic nature over the stomach of a dead zebra without making any real attempts to bury it.

When the kill has been disembowelled, the lions eat the haunches, the flanks, and the breast, swallowing the meat in big chunks, together with large pieces of skin. Neck, head, and other tough parts are left till later. The comparatively soft bones of the brisket are eaten, the ends of the ribs, as well as the nose bones gnawed off. There is, however, no crushing or cracking of the big bones. A lion uses its forepaws to hold down the parts of the kill it is tearing at.

Lions may devour a victim where it fell, though as a rule they drag the carcass into the shade of a nearby tree or bush. When they are fully gorged, they often fall asleep next to the kill or in a suitable spot not far away, so that they can resume the feast as soon as they are able to do so. I have known prides to stay with their kills for forty-eight hours. Where lions live in fear of man, they drag the kill into a dense thicket or a deep-cut river-bed fringed with bush, and afterward search out a safe retreat, quite often a good distance away, for their siesta. They may return to the carcass the following night, but a hunter cannot depend on this.

Whenever lions kill during the day, vultures, tawny eagles, pied crows, and marabou storks gather with astonishing speed and wait patiently in a wide circle on the ground or on nearby trees. As soon as the cats have gone, they come rushing in from all sides and start a spectacular and always fascinating free-for-all. It quite often happens, however, that one of the lions suddenly turns round and comes bounding back, scattering the scavengers in all directions. On one occasion, while following a pride walking away from a kill, I saw a young male stop and look up at the circling vultures. He then ran back for almost a kilometre, chased away the birds that had already settled on the scanty remains, and then lay down close by.

Should there be a pool or stream not far from where the kill was made, various members of the pride may stroll away at intervals to have a leisurely drink. Otherwise, the group will usually call at a water-hole after having finished with the kill. There they all crouch down, elbows standing out at an angle on both sides and shoulder blades raising, as heads are lowered and pink tongues lap up the water in the same way a domestic cat laps up its milk. Where lions only hunt at night, they mostly drink very early in the morning, some time before sunrise. However, in Nairobi National Park, in Tsavo National Park, and in the Serengeti, I have seen lions at the water at all times of the day and in the very middle of the night.

Having observed lions in East Africa or in the Kruger National Park, one is left with the impression that they are very dependent on water, drinking daily, or at least every second or third day, and never settling down more than about 8 (5 mi) to 14 km (9 mi) from a river or pool. In this respect, too, lions show a considerable adaptability, and H. C. Brocklehurst, a former Sudan game warden, records the following observations made in the Wadi Howar of north-western Kordofan:

> There also I found the remains of an oryx which had been killed by a lion not more than three days before. As there is no water, except in isolated wells of a depth of 30 to 40 feet, they must obtain the moisture necessary for their existence from the stomachs of the antelopes which they kill. The spoor of this particular lion went away from the kill as straight as an arrow into the desert, but owing to insufficient water I was unable to follow it.

Hunters crossing the Haud, a vast tract of land in the Somalia–Abyssinia border area that is without water for the greater part of the year, were greatly astonished to find lions 50 (31 mi), 80 (50 mi), and more kilometres from the nearest water. Sir Alfred Pease and Colonel H. G. C. Swayne came to the conclusion that these lions had to be able to go for several weeks without water, quenching their thirst with blood and the intestines of the animals they killed. J. D. Inverarity, used to conditions prevailing in India, wrote: "This is incredible to those who know how necessary water is for the existence of tigers and panthers; but that it is so, I have no doubt. I have shot them 30 miles away from water."

Lions can be encountered along the southern borders of the Sahara, where temperatures of 47° to 48° C (avg. 118° F), and soil temperatures of 65° to 70° C (avg. 152° F) are often measured. Under such conditions a lion is probably able to survive only if it spends the day quietly in a cave or under a very thick bush. The lions inhabiting the driest part of the Kalahari Desert are known at times to eat tsama melons (*Citrullus caffer* and *Citrullus nandianus*) which have a very high water content.

After having drunk, a pride will move on in search of a shady spot where they can settle down for a prolonged siesta. The stomach of a barely medium-sized lioness was found to contain 9 kg (20 lb) of meat. Hunter-naturalist F. Vaughan Kirby thought that a fully grown lion could eat up to 18 kg (41 lb) of meat at one "sitting," while Denis Lyell estimated the amount of meat a really hungry lion could put away at about 31 kg (70 lb). Feasts of this kind must, of course, be followed by periods of fasting, and fully engorged lions sometimes do not eat for four, five, and even up to six days. During this digestive siesta, they are very lazy and avoid all major efforts, even though they will change their resting place at fairly frequent intervals. At such a time you can park your car next to a pride and spend hours without getting any more action than an animal occasionally turning over on its back with its paws waving in the air, two licking each other sleepily for a while, and the whole group gradually following the shade around a tree or bush. If you are very lucky, you may see one get up and stretch luxuriously before letting itself fall on its side again. Game animals sometimes graze a mere 100 m (328 ft) from a resting pride.

The ungulates of the African veld do not live in constant fear of the big predators, as some people tend to assume, and lions strolling leisurely over the plain, obviously well fed, do not cause panic among the game animals. The herbivores watch them intently, of course, and if they happen to turn in their direction, they quietly move out of their way, opening a lane for the predators to pass through. Antelopes often follow lions for quite a long way, in order to keep them in sight as long as possible. They seem to realize that a lion they are able to watch from a safe distance can never be a danger to them. The dangerous lion is the invisible one, the one that may be lurking somewhere in thick cover or sneaking up through the high grass.

After a lion has rushed into a herd of zebra—immaterial of whether it succeeds in making a kill or not—the animals gallop a few hundred yards, wheel round, and look back, barking in high excitement. After a short time they quiet down, and soon they are grazing again.

In Africa south of the Sahara, mating takes place at all times of the year, and the same is reported from India. In Algeria mating is said to have occurred in January and February, but this interesting piece of information unfortunately cannot be checked any more. The lions inhabiting Europe during the last glaciation and in postglacial times may well have had a proper mating season, possibly in December and January like the tigers of Manchuria and eastern Siberia, with the cubs being born during the most favourable time of the year.

When a lioness comes in heat, which she does at frequent intervals, she develops a strong smell and sprays tree trunks and bushes with her urine, to which is added a secretion from her anal glands. The smell disappears as soon as she comes off heat. A courting lion often bares his teeth and wrinkles his nose, not in an angry snarl, but in a gesture common to many mammals and known to behaviourists as "flehmen."

The couple may leave the pride for a few days, but mating can also take place with all the other lions resting nearby. Lion and lioness lie close to each other, sleeping or dozing. After a while the female shows signs of restlessness, gets up, and walks away. The male jumps to his feet and follows, his nose almost touching the root of her tail. The animals may just take a few steps, but usually they cover about 30 (100 ft) to 50 m (165 ft). The lioness then slows down, rubs against the lion's hairy chest, and goes into a crouch. During the act of mating, the male holds his half-opened mouth close to the lioness's neck, without, however, biting her in the way so characteristic of many other felines. I have seen lions of just over two years grab females of the same age by the neck, but that was in play, for these youngsters had not yet reached maturity. In zoological gardens, young males have been observed doing the same thing when mating for the first time. They are said to give it up very soon, owing to the lionesses thoroughly resenting this kind of treatment.

When the act of mating is over, the lioness stretches herself, rolls about comfortably on the ground, and quickly falls asleep again, while the male stands over her for a while with his head held low, before he settles down beside her. After twenty or thirty minutes, the performance is repeated, and so it goes on for three or four days.

According to observations made in the London Zoo, the lioness generally remains in heat for four days, with actual fertilization of the egg cells only taking place during the matings of the fourth day. In the Dresden Zoo, a couple is said to have gone on for eight days, mating no less than 360 times during that period. Mating lions may utter an occasional grunt, growl, or snarl, but there certainly is much less noise and violence involved than in most of the smaller felines. When several males are after the same lioness, there may, of course, be a certain amount of brawling, but as the suitors usually are well acquainted with each other's fighting qualities, these encounters rarely result in more than a few bloody scratches.

The gestation period varies from 100 to 113 days, 105 to 108 being the most common, while 112 to 113 days can be considered as unusual. The pregnant lioness leaves the pride and chooses a hiding place, as a rule not far from a river or water-hole. During the rains, she selects higher, well-protected places among rocks, be it on a kopje or on the side of a deep gorge, but during the dry season she prefers gallery forests, reed beds, and patches of thick bush. There the cubs are born, generally three, quite often four. One, two and five have also been recorded. Litters of six seem only to occur in zoos.

A cattle-raiding lioness shot by a game warden and brought to the Kenya Medical Research Laboratory was found to carry three fully formed cubs—a male and two females—which would have been born within a few days. They weighed 1.275 (2.9 lb), 1.389 (3.1 lb), and 1.332 kg (3 lb) respectively, and had the following head-and-body and tail measurements: 34.4 (13.4 in) and 15.6 cm (6 in); 40.5 (15.8 in) and 13.5 cm (5.2 in); 22.9 (8.9 in) and 15.9 cm (6.2 in). All three were strongly marked, the spots on the body being arranged in lines, almost merging into stripes, while those on the legs were of a jaguarine type. The teeth were visible, though still covered with skin, the claws well formed, white in colour. The ears were folded forward.

The cubs are born with their eyes either closed or open. From the Dublin Zoo, famous for its lion-breeding successes, Dr. B. B. Ferrar reported two males and two females born with their eyes open after a gestation period of 104 days, while a male and female forming another litter and born after 102 days opened their eyes within twenty-four hours. In a litter of four, one male had its eyes open at birth, the other three cubs opened theirs within forty-eight hours. In the Pretoria Zoo, young lions once opened their eyes on the sixth day only. Stevenson-Hamilton writes: "Cubs are born with their eyes at least partly open, though for the first week or two they appear to see imperfectly." The milk-teeth break through at an age of about three weeks.

It happens now and then that a lioness deserts her litter, especially if it is her first one or if she is an elderly lady who has almost finished playing her part in propagating the species.

While it is certainly true that all young felines, without exception, are highly engaging creatures, small lion cubs can only be described as just about the most appealingly cuddlesome animals imaginable, sleepy eyed, woolly haired, with big paws, short, tuftless tails, and large plush ears stuck to the sides of rounded heads. The spots, usually well defined, may occasionally be almost invisible, and Stevenson-Hamilton once saw a litter of which all cubs were completely unmarked.

The cubs generally remain for several weeks in the hiding place where they were born. In order to hunt, the lioness has to leave them from time to time, and during these absences, which, when game is scarce, can extend over as much as forty-eight hours, they are, of course, exposed to considerable dangers from hyenas, hunting dogs, leopards, and even from other lions. If hunting in the immediate vicinity of the den becomes too difficult, the cubs sometimes have to leave their first shelter when hardly bigger than cats. Following the mother to more suitable hunting ground is hard and tiring work for them and can easily bring about early losses. Schaller found that "nomadic" lionesses in the Serengeti were almost never able to keep their cubs alive. Where hunting is easy, the lioness soon begins to carry lumps of meat to the cubs. In zoological gardens, mothers have been seen to disgorge partly digested meat, and there is no reason why this should not happen in the wild as well.

At the age of four or five weeks, the cubs already watch any moving object and pounce upon it in a playful manner. Soon they begin to stalk each other. One suddenly rushes forward, and next moment the two are rolling about, wrestling in the grass. After a few weeks, the cubs are taken along to kills, and when they have reached about three months, they follow their mother wherever she goes.

A lioness may rejoin the pride she left, or team up with two or three other mothers. In Nairobi National Park, where conditions are highly favourable, several lionesses remained solitary and nevertheless made an excellent job of rearing their litters. One even managed, absolutely on her own, to bring up five cubs. Within a pride, the cubs soon cease to differentiate between the various mothers and take milk from all of them. The females assist each other in hunting, and this makes life much easier. When a Nairobi Park lioness had a bad wound on her belly, probably from the horn of a wildebeest, her companion hunted alone for about a fortnight. Childless lionesses forming part of a group will play with the cubs, lick them, and behave very much as if they were mothers, too. There is a friendly and sociable atmosphere, and the members of a pride greet each other by rubbing heads whenever they meet. Cubs of various ages join in joyful games and can be seen wrestling, chasing each other, and playing "king of the castle" on a termite hill.

Lion cubs are weaned at the age of about six months. When they are seven and a half months old, their mother's teats have become very small and must certainly be dry, but if there is a lioness with younger cubs in the pride, the older ones will happily come to her until her milk, too, gives out. Cubs of one lioness have been known to suckle at another female until they were just over ten months old.

The youngsters first join hunting expeditions as spectators and sometimes behave so clumsily and carelessly that they spoil many a stalk by stampeding the game. Little by little, however, they begin to copy the lionesses' movements, and when they are about ten months old their apprenticeship starts in earnest.

The milk-teeth are replaced by the permanent dentition at the age of about one year, and this must be a very painful and miserable period in a young lion's life. The mouth is tender and bleeding and the hot nose points to a feverish temperature. Mortality is particularly high between nine and twelve months, with males apparently faring worse than the females. While males tend to predominate at birth, the proportion of the sexes is said to be reversed in favour of the females at this stage.

In the Kruger National Park, according to Stevenson-Hamilton, only 50% of the cubs survive the first two years, and out of litters consisting of two or three, one almost invariably dies, sometimes two or all three. In the Sudan, A. L. Butler found himself wondering whether even half of the young lions survived the first year. He reported that lionesses were more often seen with two cubs than with three.

The death rate depends on the general condition of the cubs and is certainly not high in such a favourable area as Nairobi National Park. Major E. W. Temple-Boreham, a former game warden of the Mara Reserve, also recorded a low mortality rate. In the Serengeti National Park, from where equally favourable reports came during the 1950s, the situation has deteriorated in course of the last eight or ten years. Cubs are now frequently in very poor condition, and the mortality rate has risen accordingly. The numbers of wildebeest and zebra have greatly increased since accurate counts were first made, but to sedentary prides these migratory animals are only available at certain times. As far as other game animals are concerned—topi, hartebeest, impala, reed-buck, giraffes—it appears to me that they were much more concentrated along the various rivers during the predominantly dry fifties and some way into the more rainy sixties than they are nowadays. Increased rainfall probably caused the non-migratory animals to spread out. In the intervals between the passing of the migratory herds, the lions of Seronera and Banagi thus have less animals to kill than in former times, and they are also forced to move about a great deal more, much to the detriment of any small cubs present at such times.

If a large pride is gathered around a kill, young cubs sometimes find it difficult to get at the meat, and in trying to push their way through the scrum, they risk being slapped by some of the greedy eaters. One may occasionally be killed by an especially savage blow, but as long as the youngsters are in good condition, this rough-and-tumble may have a fairly beneficial effect, toughening them up in preparation for a predatory existence that is, after all, a very arduous struggle for survival. From the Serengeti, however, Schaller reports even starving cubs being cuffed away from kills by hungry lionesses. Before voicing our indignation, we must remember that a litter can be replaced in a much shorter time than it takes for a lioness to grow up to maturity. Nature may be hard, but to paraphrase Shakespeare: "There's method in her hardness."

Male cubs can be distinguished from their sisters by their heavier build and broader faces. When they are one year old, the first signs of a mane begin to appear, and a few months later they sport, apart from whiskers on the side of the neck, a crest of erect hairs starting on the crown and continuing down the nape. The young females, however, generally are better and more diligent pupils, quicker in acquiring the elements of the noble art of hunting.

Adult males can be found attached to family groups where there are fairly small cubs, and I have seen a big, black-maned lion—who could behave with great brutality when it came to safeguarding his share of a kill—lick a minute bundle of spotted fur as tenderly as any lioness. On another occasion I was able to watch a cub climbing around on a dozing male who allowed it to pull his mane and chew his ears. I have, however, also known lionesses to chase away territorial males, preventing them for a considerable time from getting near the cubs.

Once the youngsters have reached an age of fifteen to sixteen months, the mothers begin to make it clear that they are not averse to having a flirtation, and from time to time one or the other will leave the pride for a few days in the company of a suitor. Soon the first signs of pregnancy become apparent, and eventually the cubs are left to fend for themselves. In a pride consisting of two lionesses and two litters of four—which all survived—the youngsters became independent within eighteen and twenty-one months respectively. One of the mothers had a new litter not much over a month later, and these cubs stayed with her for just over two years. She was not yet visibly pregnant when they left her.

Under favourable circumstances a lioness can thus have cubs roughly every two years. The period between births may occasionally be somewhat shorter, but it can also extend over two and a half or even three years. In zoos it is possible to obtain litters every year, but this apparently does not happen in the wild, for one never sees a mother with two sets of cubs less than two years old. When a lioness loses or deserts her cubs, she will usually mate almost immediately afterward.

As the cubs become independent, they form a sort of bachelors' club. Their first unaided hunting efforts are often clumsy, and they may go hungry for a prolonged period, but they soon gain experience and acquire the skills they need in order to survive. The existence of the young male is made difficult by their fathers and uncles, who will not tolerate their presence within their territories and pursue them until they leave the area, often together with their sisters, to roam about and look for hunting grounds of their own.

The age of maturity is given as two years by some authors, four years by others. Zoo lions occasionally mate succcessfully at the age of two years, but such precocity probably arises from the hypersexualizing influence of captivity. I have seen lions of about twenty months going playfully through at least some of the motions of mating, but apparently maturity is not reached before they are about three years old. Some of the young males will probably attempt to return to the area where they grew up. At first they are chased away by the male or males dominating the territory, but later on, when they have reached their prime, they may well be successful in ousting and replacing the aging rulers.

During the hot season, lions are badly harassed by stable flies, tsetse flies, and other biting pests, especially while they are resting, and they can be seen to switch their tails constantly in order to drive away their tormentors. Ticks infest their coats, with *Haemaphysalis leachi* being a very common lion parasite in the Nairobi area. From four lions—two males and two females—brought to the Medical Research Laboratory of Nairobi, I collected 53, 41, 87, and 172 specimens of this species. *Rhipicephalus appendiculatus, Rh. simus, Rh. pulchellus, Rh. parvus,* and *Rh. evertsi* were also present, but in much smaller numbers, ranging from one to five specimens per lion.

Lions carry fleas of the genus *Ctenocephalides,* and sand fleas occasionally bore into their paws. They usually have tapeworms, which they swallow as cysts with the meat of the herbivores that form their prey. The eggs of these tapeworms get into the grass with the lions' droppings and are again eaten by grazing ungulates. Dozens of round-worms may be found fastened to the stomach lining without apparently causing any trouble. One of the lions examined in the laboratory was discovered to have *Trichinella spiralis* in its muscles and diaphragm. After having killed a cow within the paddocks of the veterinary department, it ate only a little of it and then fell asleep beside the carcass. It behaved in a strangely sluggish manner when the game warden approached it and paid absolutely no attention to him. This particular lion was said by the locals to have made a specialty of killing hyenas, and it may well have contracted trichinosis in this way.

Of sporozoa, *Eimeria,* a cell parasite, and *Babesia,* a blood parasite have been found. It has been stated that the lioness Elsa died of a Babesia infection. Babesia are present in most carnivores, without causing any harm so long as the host does not develop any serious organic defect. They can, however, be made to increase enormously by, for instance, taking out their host's spleen. Elsa may therefore have been suffering from some disease or deficiency which it was not possible to diagnose after death.

Trypanosomes, causing sleeping sickness in man and nagana disease in cattle, are occasionally found in lions' blood, but their presence must be considered as more or less accidental. The nasal cavities and bronchiae may be infested with "tongue-worms." Lions can contract anthrax through eating the meat of diseased ungulates.

A lion occasionally comes to grief when hunting. I have seen several with wounds obtained in battles with buffaloes and have heard of lion and buffalo carcasses being found side by side. A lion was found dead near Simba, a railway station on the Mombasa–Nairobi line, with its skull smashed, possibly by a giraffe's hoof. Oryx antelopes, sable and roan, can all use their horns with deadly efficiency. On one occasion, a hunter following the spoor of a gemsbok—the South African oryx—into a thicket almost stumbled over the dead animal, the horns of which were covered with blood. A lion lay nearby, killed by the long, spearlike weapons. The gemsbok did not have a single scratch—the lion obviously having rushed upon the pointed horns, wounding itself fatally and at the same time breaking the gemsbok's neck.

M. S. Moore, the Serengeti game warden, once had to shoot a lion whose hind leg had been broken by a zebra. Lions, as we have seen, usually attack from the rear. My observations have left me with the impression that zebras, being able to kick out backward, have more of a chance to escape from the claws of a lion than wildebeests and hartebeests. I have often seen zebras with deep scratch wounds on their flanks and haunches which could only have been inflicted by a lion.

In the Tsavo National Park I once saw a lioness with a bunch of about six to eight porcupine quills sticking out from her side. I do not know what eventually became of her, but in Tanzania a lion was found dead, its belly pierced by innumerable quills. R. Verheyen, who made a study of the Upemba National Park in Katanga, was told of a lion that had been severely wounded by the claws of an aardvark. There have been records of lions killed and trampled by cow elephants. Packs of wild dogs and hyenas may occasionally chase and even kill one of the big cats. A lioness in Nairobi National Park one day turned up with her tail missing, and this we thought to have been the work of a crocodile. Lions' claws have been taken from crocodiles' stomachs.

The lion's worst enemy is, of course, man, who, with all the means at his disposal, has persecuted it for thousands of years, exterminating it in many areas where it used to be common. Contemporary pictorial representations show ancient Mycenaeans and Macedonians attacking lions with spears, as is still being done by African tribes, such as the Masai and the Samburu. Before motor-cars invaded Africa and fire-arms attained their present-day perfection, lion hunting was an exciting and hazardous sport that led to many fatal or near-fatal accidents. David Livingstone was badly mauled when trying to rid an African community of some cattle-raiders. He was lucky in making a good recovery in those days, long before antibiotics.

The belief that eating lion meat, and especially a lion's heart, will give you great courage is very widespread among the indigenous peoples of Africa. One of the lions brought to the Medical Research Laboratory was a young male, and I could not resist the temptation to cut off a haunch and take it home. The meat made excellent eating, being white, tender, without any offensive smell or taste, in fact, very much like veal though somewhat more coarse-grained. Lion meat was highly praised by Dr. Thomas Shaw, who travelled widely in North Africa during the first half of the eighteenth century, and also by F. C. Selous.

The average age of a hundred lions and lionesses, selected for their longevity from twenty-eight zoological gardens, amounted to thirteen years. Twenty-five years is sometimes given as the maximum, but there exists a record of one attaining an age of about thirty years in the Cologne Zoo. A lioness living in Nairobi National Park, well known under the name of Blondie, was about eighteen years—possibly between eighteen and nineteen years—old when found dead of old age.

In the Serengeti National Park I came upon a pride congregated around a kill. There were two males, one a fine strong animal in the prime of life, the other a giant with a big, dark mane, but showing visible signs of advanced age. His fangs were blunt and worn, and he found it difficult to grab and tear off hunks of meat. I was amazed that the younger lion tolerated this old gentleman within the pride. A game warden afterward told me that the two always stuck together, with the young male doing all the killing when they were not accompanying a group of lionesses. Near Mtito Andei, Kenya, a lioness made a nuisance of herself by killing chickens. She was later found to be living together with a very old lioness with whom she shared whatever food she obtained.

In the Amboseli Reserve, my wife and I once saw a very old lion. He lay on the edge of a patch of bush, sunning himself, blinking sleepily as we approached. His mane was thin, his face covered with scars, his coat looked moth-eaten and rubbed through at the elbows. He certainly was a sad sight. I have often wondered what his end may have been. There was a large pride a couple of miles from where he lay, and for some time he probably was able to subsist on the scraps left by his descendants. But I can imagine him getting weaker and weaker, with hyenas and hunting dogs circling around him, becoming gradually bolder and finally overpowering the poor old fellow.

Tiger
Panthera tigris
(LINNAEUS 1758)

The tiger is a magnificent creature. It once played the part of the "King of Beasts" in Korea, but Europeans, instead of making it a symbol of untamed beauty, came to identify the tiger with cruelty and treachery. "A violent, grim, angry, ferocious animal is the tiger," wrote Conrad Gesner, the sixteenth-century naturalist.

As far as exotic animals such as the tiger were concerned, the main source available to Gesner and his contemporaries was Pliny's *Natural History,* written about 1500 years earlier. The great Roman, while stressing the tiger's ferocity, at least had some appreciative words for the tigress, praising her devotion to her offspring.

The tiger became known to the ancient Greeks through Alexander's campaigns in Persia and India. Aristotle mentioned it in his writings, without, however, having seen a specimen. It was King Seleucus of Syria, one of Alexander's generals, who, presented the peoples of Athens with the first tiger ever to be seen in Europe. No more tigers appear to have reached the lands of classic civilization until 19 B.C., when the Emperor Augustus received some of these animals from an Indian embassy visiting him on the island of Samos. There is some mystery as to what happened to them, for eight more years had to go by before the inhabitants of Rome were shown their first tiger. We do not know whether it was one of the tigers brought to Samos, or perhaps another, more recent gift from an Indian potentate. From Pliny we only learn that it was exhibited in a cage at the dedication of the Temple of Marcellus in 11 B.C. He describes it as a very tame animal.

After this, tigers occasionally appeared in Roman arenas, but they were always something of a rarity. By far the greatest number ever seen at one and the same time were fifty-one, all of them massacred in course of the games Heliogabalus arranged to celebrate his marriage. The same emperor is said to have harnessed tigers to a chariot on which he himself posed in the guise of Bacchus. Colin Clair, in his amusing *Unnatural History,* has a tale according to which the only living creature Nero really loved was Phoebe, a tigress, which put up such a tremendous fight in the arena that he had her transferred to a golden cage in the palace grounds. An animal

180

trainer by the name of Lybius made an excellent job of taming her, and she could soon be seen stretched out at the emperor's feet when he sat on his throne.

The Romans knew well that tigers came from India and also from Hyrcania, as they called the part of Iran bordering on the Caspian Sea. The name "tigris," used by the Greeks and the Romans, is assumed to be derived from "tighri," meaning "arrow" in the language of the Aryan inhabitants of old Persia. It was applied to the swift-moving tiger, as well as to the fast-flowing River Tigris in Mesopotamia.

After the disintegration of the Roman Empire, no tigers were seen in Europe for a very long time, and the memory of the species faded away so completely that Marco Polo was greatly puzzled by the "lions" he saw at the court of Kublai Khan. "They were larger than the Babylonian lions," he said, "with good skins and of handsome colour, being streaked lengthways with white, black and red stripes." These "lions" were quite obviously tigers, and we need not worry about the "lengthways streaks," which may be due to a slip of the tongue, when the Venetian traveller dictated his story, or to a clerical error on the part of the man who wrote it all down.

The first tiger seen in Europe since Roman times seems to have been a specimen obtained by Yolanda, Duchess of Savoy, in 1478, and kept at her castle in Turin. Tigers soon afterward appeared at the court of Ferrara, and Francis I is said to have had several of them. As more and more menageries came into being all over Europe, people gradually became better acquainted with the big cat "of handsome colour." The evil reputation it received from the writings of Pliny, Gesner, and many others stuck to it until very recent times, and highly unfavourable comparisons were often drawn between the tiger and the lion.

James Greenwood wrote:

> In disposition, however, the tiger differs essentially from the lion. With all the strength of the latter, it possesses ten times its agility, and a hundred times its cunning; but for pluck, audacity and defiant carriage, he is barely fit to "hold a candle", as the ancient saying is, to the monarch of the African forest. Present to the tiger—even to *Tigris regalis* himself—your back, and you may presently expect to feel the weight of its mighty forearm, and to hear his murderous triumphant roar; but meet him with your fellow huntsmen face to face, and if he can, run he will.

Sir William Jardine's condemnation was somewhat more qualified: "He possesses no trace of the shaggy mane which adds so much to the bold and majestic-looking front of the lion, and his countenance scowling under the different passions, conveys a greater idea of treachery and wanton cruelty, than really belongs to him." While Jardine may have had some doubts about the cruelty and treachery attributed to the tiger, he certainly was fully convinced of its ferocity: "In many places he is the scourge of the country, and neither man nor beast can with safety inhabit the districts which it has selected for its own."

Linnaeus knew the tiger well and named it *Felis tigris.* Later, the generic designation was changed to *Panthera,* rightly so, for the tiger has the incompletely ossified hyoid and the roundly contracting pupils characteristic of the genus. In a book published in 1775, a naturalist named Frisch classified the tiger within a separate genus which he called *Tigris,* and Gray followed his example in the *List of Mammals in the British Museum,* issued in 1843. He at the same time changed the species name into *regalis,* probably influenced by the appellation "Royal Bengal Tiger" so very much in vogue in the literature of that period. Priority must, of course, be accorded to the species name given by Linnaeus, and Gray's *"regalis"* has been ignored by most authors. Efforts have, however, been made from time to time to revise the genus *Tigris,* but the arguments that have been brought forward in favour of such a move are by no means convincing.

Some authors would like to see *Panthera* reserved for the spotted cats—leopard and jaguar—yet lion and tiger are probably both descended from spotted ancestors. Young lions have retained these ancestral markings and their spots are sometimes arranged in rows, making them look fairly similar to little tigers. In tigers, the stripes often run in pairs, either merging into each other at top and bottom or at least forming open loops. They can thus be regarded as long-drawn-out rosettes or rings.

As a species, the tiger seems to have originated in eastern and perhaps northern Siberia, where skeletal remains have been found on the New Siberian Islands, now well within the Arctic Circle. From this centre of origin, tigers migrated south through China and Siam into Malaya, southwest through Assam into India and west through Central Asia to the Caspian Sea and Transcaucasia. They arrived at Cape Comorin after the land-bridge between Indian and Ceylon had disappeared and were never able to cross the Palk Strait. From Malaya, however, they spread to Sumatra, Java, and Bali, though not to Borneo.

The skulls of tiger and lion are very similar, and no two authorities seem to be able to agree fully on how to differentiate between the two without going into highly sophisticated osteological and dental comparisons, such as have been published by Th. Haltenorth and J. Kabitzsch.

In a general way, it can be said that the tiger's skull is massive and heavy, more vaulted and thus more catlike than the lion's, with the facial part shorter and more convex. The zygomatic arches are excessively wide and strong, the sagittal crest is present, though generally lower than the lion's. Pocock found the facial part of the tiger less massive and narrower than the lion's. Vratislav Mazak, however, describes it as more massive and broader. There obviously is so much variation within each of the two species that many of the characteristics tend to overlap. The basis line of the lower jaw is nearly straight. The first upper premolar may occasionally be absent as is the single upper molar.

Characteristics. The tiger is a massively built animal with a rounded head, a long, muscular body, powerful limbs, and a tail usually slightly shorter than half the head-and-body length. The line of the belly is not drawn in as in the lion and runs lower than the chest, while the withers are lower and the neck is somewhat longer. Frechkop has pointed out that in shape and posture the lion seems closer to the cheetah, another inhabitant of open country, than to the forest-dwelling tiger.

The tiger's ears are relatively small and rounded. Cheek whiskers are present, slight in females, but well developed in males. The density and length of the coat varies according to geographical latitude, and the hairs on the back of the neck may be long and almost mane-like.

Colouration varies from reddish orange to reddish ochre. Muzzle, throat, whiskers, chest, belly, and the insides of the limbs are purely white or light cream. The backs of the ears are black with white central spots. The vertical stripes can be grey, greyish brown, brown, or black, and their pattern is subject to almost infinite variety. Not only are no two tigers marked exactly alike, but even the two sides of one and the same individual display a very marked asymmetry. In some specimens, the stripes are much reduced on shoulders, forelegs, and on the anterior part of the flanks; in others they tend to break up into spots. This diversity of colour and pattern has led to the description of a great many subspecies, most of which have long ago lost their validity.

It must, however, be admitted that the tiger's area of distribution is much less homogeneous than that of the lion, ranging, as it does, from humid tropical jungles to Siberian forests and to strips of vegetation fringing central Asian desert rivers. It is also less contiguous, being interrupted and broken up in many places by deserts, mountain ranges, and high plateaus. While lions are confined to continental areas, tigers occur in parts of the Malay Archipelago, living in isolated insular habitats, which greatly favour the formation of subspecific characters.

The following subspecies can probably be accepted as based on reasonably safe criteria:

Bengal Tiger, *Panthera tigris tigris* (LINNAEUS)
The nominate form of the tiger is large, with a light yellowish to reddish yellowish coat and black stripes. The hairs on back and belly are 8 to 13 mm (avg. 0.4 in) and 20 to 30 mm (avg. 1.0 in) long in summer, and 17 to 22 (avg. 0.8 in) and 25 to 40 mm (avg. 1.3 in) in winter. The hairs on the back of the neck can attain a length of 20 to 56 mm (avg. 1.5 in); the whiskers are 50 to 90 mm (avg. 2.8 in) in length.

Corbett's Tiger, *Panthera tigris corbetti* (MAZAK)
This recently (1968) named subspecies has been described as smaller than the Bengal tiger, darker in colour, with shorter stripes, which tend to disintegrate into spots.

Chinese Tiger, *Panthera tigris amoyensis* (HILZHEIMER)
The eastern Chinese subspecies is smaller than the Bengal tiger, with the white areas less extensive and the black stripes broad, short, less numerous, and more widely spaced.

Caspian or Turanian Tiger, *Panthera tigris virgata* (ILLIGER)
The Caspian tiger resembles the Bengal tiger in size and background colour, but its stripes are not quite black, longer, more narrow, and set more closely together. The winter coat is longer and lighter in colour, the hairs of the back being up to 30 mm (1.2 in) long. The whiskers are very well developed, and the hairs on the back of the neck can form a slight mane.

Siberian or Manchurian Tiger, *Panthera tigris altaica* (TEMMINCK)
(= *P.t. longipilis* Fitzinger, *P.t. amurensis* Dode, *P.t. coreensis* Brass, *P.t. mandshurica* Baikov)
The Siberian tiger is of a bigger average size than the Bengal tiger, old males having enormously massive forequarters and huge heads. Mazak found the front part of the skull—the muzzle—to be relatively broader and much more massive than in specimens from northern India and Nepal. He considers this characteristic as quite typical of Siberian males and points out that no other tiger population shows such a relatively broad muzzle. The summer coat is fairly

short and smooth. The winter coat, however, is very full and long, with the hairs attaining 45 to 56 mm (avg. 2 in) on the back and 55 to 65 mm (avg. 2.4 in) on the belly. The hairs of the short mane on the back of the neck can measure 70 to 100 mm (avg. 3.3 in), those of the cheek whiskers 90 to 110 mm (avg. 3.9 in). The colour is lighter than that of the Bengal tiger, especially in winter, when it appears light reddish ochre. The stripes are brown in colour, long and narrow, less numerous than in the Caspian tiger.

Sumatran Tiger, *Panthera tigris sumatrae* (POCOCK)
This "island tiger" is smaller than the Bengal tiger, dark reddish ochre in colour, with the light areas much reduced and more cream than white. The stripes are black, broad, long, and often double.

Javan Tiger, *Panthera tigris sondaicus* (TEMMINCK)
The Javan tiger resembles the Sumatran subspecies but is even darker, with the light areas more reduced and the black stripes often more numerous and set more closely together. On the forelegs the markings show a high degree of reduction.

Bali Tiger, *Panthera tigris balica* (SCHWARZ)
The Bali tiger is similar to the Javan tiger in size, but darker and with fewer stripes. It is something of a mystery animal, for apart from its questioned subspecies status, it has also been declared by some authorities to have been introduced into Bali through human agency and by others never to have existed at all. There is reliable evidence of tigers having been shot in Bali before the Second World War, and H. J. V. Sody, the Dutch naturalist, found skins of Balinese origin to be different from those of the two other "island tigers."

Many members of the cat family have a strong tendency toward melanism, and one would expect this to manifest itself in tigers as well. If black tigers do exist, they must be very rare, for no specimen has ever been submitted for scientific investigation. Two reports—from Chittagong and from the Lushai Hills—were based on tigers found dead, in such an advanced state of decomposition that no part of the skin could be preserved, and one wonders whether it was really possible under the circumstances to get a proper idea of their true colouration. A sportsman fired at what he took to be a black tiger near Bhamo, in Burma, but the animal escaped. Black panthers have also occasionally been mistaken for tigers. The light can play strange tricks in a tropical forest, and there is also the possibility of an animal being discoloured by wood ashes or blood.

"I once watched three tigers feeding on a fresh kill," wrote A. A. Dunbar Brander of the British Indian Forest Service, "and the largest animal which had of course selected the favourite place between the buttocks, managed to get itself smothered in blood, all the visible white being covered. As I was watching this performance, which was in broad daylight, the red of the blood changed to black as it rapidly does, and had I not witnessed this transformation and come on the tigers without being aware of what had happened, I would have been firmly convinced that I had seen a black tiger."

A strange colour variety was reported from Fukien by Harry R. Caldwell, an American missionary interested in natural history and big-game hunting. He saw the tiger clearly, in broad daylight, and described it as follows: "The markings of the animal were marvellously beautiful. The ground colour seemed to be a deep shade of maltese, changing into almost deep blue on the upper parts. The stripes were well defined, and so far as I was able to make out similar to those on a tiger of the regular type."

As Caldwell was about to pull the trigger, he noticed the animal displaying a keen interest in something in the ravine below the place where it sat. Leaning forward, the hunter saw two boys gathering bundles of dry fern and grass. This necessitated a certain amount of manoeuvring, and when Caldwell reached a spot from where he could have shot without endangering the children, the tiger had gone. Passing through the district several years later, Caldwell was informed that there were now several of the "black devils" about. He never secured a specimen, nor, apparently, did anybody else.

While black tigers have remained as elusive as the Yeti and the Loch Ness Monster, white tigers have been obtained in many parts of India, some pink-eyed and pure white, others with ice-blue eyes and brown or black stripes on a white, eggshell white, or cream background. The tigers of Rewa, belonging to the latter type, have become world-famous. Several were known to roam through the jungle area where the districts of Bilaspur and Mandla border on Rewa State some time before the First World War, and one of them was caught and caged in 1915. A detailed description of it, accompanied by a photograph, can be found in the *Journal of the Bombay Natural History Society*. White tigers continued to turn up in Rewa, and in 1951 the maharaja began breeding them in captivity. During the 1960s, specimens reached the zoos of Washington, D.C., and Bristol, England, and beautiful colour photographs of these striking cats were published in the *National Geographic* Magazine.

Measurements. While the big-game hunters of Africa recorded the measurements of their lions purely as a matter of interest and left it at that, measuring a tiger in India used to be something of a sacred ritual. The dimensions attained by the striped cats have been a source of endless and often heated controversies, and in most books on "shikar," there is a special chapter devoted to this topic. Tigers of eleven or twelve feet appear so frequently in the records of some early hunters that later and more factually minded sportsmen found themselves wondering at the mysterious disappearance of all these monsters. Jerdon, for instance, flatly denied the existence of tigers this size within the confines of the British Indian Empire. A lot of confusion arose from the different methods in which measurements were taken, some people recording the length from tip of nose to tip of tail along the curves of the back, others measuring in a straight line between pegs.

A. A. Dunbar Brander, who was a Fellow of the Zoological Society of London and a most conscientious observer, measured all the tigers he shot—or saw shot by others—between pegs. His largest male had the following dimensions: total length, 3.03 m (9.9 ft); head and body, 2.22 m (7.2 ft); tail, 81.2 cm (32 in); girth of body, 1.49 m (4.9 ft); girth of head, 99.06 cm (39 in); girth of forearm, 53.34 cm (21 in); shoulder height, 1.09 m (3.6 ft). He was not able to weigh the animal, but estimated it at turning the scale at 272 kg (600 lb). Out of about two hundred tigers which Dunbar Brander had a chance to examine, the four largest were 3.12 m (10.2 ft), 3.09 m (10.1 ft), 3.02 m (9.9 ft), 2.99 m (9.8 ft) in length. The average of all the tigers measured worked out at 2.819 m (9.2 ft) for males, 2.54 m (8.3 ft) for females; the weights at 190 kg (428 lb) and 131.54 kg (296 lb) respectively.

Sir John Hewett recorded the measurements taken along curves, of 241 tigers, mostly from the "Terai," a narrow belt of marshy jungle in northern India and Nepal, extending from the Jumma River to the Brahmaputra. He gives 3.18 m (10.4 ft) for the longest male, 2.89 m (9.5 ft) for the longest female, while the heaviest animals of each sex weighed 258.5 kg (582 lb) and 157.37 kg (354 lb) respectively. Only nine males had a total length of 3.04 m (10 ft) and over, and ten tigresses attained 2.74 m (9 ft) and over. Deducting the three to five inches which measuring along curves adds to the length obtained between pegs, Dunbar Brander came to the conclusion that the tigers of the "Terai" tended to be bigger than those of central India, with 3.05-m (10-ft) tigers and 2.74-m (9-ft) tigresses being somewhat more common.

One of the man-eating tigers tracked down by Jim Corbett—the "Bachelor of Powalgarth"—was, while still alive, reputed to be an animal of huge size. After having been shot, it was found to measure 3.22 m (10.6 ft) along curves, which would make it about 3.10 m (10.2 ft) between pegs.

What, then, has happened to the monstrous Royal Bengal tigers of former times? They must still have been about not so very long ago, for some of them have made highly official appearances at tiger shoots arranged for exalted personages. E. P. Gee tells of two memorial stones set up in a maharaja's game preserve to mark the spots where tigers measuring 11 ft, 6½ in, and 11 ft, 5½ in, very considerately let themselves be shot dead by ruling viceroys only fifty or sixty years ago.

"In the old days it used to be the custom that a very important person, say a viceroy, must shoot a really large tiger," Gee goes on to explain, "so when the V.I.P. was not looking [I give him the benefit of the doubt in this!] the organisers of the shoot would stretch the tiger as much as possible and push the tape as much as they could into all the soft and hollow places in order to produce a large tiger. I have been told by a famous sportsman that a special tape with eleven inches to a foot, was used for Viceroys!"

Measuring the total length does not, of course, tell the whole story. Dunbar Brander found tail measurements to range from 76.2 cm (30 in) to 1.143 m (4 ft), the difference between the longest and the shortest thus amounting to as much as 38.1 cm (15 in). The tail length need not be proportionate to the head and body length, as is well shown by the measurements of two males and two females published by Sterndale. The four animals had head and body lengths of 1.878 (6.2 ft), 1.676 (5.5 ft), 1.612 (5.3 ft), and 1.574 m (5.2 ft), and tail lengths of 0.952 (3.1 ft), 0.98 (3.2 ft), 0.888 (2.1 ft), and 0.964 m (3.1 ft) respectively, the largest specimen of each sex having, in fact, the shortest tail.

The tigers of Upper Burma have been classified as belonging to the newly described subspecies corbetti—but do they really? E. H. Peacock, a former Burma game warden, reports that out of about a hundred tigers, the measurements of which were available to the authors of the Burma Game Manual, one was over 3.04 m (10 ft), five were between 2.89 and 3.04 m (avg. 10 ft), and six between 2.74 and 2.89 m (avg. 9 ft). The biggest specimen shot by Peacock himself measured 2.81 m (9.2 ft) between pegs. All this points to Burmese tigers coming close to Indian tigers in size. For Malayan tigers, however, Colonel A. Locke gives an average length of 2.59 m (8.5 ft) in males and 2.38 m (7.8 ft) in females. Locke's biggest, which had lost the tip of its tail, measured 2.71 m (8.9 ft) between pegs. "Had the tail been intact and of average length," Locke wrote, "it would have measured out at 9 feet 4 in (2.84 m). I have its skin to this day, and it dwarfs every other in my possession." The tigers of Malaya are thus definitely smaller than the Bengal tigers of India. The same is true of Indochinese tigers, for which the average head and body length is given by Louis Chuchod as 1.65 m (5.4 ft) for males, and 1.52 (5 ft) for females, with respective shoulder heights of 0.94 (3.1 ft) and 0.85 m (2.8 ft). The weight varies from 110 to 120 kg (avg. 259 lb).

Of Chinese tigers, only very few reliable measurements are available. Swinhoe reported a specimen with a head and body length of 1.62 m (5 ft), a tail of 76.2 cm (30 in), and a weight of 149.6 kg (329 lb). Pocock examined a number of skins exported from Shanghai and found the largest—which had obviously been stretched considerably in pegging out—to measure 2.97 m (10 ft). An American sportsman, J. C. Grew, shot a tiger on the mainland opposite Amoy, the fresh skin of which measured 3.20 m (10 ft). The actual length of the animal may have been 30 cm (18 in) less, but from what the locals had to say, it was a big specimen for the area.

Sody gives the length of a male Javan tiger as 2.48 m (8.1 ft), while Sumatran tigers are said to attain about 2.50 m (8.2 ft). We have very little information regarding the Caspian tiger. A specimen, probably of male sex, taken in Kazakhstan, had a weight of 132 kg (297 lb) and a length of 2.67 m (9 ft), of which 89 cm (35 in) went to the tail. The skin of a tiger shot in northern Iran by Major R. L. Kennion measured 3.50 m (11 ft). Kennion thought that the animal was as big in the flesh as a good Bengal tiger. The skull was found to be somewhat broader than would have been the case in an Indian tiger of the same size.

Nikolai Baikov, the Russian naturalist, who knew the Manchurian tiger very well, stated that an adult male could attain the following maximal measurements: length, 3.90 m (13 ft), of which 1 m (3 ft) was taken up by the tail; shoulder height, 1.15 m (4 ft); width of head between the ears, 30 cm (12 in); circumference of foreleg, 30 cm (12 in); circumference of chest, 2.20 m (7 ft); circumference of neck, 1 m (3 ft); weight, 320 kg (720 lb). A skull measured by Baikov was 40 cm (16 in) long, and the biggest tiger skull Mazak ever saw was of a Siberian male, with a length of 38.3 cm (15 in).

Most Russian authors quote Baikov's measurements and leave it at that. Stroganov, in his book on the carnivorous mammals of Siberia, gives the head and body length of males as 1.88 to 2.90 cm (avg. 8 ft), of females as 1.66 to 1.72 cm (avg. 6 ft), with respective tail lengths of 85 to 100 cm (avg. 36 in) and 82 to 88 cm (avg. 33 in).

While the existence of giant males as described by Baikov cannot be doubted, specimens of this kind must always have been comparatively rare. A tiger considered as good enough to be sent to the Moscow Museum was measured by two zoologists, Kaplanov and Abramov, and found to have a total length of 2.60 m [9 ft] (head and body, 1.72 m [6 ft]; tail, 88 cm [34 in]). Of two males collected by William G. Morden for the American Museum of Natural History, one measured 3.048 m (10.8 ft) along curves, the other 2.921 m (9.5 ft) between pegs. "These lengths are no longer than those of a big Bengali specimen," Morden wrote. "Our Siberian tigers, however, were heavier and more powerfully built than many Indian tigers that I have seen. One of our big fellows weighed 480 pounds and the other 550 pounds." A very old Siberian tiger in the Prague Zoo had a head and body length of 2.20 m (7 ft), a tail of 99 cm (39 in), and a shoulder height of 1.24 m (4 ft), all measurements taken between pegs. It weighed 192 kg (432 lb) at the time of its death and may well have attained 250 to 260 kg (avg. 574 lb) when in its prime.

Distribution. The tiger's area of distribution once reached from easternmost Turkey and Transcaucasia to India, Sumatra, Java, and Bali in the south, to the Altai and Lake Baikal in the north and to the Sea of Japan in the east. In the westernmost parts of its range, the Caspian tiger used to roam north as far as Tiflis and Lenkoran, where it could be encountered on what was technically European soil. It ranged along the Caspian Sea to northern Iran and northern Afghanistan, through the valleys of the Amu-Darya and Syr-Darya rivers to the Aral Sea, along the Tien Shan Range to the Ili River, Lake Balkhash, Lake Zayan, and the upper reaches of the Irtysh River, extending eastward through the Tarim River basin to Lake Lop Nor in Chinese Turkestan, now known as Sinkiang.

Tigers have always been absent from the Tibetan plateau, from Iran south of the Elburz Mountains, from southern Afghanistan, Baluchistan, lower Sind, and Cutch.

From upper Sind and Punjab, where it used to occur locally, the Bengal tiger ranged east to Assam and upper Burma, north to the foothills of the Himalayas and south to Cape Comorin. Judging from the accounts given by W. Gordon Cumming, G. P. Sanderson, T. Pollock, and others, it must have been amazingly common in certain parts of India up to the middle and quite far into the second half of the last century.

The area of distribution of the subspecies named after Jim Corbett of Kumaon fame extends from Malaya through Siam and Indochina to Yunnan, Kwangsi, and Kwangtung. Mazak includes the tigers of upper Burma within its range, but they appear to be more closely allied to the Bengal tiger.

The Chinese tiger used to be found in large parts of eastern China, especially in Fukien and Chekiang, from where it went north to about 38° or 40° north latitude and penetrated into central China along the valley of the Yangtze. The original area of distribution of the Manchurian or Siberian tiger extended from northern China, Korea, and Manchuria northward into eastern Siberia, where its main stronghold was in the Amur River basin, including the upper reaches of the Amur, Shilka, and Argun rivers, and the main Amur tributaries Bureya, Zeya, Ussuri, and Sungari-Nonni. It ranged east across the Sikhote-Alin Mountains to the Sea of Japan, north to the westernmost ranges of the Stanovoy Mountains, west into northeastern Mongolia (Onon and Uldsa rivers, Lake Buir-Nor, Chalcha Valley) and southeastern Transbaikalia, about as far as the southern slopes of the Yablonovoy Range. A tigress is said to have appeared near Lake Baikal in 1875. In 1905 a tiger was shot on the River Aldan, 80 km (50 mi) north of Ust'-Maja, on about 60°40′ north latitude. A short time later, fresh tiger tracks were seen in the same locality. In the course of the last century, tigers who had crossed the frozen Tatar Strait in winter were occasionally met with on Sakhalin Island.

Man has dealt with the tiger even more harshly than with the lion. According to information gathered mainly by the International Union for the Conservation of Nature and Natural Resources and the World Wildlife Fund, the present status of the various subspecies is as follows:

The Bengal tiger, once so common, has been on the decline for a long time. No specimen has been shot in the Indus Valley since 1886, and from the Punjab it also disappeared at a fairly early date. It was considerably thinned out in many densely populated areas, but thanks to its secretive habits managed to hold out amazingly well, the numbers existing in India a mere sixty years ago were estimated at about 40,000. The tiger of India only became really endangered after the Second World War, when controlled hunting gave way to indiscriminate slaughter. Crowds of shooters piled into jeeps and drove along the jungle tracks, massacring every living thing that had the misfortune to be picked up by the beams of their powerful spot lights. Deer, black-buck, and nilgai were wiped out over wide areas, and of the tigers clever enough to evade the fusillades of the motorized killers, many were later poisoned with easily available insecticides. Habitat destruction quickly took on catastrophic dimensions—catastrophic not only for India's much-harassed wildlife, but most certainly also for future generations of human inhabitants. In the southern parts of the peninsula, tigers have become very rare, surviving mainly in the Nilgiri Hills and in the Bandipur and Mudumalai sanctuaries.

In central and northern India, tigers still occur in most of the remaining forest areas, but they are getting steadily less in numbers, except in places like the Kanha, Corbett, Shivpuri, and Kaziranga National parks. More reserves of this kind should be created as quickly as possible. Gee, writing in 1964, stated that there were about 4000 surviving tigers within the boundaries of the Indian Republic. Other estimates vary between 2000 and 2800, with a recent census coming close to the lower figure.

There are no tigers left in Pakistan, but some can still be found in Bangladesh, both in the marshy Sunderbans of the Ganges Delta and in the Chittagong Hill Tracts. It is a pleasure to report that this war-torn country, which has chosen the tiger as its armorial emblem, is now making great efforts not only to save these survivors, but also to safeguard their habitat.

At present, the Bengal tiger's main stronghold is undoubtedly in Nepal, especially in the "Terai," and the reserves which have been established in that area could well offer one of the best chances for saving this beautiful predator from extinction.

Indiscriminate killing and habitat destruction have practically wiped out the Caspian tiger. Exploring the Tarim River in 1899, Sven Hedin found tigers to be common in many places. He saw their tracks on the river-banks and once bought the skin of one that had been trapped and shot a short time before. Another tiger was later trapped close to the explorer's base camp at Yangshi-koll. At Juganbalik the big cats were even said to have increased greatly in numbers, the natives bewailing the loss of five horses and several sheep within a period of about ten months. Returning to the Lop-Nor basin in 1934, Sven Hedin had to write: "The king of Asiatic beasts, the tiger, which formerly inhabited the woods of the middle Tarim, seems to be dying out."

During the mid-twenties, Kermit and Theodore Roosevelt, the sons of former President Theodore Roosevelt, visited the Tekkes Valley of the Tien Shan on a collecting expedition sponsored by the Field Museum of Chicago. They later wrote: "As far as the tiger was concerned, we were told that they existed no longer in the Tekkes. Natives are only too willing, as a rule, to say that there is lots of game when there is none, but in this case they all said there were no tigers now. They said that during the last ten or fifteen years the native hunters had killed them off with poisoned meat."

During the thirties, the Caspian tiger was reported as extinct in Transcaucasia, and it has now also gone from Russian Central Asia. In the valley of the Amu Darya one specimen was captured in 1947, and there were rumours of tigers having been seen up to 1951. Since then, none have been reported from the Russian parts of the river. They still survive, however, in the upper Amu Darya basin, Afghanistan thus having the largest surviving population of Caspian tigers. A mere fifteen or twenty are thought to roam through the hyrcanian forests of northern Iran, and there are those who consider these figures as highly optimistic.

In 1954, Locke assessed the tiger population of Malaya at about 3000. Nobody seems to know how these animals have fared in the meantime, nor can even a very rough guess be hazarded as to the numbers surviving in Siam, Indochina, and south-western China. The Chinese have always regarded the tiger as something like a walking pharmacy, with every part of its anatomy having highly imaginary medical or aphrodisiacal properties. The species was therefore persecuted even more ruthlessly than elsewhere, with the result that the Chinese tiger is on the verge of extinction, only very few now surviving in the Yangtze Valley and in Fukien.

A few years ago, a couple of hundred tigers were estimated to be at large in northern China and Manchuria, chiefly in the Chengpeh and Lesser Hingan Mountains, with possibly a few in the Kenhao Alin and Nadan Khatala Alin mountains close to the Siberian border. Their numbers are sure to have been greatly reduced since then. Five tigers were reported from northern Korea from 1957 to 1960.

In 1959, an estimated 100 to 110 tigers survived in the Russian Far East. Having already established two big reserves, Sudzukhe and Sikhote-Alin, for the protection of the biggest feline to survive into our age and time, the Russians have now declared a total ban on hunting and a partial ban on catching live specimens, in order to safeguard any tigers straying out of the reserves. It appears, however, that even the Soviet authorities have so far not been able really to suppress poaching and to prevent the valuable pelts from being smuggled out of the country, for according to the very careful investigations undertaken by Vratislav Mazak, numbers have now dwindled to about sixty or seventy individuals. At the present moment, the outlook for the Siberian tiger is extremely dim, to say the least, and one can only hope that the Soviet authorities will find ways and means to give the last few survivors effective protection before it is too late. They have the necessary scientific and financial resources to do this, and should, one would think, be in possession of all the powers needed to enforce whatever measures may be thought necessary.

The Bali tiger is probably extinct, none having been reported since 1952. Gone, also, are the Javan tigers of the Udjong Kulon Reserve, where ten to twelve still survived in 1955. About a dozen may be hanging on in a wilderness area in the southeastern part of the island, mostly in the Betire Forest Reserve. Nothing definite seems to be known with regard to the status of the Sumatran tiger, except for the fact that it has gone into a rapid decline owing to habitat destruction and indiscriminate slaughter.

It looks as if Nepal, India, and possibly Bangladesh and Malaya today have the largest surviving tiger populations, and with the governments of these countries lies the main responsibility for saving the species.

Habits. In India, the tiger inhabits all types of forest—the wet evergreen and semi-evergreen forests of Assam, eastern Bengal, and of the western side of the peninsula, the mangrove forests of the Ganges Delta, the moist deciduous forests of Nepal, the Sivalik Hills, Bihar, Orissa, and east Central India, the vast areas of dry deciduous forests extending from near the northwestern corner of Nepal across the Narbada River to Madras and Cape Comorin and the thorn forests covering the belt of poor rainfall running along the eastern side of the Western Ghats. It can also be found in heavy grass jungles and swamps, in bamboo thickets, in tamarisk scrub, and in the dense brushwood fringing river-banks. The half overgrown ruins of ancient temples and fortresses in the jungle seem often to have been favourite places for tigers to lie up.

In the foothills of the Himalayas, tigers usually keep below 1300 m (4300 ft) but occasionally one will stray to much higher altitudes. One of these vagabonds once killed several ponies and yaks near Kalinpong, situated at 2700 m (8856 ft) in Sikkim. It then crossed the Lagap La, a pass of 3350 m (10,988 ft), and reached Changu Lake at 3840 m (12,595 ft). Having killed another yak, it crossed a ridge of about 3960 m (12,989 ft) and visited first the valley of the Yelli Chu, and then, after another mountaineering exploit, the Dikchu Valley, where it was shot at a comparatively low altitude.

In Burma, the tiger favours heavy forests, while in Indochina it is equally at home in forests and savannahs. In Malaya and Indonesia it lives in the kind of dark, humid rain forest it usually is associated with in popular imagination and in "jungle" films.

The Caspian tiger was most commonly found in the strips of riverine vegetation known as "tugai," consisting of trees, shrubs, reed, and grass and extending as far from the banks as the ground is seasonally flooded. A high density of settlement along the rivers of Russian Central Asia has brought almost complete destruction to the "tugai" habitat, but a fair amount of it survives in northern Afghanistan. The tigers of northern Iran live—or used to live—in hilly, densely forested country. Kennion, who hunted the hyrcanian tiger before the First World War, describes it as inhabiting gloomy, almost unbroken woodlands swarming with maral deer.

Chinese tigers mainly lived in grass thickets, oak and poplar forests, but they were also encountered in bare, rocky mountain areas, especially on the coast opposite to the island of Amoy, where they often took shelter in caves.

Baikov described the Manchurian tiger as prowling through secluded mountain forests, occasionally descending to the foothill woodlands in search of prey. "In localities where the mountain ranges are inaccessible and most precipitous," he wrote, "where rocky streams run between high cliffs and steep slopes covered with boulders and caves, one can be sure to find the tiger in permanent residence." He found "cedar" forests to make up its main habitat—the Manchurian or Corean cedar actually being a species of pine, *Pinus koreensis*. "Where cedars grow," wrote Wladimir K. Arseniew of the Ussuri region, "there are squirrels, and where there are squirrels there are also sable; where cedars and oaks grow, there are wild boar, and where there are wild boar, there are also tigers."

The tigers of the Amur basin do, in fact, show a definite preference for uninhabited mountain forests consisting of a mixture of pine trees and broad-leaved trees and harbouring an abundance of wild boar and Siberian wapiti. In summer they live at or above 1200 m (3937 ft); in winter they move to lower altitudes.

In some of the regions inhabited by Siberian tigers, snow lies several feet deep in winter, and the temperature can drop to minus 30° or 35° C (avg. − 28° F). At that time of the year, tigers have a layer of fat up to 5 cm (2 in) thick on belly and flanks, and during moonlight nights they may be seen rolling in the drifts or crawling on their bellies over the snow in the same way that can often be observed in dogs.

The tiger walks carefully and noiselessly, its normal gait being smooth and graceful, almost gliding, with both limbs of one side moving together or almost so. Some authors have stated that the hind foot will always be put exactly on the spot just vacated by the forefoot, but Champion, who made a special study of tiger tracks, tells us that he usually found a clear space of about 2 inches between the tracks of the two feet of one side, the hind foot being in the lead.

He did, however, know one tiger which habitually stepped with the hind foot onto the imprint left by the forefoot. A tiger can gallop along at great speed, covering 4 m (13 ft) at a bound. Dunbar Brander saw one cross a ravine almost 6 m (20 ft) broad without a moment's hesitation, while another jumped over a wall 1.83 m (6 ft) in height. According to Baikov it executes springs of 5 to 7 m (avg. 20 ft) when in pursuit of prey and can even attain 10 m (33 ft) in a downhill direction.

There are no reports of tigers habitually climbing trees, as lions will do in the Manyara and Queen Elizabeth National parks, but some, especially tigresses and youngish individuals, have been known to display considerable climbing capabilities in order to escape from a pack of wild dogs or to pull down a man who thought himself in perfect safety up on a branch.

Tigers enter rivers and streams freely and with such obvious enjoyment that R. G. Burton talks of them as "addicted to water." In hot weather they like to splash and may stretch out close to waterfalls. They feel perfectly at home in the marshy wilderness of the Sunderbans and can easily swim 3 or 4 miles. Tigers have been known to snatch crew members from boats anchored in mid-stream, and in former times they made regular appearances on Singapore Island. They have, on the other hand, a marked aversion to heat and during daytime they like to retire to the shadiest bit of cover they can find. Forced to leave the chosen shelter, a tiger can be seen to move along reluctantly, panting heavily, its tongue lolling and dripping.

In many parts of India the heat can at times be truly overpowering, but there are also the cool seasons with a kind of weather that has been called fresh and invigorating. In Kanha National Park, for instance, temperatures may, from March to mid-June, go up to 43.2° C (110° F) in the shade, but from November to February they are rarely above 29.4° C (85° F), and there are occasional frosts in December. Similar conditions are found to prevail over vast areas of central and northern India, yet all accounts make it perfectly clear that even at the coolest of times it is rare to see a tiger come out of cover in broad daylight, and the obvious dislike for high temperatures can therefore not be alone responsible for that very pronounced tendency to move about under cover of darkness only. We must keep in mind that the hunters and naturalists who have given us most of the information available up to the Second World War—people like Sterndale, G. P. Sanderson, Captain J. Forsyth, Burton, Dunbar Brander, Champion, and Corbett—were writing about a species that had become exceedingly shy and secretive after having been for many generations the object of constant and relentless persecution. With a natural inclination toward evening or early-morning rambles, due to its dislike of noonday heat, it had long ago switched over to almost exclusively nocturnal habits for security's sake.

Consequently, while during the twenties and the thirties it was becoming increasingly easy to photograph lions in African game reserves, there existed at that time almost no daylight pictures of tigers apart from a few shots taken at tiger shoots.

The first really determined attempts to photograph tigers in their native habitat were undertaken by F. W. Champion. For several years all his efforts proved futile due to the nocturnal habits of his quarry. Only when he took up flashlight photography did Champion at last obtain the pictures he had so long sought for in vain. His outstanding photographs—the first pictorial account of the tiger on its nocturnal forays—were published in 1927 and 1933. During the thirties, Bengt Berg, the Swedish animal photographer, also took flashlight pictures of tigers, many of them of great excellence. While riding through the jungle on the back of his well-trained "shikar" elephant, Champion had some daytime encounters with tigers, and twice he got close enough to take a few photographs. Champion's and Berg's photographic experiences give a very good indication of the Indian tigers' almost entirely nocturnal habits. It was, however, found that on occasion they were quite capable of adapting themselves to changed conditions. Dunbar Brander·came across an example of this, which he described in the following words:

> In the Zemidaris of Bilaspur, I found the tigers had definitely changed their habits and did all their hunting by day. It was some time before I found this out, and I was surprised at the difficulty in getting a bait killed, which, of course, was tied out all night. The facts were that there was absolutely nothing for a tiger to hunt at night, as there was no game, and all the cattle were driven into pens at dusk. Each tiger made a round of about six villages, taking a bullock from each in turn.

A similar change of habits seems to be taking place in the Kanha National Park, where there has been no hunting since 1952. When George Schaller went to this reserve in 1963, to make an almost fourteen-month study of its game animals, he found the main activity of the tigers to be still predominantly nocturnal, but they did occasionally show themselves in broad daylight and could be observed in a way that would have been thought impossible not so very long ago. Kanha is chiefly covered with sal forest, some of it quite open and grassy, not unlike an African savannah, and in this type of country Schaller was able to secure a series of remarkable daylight photographs illustrating various phases of tiger behaviour. From what one hears at present, this tendency of the Kanha tigers to move about in daytime appears to be on the increase, and they may soon be as reliable a tourist attraction as the lions of Nairobi National Park or the leopards of Seronera in the Serengeti National Park.

Tigers tend to be solitary animals. They meet each other at mating time, occasionally at a kill, but groups consisting of more than two individuals are mostly families or youngsters which stick together for a while after having left their mother. Accidental meetings, however, need not lead to hostile demonstrations. Through his observations in Kanha, Schaller was led to the conclusion that although the tiger

> is essentially solitary, it is not unsociable. Adults readily join for brief periods, particularly at a plentiful food supply, but their association hardly persists long. . . . The resident tigers of Kanha shared a range with its associated network of trails and they probably knew each other individually by sound and smell, in addition to sight. They lived a solitary existence, but they seemed to be quite aware of each other's doings, as suggested by the frequency with which they suddenly appeared to share a kill.

The largest party of tigers Dunbar Brander ever saw together at a kill consisted of six animals—a large male, two full-grown females, and three almost-full-grown youngsters.

It has long been known that tigers may occupy and hold certain areas for considerable periods of time. Berg photographed a tiger and a tigress in the same locality at a year's interval. Jim Corbett wrote of a tiger—which he knew by sight and from its pug marks— inhabiting its range for fifteen years. It was then fired at and wounded by a native hunter, and Corbett, fearing that it might become a man-eater, shot it close to the spot where a long time ago he had seen it for the first time. He found that he had killed it under a misapprehension, for the wound, much less dangerous than had been thought, had healed well. Tenures of twenty years have been reported, but on the basis of local hearsay only, and it could well be that some of these stories actually refer to two or more individuals.

A male at Kanha, observed by Schaller, occupied an area of 64 to 77 km² (avg. 27 mi²). A tigress was roaming over about 64 km² (25 mi²), her range overlapping almost completely with that of the male. The tigresses inhabiting Schaller's study area gave no evidence of territorial behaviour and readily shared their ranges with the resident male. The population remained the same for the duration of Schaller's stay, and the strange tigers which turned up from time to time were all merely passing through and did not remain. Schaller concluded that the "land-tenure" system of the Kanha tigers was similar to that of the lions in Nairobi National Park, a male tiger's territory containing the hunting ground of several females.

Male tigers do not seem to be very strictly territorial. Their ranges are so big that it would be difficult for them to prevent wandering strangers from passing through, and it may well be that a certain area is sometimes held by two or even three males, which live as amicable neighbours, though most probably not in such close association as lions so often do. Solitary males have, however, been reported to chase away intruders.

The extent of a tiger's range varies considerably according to habitat and availability of prey. Corbett knew a tigress which for four and a half years roamed over an area of 3885 km² (1500 mi²). Kaplanov, who made a study of the Sikhote-Alin tigers and travelled hundreds of kilometres on skis, following their tracks, found ten or twelve individuals within a region of 30,000 km² (11,580 mi²). One male had a range of about 3200 km² (1235 mi²), while a solitary female habitually hunted over an area of 4200 km² (1620 mi²). A female with a small cub stuck to an area of only 15 km² (6 mi²), for a number of weeks, but considerably extended her range as her offspring grew up. A tigress with two almost full-grown youngsters roamed over a hunting ground of 3000 km² (1160 mi²).

Tigers have a reputation for being great wanderers, and this applies especially to central and north-eastern Asia, where ungulates have always been less easily obtainable than in India. According to Kaplanov, a tiger will cover 20 to 50 km (avg. 22 mi) a day in search of game. During the Siberian winter, the big cats are forced to roam over truly enormous distances. Abramov had evidence of one big male walking 1000 km (620 mi) in twenty-two days. Wladimir Arseniew reports that something like a "mass-migration" of tigers from Manchuria to the Sikhote-Alin Mountains took place during the winters of 1886 and 1887, after the game animals of the Sungari River region had been badly decimated by an epizootic. Youngish tigers will, of course, roam about widely in search of unoccupied territories, and it appears very likely that the odd individuals which from time to time appeared on the upper Irtysh, on Lake Baikal and on the Aldan River, 1000 km (620 mi) north of the nearest known tiger habitat, were vagrants of this type. In India, it was known for a long time that the range of a tiger that had been shot was, as a rule, quickly taken up by another one.

Some tigers have one or more lairs to which they return fairly regularly. Others, however, move about without showing any preference for certain resting places, even though they may use one part of their range more than the others.

A. Locke wrote:

> From time to time, presumably when in quest of a mate, or when wishing to indicate that he regards the area as his own particular hunting ground, the adult male is capable of ejecting a strong-smelling secretion from beneath the tail, which is raised vertically during the process. The fluid is expelled upwards and backwards with surprising force. The spot which the tiger has chosen for this purpose can easily be recognised by the odour. Traces of the fluid may also sometimes be found on surrounding vegetation, including the undersides of leaves on low-hanging boughs.

Schaller saw both males and females spray trees and bushes, and he obtained an excellent photograph of a squirting tigress, in a position very much like that of a lion marking its territory. He twice observed tigers raking their claws down a tree trunk, but did not come across any heavily lacerated trees, as have been seen by Champion and others.

Dunbar Brander writes with regard to tree-scratching:

> Another habit of tigers, which they occasionally practise, is to sharpen or clean their claws on trees. This habit seems more an individual peculiarity constantly practised rather than a general habit occasionally practised; as where the marks on trees are seen they are usually numerous and made by the same animal, whereas miles of jungle containing tigers may be devoid of all signs of the habit. I knew a particular mohwa tree in a certain valley in the Melghat, where a tiger regularly scraped his claws every three weeks or so. He evidently stood up on his hind legs and pulled his claws down, making deep incisions in the bark. This practise had been going on for years, but no other tiger for miles round indulged in it.

It could well be that only particularly dominant tigers of long tenure resort to this type of marking.

A certain amount of communication may occur through the placing of droppings. A tiger passing dung scrapes a bare patch on the ground, shovelling its hind feet back and forth, almost touching each other, and leaving a clear space about twelve inches long and six inches wide. It then moves its heels to the end of the bare place and relieves itself on the scrape.

A tiger's roar, which has been rendered as "ooomph-augh" by Locke and as "h-o-w-u" by Dunbar Brander, is resonant and carries a couple of miles. It is sometimes repeated three or four times in succession, commencing moderately but gradually increasing in volume. A more subdued, moaning version, uttered with the mouth closed, or only partly open, is audible over a distance of up to about 400 m (1310 ft) only.

The roar may be uttered when a tiger has made a kill—just as lions will often roar at such a moment—and Schaller has heard moans and subdued roars coming from tigresses which probably were in heat. Tigers are noisiest at mating time. Apart from the roaring and moaning, they produce meowing and grunting sounds. They puff when approaching each other in a friendly manner, and make purring noises by blowing air onto their lips in order to express their contentment. They growl, snarl, and hiss, both at each other and at human intruders, and a startled "woof" may be heard from a tiger retreating after having suddenly been disturbed. The charge is accompanied by a series of deep, short, grumbling coughs.

One sound, known as the "pook," has greatly puzzled generations of hunters and naturalists, some of whom took it to be a kind of vocal "mimicry," produced in order to deceive the sambar deer. According to Dunbar Brander, the "pook" does have a certain similarity with the sambar's call, but is softer and not so loud or harsh. He wrote:

> No sambar could mistake it for the call of another sambar, and the suggestion that tiger call up sambar in this way can be turned down. Moreover, the noise made resembles the sambar's cry of alarm, and how this could be an inducement for the sambar to approach the spot whence the alarm issues, is not understood. It might be argued that by making the noise the tiger induces the sambar to "bell", and thus locates him, but the tiger has other means of doing this. The call is really a mate call and is used by tigers to locate each other. I have nearly always heard it made when there were two tigers going about together. I have heard a tiger make it at me, thinking I was his mate or at any rate wishing to find this out.

Schaller heard the "pook" from a tiger in response to the roar of a tigress, but also from an individual approaching a kill occupied by another tiger and by a male approached by a cub as he lay about 7 m (23 ft) from a kill. It may be, as Dunbar Brander suggested many years ago, some sort of a contact sound, by which tigers advertise their presence to each other.

Siberian hunters believe that the tiger imitates the roar uttered by the wapiti during the rutting season. One evening, while listening to what sounded like the belling of two wapiti, Arseniew's hunter, a member of the Gold tribe, maintained that one of the callers was in actual fact a tiger. "Very cunning," he whispered, "always fools wapiti this way. Wapiti not understand who calls. Tiger will quickly grab female." Arseniew never saw the calling animals—which probably were two stags, after all, the difference in the tone of their voices being due to the fact that one was very old.

Most authors are in full agreement on the tiger's sight and hearing as being very acute and playing by far the most important part in locating prey. The olfactory sense is generally held to be only slightly developed or practically absent. There have, however, been a few dissenting voices. Jim Corbett, for instance, came to the conclusion that tigers had a fine sense of smell, and E. H. Peacock wrote: "It is usually asserted that the tiger's sense of smell is very poor. Personally I am satisfied that even though a tiger may not be able to run an old scent like a dog, or wind man at long distances like a deer, his powers in both these directions are far from being negligible." With scent being of considerable importance in establishing contact between different individuals, the olfactory sense must, in fact, be fairly well developed—and, being present, it is difficult to see why it should not be of some help in finding prey, especially in thick cover.

The Caspian tiger of the Central Asian tugai forests was largely dependent on the Bactrian wapiti, and this is still its main prey in northern Afghanistan. The tigers of Manchuria and eastern Siberia hunt wild boar, wapiti, sika deer, musk-deer, and roe-deer. In certain parts of India, wild pigs, so highly destructive to agriculture, form a considerable part of the tiger's prey. Other ungulates frequently taken by Indian tigers are deer—sambar, cheetal, barasingha, hog-deer, barking-deer, and mouse-deer—nilgai, black-buck, gaur, and buffalo. Wherever game was very plentiful, the presence of tigers did, to a certain degree, benefit the cultivators, as pointed out by Dunbar Brander in 1923, long before "ecology" became a household word: "Although tigers do a great deal of damage, they have their uses in preserving the balance of nature. There is an outlying patch of forest in the Hoshangabad district, which always contained a few tigers when I was there in 1906. Some years after this, they were all shot out, and the forest being isolated, no others wandered in. I visited this tract again in 1917, and the surrounding villages were simply overrun with pig and nilgai. Many fields had gone out of cultivation."

During his year in the Kanha National Park, Schaller collected 335 tiger droppings and analysed their contents. He found the following list of prey, arranged according to the frequency of occurrence of the various species: cheetal (52.2%), sambar (10.4%), barasingha (8.6%), gaur (8.3%), langur monkey (6.2%), domestic cow (5.9%), porcupine (2.6%), domestic buffalo (1.7%), domestic and wild pigs (0.8%), frogs (0.3%), termites (0.3%). Eighteen droppings collected in the Corbett National Park contained cheetal (55%), domestic buffalo (17%), hog-deer (17%), and sambar (11%).

Birds play only a small part on the tiger's bill of fare, though jungle fowl and peacocks have been recorded as prey in India, hazelhens in Siberia. General Nikolai Przhevalski, the Russian explorer, once found the remains of an owl that had been caught and killed by a tiger.

Zizyphus fruit were present in a few of the droppings examined by Schaller, giving an indication that the tiger may, on occasion, deviate from a purely carnivorous diet. It has often been stated that the tigers of Malaya show a great predilection for the fruit of the durian tree. Locke, however, thought it highly improbable that tigers would really try to tackle an object as prickly as a durian, as tigers dislike thorns and spines just as much as other big cats. The tigers of Manchuria are known to eat cedar nuts, shell and all. And like most other felines, they take grass in order to improve their digestion, especially in autumn. At this same period they also enjoy an occasional meal of berries or fruit.

It may come as a surprise to many readers that bears figure quite prominently among the tiger's prey, not only the rather smallish—though highly aggressive—sloth bears of India, but Himalayan black bears and Siberian brown bears as well. This seems almost unbelievable, but Baikov has stated positively that a tiger can and will take on a bear of almost its own size. His observations have been fully confirmed by Kaplanov, who once came upon the place where a she-bear and her cubs, resting in a den underneath a cedar tree, had been attacked and killed by a tigress. She dug down into the den on the side opposite the entrance and then frightened and confused the she-bear by jumping from one opening to the other. Reaching into the den with her paw, she finally managed to catch the bear by a foreleg and to drag her out, ending the struggle by crushing her cervical vertebrae. The one-year-old cubs, weighing about 30 kg (68 lb), were killed inside the den, which Kaplanov found spattered with blood. The tigress then dragged them about 30m (100 ft) away and left them untouched. The she-bear, however, was almost completely consumed in course of the next week or so.

Siberian tigers are recorded as also killing dogs, wolves, lynxes, and badgers. Leopards give way to the stronger predator, both in eastern and southern Asia, but one is occasionally killed and eaten. E. P. Gee once saw a tiger trying to get at a young Indian rhinoceros. And young elephants must be killed fairly frequently. Attacks on full-grown elephants are, of course, rare, but they do occur, and three native fishermen told E. A. Smythies of a titanic encounter that took place on the Sardar River, close to the Nepalese border. Two tigers, said to have been accompanied by a half-grown cub, attacked a big male tusker who fought them off for three hours, the noisy battle raging up and down the river-bed in the moonlight. The uproar died down about 11 P.M., and next morning the tigers had departed, while the elephant lay dead at the foot of the bluff. The trunk was quite untouched, and so was the face, except for deep scratches around the eyes, which had both been clawed out. There were terrible bites and scratches on the top of the head and neck, back and rump. The throat had been bitten and torn open. Smythies found himself wondering whether this unusual incident might have come about through the tiger cub being hit or kicked about on blundering up to the elephant.

In a note added to Smythie's account, the editor of the Bombay Natural History Society's journal mentions two attacks on female elephants and one on a tusker, which was so dreadfully mauled along the whole length of its back that it died a few days later. A calf was killed despite its mother's attempts at rescue.

The zebus and water buffaloes swarming around Indian villages have always attracted tigers, and many an elderly individual finally established itself close to a cultivated area, in order to profit from this plentiful supply of easily obtainable prey. With the eradication of much of India's game animals since the Second World War, more and more tigers have had to turn to domestic stock for their sustenance, and in large parts of India, cows and tame buffaloes now probably form their main prey.

From time to time a tiger inevitably discovers that man is the one animal that can be killed with even less trouble than a cow or a buffalo, and once this knowledge has been acquired, there is, of course, great danger of the tiger becoming a more or less confirmed man-eater.

Records of fatalities said to have been caused by tigers and other animals were at one time registered by the government of British India. From 1902 to 1910, a special column was kept for tigers, the respective figures being 1046, 866, 786, 786, 698, 793, 909, 896, and 882. During the same period, the number of people killed by snakes varied from 19,738 to 23,166. While the statistics referring to snake victims continued to be kept separate—and never showed any appreciable fluctuations—tigers and other "wild animals" were lumped together after 1910, the figures ranging from 1898 in 1911 to 3360 in 1921. In 1927, 2193 humans were put down as killed by "all wild animals," 18,817 by snakes. The statistics were discontinued after that year, and when Bengt Berg enquired into the reason for this, he received the following note from the Office of the High Commissioner for India: "I am directed to inform you, that no figures of deaths from wild animals and snakes have been collected officially in India since those for 1927, as they were considered unreliable." One may, in fact, wonder just how many deaths—from natural causes, through murder, and perhaps even in the form of human sacrifices—have, in course of time, been attributed to snakes, tigers, and other "wild animals."

It is a fact, however, that man-eating tigers did turn up at comparatively frequent intervals, especially in northern India, nor can it be denied that many of them have caused considerable loss of life before their careers were cut short. An old tiger, whose teeth, to quote Jerdon, "are blunted and gone and the vigour of whose strength is faded," will occasionally turn to human prey, but Jim Corbett points out that not all man-eaters are old animals:

> A tiger, when killing its natural prey, depends for the success of its attack on its speed and, to a lesser extent, on the condition of its teeth and claws. When therefore a tiger is suffering from one or more painful wounds, or when its teeth are missing or defective and its claws worn down and it is unable to catch the animals it has been accustomed to eating, it is drawn by necessity to killing human beings. The change over from animal to human flesh is, I believe, in most cases accidental.

One man-eating tigress shot by Corbett had had an unfortunate encounter with a porcupine, in which she lost an eye and got fifty quills embedded in her right foreleg and paw. She killed two people who stumbled upon her as she lay starving, licking her festering wounds and trying to extract the quills with her teeth. The first victim she left untouched, but ate a small part of the second, and from then on she took to hunting humans systematically, killing twenty-five persons before, as Corbett wrote, "she was finally accounted for." The dangers, trials, and tribulations of tracking down man-eating tigers have often been described, but never more factually and modestly than by Jim Corbett himself.

Man-eaters have been reported not only from India, but also from Sumatra, Malaya, Indochina, and China. They appear always to have been uncommon in Manchuria and Siberia, the last report of a man-eating tiger in the Russian Far East dating back to 1917. All attacks on human beings which came to Abramov's notice during thirty-five years spent in eastern Siberia were purely accidental and most often due to animals charging after they had been shot at and wounded.

The great majority of tigers will, in fact, go to any length in order to avoid man. Champion had good evidence of this when he first took up flashlight photography. As long as he kept setting up his apparatus near a tiger kill during late afternoon, in order to minimize the chances of its being set off by birds or jackals, tigers very rarely came back for another meal. He finally realized that they had watched his activities and then quietly stolen away, deserting their kills in preference to risking an encounter with a human being. Once Champion began to take advantage of the knowledge that a tiger's period of minimum activity lasted from about 11 A.M. to 3 P.M., his successes became more frequent.

Major Sherwill, one of Jerdon's correspondents, did not hesitate to call the average tiger a "harmless and timid" animal, and Captain J. Forsyth, whose book, *The Highlands of Central India,* will always remain a classic, wrote:

> For the assurance of the timid I may as well say that I have never had my camp actually invaded by a tiger, though constantly pitched, with a slender following and without any sort of precaution, in the middle of their hàunts. It strikes a stranger to jungle ways a little oddly, perhaps, to see a man in the warm summer night calmly take his bed out a hundred yards from the tents, lie down under the canopy of heaven, listen, pipe in mouth, for half an hour to the noises of wild animals and then placidly fall asleep. He soon learns to do the same himself.

The tiger is a lone hunter, and there are only very few observations to indicate an occasional co-operation between different individuals. There is, of course, the story of the two tigers attacking an elephant, and Dunbar Brander had evidence of a couple of tigers teaming up to kill a fairly large buffalo. He also knew of two or more having gone after the same sounder of wild pig, and the same has been reported by Baikov. Some Manchurian hunters say that tigers will "herd" wild pigs as if they were a flock of sheep. It would, of course, seem quite natural for a more or less accidental co-operation to develop between a tigress and her full-grown cubs, or between youngsters that have not yet split up after separating from their mother, but this does not appear to happen very often.

Becoming active at dusk, the tiger roams through its range at a slow pace, moving silently and with great stealth, stopping from time to time to listen, to look and perhaps also to sniff. Some tigers have definite "beats," which they patrol at fairly frequent intervals, but it would probably be rather hasty to generalize on this point. They certainly like to walk in the beds of forest streams or along man-made jungle tracks, especially during the cold season, when the grass can be clammily wet. Champion had various indications of how highly keyed up the senses of these prowlers must be, for of the tigers passing in front of his flashlight camera, one carefully stepped over the trip wire, another was photographed in the act of biting through it, while a third suddenly took alarm, crouched and leaped toward the camouflaged camera, just failing to knock it over.

Prospective prey is first stalked and then rushed from a distance of about 9 to 25 m (30 to 83 ft). The actual method of killing varies not only according to prey species and to hunting experience, age and individuality of the tiger, but also depends a great deal on the circumstances of the moment, on the chances the tiger gets to time its rush properly and to catch a firm hold of its victim. It can be said in a general way that the back of the neck is usually grabbed with the fangs, while the claws of the forepaws are driven into shoulder, chest, forehead, or muzzle in an effort to pull the animal down to the ground or to bowl it over. The neck may be crushed or dislocated in the struggle, but, if this does not happen, the tiger will usually shift the grip of its fangs to the throat as soon as the animal has fallen and kill it by strangulation.

Cows and domestic buffaloes are generally brought down quite easily and efficiently, but the latter will sometimes bunch together and chase a tiger away from a freshly killed member of the herd. Sterndale even reports an incident, in which the life of a herdsman was saved from a man-eater by the very animals entrusted to his care:

> I had made a detour in order to try and kill this man-eater, and had sent on a hill tent the night before. I was met in the morning by the "khalasi" in charge, with a wonderful story of the tiger having rushed at him, but as the man was a romancer, I disbelieved him. On the other side of the stream was a gentle slope of turf and bushes rising gradually to a rocky hill. The slope was dotted with grazing herds and here and there a group of buffalos. Late in the afternoon, I heard some piercing cries from my people of "Bagh! Bagh!" (Tiger! Tiger!). The cows stampeded, as they always do. A struggle was going on in the bush, with loud cries of a human voice. The buffalos threw up their heads, and grunting loudly, charged down on the spot, and then in a body went charging through the brushwood. Other herdsmen and villagers ran up, and a charpoy [cot] was sent for and the man brought into the village. He was badly scratched, but had escaped any serious fang wounds from his having, as he said, seen the tiger coming at him and stuffed his blanket into its mouth, whilst belabouring it with his axe. Anyhow, but for his buffalos he would have been a dead man in three minutes more.

To force a wounded tiger out into the open, a herd of buffaloes is sometimes driven through the thick cover it has chosen to hide in, and Rudyard Kipling has immortalized the big bovines' collective aggressiveness by having Mowgli contrive the death of Sher Khan, the lame man-eater, under their thundering hooves.

It has been stated that tigers will never tackle a full-grown male gaur—the "bison" of Anglo-Indian sportsmen—but R. C. Morris knew of at least six solitary bulls killed by them. Gaurs, water-buffaloes, camels, and young elephants are often hamstrung. One old gaur that did get away was severely mauled on its head, neck, and shoulders. It had the rear hind leg bitten through, the bone being completely severed, and one can only wonder how it managed to throw off the attacker and make good its escape.

Tigers are by no means infallible hunters. Morris had evidence of at least half a dozen unsuccessful attacks on bull gaur, one being the near-victim mentioned above. In Kanha, where tigers mainly prey on deer, Schaller found that for each animal captured, at least twenty unsuccessful attempts were made. It was quite common, he tells us, in the morning to see tigers with bellies so lean that they could not have eaten a substantial meal for the previous two or three nights.

Killing a wild pig can be as difficult as tackling the mighty gaur. Walter Elliot, as quoted by Jerdon, once found a full grown tiger newly killed, evidently by the rip of a boar's tusks, and he heard of a similar instance from a friend who had witnessed the encounter. Sterndale records a boar not only ripping a tiger to death, but gnawing and crushing its chestbone after life had become extinct. Manchurian tigers seem to have evolved a special technique in dealing with the wild pigs that form a very substantial, if not the major, part of their prey. They lay in ambush on a cliff and jump onto them from above, crushing the neck vertebrae between their fangs.

Locke once saw a tiger chase after a boar, both animals appearing tired out by their exertions. As a rule, however, a tiger having miscalculated its rush makes no serious effort to pursue the escaping animal. A tigress which Schaller saw, bounding at full speed after a jackal for about 400 m (1300 ft) may have done this more or less for the "sport" of it. Deer certainly seem to feel quite safe at a distance of about 30 m (100 ft) from a visible tiger.

The accounts of many observers and the colour photographs recently taken by Werner Fend make it abundantly clear that the tiger's colouration blends in very well with the surrounding vegetation and can therefore be considered as a factor improving its performance as a stalker. The often-raised objection that concealing colouration is of little or no use to a predator hunting mainly at night

has no real validity. The pattern of stripes is sure to have a concealing effect in bright moonlight, and it must not be forgotten that
in the northern parts of its area of distribution, where summer
nights are short, a considerable amount of hunting will have to be
done during the long periods of dusk and dawn, when visibility is
fairly good. And, what is most important, we do not know whether
tigers have always been so exclusively nocturnal as they were during
the last 150 years or so. What seems to be happening in Kanha, and
what has happened with lions and leopards in various African and
Asiatic reserves, can be taken as a strong indication that they were
not.

A tiger usually drags or carries its kill into some cover, occasionally over a distance of up to 200 (650 ft) or even 500 m (1600
ft). In the case of a buffalo weighing about 200 kg (450 lb), this is an
effort which well illustrates the big predator's tremendous strength
and power. The meal is then begun immediately, generally from between the victim's buttocks. Dunbar Brander found that the stomach
is often torn out and left uneaten, a habit which, according to Locke,
seems to be the general rule in Malaya. The tigers observed by
Schaller in Kanha mostly ate both the entrails and the stomach after
having emptied them of their vegetable contents.

Locke puts the amount a tiger is able to eat at one sitting at 18 kg
(41 lb), Sanderson at 30 kg (66 lb), and Baikov at 30 to 50 kg (avg 90
lb)—the three authors, of course, writing of Malayan, Indian, and
Manchurian tigers respectively. Schaller reports a male tiger in
Kanha polishing off a 113 kg (254 lb) barasingha in three nights
consuming a total quantity of about 72 to 79 kg (avg 167 lb) of meat,
or 24 to 26 kg (55 lb) per day. Two tigresses ate 40 kg (88 lb) from a
cow in one night. Tigers, according to Schaller, make little use of
their forepaws while eating a large prey, although a small piece of
meat may be held down while the animal tears at it.

After the first meal, a tiger usually goes to the nearest stream or
water-hole to have a drink, and then returns to lay up for the day in
the vicinity of the kill. It will sometimes tear up grass with its claws in
order to cover up what is left of the carcass. Dunbar Brander once
surprised one in the act of doing so. He also saw a tiger lying down
and falling asleep on top of a dead buffalo, thus protecting it from
the vultures and crows.

A tiger resting close to its kill may suddenly rush in among the
scavengers and chase them away, as has been well shown in some of
Werner Fend's movie shots. If the tiger feels safe, it may return for
an occasional snack during the day, but more often it will wait until
dusk before having another feed. It will sometimes visit a kill until

the last scraps have been consumed, and long before that has happened, the carcass will, of course, be very high and swarming with maggots.

The often repeated assertion that tigers always kill for themselves and refrain from touching carrion was categorically denied by as early a writer as Jerdon, and Dunbar Brander wrote later:

> Besides killing for themselves, tigers will eat any fresh carcass they may happen across, and I have even known them to eat animals which were absolutely putrid. I have already mentioned six tigers on a putrid cheetal stag. This animal was one I had wounded and lost, and it had been lying dead in the long grass for a week. I discovered it by the smell. The men sent to fetch the head returned in great excitement, reporting several tigers on the carcass, and when I arrived I found that the body was a mere shell and that the tigers had been scooping out the inside which consisted of smell, maggots and putrid flesh.

Locke knew a hungry tiger to eat the tainted earth on which a highly decomposed buffalo had been lying. After thoroughly gorging itself, a tiger may not hunt again for several days, and Dunbar Brander thought it probable that, on the average, the big cats do not kill more than once in four or five days. Among the Sikhote-Alin Mountains, Kaplanov found tigers to remain near their victims—eating and digesting—for five, six, or even ten days. He calculated that an adult Siberian tiger kills an average of thirty large animals, about 100 kg (220 lb) in weight, in the course of every twelve months.

The tigers of southern Asia mate at all times of the year, although their sexual activities do seem to reach definite peaks at certain periods—in southern India in April and May, and to a lesser degree in October and November, in Kanha from November to February, in Kumaon from November to April, in Malaya from November to March, and in Indochina from November to April. In Manchuria and eastern Siberia the great majority of matings take place in winter, at the end of December and in January. It is during mating time that tigers are the most vocal. As Baikov says:

> The males wander over mountains and through forests, searching for the females. One tigress may be pursued by several males, which then fight each other for her favours, the strongest keeping the others away until he has mated with her. The battles between males are fierce and the ground becomes spattered with blood flowing from deep scratches. But these encounters are never continued to the death, for the weaker gives way to the stronger and goes off in search of new adventures.

Forsyth has given a wonderful description of the tremendous uproar that accompanies the tiger's courtship:

When I was encamped near Matin, I listened one night to the most remarkable serenade of tigers I ever heard. A peculiar long wail, like the
drawn-out mew of a huge cat, first rose from a river course a few
hundred yards below my tent. Presently from a mile or so higher up the
river came a deep tremendous roar, which had scarcely died away ere it
was answered from behind the camp by another, pitched in a yet deeper
tone startling us from its suddenness and proximity. All three were
repeated at short intervals, as the three tigers approached each other
along the bottom of the deep, dry watercourses, between and above
which the camp had been pitched. As they drew together the noises
ceased for about a quarter of an hour; and I was dozing off to sleep
again, when suddenly arose the most fearful din near to where the
tigress had first sounded the love note to her rival lovers, a din like the
caterwauling of midnight cats magnified a hundredfold. Intervals of
silence, broken by outbursts of this infernal shrieking and moaning, disturbed our rest for the next hour, dying away gradually as the tigers retired along the bed of the river. In the morning I found all the incidents
of a three-volume novel in feline life imprinted on the sand; and marks
of blood showed how genuine the combat part of the performance had
been.

Two tigresses in the Basel Zoo were found to come in heat at
very irregular intervals, ranging from 20 to 84 and 27 to 83 days respectively, the average being 51.9 and 54.2 days. Receptivity usually
lasts five to seven days.

Various authors have described mating mostly from observations
in zoological gardens. The tigress appears particularly excited, snorts
like a horse, touches the male's vibrissae with her own and rolls on
the ground, waving her paws in the air. She then crouches on her
belly, and the tiger, which up to that moment has watched her in
what to one zoologist appeared as a "surly manner," now stands over
her, utters a series of coughing roars, and usually seizes her neck
with his fangs, without, of course, piercing the skin. When the act of
mating is over, the tigress will often jump to her feet with lightning
speed, and go for her spouse, trying to hit him with her paws. If he
does not instantly retreat into the farthest corner of the cage, he may
get badly scratched in the process. This love-play takes place dozens
of times in the course of one day. In the wild, tiger and tigress stay
together for five or six days, and during this period the couple
moves about restlessly, though staying within a fairly limited area.
The animals then separate, and the male may go in seach of another
tigress.

The tigress drops her cubs in some dense cover, among rocks, in
a cave or in a hollow tree. Figures given for the length of gestation
vary from 95 to 112 days, though 103 to 105 days can probably be

regarded as a good average. Litters consist of from one to six cubs, two to three being the most common number. Litters of six are rare, but one has been reported from the Edinburgh Zoo, and six embryos have on several occasions been taken from tigresses shot in India. The Honourable J. W. Best even records a case of a tigress containing seven unborn cubs. The sex ratio is practically even at birth, but switches in favour of the females later on.

Two new-born tigers examined by Mazak had a head and body length of 31.5 (12.2 in) and 33.8 cm (13.2 in), a tail length of 13.9 (5.4 in) and 15.0 cm (5.9 in), and a weight of 925 (32 oz) and 1195 g (42 oz) respectively. Stroganov allows a variation in weight ranging from 785 to 1500 g (avg. 40 oz). Three tigers of the Bronx Zoo, in New York, two males and a female, weighed 1162 (40.7 oz), 1133 (40 oz), and 1218 g (42.6 oz) at birth and increased their weight to 66.67 (147 lb), 70.76 (156 lb), and 58.05 kg (128 lb) within nine months. At the age of two years they had attained 198.66 (437 lb), 197.76 (435 lb), and 141.06 kg (310 lb).

Tiger cubs are born blind, opening their eyes after about one week. The milk teeth break through at the end of the second week, while the definite dentition is acquired after about one year. The cubs are marked with stripes, but the background colour is somewhat lighter than that of their parents. It darkens three and a half to five and a half months after birth. Lactation lasts for five to six months, the cubs beginning to eat small quantities of meat when they are eight weeks old.

Young tigers are lively creatures, and their playfulness comes out at a very early stage of development. Helen Martini, who brought up so many waifs and strays for the Bronx Zoo, has given a charming description of the behaviour of three cubs less than a month old:

> To watch the three of them at play was endlessly fascinating. They would box each others faces with their fat little oversized paws; then they would start a game of wrestling, rolling on top of each other and trying to keep one another down. Rajpur was always good-natured about having the other two roll on him, but Raniganj would struggle and cry if he got pinned down, and when he wriggled free, he would reward his tormentors with a nip and a snarl, which invariably set off another rough-and-tumble. Raniganj enjoyed the game only when he was winning; and often I had to pick him up and put him back in his box, with a rubber ball and one of my shoes. Little Dacca, on the other hand, never tired of teasing her brothers to wake up and play, and she was always the leader in the rough-and-tumble that followed.

At the age of thirty-six days, Helen Martini's tigers began to show a keen interest in what was going on outside their play-pen. When they were forty-four days old, they started to romp about and to stalk each other, as well as their human foster-mother whenever she turned her back. Their curiosity knew no bounds, and they were always eager to explore the mysteries of doors and cupboards.

A tigress may take her cubs away from the original den when they have reached the age of about two months, and she will then lead them from one hiding place to another. They remain concealed, keeping very quiet, while she goes out hunting. After she has made a kill, she takes them out to the carcass, and the whole family may remain there until all of it is eaten. The playfulness which Helen Martini found so delightful in her small cubs is, at that time, still very much in evidence, and the youngsters can be seen to indulge in prolonged periods of romping.

Authors such as Sanderson, Burton, and Corbett have pointed out that young tigers tend to take up hunting at a relatively early age. Corbett, for instance, knew of a male which, after having been abandoned by its mother when only one year old, managed to subsist by killing pea-fowl, small pigs, barking deer, and an occasional cheetal hind. He made his home in a fallen and hollowed-out forest giant, and to this den he brought most of his kills. The male cub of a family of Kanha tigers, kept under close observation by George Schaller, became semi-independent at the early age of eleven months. He occasionally hunted on his own and one day managed to snatch a pig from a village hut, even though the female cubs were, at that time, still wholly dependent on their mother for food. Schaller's tiger family began to show signs of breaking up when the youngsters were sixteen months old. The male was then able to kill a buffalo almost as efficiently as his mother, and he often hunted by himself, staying away from the family for prolonged periods. There still was a certain cohesion, however, between the mother and her cubs when Schaller's study came to an end. He thinks that the male most probably became fully independent at an age of about eighteen to twenty months, while his sisters remained with the mother for an additional three to four months. Most authors writing on the subject of Indian tigers have indicated the separation of cubs from their mother to take place when they are about two years old. It appears, however, that families of Siberian tigers can remain together for three or even four years.

On rare occasions, tigresses have been seen with cubs belonging to two different litters. Abramov and Sludski reported observations of this kind from Russian Asia, Dunbar Brander from India, and Sir John Hewett wrote of a tigress which was found to carry unborn young while having a litter of cubs about ten months in age. As a rule, however, the new litter is dropped after the family has disintegrated, usually over two years, perhaps even three or four years after the birth of the preceding cubs.

In zoological gardens, young tigers sometimes mate at two or two and a half years. In the wild, the age of reproduction is probably reached at three or four years. Sludski, writing of Central Asia, thought that males only became mature between four and five years. Corbett, on the other hand, had evidence of a male mating at the age of three years. Tigers grow until they are about five years old and then fill out for many years after that.

Russian authors have tended to overestimate greatly the tiger's longevity, crediting it with attaining a ripe old age of forty to fifty years. Ages of up to sixteen and eighteen years have quite often been recorded in zoological gardens, but a Siberian tiger that died at the age of twenty-six years showed clear signs of advanced senility, and was found to have suffered from debility of the heart and lungs. Reserves such as the Kanha National Park will perhaps make it possible to discover how long a tiger can live in the wild—but it seems most unlikely that the life-span will be found much to exceed nineteen or twenty years.

For a long time the main factor limiting the life expectancy of tigers has, of course, been the hand of man. The literature on tiger hunting—on foot, from a machan, from the back of an elephant—is vast and often very readable, and there is no need to deal with this topic any further.

According to Dunbar Brander, the flesh of a tiger "much resembles veal and retains none of the disgusting odour of the animal before skinning." It is eaten by the Tharus of the Nepal Terai, but the Gond inhabiting the wilder parts of Central India will not touch it. In Malaya, it is recommended for debility of the spleen or stomach.

"The tiger is not always monarch over all the beasts of the field," wrote Sterndale. "He is positively afraid of the wild dog (*Cuon rutilans*), which readily attacks him in packs." Some authors have doubted the possibility of a tiger being overwhelmed by wild dogs, but Dunbar Brander once arrived at a jungle village three days after a pack attacked a tigress immediately after she had killed a sambar. When the noise of the battle had died down, the villagers approached the spot and found the tigress and two dogs dead. Kenneth Anderson, a renowned slayer of man-eaters, saw a tigress involved in a running battle with half a dozen dogs forming the advanced guard of a big pack. She killed one of them and then bounded away, hotly pursued by the five remaining dogs. They were just out of sight when the main pack, consisting of twenty-three individuals, streamed by. On the following day, and five miles from where he had witnessed the beginning of the drama, Anderson found the dead and partially eaten tigress surrounded by five dead dogs.

While their mother is away hunting, tiger cubs may occasionally be found and killed by prowling predators, including male tigers, while half-grown individuals have been known to be killed by brown bears. Abramov heard of a bear in the Shushi-Pokto Reserve near Khabarovsk killing a three-year-old tiger which had separated from its mother to remain at a dead pig. Two similar cases were reported from the Sikhote-Alin Reserve in 1960 and 1963. Adults are occasionally killed or incapacitated in hunting accidents.

Diseases and parasites do not appear greatly to affect tiger populations. Two cases of rabies have been reported from India, another from Russia. Trichinella infections, which have been diagnosed in captive tigers, could possibly occur in the wild, especially in Siberia. Droppings collected in Kanha contained two species of tapeworm, and a tapeworm (*Taenia bubesei*) was also taken from a tiger shot in Tadzhikistan. One trematode and a couple of nematodes (filaria) have been reported from Siberian tigers.

Indian tigers are always heavily infested with ticks, which will crawl onto the people skinning them. The irritations caused by their virulent bites take long to disappear, and Fend even maintains that on such an occasion he contracted a high fever. A Russian zoologist took 339 ticks from a Central Asian tiger, of which 328 belonged to the species *Rhipicephalus turanicus*. The other species obtained were *Boophilus calcaratus, Hyalomma detritum,* and *Hyalomma marginatum.*

In captivity, tigers can become remarkably tame, and they often figure in circus acts.

Leopard, Panther
Panthera pardus

We have to stretch the powers of our imagination to visualize England, Spain, France, and Germany inhabited by that most exotic of felines, the leopard. However, the leopard formed part of the European Pleistocene fauna, and made its appearance during the Cromer Interglacial, more or less simultaneously with the lion. At that early period it already had a very wide distribution, as shown by skeletal remains found in Transvaal, on the island of Java and at Choukoutien, the Chinese locality famous for the discovery of Peking man. While the Pleistocene leopards of Africa were of about the same size as the ones living there today, the bones excavated in Europe and China must have come from animals of a considerably larger size. In Europe it was probably less common than the lion, as remains of the latter species turned up at about three times as many sites than those of the leopard. It was also less widely distributed, its northward range only extending to a line running roughly from Liège through Thuringia and Moravia to the Transylvanian Alps. It vanished at the end of the Würm Glaciation, and there is no evidence of the leopard lingering on in southeastern Europe as did the lion. The ancient Greeks only knew it from skins and live specimens shipped over from Asia Minor.

The Romans obtained their first leopards from North Africa, where they were very common, and the species was referred to as "panthera" in republican times, a name derived from *panthēr,* a Greek word of doubtful etymology. George Jennison, a recognized authority on the animals of the antique world, suggests that *panthēr* might originally have meant the genet cat and was later transferred to the leopard, but genets do not occur in Greece and Italy, as he mistakenly assumed, nor could these secretive and strictly nocturnal viverrids have made much of an impression on Greek traders visiting Palestine, North Africa, or Spain.

A much coveted political post in ancient Rome was that of the Aedile, an appointment which included the responsibility for the staging of the highly popular circus games. For an ambitious politician, a good knowledge of where to obtain an impressive number of "bestiae africanae," as lions and leopards were called, was of prime importance. The Roman expansion into the eastern Mediterranean drew attention to Asia Minor as an alternate source of "pantherae," and when Cicero was proconsul of Cilicia, he found himself bombarded with letters from one Marcus Caelius, a newly elected Aedile who expected the governor to drop everything in order to provide him with leopards. "About the leopards," he wrote, "set the people of Cibyria to work and see about their transport to me." A month later, he dispatched an even more urgent letter:

> In nearly all my letters to you I have mentioned the subject of leopards. It will be a disgrace to you if, when the merchant Patiscus has sent ten to the Tribune Curio, you don't get many more. Curio has made me a present of those ten and of another ten from Africa. If you will only remember to set the Cibyrates to work and to write to Pamphylia—for they say that more are caught there—you will get what you want done. Do please see that you attend to this. In this affair the trouble for you is only to talk—I mean to issue orders officially and to promise commissions. For as soon as the leopards are caught, there are my own people to look after the animals' keep and to bring them to Rome.

More letters in the same vein followed, but Cicero obviously was of the opinion that the inhabitants of his province had more important things to do than to chase leopards. The Aedile being an influential personage, he finally composed a letter which any civil servant can take as a model of how to deal with a bothersome politico:

> About the leopards, the professional hunters are busy, acting on my commission. But there is an extraordinary scarcity of the beasts, and it is said that those that are here complain bitterly that they are the only living creatures in my province against whom any harm is meditated. So they are said to have decided to leave my province and move into Caria. Still, the business is being carefully attended to, especially by the merchant Patiscus. Whatever is got will be for you, but what there is to get, we do not know.

In imperial Rome, the leopard came to be called "pardus," while "panthera" was generally used for the cheetah. There was at that time a fairly widespread belief that these two animals were the male and female of the same species. The name "leopardus" was also in use, not for the animal we now know as leopard, but for maneless or scantily maned lions, most of which must have been young and therefore distinctly spotted beasts. It was probably for this reason that they were thought to be the offspring of male "pards" and lionesses. "Lions born from lions and lionesses will at a certain age get a full mane," Pliny wrote, "but this is never acquired by lions born from lionesses and pards." He maintained that hybrids of this kind were quite common, especially in the African deserts, where the different sorts of animals had to gather at the very few rivers there were. After mating with a "pard," the lioness was thought to bathe in order to remove the smell of her illicit lover and thus hide her adultery from the lion.

After Rome had fallen, "pards" continued to be massacred in the arenas of Byzantium. Crusaders must have come in frequent contact with leopards, and in medieval Europe it was quite the fashion for kings and princes to possess a few of these highly decorative cats, although some may actually have been cheetahs. There are records of leopards having been on display at the Burgundian court of Dijon at the time of the Duchess Margaret, and some were kept at the castle of Plessis by King Louis XI of France.

Linnaeus described the leopard from a specimen of uncertain origin and named it *Felis pardus*. As more and more skins and skeletons became available for scientific examination early in the nineteenth century, zoologists noticed a range of variability which appeared too wide to fit their pre-Darwinian concept of a nicely pigeon-holed and immutable species. Had not Oppian, the Greek writer, stated that leopards came in two kinds, one large with a short tail, the other small and long-tailed? And had not Aldemiri, the learned Arab, supported this view in 1371? Cuvier came to the conclusion that there were in actual fact two species of "pards," the panther, *Felis panthera,* and the leopard, *Felis leopardus*. Temminck agreed with him and maintained that the tail of the leopard contained twenty-two vertebrae, and that of the panther twenty-eight. Sir William Jardine expressed doubts as to the validity of this distinguishing character, giving it as his opinion that the number of caudal vertebrae varied in many well-established species. He was perfectly right in this, for it has since been established that in a leopard's tail there may be any number of vertebrae from twenty-two up to twenty-eight. As a whole, however, Jardine nevertheless accepted the findings of Cuvier and Temminck.

After the great pundits of zoology had spoken, it was hardly surprising that many sportsmen and field naturalists made gallant attempts to distinguish their "pards" as panthers and leopards. Walter Elliot, as quoted by Jerdon, described the panther as large, light in colour, and inhabiting more open country, the forest-dwelling leopard as smaller, long-tailed, and dark. The skull of the first, he thought, was longer, less rounded, and more pointed. Sterndale, on the other hand, used the name leopard for the bigger, and panther for the smaller and darker of the two.

Agreement, however, was not general. Blyth, for instance, refused to accept the two species. Andrew Smith, the author of *Illustrations of South African Zoology*, admitted the great variability of these animals, of which, as he said, it was difficult to find two individuals which exactly resembled each other, but declared himself unable to regard leopard and panther as specifically different. William Cornwallis Harris, well acquainted with the leopard of both India and Africa, agreed with Smith, and G. P. Sanderson, while admitting the existence of the two types described by Elliot, Sterndale, and many others, regarded them as varieties of one species only. Finally, in 1891, Blanford summed up the problem: "I cannot help suspecting that the difference is very often one of age . . . for young leopards have rounder heads, without any occipital ridge to the skull and rougher fur than older animals. I have for years endeavoured to distinguish the two forms, but without success. The size of the animal, the number, form and closeness of the spots and the length of the tail are all extremely variable characters."

This, one would think, should have settled the dispute, but firmly established misconceptions are slow to die, and as recently as 1918, General R. G. Burton wrote: "It is curious that the idea that there is in India more than one species of panther is still prevalent, even in quarters where more enlightenment might be expected. An experienced sportsman only a few years ago produced an interesting book of reminiscences in which he maintains that there were not merely two but three species of panther and these inhabiting the same districts! He even went so far as to give the name of 'pantheret' to the smallest of these supposed species."

There is, in fact, one species only which, in English, can be called either leopard or panther. In accordance with Oken's classification of 1816, it now has the scientific name of *Panthera pardus*. The pupils are round and the hyoid is only partly ossified.

The skull is relatively elongate, rather flat above, less arched than that of the tiger. The teeth are robust, the canines, especially the upper ones, very well developed, and the post-canine spaces wide. The first premolar is always present.

Characteristics. The leopard can surely be described as the most perfect of the big cats, beautiful in appearance and graceful in its movements. The elongate body, lithe and well muscled, is carried by massive limbs of moderate length. The paws are broad and rounded, the ears short. The tail is proportionately longer than that of the tiger. The coat is short and sleek in tropical specimens, deep furred in animals from cold climates. The pelage of the Anatolian leopard, for instance, is described as thick, soft, and in winter remarkably like the snow leopard, long and hairy with considerable under-wool.

The ground colour varies from pale straw and grey buff to bright fulvous, deep ochre, and even chestnut. Throat, chest, belly, and the insides of the limbs are white. The backs of the ears are black with white spots situated centrally, marginally or at the tips. Head, throat, and chest are marked with small black spots, the belly with large black blotches. On shoulders, upper arms, back, flanks, and haunches, the spots are arranged in rosettes which usually enclose an area of a shade somewhat darker than the background colour. The rosettes can be small or large, thick-rimmed or thin-rimmed, and some may have a small dot in the centre. In the Amur leopard they are ringlike and can have a diameter of about 65 mm (2.5 in). The rosettes continue onto the tail, changing into large spots and transverse bands toward the tip. The underside of the end part is white or yellowish white.

African leopards inhabiting hilly or mountainous areas are usually bigger than lowland animals. In Uganda, forest leopards are said to be smaller, darker, and marked with bigger spots than those inhabiting open country. To a certain degree, these two types can also be distinguished in Kenya and Tanzania.

The almost infinite variability which so greatly puzzled nineteenth-century authors has led modern taxonomists into describing and naming about thirty subspecies, of which Allen lists twelve for the African continent. No less than three subspecies are supposed to occur in India alone, and one cannot help wondering whether the confusion is any less now than it was a hundred years ago. A leopard collected near Lake Manyara in Tanzania was given the subspecific name *suahelica,* while a specimen from the Loita Plains in Kenya served as type for the description of subspecies *fortis.* Pocock, after having gone through a tremendous amount of material, declared himself unable to distinguish leopards from East Africa in size, colour, markings, skull, and dental characteristics from the leopard of Bengal, *Panthera pardus fusca.* He relegated *suahelica* and *fortis* to the status of synonyms, and we now have the rather grotesque situation of the leopards from Bengal and East Africa being considered as identical, although separated from each other by a whole string of northeast African and southwest Asian subspecies.

While there are perfectly good reasons for according subspecific distinction to well-defined populations, such as the leopards of Java and the Kangean Islands, of North Africa, of Anatolia, Arabia, and Manchuria, one cannot get away from the fact that the thing has been overdone, with little or no attention being paid to the spectrum of individual variation which is so especially broad in this species.

These variations can, on occasion, take on truly extravagant forms. In a paper on the panthers and ounces of Asia, Pocock reproduced the photograph of an aberrant leopard skin from southern India which resembles that of a jaguar or clouded leopard, with large, black-rimmed blotches, each containing a number of dots and spots. Another skin shown by Pocock, also from southern India, has the normal rosettes broken up and fused to such an extent that, supplemented with additional pigment, they convey the impression of a black leopard streaked and speckled with yellow. It can be taken as an extreme example of the not-uncommon extension and multiplication of markings known as nigrism and abundism.

Leopards have a strong tendency toward melanism, a general increase in pigmentation, in which the background colour turns to dark glossy brown or black, while the markings, which even in the blackest specimens become visible with the light at a certain angle, remain perfectly normal. Black leopards can be found in one and the same litter with spotted ones, and contrary to popular belief they are not more ferocious than their normally coloured brothers and sisters. Melanistic specimens turn up most frequently in moist, densely forested areas and have often been reported from southwestern China, Burma, Assam, and Nepal, as well as from Travancore and other parts of southern India. They are common in Java and particularly in the southern parts of the Malay Peninsula, where black leopards are said to be more numerous than spotted ones.

Black leopards are scarcer in tropical Africa than in southern Asia, but they appear to be not uncommon in Abyssinia. In Kenya, they are mainly found in the forests of Mount Kenya and the Aberdares. Odd individuals have been recorded from Kikuyu Forest, Maralal, and Barsalinga. The last locality is at low altitude in dry and rocky country, but the specimen shot there might well have come from Mount Kenya or the Mathews Range. Black leopards have also turned up on the Virunga Volcanoes. One would think melanistic mutations to be fairly numerous in the equatorial forest belt, but the only record I have come across so far is of one seen in Cameroon by Peter Turnbull-Kemp.

A white to cream-coloured leopard with pale spots and sky-blue eyes was shot at Sarsaran, in the Maharaja of Dumraon's jungle. Semi-albinos of a similar kind have been recorded from southern China, from Hazaribagh in India and from Rhodesia. Pocock saw one purely white skin, apparently from East Africa, in which the spots were only visible in reflected light.

Measurements. Leopards vary greatly in size, as is well exemplified by Sterndale, who gives for the animal he names the "pard" a head and body length of 1.37 to 1.67 m (avg. 5 ft) and a tail length of from 76.2 to 96.5 cm (avg. 34 in); for the "panther," a head and body length of 0.91 to 1.06 m (avg. 3 ft); a tail length of 76.2 cm (30 in); and a shoulder height of 45 to 60 cm (avg. 21 in). In the Golis Range of what is now part of Somalia, R. E. Drake-Brockman shot a fine male with a head and body length of 1.21 m (4 ft), a tail length of 78.7 cm (31 in), and a weight of 34.9 kg (79 lb). He saw a skin from Hargeisa which had a total length of 2.64 m (9 ft). It did not look unduly stretched, and the animal in the flesh probably measured a little over 2.43 m (8 ft). From the Wadi Nogal, also in Somalia, Major Dunn obtained a male and a female, the stretched skins of which measured: total length of male 1.80 m (6 ft); head and body length, 1.15 m (4 ft); tail, 65 cm (25 in); total length of female, 1.65 cm (5.4 ft); head and body length, 1.07 m (3.5 ft); tail, 58 cm (23 in). These leopards made the type-specimens of a subspecies, *Felis pardus nanopardus,* the "pygmy leopard," which is still regarded as valid.

A record specimen with a total length of 2.92 m (9.6 ft) came from Ruanda. A leopard from southern Nigeria had a head and body length of 1.91 m (6.3 ft); tail, 90 cm (35 in); weight, 75.7 kg (170 lb). Leopards 2.75 and 2.74 m (9 ft) in total length have been obtained in Malawi and Kenya. According to Stevenson-Hamilton, average males from the Transvaal Low Veld do not much exceed 45 kg (101 lb) in weight, though some may attain 54 kg (122 lb). Females average 9 to 13 kg (avg. 25 lb) less.

Dunbar Brander found the average male from central Indian to have a total length of 2.03 m (6.7 ft) and a weight of 50 kg (113 lb). Large males measured from 2.18 to 2.36 m (avg. 7 ft) in length, weighing up to 68 kg (153 lb). The shortest and longest tails measured by Dunbar Brander were 71.12 (28 in) and 96.52 cm (38 in) in length.

For the Amur leopard, the following measurements are given by Stroganov: head and body, 1.07 to 1.36 m (avg. 4 ft); tail, 82 to 90 cm (avg. 34 in); shoulder height, 64 to 78 cm (avg. 28 in); and weight 32 to 40 kg (avg. 81 lb).

Distribution. With the exception of some absolutely waterless desert tracts, the leopard's African area of distribution originally extended from the Cape of Good Hope to the Mediterranean. Specimens from the island of Zanzibar, where the leopard is now most probably extinct, were given subspecific distinction under the designation *Panthera pardus adersi.*

In western and Central Asia, the species ranges from the Sinai Peninsula, Arabia, Asia Minor, Transcaucasia, and the Caucasus—where it used to occur on the European side as well—through southern Turkmenistan, southeastern Uzbekistan, southwestern Tadzhikistan and Iran to Baluchistan, Sind, and Kashmir. From Nepal, Sikkim, Bhutan, and Assam it extends south through the Indian peninsula to Cape Comorin and Ceylon, southwest through Burma to the Malayan Peninsula, and Java and east through Siam and Indochina to China. E. Schaefer found it widely but sparsely distributed over the mountain areas of the Chinese-Tibetan borderlands, but nobody seems to know just how far west it goes into Tibet itself. Burrard saw tracks to the north of the main Himalayan axis, and a skin given to Colonel F. M. Bailey by a Tibetan was said to have come from near Shigatse, about a hundred miles north of Sikkim. It was clearly a winter skin, and Pocock declared it to be one of the most beautiful leopard pelts he ever handled.

From northern China, the leopard ranges through Manchuria to Korea and to about 50° north latitude in easternmost Siberia. It appears always to have been somewhat local and uncommon in the Russian Far East. Baikov, writing between the two wars, reported short-haired "Chinese" leopards from northern China, Korea, and from the extreme south and southeast of the Ghirin and Mukden provinces, long-haired Manchurian or Amur leopards from southeastern Manchuria and from the northern part of the Ussuri Territory, about as far as the Imam River, with vagrants occasionally straying into the Little Khingan Mountains, to Transbaikalia and into the Amur basin. The occurrence of the species on Sakhalin Island has never been confirmed.

A great deal of confusion was created by a skin bought in Japan and classified as the type specimen of a subspecies *japonica.* As leopards have never inhabited any of the Japanese islands, the skin in question probably came from northern China, Korea, or Ussuri, but it certainly did mislead a number of authors into including Japan within the leopard's area of distribution.

Accounts of leopards seen or shot in Sumatra must have originated in mistaking the clouded leopard for the common species, for according to A. Hoogerwerf, none of these reports have ever been substantiated. Th. Haltenorth informs me that he, too, has not been able to find any evidence of the leopard having occurred on the island within historic times. As Sumatra forms an obvious geographical link between the Malay Peninsula and Java, it is difficult to understand why the species should never have established itself there, or, if it ever did, why it has not been able to survive. Its presence on the island of Ceylon and Pleistocene fossil remains found in Java show the leopard to have been an inhabitant of southern Asia for a very long time. Equally puzzling, of course, is the fact that it got to the Kangean Islands, but never became a member of the Balinese fauna.

Leopards have long been hunted for their skins. H. E. Wilson, the botanist-explorer, writing in 1913, reported meeting three men laden with over a hundred leopard skins in the upper Min River valley of Szechwan. The skins came from Kweichow, they told him, and were being taken to Sungpan to be used as robes and girdles by the Sunfan and other tribespeople.

In Baikov's time, about a hundred leopards were killed annually in Manchuria, the skins fetching from 50 to 150 dollars on the markets of Ghirin, Ningan, Mukden, and Tientsin. Large-scale persecution of this kind was fairly localized, however, and a real threat to the species only developed when leopard skins became "big business" on a world-wide scale, through the mania for spotted fur coats a few years ago. The beautiful animals were trapped in tens of thousands so women could wear their pelts.

The International Union for the Conservation of Nature and Natural Resources and the World Wildlife Fund have had to list several subspecies as in imminent danger of extermination. The Amur leopard, *Panthera pardus orientalis,* is practically extinct, with about ten to fifteen survivors in eastern Siberia and an unknown—though certainly very small—number in Korea. Of the Anatolian leopard, *Panthera pardus tulliana,* three to five individuals may survive in Transcaucasia and in the Caucasus—where one was reported in 1956—and less than a dozen pairs in Turkey, some of them in the Taurus Mountains on the northern limits of Cicero's old province of Cilicia. Once common and widely distributed, the Barbary leopard, *Panthera pardus panthera,* of North Africa has its last stronghold in Morocco. Extinct in the Rif and on the Upper Atlas, where it could still be found during the 1920s and 1930s, between fifty and one hundred are said to survive in the Central Atlas and in the mountain forests of Oulmes. In Algeria, the Akfadou National Park appears to be the only area which still contains a small, though steadily dwindling population. In Tunisia, a few are believed to hold out in the forests between Bizerte and Tabarca and in the impenetrable mountain thickets of Tamerza.

In comparing its decline with that of the lion and the tiger, it must, however, be admitted that the leopard has succeeded in hanging on with quite astonishing tenacity in places where the two larger species were wiped out a long time ago. The last tigers of Transcaucasia were killed off at the beginning of the 1930s. Lions disappeared from Algeria during the 1890s, from Morocco around 1925. In Egypt, they were fading away toward the end of the eighteenth century, while leopards were reported from the Western Desert, between Siwa and Dabaa, as recently as 1932.

Although scarce everywhere, the leopards of Arabia (*P.p. jarvisi*, *P.p. nimr*, and *P.p. saxicolor*) are still quite widely distributed. David L. Harrison reports that there have been a surprising number of recent occurrences, and this among a well-armed and trigger-happy population only too keen to blast away at anything that moves.

In 1961 while visiting the game farm of Jonckers Hoek, situated in a picturesque valley of the Sneeukop Range, not far from Stellenbosch, I was told of a leopard that lived on the steep, rocky mountainside above the farm and made itself useful by keeping down the destructive baboons. There have been reliable reports of a few leopards roaming over the Langeberg Mountains just north of the road connecting Cape Town with Swellendam. One solitary hare was all the "game" I saw in 1968, during six weeks spent in Lesotho, yet shortly after my departure a leopard was killed close to Maseru, the capital of the mountainous little country. In East Africa, according to a recent survey, leopards are holding out amazingly well, even though thousands of skins must have been smuggled out through Somalia and Abyssinia.

Habits. The leopard is a highly adaptable species, able to exist comfortably wherever it finds enough food and a sufficiency of cover. Within its enormous area of distribution, there are very few habitats in which it has not successfully established itself. In Africa it occurs in every type of forest, evergreen, deciduous, and riverine, in woodlands, savannahs, acacia grass lands, in thorn-bush and semi-deserts, on kopjes and cliffs. It feels equally at home in swampy tropical forests as on rugged mountains. The explorers Barth and de Bary found leopards common in Air. It has now become rare in that part of the Sahara, and Henri Lhote, in the course of all his many expeditions, encountered only one, to the north of Taboua. Among the bare peaks and valleys of Hoggar and Tassili, Turnbull-Kemp has, however, come across signs of leopard relatively recently.

On Mount Kenya, leopards roam right up to the snow line. In 1926, Dr. Reusch discovered a frozen carcass at 5638 m (18,500 ft) on the rim of Kilimanjaro's Kibo Crater. A photograph taken a few years later by H. W. Tilman shows it not embedded in the ice, as is often stated, but lying on top of a rocky pinnacle. A leopard was recently seen at 4572 m (15,000 ft) on the southern slopes of Kibo, and a party of climbers heard one at 4205 m (14,000 ft) on Mawenzi, the second highest peak of Kilimanjaro.

Throughout Arabia, the leopard is an inhabitant of mountain uplands and hilly steppes, rarely venturing out into the open plains and deserts. In the Caucasian region it is—or was—found in dense forests as well as on bare crags, while in summer it used to go up to the alpine meadows, its vertical distribution thus extending from sea level to about 2500 m (8200 ft).

Indian leopards are more tolerant of the sun than tigers and will live not only in forests, but also in scrub jungles and in any type of broken and rocky country. In Burma, the species is more common in the dry zone than in the heavy forests. In Kashmir, according to Ward, leopards do not mind a certain amount of snow, but prefer not to winter at high altitudes. They probably do not surpass 3000 m (10,000 ft) in the Himalayas. The leopards of Manchuria give preference to rocky mountains covered with mixed or broad-leafed forest. In the neighbouring Ussuri region, too, they mainly roam through hilly woodland tracts.

The leopard in movement combines utmost grace with considerable muscular power. It comes along silently, its steps soft and resilient, the head held low, with the jaw often hanging slightly relaxed, the tail bent upward in an elegant curve, its tip higher than the line of the back. In its easy, almost ambling walk, the leopard probably does not often attain much over three miles an hour. It can, however, change over to a fast walk which, according to Peter Turnbull-Kemp, increases its pace to about four miles an hour. From time to time a trot may be adopted, but this does not seem to be a popular gait and is soon dropped in favour of either the walk or a fast gallop. Speculating on the maximum speed attained, Turnbull-Kemp considers it as improbable for a running or charging leopard to exceed 64.3 km (40 mi) an hour, even over short distances, with the normal running speed probably not much in excess of 60 km (37 mi).

Although the leopard is not built on the lines of a specialized jumper, such as the puma, it has been known to approach the American cat's performances. For a vertical spring, A. Jeannin considered 3 m (10 ft) as a maximum, for the long jump 3 m (10 ft) from a standing position, and 4.50 m (15 ft) while on the run. Turnbull-Kemp, however, records a big male at full gallop crossing a washed-out ravine in a clean leap of 6.60 m (22 ft), and he saw a small female spring to a tree fork 3.42 m (11 ft) above ground, launching itself from a point about 2.40 m (8 ft) from the base of the tree. A third athletic feat he mentioned is of a modest-sized individual leaping down into a road cutting from 7.16 m (23 ft) up and immediately springing to the top of the opposite bank, which had a vertical height of 3 m (10 ft).

The leopard climbs with perfect ease and agility, running up a tree trunk like a huge cat and usually coming down head-first, jumping to the ground from a few metres up. Only once have I seen one climbing down backward and with considerable difficulty, and that was an individual with a bad limp, probably due to a thorn or a porcupine quill in one of its paws.

Leopards are strong swimmers, but do not lie in the water as tigers so often will. They avoid rain pools carefully and display all the domestic cat's dislike for getting wet. An exception was made by a tame cub of Turnbull-Kemp's, which readily entered his bath with him—at least until it once ate the soap. From that moment on, it refused to have anything further to do with the bath.

Silent as leopards generally are, they will at times betray their presence by uttering a harsh, sawing call repeated several times in quick succession. I have heard it only at night, sometimes quite soon after sunset, and it is difficult to render it in writing. South African artist-naturalist C. T. Astley Maberly's rendition of "grunt-ha! grunt-ha! grunt-ha!" is very close. It is, in Maberly's description, an extremely harsh-toned coughing grunt and the air drawn in after each grunt gives it that double effect reminiscent of the sound of sawing wood. The call of the male is deeper and harsher than that of the female. Maberly reports having also heard an occasional short roar, which he suspected to be a note of greeting between individuals.

Turnbull-Kemp mentions a variety of grunts, some vaguely pig-like. He frequently heard leopards grunt as they approached a kill and grunt explosively when alarmed. A leopard brought to bay or caught in a trap will growl and snarl like any other big cat, but one treed by a pack of dogs was heard to give vent to a most miserable burst of caterwauling. While charging at a gallop, two or three short coughs are usually given, similar to those of the tiger but of lesser volume.

In trying to sum up what is known of the leopard's doings, one must be careful to remember that the species is highly flexible in its habits. Behaviour observed in one locality may not necessarily be exactly the same in another, nor can we be sure that what is being recorded in a certain place today will still apply ten years hence. Some authors depict the leopard as strictly a prowler after dark, while others regard it as very much less nocturnal than the tiger. As

Turnbull-Kemp rightly remarks, leopards may be seen at any time of the day and will regularly hunt on overcast or misty days, but where they are hunted, the degree of nocturnal activity increases, and they may never be seen in daylight. The opposite is just as true, and a newly acquired sense of security eventually induces them to become diurnal to such a degree that they quite frequently hunt in bright sunshine.

Leopards have an amazing ability to go on living in very densely populated areas. In India, as Dunbar Brander points out, a ravine surrounded by cultivated ground suffices for shelter. About twenty-five years ago, a leopard put on display at an agricultural show in Nairobi broke out of its cage, and the game scouts of Nairobi National Park were called in to search for it. The leopard in question returned to its cage all by itself, but the tracks of four or five others were found in parks and gardens. For several years my wife and I lived in a part of Nairobi where a leopard could often be heard at night. And the *East African Standard* of January 22, 1961, ran the following account: "Two Africans were mauled by a leopard lurking in the swamp area of Fort Hall Road, in the middle of Nairobi, last night. Both had been walking home and apparently surprised the leopard whilst it was lying in the thick reeds and bushes. One man was seriously injured."

The spotted cat's stealth and its incredibly secretive ways have become almost proverbial. A village shikari in Bundelkhand, India, asked by an English sportsman whether a particular leopard was cunning, exclaimed in reply: "Sahib! Where that leopard walks, he brushes out his tracks with his tail!"

Even where they live virtually among humans, they know how to remain invisible, and before they were protected and could be seen in national parks, it was not at all unusual for somebody to spend twenty or more years in Africa without ever catching a glimpse of a leopard. And this in spite of the fact that these animals were then infinitely more common they are today. As C. G. Schillings, the pioneer photographer who travelled in East Africa at the turn of the century, put it: "Vastly more numerous than the lion, the leopard is literally everywhere and nowhere!"

In the region we now know as the Ambolesi Reserve, Schillings obtained what certainly must have been the first photograph of a leopard in the wild. The flashlight flared up around midnight, and when Schillings developed the plate it showed a big male on its way to the water. Between the two wars, excellent flashlight photographs were obtained by Martin Johnson in East Africa and by F. W. Champion and Bengt Berg in India.

F. W. Champion wrote:

I have found that leopards are much more difficult to photograph on paths than tigers, partly because they use them so very much less, but largely because they nearly always seem to find the trip-wire and step over it without touching it. It seems to be quite useless to attempt to catch a leopard on a path in a moonlight night, and even on dark nights they will find any but the darkest and thinnest wires.

Authentic daytime photographs remained rare, however, and it may be considered as significant that on her visit to East Africa in 1951, Ylla, the then world famous animal photographer, had to be content with taking pictures of a captive specimen.

Leopards must always have been numerous on the Serengeti Plains. Between the two wars, Audrey Moore knew one old female which liked to resort to a certain big tree. The animal could often be seen sitting hunched in a fork, but Audrey Moore never obtained a photograph, nor did she apparently ever see a leopard kill its prey, for in her charming book on the wildlife of the Serengeti, she had to give what she very honestly called "a reconstruction" of the spotted cat's way of hunting.

On our first visit to the Serengeti in 1949, at a time when Seronera Lodge did not exist and few tourists undertook the long and arduous trip from Ngorongoro to Banagi, we one day saw a leopard climb an acacia tree, carrying a Thomson's gazelle in its mouth. At the foot of the tree there were two spotted hyenas which had apparently tried to rob the cat of its prey and now seemed to be quite ready to resort to siege tactics. While I got my camera ready, my wife discovered a second leopard, hiding among the branches, but long before we were close enough for a photograph, the first leopard dropped the gazelle, which hit the ground close to one of the hyenas, jumped off the tree, and vanished in a thicket, followed by its companion, of which I had only a very quick glimpse.

In the course of the following years, we had many leopard encounters in the Serengeti, but it always was the same story: a cat jumping off a tree and bounding away in the direction of the nearest patch of bush, or glimpsed for a couple of seconds among the high grass and scrub fringing a river-bed and never found again.

One big male then began to realize that motor cars were harmless things—noisy, smelly, and uneatable, to be sure, but also perfectly inoffensive. He tamed down amazingly quickly and was soon known as Good as Gold. We came face to face with him on October 10, 1962. Good as Gold lay peacefully on a thick, almost horizontal branch of a yellow-barked acacia and near him hung the skin of a baboon he had killed on the previous day. He hardly ever looked at us, and I was able to take dozens of pictures of the famous leopard. After this we saw Good as Gold on several occasions and for the last time in 1964. By that time, other leopards were changing their normally so secretive ways, especially youngish animals which had become acquainted with cars at a very early age. Some have become as tame—and even tamer—than Good as Gold.

Leopards in the Mara Reserve and in Nairobi National Park also show an increasing disregard for motor cars. The one place in the world, however, which at the moment seems to rival the Serengeti National Park in the opportunities it offers for observing and studying leopards is the Wilpattu National Park in Ceylon. Dr. F. Vollmar tells me that in this area he once saw no less than eight leopards in one day. The animals obviously knew what they owed to the director general of the World Wildlife Fund.

From 1967 to 1974, my wife and I were able to pay fairly regular visits to the Seronera region, sometimes three to six in one year, and on every occasion we have been able to see leopards. In March 1967 we stayed for ten days and had wonderful luck. Along a three-mile stretch of the Korongo ya Makindu, a tributary of the Seronera River, we almost every day met the same five leopards, three of which were solitary animals, the two others a mother and her almost full-grown male cub.

While it is certainly rare nowadays not to find any leopards at all in the vicinity of Seronera, one can, of course, not always count on such a high population density. The cats sometimes spread out over a much wider area, and if none are met with on the yellow-barked acacias and sausage trees along the Seronera and its tributaries, it is worth while to visit the granite kopjes dotted over the plain, where leopards quite often lie on the big boulders. Even though certain individuals may be encountered in the same places for months or even years, leopards will, as may be expected of animals with such a high degree of adaptability, not hesitate to move to other parts, either permanently or for the time being, if circumstances force them to do so. Good as Gold, for instance, usually hung out on the Seronera River, not far from Seronera Lodge, but I once photographed him eight miles from his favourite haunts.

C. T. Astley Maberly tells of two leopards suddenly turning up on his farm Narina at Duiwelskloof. One was shot on a neighbouring property, the other, however, remained for two years before it mysteriously disappeared. During that period it kept patrolling a fairly regular beat, appearing near Maberly's house every third or fourth week, but never staying more than about six or seven days.

My impressions of the leopard, formed over many years, are of an essentially solitary animal with fairly sedentary tendencies. This, and the fact that on various occasions I saw individuals place scent marks, made me assume that the species was definitely territorial in its habits. While studying the Serengeti lions, George Schaller often encountered leopards, and he, too, came to regard them as territorial. He found their ranges to overlap a great deal, but they had a tendency to focus their activity on an area that was at the moment little used by others. As a whole, they displayed a strong mutual avoidance, probably based on visual contact and scent markings. Schaller once saw three non-courting adults together, but as a rule, adults kept at a distance of at least a quarter mile from each other. Schaller calculated that the Serengeti leopards had ranges of about 22 to 26.5 km² (avg. 9 mi²). This agrees well with Turnbull-Kemp's estimate of 18 to 26 km² (avg. 8 mi²). In the Wilpattu National Park, according to Eisenberg, leopard ranges are much smaller, varying from 8 to 10.5 km² (avg. 3 mi²).

I have seen leopards spraying bushes and tree trunks. Schaller reports them ascending trees to mark the branches, and he thinks that females squirt more frequently than lionesses. The Wilpattu leopards studied by Eisenberg scraped the ground, sprayed urine, and scratched trees, especially such as had a leaning trunk or a very large limb approximately six to eight feet from the ground. A leopard approaching its scratching tree first sniffed the base and then climbed up the oblique trunk or sprayed onto the branch. It paused to sniff at previous scratch marks, and after extending itself along a limb, either tensed its shoulder muscles and began scratching with its forepaws, or went into a crouch and scratched backward with its hind legs. It sometimes sprayed urine around the base of the tree and afterward impregnated the branch with its exudates as it scratched or reclined on its belly.

It must, however, be mentioned that Dunbar Brander described leopards as less solitary than the tigers, with three or four sometimes being seen together.

The sawing call, mentioned earlier, must be an important means of communication. By following this sound one morning in the Burmese jungle, C. H. Stockley came upon two obviously courting leopards. He watched them through the leaves for a little while, but they were moving about a lot and eventually, in trying to get a better view, he stepped on some dry bamboo and frightened them away. This observation seems to indicate that the call can serve to bring the sexes together. Listening to the "grunt-ha! grunt-ha!" in Langata outside Nairobi, and at the foot of Ngulia Mountain in the Tsavo

National Park, I always had the feeling that it was uttered by a solitary animal, as a means of acoustically marking its home range.

Dunbar Brander came to the conclusion that leopards have even better eyesight than tigers. Their hearing he thought to be exceedingly acute, too, but perhaps just a little less so than the tiger's. Turnbull-Kemp considers the leopard's sense of hearing quite on par with what he calls its "superlative" sense of sight:

> To watch an alert leopard is to realise that not only the sight is in constant play, but also the hearing. One gains the impression that every sound is carefully sifted. The chattering alarm-calls of the minor inhabitants of the forest, jungle or bush are each noted; but additionally there is the feeling that the most insignificant trifles of sounds are being registered and analysed. In sound range the hearing of a normal human is confined to frequences of 15 cycles per second to 20,000 cycles per second. The hearing of a leopard ranges from about the same low limit to approximately 45,000 cycles per second. An additional feature of such fine hearing is the ability of the leopard to detect the precise origin of a sound.

The sense of smell is described as "poor" and "limited" by most authors. Dunbar Brander, however, regards it to be somewhat better than the tiger's and reports having seen leopards using their noses. With scent markings playing an important part in intraspecific communication, the olfactory sense is probably more highly developed than generally assumed, and it is hard to believe that it should play practically no part in hunting. It has, after all, brought bad luck to many a leopard by leading it to a bait.

A number of years ago, when a parasitologist of the Kenya Medical Research Laboratory wanted some hyenas for examination, I went out and set a big cage trap at the foot of Lukenya Bluff, 40 km (25 mi) from Nairobi. My African assistants slightly roasted the lump of meat we were going to use as a bait, explaining that this would make the odor spread over a wider area. The first animal to enter the trap, however, was not a hyena, but a leopard, a small female with worn teeth, whose nose had obviously been quite sharp enough to pick up the enticing smell and to lead her to its origin, ahead of the notoriously keen-scented hyenas which we knew to be numerous in the vicinity. The parasitologist thought this too good an opportunity to miss, and I had to stand by while one of my colleagues blasted the poor old cat with a shot-gun. A few filarial worms were all that parasitological science got out of her.

The trap was reset, baited again with a lump of slightly roasted meat, and two days later it contained a big male leopard. I was able to convince the parasitologist that a few more filarial worms were not worth the life of this splendid animal, and it was handed over to the national parks authorities, who released it in the Tsavo National Park.

As a rule, a leopard lies up during the day in thick bush, among rocks, on a tree, sometimes even on a vulture's nest and becomes active around sunset. On one occasion, in the Serengeti, we spent an hour or so watching a female stretched out on a horizontal branch, with her legs dangling on both sides of her support. From time to time she opened her eyes, yawned, cast a drowsy look around, and fell asleep again. It was late in the afternoon, with black storm clouds coming up from the west. As the first drops fell, the leopardess came fully awake, climbed down from her tree, and set out to hunt.

At first she displayed considerable interest in some reed-buck a few hundred metres away, but when they disappeared, she systematically visited all the patches of scrub and bush where, as we well knew, reed-buck often lay. She worked those places exactly like a sporting dog and was obviously out to rise any game there might be. Discovering a reed-buck crouched among some medium-high grass, the leopardess took cover behind our Land-Rover, literally using it as a "stalking horse." At a given moment, she sneaked round the hood, then traversed a stretch of short grass in a low-slung run, and crept into a patch of high grass not far from her prospective victim. The buck, however, became aware of the approaching danger, and, before the cat could manoeuvre into position for the last deadly rush, it jumped to its feet, uttered a whistling alarm call, and bounded away.

Among the big cats, the leopard is certainly the most accomplished stalker. There was a highly instructive demonstration of this one morning at about ten in Nairobi National Park. Walking along the Athi River, I discovered a concentration of game on the opposite bank—a big herd of impala, two dozen water-buck, two eland—and stopped to enjoy the pleasing spectacle. All at once, an impala standing in the high grass interspersed with light scrub reared up, and I caught a glimpse of a leopard with its fangs fastened to the antelope's throat and the paws around its shoulders. Within a couple of seconds the attacker and the victim had vanished from sight, swallowed up by the high grass and scrub.

I was greatly impressed with the incredible stealth displayed by the hunter. It must have crept unnoticed to within almost touching distance of the impala, and there had been practically no rush at all. To me it certainly looked as if the leopard had suddenly materialized alongside the antelope. There was, of course, a general stampede, the impala and water-buck rushing out of the scrub and then stopping about 60 m (198 ft) away in order to look back. They uttered a weird chorus of alarm notes, the water-buck grunting and the impala going "grrr-grrr-grrr." For a long time I searched the area with my field-glasses, but I never saw the leopard again.

In this case, high grass and scrub had facilitated the stalker's approach. Another leopard used the cover afforded by a jumble of rocks to get within a couple of metres of its prey. This happened in the Tsavo National Park at 10:30 on a bright and sunny morning. There was a lot of game about—wildebeest, zebra, water-buck, Grant's gazelle—mostly between our Land-Rover and one of those old lava streams which form such a feature of certain parts of Tsavo West. The wildebeests, which were grazing close to the lava stream, suddenly stampeded up a hillside, taking all the other animals along in their headlong flight. After having galloped a few hundred metres, the mixed herd came to a halt, its members wheeling round to face in the direction from where they had come. The wildebeests scampered about in high excitement, and some even went back part of the way, all staring intently at the same place. Focusing my glasses at the spot thus indicated, I discovered a leopard standing over a wildebeest calf which it had just killed near the rocks.

As we approached, the cat grabbed its victim and began to drag it up the steep and rugged side of the lava stream. It held the dead animal by the neck, with the body trailing between its forelegs. About half-way up, it stopped, looked down at us, and through the view-finder of my camera, to which was screwed a 640-mm lens, I could see it pant violently. It was a very beautiful leopard, dark in colour and most strikingly marked. I managed to expose a few pictures before it again took hold of the kill and dragged it farther up. Having negotiated some particularly big boulders, it stopped again, panting as before, and turned its head toward us, giving me a chance for some further photographs. Another effort—but before it disappeared over the top it had to put in one more breathing spell.

More than seventy years ago, M. A. Wallinger, a divisional forest officer stationed at Dharwar in India made some detailed notes on how goats tied out as bait were killed by leopards, but his observations, published in the *Journal of the Bombay Natural History Society,* do not seem to have received the attention they deserved. In summing up what he had learned, Wallinger stressed the following points: the stalk is a quiet and stealthy process, with the victim unaware of its impending death; there is practically no spring if the cover available will allow the predator to stalk right up; the victim is seized by the throat, strangulation, not dislocation of the vertebrae, being the direct cause of death; there is an instinctive desire to drag the carcass away; the leopard starts to feed at the pelvis; it drinks after having fed. Sitting up over a goat tied up at some distance from the nearest cover, Wallinger heard two leopards approach. One of them suddenly sprang out a distance of 6 m (20 ft) and seized the goat by the throat, the impetus of the attack throwing both animals to the ground.

On a recent visit to the Serengeti National Park I saw a leopard rush a Thomson's gazelle over a distance of about 40 (130 ft) to 50 m (165 ft). In the course of three or four hours it undertook three attempts to secure a kill, displaying great stealth and almost infinite patience, and making the fullest use of every bit of cover it could find along the uppermost part of the Seronera River. The first bunch of thomies it tried to stalk apparently got its wind, for they suddenly jumped and scampered away. Shortly afterward, the leopard managed to get very close to another herd. My position was right behind the stalking cat, and, for a considerable time, my field-glasses showed me the top of its head together with the gazelles which were grazing with complete unconcern about 12 m (39 ft) from the crouching predator. Any moment I expected the cat to pounce upon one of them, for everything appeared to be in its favour. The leopard, however, did not seem to think so, for it never moved, and the thomies gradually drifted away and out of reach.

A couple of hours later, the leopard was at it again, stalking up to half a dozen gazelles, possibly the same it had been after earlier in the day. For about twenty minutes it gradually, ever so gradually, inched nearer and nearer, sliding on its belly from one patch of scrub to the next—and then it suddenly bounded forward. Seen through the field-glasses, it seemed to move at the speed of lightning—but the thomie reacted so quickly that the cat literally missed it by inches. As the gazelle raced to safety, the leopard flopped down, and when we drove up to it, we found it gasping for breath, almost choking in its efforts to fill its lungs.

Kruuk and Turner noticed both throat and nape bites on leopard kills; probably an animal jumped at from behind might well be grabbed by the back of the neck. The nape bite is sure to be used in dispatching small prey—gazelle kids, jackals, baboons, and perhaps also when a leopard jumps down on its victim from a tree. This way of hunting from ambush has been reliably recorded on a number of occasions.

My observations in the field have fully convinced me of the high degree of camouflage a leopard obtains from its colouration and markings. On many occasions I have looked at a small bush only a few yards away, knowing full well that there was a leopard inside, and it has taken me an incredibly long time to make out the outlines of the cat. In the Ngare Nanyuki region of the Serengeti National Park, we once put up a mother with a half-grown cub. This was before the leopards had become indifferent to cars, and the two animals immediately disappeared in a small patch of very low scrub not more than 6 or 7 m (abt 21 ft) in diameter and easily overlooked from the roof hatch of our car. We circled it several times, scanning every part of it, but even the eagle-eyed game scout was unable to detect any signs of the leopards. We continued the search until somebody discovered the mother right out in the open, half-way between the scrub and an extensive belt of thick bush. She had achieved the incredible feat of sneaking out of the sparse cover literally under our very eyes and to get away unnoticed, although five people were looking for her. We drove after her but were unable to head her off. We never found the cub again—but I am sure that all the time it lay motionless just a few yards from us.

Authors doubtful of the concealing and selective value of the leopard's colouration point to black panthers, which, they say, survive just as well as spotted ones, but it must not be forgotten that melanistic specimens are mainly found in areas of dense, deeply shaded forest jungles, where a black or dark brown skin has, in fact, the same camouflaging effect as a yellow, dark spotted one in scrub, dry bush, or among the leaves of a savannah tree.

The leopard's diet is enormously varied. I have myself noted the following animals as prey: wildebeest calf, half-grown topi, impala, reed-buck, Thomson's gazelle, Grant's gazelle, black-backed jackal, baboon, and European stork. The greatest number of kills seen by me were of reed-buck, but these antelopes are especially common along the Seronera River and its tributaries, where I have mainly studied the spotted cats. When the plains west of the Seronera River are literally swarming with migrating Thomson's gazelles, the leopards will kill almost nothing else.

The occurrence of the black-backed jackal among the victims is by no means unusual. A leopard in Ngorongoro Crater has been recorded as killing no less than eleven jackals within one month. One can, in actual fact, speak of a marked preference for small canines, both wild and domestic, and the leopards of India and Africa often perform amazing feats of boldness and effrontery in order to snatch a dog from the very feet of its master.

Genet cats and civets are frequently taken, and even cheetahs are not immune. In the Serengeti National Park a leopard descended from a tree and grabbed a lion cub that had just been left by its mother. As the lioness came running back, the loepard dropped the dead cub and darted back up the tree to safety.

From data collected between 1957 and 1965, Kruuk and Turner compiled the following list of animals killed by Serengeti leopards: wildebeest adult, 2% of total; wildebeest yearling, 4%; wildebeest calf, 4%; topi yearling, 2%; impala, 16%; Grant's gazelle, 4%; Thomson's gazelle, 27%; reed-buck, 11%; bush-buck, 2%; zebra foal, 7%; cheetah, 2%; black-backed jackal, 2%; rock hyrax, 2%; baboon, 4%; spring hare, 2%; secretary bird, 2%; European stork, 4%; guinea fowl, 2%; vulture chick, 2%; python, 2%.

Working in the same area from June 1966 to September 1969, Schaller listed as food items: Thomson's gazelle, 63.4%; Grant's gazelle, 6.1%; reed-buck, 11.6%; wildebeest, 6.7%; topi, 1.8%; hartebeest, 1.2%; zebra, 1.2%; water-buck, 0.6%; wart-hog, 0.6%; baboon, 0.6%; golden jackal, 0.6%; black-backed jackal, 0.6%; bateared fox, 2%; serval, 1.2%; European stork, 2.4%.

Lists of prey will, of course, differ greatly according to habitat and geographical region. In some places, leopards are known to kill a lot more hyraxes than they do in the Serengeti. Droppings which Schaller picked up at Kabara, in the saddle between Mount Mikeno and Mount Karisimbi, two peaks of the Virunga range, consisted entirely of remains of tree hyraxes and duikers.

The Virunga Volcanoes are the home of the mountain gorilla, and there have been persistant rumours of leopards attacking the big apes. Ben Burbridge, who went to the area before it was a national park in order to catch some live gorillas, was told of a terrible fight that lasted all night and ended with the death of the cat. Zoologists were inclined to disbelieve these accounts, until Walter Baumgärtel of the Traveller's Rest Hotel at Kisoro, informed the Uganda Game Department that Reuben Rwanzigire, his famous gorilla guide, had come across two apes, a male and a female, quite obviously killed by a large leopard. Soon afterward an American biologist, Dale Zimmermann, was fortunate enough to see a black leopard stalk a troop of gorillas at about 3600 m (12,000 ft) on Mount Muhavura, not far from where the dead ones had been found. It did not carry through its attempts to get close to the apes.

The chimpanzees of Budongo Forest, studied by Vernon Reynolds, did not seem to be molested by leopards. In certain areas, however, they must be preyed upon, A. Kortlandt's observations giving clear evidence that chimpanzees regard the spotted cats as enemies. Eugene N. Marais, studying the baboons of the Waterberg Mountains, saw leopards snatch individuals from the outskirts of the troops. Pursued by the big males responsible for the safety of baboon communities, the cats would drop their dead or crippled victims and escape, to come back for their prey after the angry primates had moved on.

In the Kafue National Park, in Zambia, reed-buck, puku, and duikers form nearly 50% of the leopard kills, but several full-grown hartebeests and one very old greater kudu have also been listed. In the Kruger National Park, impala at present make up 75% of the prey. Thirty years ago, Stevenson-Hamilton recorded reed-buck, impala, bush-buck, duiker, baboon, vervet monkey, cane rats, and other rodents, guinea fowl, francolins, and any other bird that could be caught. An individual on the Nuanetsi River that was kept under close observation for several months was found to prey entirely on small mammals and birds, killing nothing bigger than cane rats.

Droppings collected on Kilimanjaro show that leopards can, at least temporarily, subsist on a diet of small rodents. Four-striped mice, *Rhabdomys pumilio*, and mole-rats, *Tachyorictes daemon*, are so common on Africa's highest mountain that climbers without any zoological aspirations will comment on their presence. Swamp rats, *Otomys irroratus*, have been recorded up to 4800 m (15,700 ft), and the same altitude is occasionally attained by porcupines.

Fish are often taken, and in the case of leopards marooned on various islands in Kariba Dam, they eventually made up a prominent part of their diet. On some of these islands food became so scarce that leopards took to stealing cat-fish from fish eagles. It is this ability to live on small fry of the most different kinds that allows the leopard to exist in places where all the game has long ago been exterminated.

Leopards living in populated areas will, of course, prey on domestic stock, especially goats and sheep. Cows are occasionally taken, and a Kenya Game Department report tells of a full-grown mule being killed by a small "forest leopard" at Marsabit.

Of the prey taken in central India, Dunbar Brander wrote:

Their food is exceedingly varied and consists of almost anything they can catch and master. This includes sambar, nilgai and all the larger deer and antelopes, except bull nilgai and stag sambar and barasingha. These I have never known killed by leopard, simply because few leopards are big enough to tackle them. They kill sows and small pigs, cattle, calves, donkeys, ponies, young buffalos, goats, sheep, dogs, jackals, blackbuck, chinkara, four-horned antelope, barking deer, mouse deer, monkeys, hares, peafowl, jungle fowl, porcupines and even crabs, snakes and lizards—a fairly comprehensive menu. Their relation towards porcupines varies, as although they will kill and eat them, I have known them to occupy the same earth apparently on relations of mutual trust.

When hunting monkeys—langur in India and baboons in Africa—a leopard may climb a tree and force the panic-stricken primates to leap to the ground. Dunbar Brander once saw two of them at this game, one on the first branch of a large pepul tree, the other higher up, with langurs dropping from the outer branches. The cats unfortunately became aware of the observer and bolted before Dunbar Brander could find out just how much of a cooperation, if any, might have developed between them. It is rare to see leopards hunt in company, though Selous has recorded a pair going after a young giraffe.

The leopards of the Caucasus were always found near areas sheltering chamois, European bison, deer, and wild goats, while those inhabiting the slopes of the Talysh Mountains and the plains of Lenkoran mainly killed wild pigs, especially youngsters. On the Kopet Dagh Mountains the leopards live at a high altitude where wild sheep and wild goats are abundant. Russian observers also report the cats as killing porcupines and eating animals as small as mice.

The Manchurian leopard preys upon roe-deer, wapiti, wild pigs, musk-deer, and gorals, as well as on game-birds such as pheasants, black grouse, and hazel-hens. Baikov states that Chinese leopards quite often attack humans and are considered as more dangerous than tigers.

Dunbar Brander wrote:

> The same causes which tend to produce man-eating tigers act equally on leopards, but in the case of the latter animal difficulties in the way of obtaining food are much less, and man-eating leopards must more often be animals having a definite liking for human flesh. Some leopards, like some tigers, are occasional man-eaters, others confirmed man-eaters, and when an animal of this nature frequents a particular tract, no one is safe, as owing to their knowledge of man's way and being habituated to enter villages at night, they will enter a hut and drag out their victim from his cot. Man-eating tigers will not venture to do this, or at any rate only on very rare occasions. From a man-eating leopard, therefore, people have no security at all.

In 1857, Sterndale, while stationed at Seoni, heard of a man being killed by a big cat, assumed to be a tiger. He immediately arranged a beat and, as the drive proceeded, a leopard came out, went on, was turned back by an elephant, and came out again. The culprit being thought to be a tiger, no shot was fired at it, and it was only later, on examining the body of the victim, that Sterndale discovered the man-eater to have been a leopard, the very leopard that had been allowed to escape. During the following three years, this leopard, known as the Kahani man-eater, devastated a track of country about eighteen miles in diameter, killing over two hundred people. Sterndale himself, and other sportsmen as well, went after it on many occasions, but it thwarted all attempts on its life with such uncanny ease that the local population came to regard it as a "were-leopard." It was finally killed quite accidentally by a native shikari who mistook it for a pig.

The "Leopard of Rudraprayag" terrorized a part of Garhwal for nine years and accounted for at least 125 human victims before it was shot by Corbett after an arduous campaign lasting several months. The place where it fell on May 2, 1926, is marked by a plaque, and even today the inhabitants of the area still bless the name of Corbett Sahib, who delivered them from the killer. The leopard measured 2.28 m (7.5 ft) between pegs, 2.38 m (7.8 ft) along curves. Its teeth were worn and discoloured, with one canine broken off, and on the left hind foot, due to a shot fired at the animal about the time when it started its depredations, one toe and claw were missing. Corbett's account of the hunt is a classic.

An African leopard will occasionally snatch a child from a village as it might snatch a goat or a dog, but real man-eaters are scarce, and none have achieved anything like the sinister reputations of the man-eating leopards of Kahani and Rudraprayag.

Leopards do not hesitate to feed on carrion, and Champion found them to steal quite frequently from tiger kills. He got a flash-light photograph of a small individual at a buffalo killed by a tigress, looking very apprehensive, as if expecting the owner to make a wrathful appearance at any moment.

Having brought its stalk to a successful conclusion, a leopard often takes its kill up a tree, as otherwise it risks being deprived of its prey by other carnivores. In the Kruger National Park four hunting dogs drove one from a freshly killed impala and began tearing at the carcass. In this case, the cat suddenly came back, sprang amongst the dogs, growling angrily, grabbed the impala and climbed a nearby tree. Had the dogs been more numerous, it would most certainly not have acted so aggressively. Leopards will also give way to hyenas and to lions. A leopard comfortably settled down on a high tree in Nairobi National Park became so alarmed at the appearance of a lioness, that it slipped down to the ground and quickly ran up a steep slope, vanishing from sight over a low cliff. I don't think the lioness was aware of its presence at all.

Really to appreciate the leopard's muscular power, one has to see it run up a tree carrying a gazelle or reed-buck as large or even larger than itself. It holds the carcass by the neck and, having negotiated the tree trunk, drags it along the branches in order either to wedge it into a fork or simply hang it over a branch. It then remains in the vicinity of the kill for one, two, even up to three or four days, feeding on it at intervals, and sleeping in between, stretched out on a thick branch. It may carry the kill around in the tree, hanging it now higher, now lower, without any apparent reason. It consumes the carcass in such a way that it is gradually reduced to back, neck, and head, with the legs dangling loosely from strips of skin. Even though the cat may now and then gnaw at the upper heads of the leg bones, it almost appears as if it were careful not to sever completely the limbs from the carcass. Any part becoming detached will, of course, fall to the ground and may then be lost.

Once only have I observed two adult leopards at the same kill, a male and a female which at that time seemed to inhabit a joint home range on a tributary of the Seronera without, however, showing any signs of courting. When seen for the first time, they were both busy on a reed-buck hanging in a fork. Later we found the male asleep on a tree about a mile away, while the female was still greedily feeding. After a short while, the male returned and climbed up to the carcass. The female received him threateningly, baring her fangs and uttering a menacing "piupupiupiupiu," similar to the sound often heard from two domestic toms circling each other on stiff legs. She eventually withdrew from the kill, and the male spent some time trying to drag the reed-buck higher up into the tree, but did not make any progress, as the head was tightly wedged in a fork. When he finally gave up and stretched out on a branch, the female quickly came back to the kill, put her head between the antelope's forelegs, and began chewing a hole into the chest.

The habit of treeing kills is widespread in Africa. Drake-Brockman reported it from Somaliland, where he saw as many as three sheep on one and the same tree. Stevenson-Hamilton refers to it in connection with the Kruger National Park, and mentions one of his game wardens seeing a giraffe calf weighing 90 kg (203 lb) lying across a branch 3.60 m (12 ft) above the ground. Even human bodies have been dealt with in the same way. In the Sudan, Romolo Gessi, one of Gordon Pasha's lieutenants, had a man carried off from one of his camps. The poor wretch, he tells us, was found next day, hanging half eaten upon a tree. Wilhelm Kuhnert heard of a similar case in what was then German East Africa.

A leopard's larder is perfectly safe from vultures, hyenas, hunting dogs, and usually also from lions. There have, however, been a few instances of lions climbing trees in order to pull down a kill. While the leopards of Seronera seem to tree most of their kills, it cannot be said that they will invariably do so. On one of the tributaries of the Seronera, we one morning came upon a big, golden brown male walking parallel to the bank without paying the slightest attention to our car. From time to time he sat down to scratch his chin with a hind paw. He had a beautiful tail, which he carried curved upward in the way leopards always do, and when he was walking through scrub, he lifted it so high that we could follow his march simply by watching the white spot on the underside of the tip gliding along above the bushes. We thus had an excellent demonstration of what a useful guiding star this white spot must be for any leopard—young or adult—following another.

We accompanied the male down-river, overtaking him several times. Nothing, however, could make him deviate from his course and perfectly sure of where he wanted to go, he finally approached a clump of bush, slipped inside, and came out almost immediately carrying a dead thomie in his mouth. There could be no doubt that he had stored the gazelle in this thicket after killing it earlier in the day.

He now retraced his steps up-river for about 40 m (131 ft) and then settled down to eat his prey under a thick bush overhanging on one side and forming something like a shady cave, into which the leopard fitted quite snugly. Most of the time he fed in a crouching position, but at times he sat up on his haunches. He held down the carcass with his forepaws, pulling and chewing the flesh from the bones with his head held inclined sideways, so as to make the best use of the cutting edges of his cheek teeth. For a time he chewed assiduously on a leg, and once he pulled off a big bunch of white hairs from the thomie's belly, which stuck to his lower lip like a false beard. He shook his head violently to dislodge the encumbrance, and downy puffs floated away into the grass. He licked himself for a while, and then continued feeding.

This went on from 11.15 to 11.45 A.M. and then the leopard suddenly got up, came out from underneath the bush and walked away up-river. He stopped shortly, threw up his tail, and sprayed a bush, then went on another 50 m (164 ft) or so and lay down in the open to wash himself thoroughly and very elaborately, as leopards have a habit of doing at very frequent intervals. Getting to his feet again, he proceeded at a very leisurely pace, keeping right out in the open.

Twice more he placed scent marks on bushes, and then descended into the river-bed to drink from a small pool. Shortly afterward we lost him in thick bush, not far from the spot where we had met him.

As far as Indian leopards are concerned, treeing kills has been mentioned by Forsyth, who once found the body of a child in a fork of a tree, by Blanford, Dunbar Brander, Champion, and others; but the way they have recorded their observations and the recurrent letters on the subject published in the *Journal of the Bombay Natural History Society* make one suspect the habit to be less common than in Africa. Dunbar Brander thought that leopards mainly resorted to storing their kills above ground level where tigers were especially numerous.

The leopard's spotted coat blends most marvelously with the foliage of trees, but the one thing that often gives away his presence is the long tail hanging below the branch on which the animal rests. One morning, in the Serengeti National Park, we spotted a female in this way and parked the car a short distance from the tree on which, as we thought, she had decided to lay up for the day. After only a few minutes, however, she climbed higher into the upper branches of the tree where she began to pull around a half-eaten kill—a young topi—which we had not at first noticed. Grabbing the carcass by the neck, she came down again. At the lowest fork, she jumped to the ground and then dragged the kill through the grass, with the body between her forelegs. She paid no attention to us, except for once, when she ran a few paces because we had swung toward her somewhat too abruptly; but she immediately quietened down again. She let go of the kill several times in order to have a short rest, and all the while she was heading toward a kopje. She finally dragged the kill up over stones and through scrub to the base of an enormous granite boulder, and, as she disappeared in the high grass growing around the base of this rock, we distinctly heard the mewling sounds uttered by her cubs.

In Africa and India leopards mate at all times of the year, while in Manchuria and eastern Siberia there appears to be a definite mating season in January and February. In the Caucasus, leopards used to mate in early spring. According to observations made in zoological gardens, females come in heat at intervals of 20 to 50 days, which averages out at 45.8 days. Heat lasts for about six or seven days. Several males have been seen to pursue one female and fight over her. The game warden of Nairobi National Park was fortunate enough to watch a couple's mating behaviour, which he described to me as very similar to that of lions.

The gestation period is variously given as 90 to 105 days. The litter consists of one to six, mostly two to three cubs, but the early mortality is rather high and it is rare to see a mother with more than one or two. The den may be situated in a cave or crevice among boulders, in a hollow tree, in a reed-bed, or in a dense thicket. The cubs open their eyes after ten days. Their fur is longer and more woolly than that of adults, pale greyish fawn in colour with small, rather ill-defined spots.

"Leopard cubs at this early age are nervous, wide eyed and playful little souls, behaving much like the kittens of the domestic cat," wrote Turnbull-Kemp. "They will pat at dry leaves fluttering in the wind, bounce pot-bellied on too unsuspecting crickets and grasshoppers, or scramble over a tolerant mother—making lurching assaults on her tail or paw to the accompaniment of cracked and treble growls of wrath."

If the cubs have to be moved to another hiding place, the mother will carry them one at a time, holding them by the loose skin of the back, and, if necessary, she does not hesitate to swim a river in the process.

I have never seen a male leopard close to a female with smallish cubs and should, on the basis of my own experience, consider it as highly unusual for one to show an interest in his family. Armand Denis, however, reports having seen a male, female, and cubs perched together on a tree, feeding upon a kill brought there by one of the adults. E. Cronje Wilmot knew of a male not only sharing a hiding place with a nursing female, but dragging meat to the family, and Turnbull-Kemp wrote: "The most exceptional sight known to me occurred in Eastern Transvaal, where it was possible to see two well grown cubs from previous litters, four small cubs, and both parents all sharing the same cave-like recess in a granite outcrop. This last case, it should be mentioned, was noted in an area which is rich in game and heavily populated by leopards." Dunbar Brander considers the leopard more "conjugally inclined" than the tiger.

The cubs are weaned at about three months, but can be seen to suck, or try to do so, for some time longer. At that age they begin to leave the den and to follow their mother about on her prowls. Female leopards are devoted to their offspring, and one occasionally gets delightful glimpses of family life. On the Seronera River, I recently came across a mother with two cubs. She was on a tree where she had a kill—a Grant's gazelle—and one of the cubs lay stretched out on a neighbouring tree, sunning its fat little stomach. The second cub, after rustling around for a while among the undergrowth surrounding the base of the tree, suddenly ran up the trunk to join the mother. It snuggled up against her, and she licked it continuously for at least ten minutes.

Late one afternoon in the Mara Reserve, we found a three-quarter-grown cub lying on the bank of a dry river-bed. We had a game ranger along with us who knew the youngster and thought that its mother might not be far away. After a short time the cub suddenly got up and ran along the river-bed, uttering a series of twittering calls. Seeing its mother come out of a strip of bush, it joyfully bounded toward her. Moving on together, mother and child began to play in a most delightful manner, pawing and chasing one another like kittens, jumping over each other's backs, the cub frequently turning regular somersaults. It was most probably of male sex, still distinctly smaller than the mother and with a childish look on its face, very different from the alert expression the mother retained, even while at play. As they gambolled about, they both carried their tails curved up, with the white tips well visible.

Cubs have been reported to kill small fry when about five months old. They may possibly be able to fend for themselves at the age of one year, but will usually stay with the mother for a period of eighteen months or up to two.years. A male cub kept under observation by Schaller began periodically to roam about on its own when it was over fifteen months old, and it was virtually independent at twenty months. It still hunted in the same area as its mother, however, and the two met occasionally. The cub was even seen to take a kill away from her with impunity. Schaller reports a Seronera female, which gave birth to a cub in January 1967, having another litter in May or early June 1969. She must thus have conceived in late February, about twenty-five months after the birth of the previous litter.

At Seronera, subadult and adult females were found to outnumber males by about two to one. With the sex ratio about fifty-fifty at birth, male cubs must therefore have a very much higher infant mortality than their sisters, a phenomenon similar to what has been noticed in lions and tigers.

Life-spans of up to twenty-one and twenty-three years have been recorded in captivity. Certain man-eaters, which must have been at least three years old—probably older—when they embarked on their careers, and which were destroyed before they reached senility, have been known for seven, eight, and nine years. In 1946, Turnbull-Kemp was shown the spoor of a male whose foot had been caught and mutilated in a trap in 1935, when it was already a big and fully adult animal.

Leopards are occasionally killed by lions, tigers, and crocodiles.

An individual unable to dash up a tree may well be surrounded and torn to pieces by a pack of Indian wild dogs or African hunting dogs. In the pursuit of prey, accidents will happen to leopards as they do to tigers and lions. Attacks on baboons sometimes result in the spotted hunter being overwhelmed and badly injured or killed by the big males of the troop.

Man is the leopard's worst enemy. It is thought that 75% of the leopards shot by sportsmen in India were killed over bait, 20% in beats, and 5% in chance encounters or after having been systematically tracked down. It is safe to assume that practically all of the tens of thousands deprived of their skins to satisfy the fur industry were trapped or snared, mostly under circumstances of extreme cruelty.

Anthrax has been noticed as a cause of death in the Kruger National Park, and a leopard in Nairobi National Park was found to have died of severe pulmonary haemorrhage and necrosis similar to what can be observed in a rather obscure canine affliction known as the "Nairobi Bleeding Disease." Cases of rabies have been of rare occurrence. A form of typhoid often turns up in captive individuals. The parasites taken from leopards include fleas, lice, ticks—for instance *Amblyomma tholloni, A. variegata, Haemaphysalis leachii,* and *Rhipicephalus simus*—mites, pentastomids, flukes, tapeworms, and roundworms. Two tapeworms—*Taenia ingweni* and *Taenia pisiformis*—turn up quite commonly and may be of some pathological importance.

Young leopards brought up in captivity can turn into amazingly tame, affectionate, and docile pets, but it is well to remember that individuals may vary greatly in this respect. While playing with a tame leopard in front of a camera, Jean Lester of Lobatse, Botswana, was suddenly dragged down and badly clawed. So quick was the changeover from play to aggression, that the photographer exposed several more frames before he fully realized what was happening and dropped the camera in order to lend a hand in dragging the animal off the girl.

Leopards breed well in captivity and can be found in most zoological gardens. They occasionally appear in mixed groups of trained circus animals.

Jaguar
Panthera onca
(LINNAEUS 1758)

The jaguar was first reported by Amerigo Vespucci, who, in 1500, mentioned "panthers" among the animals of Venezuela. Four years later, writing about South America in general, he made the very pertinent remark: "Few are like ours, except the lions, panthers, stags, boars, goats and deer; and even these have some dissimilarities of form."

The jaguar is a spotted cat, and Vespucci cannot be blamed for having mistaken it for a panther. His successors, however, soon began to refer to the animal as a tiger. A map of South America, published by Hondius in 1599, may have contributed to this error, for it not only shows a fully maned African lion, but also a striped Asiatic tiger. Even today, all over Spanish-speaking America, the jaguar goes under the name "El tigre."

The word "jaguar" was borrowed from one of the Tupi-Guarani languages, spoken within an area that extends from the Amazon to Paraguay and to the eastern slopes of the Bolivian Andes. It originally was "yaguara" and is said, perhaps somewhat fancifully, to mean the "wild beast that overcomes its prey at a bound." Among the Guarani of Paraguay, the species is known as "yaguarete," which Rengger translates as "body of a dog." According to a more recent author, Hans Krieg, a German zoologist, "yaguá" does, in fact, stand for "dog," the puma, for instance, being called "yaguá pitá," or "red dog." The Brazilians call the jaguar "onça." Linnaeus must have been aware of the name current in Portuguese-speaking America when he chose *Felis onca* as the jaguar's scientific designation. On the basis of such characteristics as the partly ossified hyoid and the roundly contracting pupils it has later been included in the genus *Panthera*.

The remains of a giant jaguar, *Panthera athrox*, have been found in Pleistocene deposits all over North America from Alaska to Mexico. It rivalled the European cave lion in size, and J. Leidy, the pioneer palaeontologist who described it from bones excavated at Natchez, Mississippi, regarded it as an American lion. It was only quite recently, in 1941, that George Gaylord Simpson was able to prove its close affinity to the present-day jaguar. At least seventy-six individuals have been recovered from that palaeontological treasure-house, the tar pits of La Brea, California. The present-day jaguar has also been recorded from the Pleistocene of North America, in specimens averaging somewhat larger than the biggest modern subspecies.

The jaguar's skull is large, with the brain-case comparatively broader than a tiger's, and the frontal part of equal relative height. The facial part, however, is shorter than in either the tiger or the lion. The dentition is robust, with the canines so well developed that Haltenorth considers them as relatively the strongest of any of the big cats.

Characteristics. "A big powerfully built creature, giving the same effect of strength that the tiger or lion does, and that the leopard and puma do not"; thus Theodore Roosevelt characterized the largest of American cats. The jaguar is, in fact, more heavily and powerfully built than the leopard, with a large rounded head, a deep-chested, barrel-like body, relatively shorter than that of a lion or tiger, rather short, though very massive limbs, and a tail not longer than about one-third of head and body. The colouration varies from pale yellow through reddish yellow and yellowish red to reddish brown and rich rusty red, paling to white or light buff on cheeks, throat, lower neck, chest, belly, and inside of limbs. There are black spots on head, neck, and limbs, and large black blotches on the underparts of the body. Shoulders, back, and flanks are marked with spots forming large rosettes which enclose one or several dots in a field somewhat darker than the ground colour. Along the middle of the back there runs a row of elongate black spots which tend to merge into a median line. The backs of the ears are black with a small whitish or buffish central spot. The tail, white for all its length on the underside and toward the end on the upper surface as well, carries more or less crescentic or circular spots and two or three black rings in the terminal third. The tip is usually black. Colouration and markings are as variable as in the leopard. After having handled hundreds of pelts, Krieg came to the conclusion that specimens from savannah regions were generally lighter in colour than forest jaguars.

Melanistic individuals, dark brown or black, with the markings visible in oblique light, are by no means uncommon and were at one time regarded as a separate species. Alexander von Humboldt encountered this interesting colour phase at Esmeralda, Venezuela, and near the place where the Casiquiare branches off from the Orinoco.

The Indians told him that black "tigers" were very rare, never mingled with the common jaguars, and formed "another race."

Humboldt obviously had his doubts on this point, but thought that only somebody residing on the Orinoco and accompanying the Indians of Esmeralda on the "perilous chase of the tiger," would be able to decide whether it was a variety or a species. The information Prince Maximilian of Wied obtained regarding the black jaguars of south-eastern Brazil was equally inconclusive. Another early explorer, Eduard Poeppig, coming down from the Andes in the 1830s, heard of the black "tiger" along the Huallaga, a tributary of the Marañón. According to local opinion, it was "bigger and more ferocious" than the spotted jaguar, and Poeppig assumed it to be a species in its own right. Rengger, however, who saw a few black and chestnut skins in Paraguay, immediately recognized them as mere colour variations.

Henry Walter Bates met a black jaguar on the banks of the upper Amazon near the mouth of the Tefé River, and during his prolonged stay at Ega (or Tefé) he found black specimens to be more common in the neighbourhood of that place than spotted ones. The Marquis de Wavrin heard of black jaguars on the Putumayo and saw skins in the Mato Grosso and in the country of the Jivaros Indians. From all available records it appears that melanistic jaguars, like black leopards, seem to turn up most frequently in dense, humid tropical forests, from the Brazilian state of Paraná, northern Paraguay, and Mato Grosso in the south to Darién in the north.

Albinotic or partly albinotic skins have been reported from Paraguay. Don Félix de Azara, Spanish soldier and naturalist, described one that was so pale that the rosettes could only be seen in certain lights. Rengger was shown a greyish white skin, with faint shades of markings visible on belly and flanks. The hunter who shot the animal told him that the claws had been white.

Based on differences in size and in the cranial structure, no less than sixteen subspecies have been described.

Measurements. An average male has a head and body length of about 1.82 m (6 ft), a tail length of 50 to 56 cm (avg. 21 in), and a shoulder height of 68 to 76 cm (avg. 28 in). Hall and Kelson give the total lengths of six males as varying from 1.72 to 2.41 m (avg. 7 ft), of five females from 1.57 to 2.19 m (avg. 6 ft), the respective tail lengths being 52.3 to 66.5 cm (avg. 23 in) and 43.2 to 60.4 cm (avg. 20 in). Males from Mexico, according to Jack O'Connor, an American sportsman, average about 54 kg (122 lb) in weight, the heaviest he ever heard about attaining 73.47 kg (165 lb). Females from the same area average as little as 36 kg (81 lb). A male from Brazil—probably from Mato Grosso—is recorded as having weighed 131.8

kg (297 lb) and Sasha Siemel, the famous jaguar hunter, published the photograph of a very big specimen that had a weight of 158 kg (356 lb). Hans Krieg writes of seeing big males in the Argentinian Chaco which were as heavy as an Indonesian tiger.

Rengger was probably the first to draw attention to regional differences in size. He found the jaguars of northern Paraguay to be noticeably smaller than those farther south, skins from the Entre Rios Province of Argentina, for instance, measuring two, three, or four inches more in length. Skins he examined in northern Brazil, in Bahia and Pernambuco, were all, however, much smaller than those from northern Paraguay.

According to the findings of American taxonomists, the smallest jaguars occur in Central America, from Yucatán to Colombia. Today, the largest are probably found in the southern Mato Grosso and in the Argentinian Chaco.

Distribution. When John James Audubon and John Bachman were collecting materials for their monumental work *The Viviparous Quadrupeds of North America,* General Sam Houston informed them that he had encountered jaguars east of the San Jacinto River. The species thus could at one time well have reached lower Louisiana, as stated by several authors. Houston also reported the jaguar as occurring "abundantly on the headwaters of some of the Rio Grande's tributaries." During a visit to San Antonio in 1845, John Woodhouse Audubon heard of jaguars lurking about the watering places of the mustangs and deer.

A few jaguars have been shot and trapped in New Mexico, from the border areas to about the 35th parallel, while in Arizona the species once ranged as far north as the Grand Canyon. Two jaguars with a cub were reported in the Tehachapi Mountains north of Los Angeles in 1855 by James Capen Adams, a trapper, who became famous for travelling around the wilderness in the company of a tame grizzly bear. The last California jaguar was killed at Palm Springs in 1860. It is rare today for a jaguar to make an appearance north of the Mexican border. The last New Mexico records seem all to go back to the first decade of the twentieth century, but one was killed in Texas in 1946, another in Arizona in 1949. From southeastern Texas, the jaguar's area of distribution extends south along the Gulf coast to southern Vera Cruz; from Sonora, possibly from southernmost Arizona along a narrow strip of country on the Gulf of California to Oaxaca. In 1955, a specimen was shot in Baja California.

From Chiapas and Yucatán, the species ranges through Central America to Venezuela, the Guianas, and Brazil, as well as to eastern Colombia, eastern Peru, eastern and southern Bolivia, going as far west in all these countries as the first ramparts of the Andes. The jaguar's range originally extended south into Paraguay, Uruguay, and Argentina, where it included the Pampa Central.

There are authors who assume the jaguar to have ranged even farther south, at least up to the end of the eighteenth century, all through Patagonia and right down to the Strait of Magellan. This has been denied most emphatically by Hans Krieg, who points out that there is not a shred of evidence to prove that Patagonia was ever inhabited by jaguars since the region took on its present aspect after the end of the last Ice Age. Nor does Krieg accept the species as having occurred around Lake Nahuel Huapi. Krieg's view is accepted by the great majority of zoologists.

The jaguar disappeared from Uruguay during the early years of the present century, and in 1925, von Colditz reported it as practically extinct in the Pampa Central of Argentina. Today, distribution within that country is restricted to the far north, to northern Corrientes, and the Chaco of Santiago.

In Humboldt's time, about 4000 jaguars were recorded killed annually throughout the vast extent of Spanish America, with 2000 skins being shipped to Europe from Buenos Aires. During the 1930s a skin could be bought in Argentina for as little as 100 to 150 pesos. Prices have since soared to fantastic heights, and the jaguar has been as badly hit as other spotted cats. In a recent issue of the *National Geographic* Magazine, there was a photograph showing piles of jaguar and ocelot skins in a warehouse at Manáos, at the confluence of the Amazon and the Rio Negro. During the last fifteen years or so, hundreds, perhaps thousands of similar warehouses and trading posts must have been doing a roaring business in skins along the Amazon, the Orinoco, and their tributaries, all over the Mato Grosso, and throughout the jaguar's Mexican range. During the first eight months of 1968, no less than 7238 jaguar skins, valued at 864,000 dollars, reached the United States.

In Brazil, the jaguar, as well as the ocelot and the margay, are now protected by law, but to really control the activities of poachers will be very difficult indeed. One can only hope that the world-wide outcry against the mass slaughter of these magnificent animals for no other reason than to satisfy the eccentric demands of a small minority will kill the cat-fur fashion once and for all. With the demand for its skins gone, prices are sure to tumble, and poaching will no longer be a paying proposition.

Habits. Jaguars are found in tropical forests and savannahs, especially in the neighbourhood of rivers, streams, backwaters, and morasses. Along the Rio Paraguay and its tributaries, they inhabit riverine forests and swampy ground covered with reeds and high grass. Around Ega, on the upper Amazon, Bates found them living on the strips of forest land which remain dry during the widespread floods of the wet season. They freely traverse marshy jungles quite impenetrable to man.

Richard Spruce, the botanist, never encountered jaguars in the cinchona forests of the Ecuadorian Andes, but found them plentiful at about 1000 m (3280 ft) at Tarapota in the Cordillera Oriental of the Peruvian Andes. Wilfred H. Osgood saw jaguar spoor at 2100 m (6900 ft) in northern Peru, and this may be about as high as the species will go, although there is one record of 2700 m (8860 ft),from Bolivia.

In northwestern Mexico, jaguars can be encountered among low scrub in fairly arid country, and they have been known to enter the Sonora Desert, one of North America's driest regions. As a whole, however, one certainly has to agree with von Colditz that the jaguar "needs water, a lot of water." It is an excellent swimmer and can be seen crossing the Rio Paraguay, with the head and the whole of the spine above the surface, paddling in an almost straight line across the broad expanse of water. Having climbed out on the opposite bank, it looks around, shakes its body, then each of its paws separately. It shows an even greater liking for playing about in the water than the Indian tiger, so much so that one might almost be tempted to regard it as semi-aquatic in some parts of its range.

Owing to the jaguar's very marked preference for the immediate vicinity of watercourses, the early naturalist-explorers, who travelled by water and collected specimens along the river-banks, obtained some fascinating glimpses of this usually shy and highly secretive cat. A good example is given by Alfred Russel Wallace in his account of the uppermost reaches of the Rio Negro:

> In the evening I took my gun, and strolled along the road a little way into the forest, at the place I had so long looked forward to reaching, and was rewarded by falling in with one of the lords of the soil, which I had long wished to encounter. As I walked quietly along, I saw a large jet black animal come out of the forest about twenty yards before me, which took me so very much by surprise that I did not at first imagine what it was. As it moved slowly on, and its whole body and long curved tail came into full view, in the middle of the road, I saw that it was a fine black jaguar. I involuntarily raised my gun to my shoulder, but remembering that both barrels were loaded with small shot, and that to fire

would exasperate without killing him, I stood silently gazing. In the middle of the road he turned his head, and for an instant paused and gazed at me, but having, I suppose, other business of his own to attend to, walked steadily on and disappeared in the thicket. As he advanced, I heard the scampering of small animals and the whizzing flight of ground birds, clearing the path for their dreaded enemy. This encounter pleased me much. I was too much surprised and occupied too much with admiration to feel fear. I had at length had a full view, in its native wilds, of the rarest variety of the most powerful and dangerous animal inhabiting the American continent.

Most people who have been fortunate enough to observe the jaguar in its habitat agree that in its movements it does not give that impression of lithe grace so characteristic of the leopard and may even appear somewhat clumsy by comparison. It normally walks along with fairly long strides—50 cm (20 in)—and while it has been said not to carry its tail curved up in the way of the leopard, various descriptions—like the one taken from Alfred Russel Wallace's book—and a good number of photographs give evidence of its doing so fairly frequently. Attacking prey in a series of short, quick bounds, or running for cover, it is able to attain a considerable speed. According to de Wavrin it can outdistance a horse over a short stretch, but will tire very quickly.

Although not such an expert tree climber as the puma, it is nevertheless much more at home among the branches than the tiger or the lion, probably not far behind the leopard in this respect, and it may occasionally take to the trees in order to grab a sloth, a sleeping bird, or a monkey. Most of the jaguar's hunting, however, is done on the ground, at dawn or dusk, during bright nights of moonshine or starlight, more rarely during very dark nights or in the middle of the day. In remote, practically uninhabited regions, it can be seen on the move at sunset and till about nine o'clock in the morning, but fear of man will turn it into an almost entirely nocturnal creature.

In north-western Mexico, the jaguar occasionally kills mountain sheep, which proves it to be a hunter of as much stealth and stalking ability as any of the other big cats. It takes a fair number of deer—for instance swamp deer in the marshes of the southern Mato Grosso—but it is by no means such a confirmed deer-slayer as the puma. Its preferred prey, by far, are peccaries and capybaras.

It is perhaps significant that the jaguar's former range within the southernmost parts of the United States coincided closely with that of the javelina, or collared peccary, a wild pig. The white-lipped peccary occurs from southern Mexico to Argentina and roams through the tropical forests in herds of up to a hundred or more. The boars have a reputation of being fierce fighters, and jaguars are generally said to follow the troops at a safe distance or to watch them from vantage points in order to pounce upon stragglers and strays.

Even more than on peccaries, however, the jaguar depends for its sustenance on the capybara or chiguire, a tailless creature that looks like an overgrown guinea pig. It has a shoulder height of about 50 cm (20 in) and a length of 1 mc (3 ft). It is the biggest of all living rodents. It swims and dives well, and is generally encountered in small herds which bask on the sand-banks like miniature hippopotamuses. "The capybara is the jaguar's daily bread," says Hans Krieg, and with these bristly coated animals swarming along South American rivers, streams, and lakes in enormous numbers, the big cat finds its table permanently and plentifully set.

Rengger made full use of the unique opportunities he had for studying the jaguar's hunting behaviour on the banks of the Rio Paraguay, and he has given an excellent account of what he saw:

> The jaguar sneaks along the river's edge, searching for capybaras and otters. From time to time it stops as if listening, and looks around attentively, but never did I see one follow a spoor with its nose on the ground. Should it discover a capybara, the jaguar will stalk it with incredible patience and circumspection. Serpent-like it winds its way over the ground, pausing for a minute or so to observe its quarry, often making a considerable detour in order to approach it from another direction where there is less risk of being detected. After it has been successful in getting close to its prey, the jaguar pounces on it in one, rarely two bounds, presses it against the ground, tears out its throat and carries it, still struggling, into a thicket. The jaguar often finds its movements betrayed by dry grasses crackling under its weight, a noise to which, incidentally, the boatmen camping on the river banks pay great attention. The capybara may also get the stalker's wind when it is still far away and will then rush into the water, uttering loud cries of alarm. Jaguars have been seen to jump into the river after a capybara and catch it before it could dive to safety. Having failed to catch its quarry, a jaguar immediately walks on, as if ashamed, without looking round. While stalking, its attention is fully concentrated on its prey, and it pays almost no heed to what is going on all around, ignoring even fairly loud noises. If it finds itself unable to approach its prey without being noticed, it lurks among the bushes in the position of a cat watching a mouse, crouched ready to spring, eyes fixed on the object of its rapacious greed, with only a twitch now and then of its outstretched tail. It does not catch all its prey by stalking, but also hides among the reeds, waiting for animals to come to drink.

Hunting along the river-banks, the jaguar also takes otters and, according to Hermann Burmeister, coypus. Tapirs are frequently preyed upon, although killing one of these big, thick-skinned ungulates does not seem to be too easy a task. If not brought down at once, a tapir crashes toward the near-by river, and in its headlong rush, the jaguar may be brushed off by the dense vegetation or dashed against a tree. Even if it hangs on, it will have to let go when the victim submerges. Tapirs which managed to escape from a jaguar's claws, with deeply lacerated hind-quarters, have been shot on various occasions.

The great ant-eater is able to give a good account of itself when attacked by a jaguar, rearing up and spreading wide its powerful and well-armed forelimbs in readiness for a welcoming embrace. Caught in the iron grip of those powerful claws, the cat will not escape without serious injury and may even be killed.

Jaguars naturally catch a lot of small game. Rengger found the remains of rats and agoutis in their stomachs, and Azara took the spines of prehensile-tailed porcupines from droppings. Wild turkeys and other game-birds are often killed, and probably various kinds of marsh birds as well. Claes Chr. Olrog, the Swedish naturalist, reports coming across the empty carapaces of innumerable armadillos, which had been eaten by jaguars, and he regards the big cats as the worst enemies of these otherwise so well-protected animals. The jaguar is, however, able to break through the even stronger armour of the river turtle, *Podocnemis expansa,* and when picking up the remains of some of these reptiles, opened and devoured a few hours before his arrival, Eugene André, like Humboldt before him, marvelled at the strength required to tear asunder the firmly linked carapace and plastron, a feat which the jaguar seems to perform with apparent ease.

In former times, huge crowds of these turtles used to visit the sandy beaches of the big rivers at breeding time. On his trip up the Orinoco, Humboldt was told by the Indians that the concentrations of turtles always attracted many jaguars, who not only killed the reptiles themselves but also dug out their eggs. This was confirmed over a hundred years later by an American naturalist, Leo E. Miller, who wrote:

> The hoarse cough of jaguars was heard almost nightly; it was the season when great numbers of turtles left the river at nightfall to deposit their eggs in the sandbanks, and the jaguars left the forest at dark to dig up and feed on these eggs. One night, just as the boat had drawn up to the higher sand-bank, preparatory to tying up, one of the huge cats was discovered sitting ten feet above us, quietly surveying the scene on deck; there was a rush for guns, but when they were secured, the jaguar had disappeared.

The river turtle has been almost exterminated in many parts of its range—not by the jaguars, of course, but by that greediest of predators, man. Jaguars have been known to kill snakes, including boas and anacondas, and it may well be that one occasionally bites off more than it can chew by tackling an individual of the latter species too big to cope with. One traveller maintains that he found the carcass of a "tigre" which showed every sign of having been killed by a constricting snake.

When Humboldt reported jaguars as killing and eating crocodilians, there was a certain amount of polite disbelief, but this assertion of his has long since become a well-established fact of South American natural history. Bates, for instance, came across a freshly killed caiman in the Amazon forest, pounced upon by a jaguar while guarding its nest. George K. Cherrie, one of the naturalists accompanying Theodore Roosevelt on his Brazilian expedition, examined a six-foot caiman killed by a jaguar and concluded that the cat had sprung upon its back, crunched the vertebrae of the neck with its powerful jaws, and then torn open the paralyzed reptile's chest.

From catching turtles and caimans, there is only a small step to fishing, and fish can, in fact, be considered as forming a not inconsiderable part of the water-loving jaguar's diet. The observant Rengger was able to contribute some very interesting notes concerning "el tigre's" piscatorial habits:

> Regarding the manner in which the jaguar catches fish, many fabulous tales are current in Paraguay. It is said, for instance, that it attracts fish by the froth of its saliva, or by touching the surface of the water with the tip of its tail. A very reliable hunter, to whom I am indebted for many noteworthy observations and much good advice in my travels, taught me better, and my own observations later confirmed the veracity of his words. One sultry summer's evening, I was returning home in my boat at the approach of a thunderstorm, when my companion, an Indian, noticed a jaguar on the edge of the river. We drew nearer and took cover under the overhanging willow trees in order to observe his actions. It was sitting crouched on a spit of land, where the water was running rather more swiftly, the kind of place favoured by a predatory fish known in Paraguay as "dorado." Occasionally it bent forward, its eyes fixed on the surface of the river as if it wished to penetrate the depth below. After about a quarter of an hour, I saw it slap the water with its paw and throw a large fish on to the bank. It was fishing in exactly the same way as our domestic cat.

The story of the jaguar luring fish within reach, which Rengger found current in Paraguay, has cropped up in many other parts of South America. Herbert M. Smith, as quoted by E. W. Gudger, wrote of the jaguar of Brazil:

The Indians have a curious story about his fishing. The jaguar, they say, comes at night and crouches on a log or branch over the water; he raps the surface with his tail, gently, and the "tambakis" or other fruit-eating fish, come to the sound, when he knocks them out with his paw. I do not take it upon myself to say that this story is true, but I have heard it from all sides, and from persons who aver that they have seen the fishing.

On the Rio Guayapo, Karl Weidman, the animal photographer, obtained a splendid picture of a jaguar lying on a dead tree that fell into the river, and it looks as if it might have been after fish when surprised. As a leopard watches its quarry, the tip of its tail keeps twitching, and Rengger reported the same for the jaguar. One could imagine a fishing jaguar going through the same motions, and in the case of the animal photographed by Weidman, the tip of the tail would just about have touched the surface. This might, without any intention on the jaguar's part, have attracted some fruit-eating fish. Quite often threads of saliva can be seen hanging down from the lips of both lions and leopards. A few droplets falling into the water beneath the jaguar's resting place could make a fish raise in order to investigate and thus—quite accidentally, of course—bring it within reach of the cat's paw. In both cases it would be very easy for a casual observer to imagine the jaguar as having acted with full premeditation. In the Amazon and Guiana forests, jaguars will enter shallow pools in order to catch the large fish known as pirarucu or arapaima, which can reach a length of up to 4 m (13 ft) and a weight of 200 kg (450 lb).

It may seem strange that a predator so well equipped as the jaguar—with a dentition as big as that of a small lion, with an enormously muscular neck and big, powerful paws—should feed largely on small wild pigs, large rodents, and fish. South America, however, is not a continent teeming with big game. There are no herds of antelopes or zebra, no buffaloes or gaur. Of the indigenous deer, most species are small, and the few big ones—such as the swamp deer and the pampas deer—live in small troops. The tapir, the largest South American ungulate, is an animal of solitary habits. As far as the regions inhabited by the jaguar are concerned, the peccaries and the capybaras are the only mammals encountered in really large numbers.

It must be remembered that the jaguar is a comparatively recent immigrant into South America, a continent which, for about 60 million years, from early Palaeocene to late Pliocene, was completely cut off from the rest of the world. In the isolation of this huge land mass, there evolved a fauna different from that of any other continent, with carnivorous, sabre-toothed marsupials, giant ground sloths, giant armadillos, with rodents the size of rhinoceroses and strange ungulates such as the long-nosed *Macrauchenia* and hippopotamus-like *Toxodon*. When the Isthmus of Panama came into being, linking the two Americas, it formed a bridge over which some of the South American animals—ground sloths, giant armadillos, and opossums—migrated north to mix with a very different fauna, closely allied to that of Eurasia. In course of the Pleistocene, however, North American animals, perhaps driven by the recurrent glaciations, traversed that same land-bridge into South America, and among them there were such predators as sabre-toothed tigers, pumas, and jaguars, which had hitherto preyed upon ungulates well used to their presence, forced, of course, to pay their tribute, but not to the extent of being wiped out. The large animals of South America, on the other hand, were unable to stand up to carnivores of such high efficiency, and many of them went into a steady decline. What the big cats had started was probably finished by man, entering South America from the north at the end of the Pleistocene. Thus it came about that the jaguar, fitted out like the lion and the tiger for killing large ungulates, eventually had to content itself with comparatively small game such as peccaries and capybaras.

Man may have wiped out the last ground sloths and giant armadillos, but many thousands of years later, with the advent of European settlement, it was man who introduced a whole set of ungulates hitherto unrepresented in South America, and thus provided the jaguars with an abundance of large prey very easy to kill. It is hardly surprising that from Argentina to Mexico, wherever the country was suitable for ranching, the big cats took to decimating the herds of domestic stock. In Rengger's time, the inhabitants of Paraguay complained bitterly of their depredations. Bulls were rarely attacked, but the losses in calves, heifers, cows, horses, and mules were heavy. Azara had stated that jaguars killed these animals by breaking their necks, but Rengger could not confirm this, either by direct observation or through examining kills. Large animals, he found, had their throats bitten, small ones were killed by a bite in the back of the neck.

The sudden influx of ungulates probably brought about a considerable increase in the numbers of jaguars. Rengger thought that the big cats were the most common in the regions of Buenos Aires, Uruguay, Entre Rios, and Paraguay, where the plains were literally covered with enormous and rather negligently guarded herds of cattle.

In course of time, ranching spread north, up the Rio Paraguay and into the "pantanal" country of southwestern Mato Grosso. When the Roosevelts visited this area, they found jaguars so abundant that Kermit Roosevelt later wrote: "In the vast marshlands of the Mato Gross where I hunted jaguar with my father there was a better opportunity of coming across them in the open as one does lion in Africa." This remark, astonishing to the present-day reader, not only gives an idea of the number of "tigres," but also shows how secretive the lions in Africa had become during the first decade of the century.

Even though some Mato Grosso ranchers were said to lose up to 6000 head of cattle a year, it would be very wrong to imagine all the jaguars of the region indulging in one vast orgy of stock killing. Predators have a very strong tendency to stick to the prey they are used to, and in the area where the Roosevelts hunted for the American Museum of Natural History, there was so much game that the domestic animals were little molested by the ordinary jaguars who might just kill a calf now and then. The confirmed cattle killers were mostly old males. Roosevelt did, however, hear of a neighbouring ranch where the jaguars lived almost exclusively on horses and cattle. Krieg, like Roosevelt, found old, fat jaguars with blunted teeth to be the main offenders as far as domestic stock was concerned.

Until the day some wretched fashion designer thought of coats made from the skins of spotted cats, jaguars were mainly killed because of the damage done to livestock. They were invariably hunted with dogs and could, as a rule, be shot without much trouble once they had been brought to bay against a bush or rock or up a tree. "El tigre" is generally far less bold and aggressive than the leopard, but while some individuals are excessively timid, others will put up a fight when cornered. In the pantanales, especially between the Rio San Lorenzo and the Paraguay, where the boldest jaguars are said to occur, the ranchers used to employ professional hunters—called "tigreros"—to deal with known cattle killers. Operating in very difficult country covered with tall grass and tangled jungle thickets, these "tigreros," mostly Indians and half-breeds, were for a long time inclined to put more trust in a stout spear than on a fire-arm. A man with a gun, they argued, might not have another chance if the first shot failed to drop the "tigre." Frequently, too, the charge came so fast and out of such thick cover that the hunter was knocked down before being able to shoot. The spearman, however, could present his weapon in such a way that the attacking jaguar impaled itself. This, at least, was the theory—but accidents did happen, even to very experienced "tigreros." An excellent account of spear-hunting has been given by Sasha Siemel, probably the only European really to master this dangerous form of sport.

In attacking a human being, a jaguar usually rises up on its hind legs, so as to be able to reach the head with its paws, and Richard Spruce knew a man who had been literally scalped in such an encounter. He lived at Santarém, Brazil, in 1850, and always wore a black skull cap, his head still being very tender. Casual meetings between man and jaguar generally pass off as the one described by Alfred Russel Wallace, though there have been instances of a cat following a human intruder, either out of curiosity or to make sure that he left its hunting range.

Most authorities regard unprovoked attacks on man as extremely rare. Edward W. Nelson, for instance, wrote of the jaguar of Mexico:

> During the years I spent in its country, mainly in the open, I made careful inquiry without hearing of a single case where one had attacked human beings. So far as I could learn, it had practically the same shy and cowardly nature as the mountain lion. Despite this, the natives throughout its tropical home have a great fear of "el tigre", as I saw evidence repeatedly in Mexico. Apparently this fear is based wholly on its strength and potential ability to harm man if it so desires.

Leo E. Miller, with a long and very extensive experience of travel and natural history collecting in South America, expressed himself astonished at the abundance of jaguars and their harmlessness under ordinary circumstances, but added: "At times they will attack human beings. At one of the rubber camps we were shown the skin of a recently killed animal which had stalked a two-year old child at play not far from the hut; the mother, a negress, seeing the animal in time, attacked it with a 'machete' and killed it."

Rengger thought that jaguars were shy and retiring in practically uninhabited regions, but bold and sometimes aggressive where they had become used to the presence of man, particularly along the big rivers with their heavy boat traffic. Both he and Darwin heard of a number of accidents on the banks of the Rio Paraná and Rio Paraguay, the victims most often being wood-cutters and boatmen.

The classic story of an unprovoked attack goes back to 1825 and refers to a jaguar driven by high water to seek shelter in the chapel of the Convent of San Fernando at Santa Fe. Two monks, entering one after the other, were killed, while a third, who came to see what was the matter, only escaped with great difficulty. The animal was then locked in and shot. There are several versions of the incident, some authors adding the information that it was a Senator Iriondo, on a visit to the convent, who had the doors of the sacristy locked and called in a hunter. One also gets the impression that the tale—like the traditional fisherman's tale—got bigger and better as time went by, with the jaguar's score increasing to three and even four monks.

It may have been these inconsistencies which made somebody go to Santa Fe, New Mexico, in order to do a thorough check-up on the story. And what did our investigator find? There was no Convent of San Fernando at Santa Fe, and there never had been, nor were there any records of monks or lay brothers in New Mexico at the period in question. As for Senator Iriondo, the local historians declared him to be entirely fictitious. Another piece of debunking had thus been brought to a satisfactory conclusion, and one more famous story, quoted in practically every account of the jaguar for over a hundred years, had turned out to be nothing but a hoary old legend. There was only one thing wrong with this very elegant piece of work. The investigator had been out in his reckoning by about five thousand miles—he should have gone to Santa Fe, Argentina, and not to Santa Fe, New Mexico.

The first European to record the story of the church-going jaguar was, in fact, none other than J. R. Rengger, who arrived in Santa Fe a few days after the event. He, incidentally, mentions only one person as killed by the animal. Darwin heard the tale a few years later, when travelling around Argentina and included it in his famous book on the voyage of the *Beagle*.

Man-killing, in fairly rare occasions, can be taken as proved, but what about man-eating? There was talk along the Rio Paraguay in Azara's and Rengger's times of certain jaguars having taken to man-eating, but there seems to have been little substance to these stories, and they can probably be put down as mere rumours. Sasha Siemel makes it quite clear that the jaguars he was hunting professionally were cattle killers and not man-eaters. On the Rio Putumayo, de Wavrin heard of jaguars occasionally entering huts and carrying off human victims.

Even though jaguars may, now and then, snatch away and eat a child or kill a lonely wanderer, more or less in mistake for other game, none seem ever to have taken to hunting humans for food systematically, as tigers, lions, and leopards will occasionally do, with the one, rather vaguely reported exception of an animal on the west coast of Mexico, which apparently killed twelve people before it was shot. No details are given, and we do not know for certain whether the victims were eaten or not. The jaguar in question could have been either crippled or rabid.

After killing a small prey, a jaguar will devour it at once, skin, bones, and all. Of a large animal, such as a cow or a horse, it makes a copious meal, feeding, according to Rengger, in a crouching position, its paws on the kill, and chewing off piece after piece with its head bent sideways. It apparently does not touch the intestines. As a rule, the "tigre" then resorts to a hiding-place not very far away, settles down for a digestive rest, and returns for a second meal the following night. Some individuals, however, having become excessively wary through frequent contacts with man, will abandon the carcass after having fed on it once.

If the kill has been made right out in the open, the jaguar usually drags it into the nearest thicket, and it is on such occasions that some idea can be gained of the big cat's muscular powers. Colonel Candido Rondon, one of the members of Theodore Roosevelt's Brazilian expedition, knew of a horse that had been dragged for over a mile, and A. S. Leopold refers to carcasses of 200 kg (450 lb) being moved over distances of 2 or 3 km (avg. 1.6 mi). Rengger quite rightly expresses disbelief in the famous story, reported by Azara, of a jaguar swimming across a river with a horse in its mouth, but he admits that after having killed one of two horses or mules harnessed together, the "tigre" occasionally drags the living animal away with the dead one. The kill is taken into cover partly for shade and security, partly, however, to safeguard it from vultures, which appear as quickly as they do in Africa and India. Cherrie tells of locating jaguar kills in the pantanal country by watching the vultures, in exactly the same way as lion kills are found on the plains of East Africa.

Jaguars have long been known to be solitary and more or less territorial in their habits. "During most of the year," Rengger stated, "each jaguar lives alone within a certain area." Similarly, Theodore Roosevelt wrote of the jaguar of the southern Mato Grosso: "In these marshes, each jaguar had a wide irregular range and travelled a good deal, perhaps only passing a day or two in a given locality, perhaps spending a week where game was plentiful."

The actual extent of a jaguar's home range varies greatly according to habitat and geographical latitude. From his own observations and from those reported by some of his friends, Jack O'Connor came to the conclusion that male jaguars in northwestern Mexico spend their entire lives within home ranges with a radius of about 16 to 32 km (10 to 20 mi). He was, however, told by Dale Lee, an experienced jaguar hunter, that in South America one male could be found ruling over a large area containing several adult females and two or three immature males.

Young males, not yet established in a home range, and old ones, which have been deprived of theirs, will, of course, roam far and wide, covering hundreds of miles and sometimes making appearances far outside regularly inhabited jaguar country.

Jaguars are sure to delineate their home ranges by placing scent marks, but very little is yet known of their territorial behaviour. One form of marking, however, was recorded a very long time ago. Darwin wrote of the jaguar:

> One day, when hunting on the banks of the Uruguay, I was shown certain trees, to which these animals constantly recur for the purpose, as it is said, of sharpening their claws. I saw three well known trees; in front the bark was worn smooth as if by the breast of the animal, and on each side there were sharp scratches, or rather grooves, extending in an oblique line, nearly a yard in length. The scars were of different ages. A common method of ascertaining whether a jaguar is in the neighbourhood is to examine these trees.

Darwin later was the first to suggest that tree scratching might have something to do with the demarcation of an animal's home range.

Travellers and naturalists speak of the jaguar as a decidedly noisy animal, whose voice is often heard at night. Jack O'Connor likens its roar to the last phase of a lion's roar, and this fits in very well with the descriptions given by Rengger, Nelson, and others, as a sequence of five or six guttural notes, something like "Uh, uh, uh, uh, uh, uh." The sound carries far—to half an hour's distance, Rengger says—and besides being a mating call it could well have a certain significance in territorial marking.

In India, some hunters have acquired the ability to attract the tiger by imitating its voice, and similar practices are current in various parts of the jaguar's range. Nelson wrote:

> In one locality, on the Pacific Coast of Guerrero, I found that the hardier natives had an interesting method of hunting the "tigre" during the mating period. At such times, the male has a habit of leaving its lair near the head of a small canyon in the foothills early in the evening and following down the canyon for some distance, at intervals uttering a subdued roar. On moonlight nights at this time the hunter places an expert native with a short wooden trumpet near the mouth of the canyon to imitate the "tigre's" call as soon as it is heard, and to repeat the cry at proper intervals. After placing the caller, the hunter ascends the canyon several hundred yards and, gun in hand, awaits the appearance of the animal. The natives have many amusing tales of the sudden exit of untried hunters when the approaching animal unexpectedly uttered its roar at close quarters.

Jaguars growl and mew, and when cornered by dogs they will snarl. On such occasions von Colditz also heard a sound which he rendered as "huarr."

Over most of its area of distribution, the jaguar's reproduction is not tied to any definite season. In the utmost north of its range, however, mating usually takes place in early spring, perhaps even in January, while in Paraguay, according to Rengger, there is a mating season in August and September. At no other time, he says, can the roar of the jaguar be heard quite so permanently. Several males may pursue one and the same female, and this can lead to some fighting, with the weaker contestants quickly giving way to the dominant one. Mating itself is a fairly noisy affair, possibly with some exchange of blows between male and female. Rengger was led to believe that the sexes did not stay together long, up to four or five weeks at the utmost. He did stress, however, that during that time male and female never hunted together.

The gestation period varies from 93 to 105 days, and the litter consists of from one to four cubs, which are dropped in some dense thicket, in a cavity under a partly uprooted tree, under a river-bank, or among rocks. Born blind, they are about 40.6 cm (16 in) in length, weigh 5.4 kg (12 lb) and have a rather long, coarse pelage, buff in colour and marked with large, black spots which may have faint indications of pale centres.

During the first days the mother hardly leaves the den at all, and the slightest disturbance will cause her to carry the cubs to another shelter. They are said to begin following her about when approximately six weeks old, remaining hidden in thick cover while she is after game. The youngsters take on the colouration of the adults at about seven months, and at the age of nine or ten months they have the appearance of being almost half grown. They probably stay with their mother for about two years and may be fully adult at three years. According to mammalogist George G. Goodwin there is some evidence that the male occasionally takes an interest in its progeny and even helps to provide the cubs with food. From all that has been written about jaguars, however, such a paternal concern for the family must be considered no less exceptional than it probably is in the leopard. Goodwin himself says that the father is not allowed into the nursery while the cubs are small, and de Wavrin writes of the mother protecting her young from the male.

A captive female, just over three years old, gave birth to her first cub on November 10, mated again between December 23 and January 3, and produced a second litter on April 11. Reproduction is hardly likely to occur at such a quick rate in the wild, but Hans Krieg once shot a female that contained three tiny embryos and had a youngster at foot estimated to be about nine months old. She would thus have had a new litter with her present cub only about a year old, but this may have been an exceptional occurrence.

Jaguars have been known to live in captivity for up to twenty-two years. This fits in with a statement made by one of Rengger's Paraguayan friends to the effect that the big cats could attain an age of over twenty years. Rengger himself was not prepared to accept this, and, as far as life in the wild was concerned, he was probably right. "In inhabited areas," he wrote, "there will not be much of a chance for a jaguar to die a natural death. Yet very aged animals are occasionally killed. Four hours out of Asunción, M. Longchamp shot an old female near a farm house, with a mangy skin and worn teeth. She had already lost the hindmost cheekteeth of both upper jaws."

According to Colonel P. H. Fawcett, the explorer, a man living near Rurrenabaque in Bolivia had a fairly large jaguar which he allowed to wander about the house like a dog. Being something of a practical joker, he used to take his pet out along the trail to the town and waited for travellers on muleback. At a signal, the jaguar leaped out from the bushes, and the mule would shy, usually throwing off his rides, whose terror at finding himself face to face with a "tigre" can be imagined.

Keeping jaguars about the house seems to be an old Latin-American custom, for in course of his travels in Paraguay and along the Rio Paraná, Rengger came to many farm-houses where there was a cub tied to a tree in the court-yard with a piece of string or a leather strap. After about three years, these captives, especially those of male sex, tended to become dangerous, and Rengger witnessed an incident in which a girl had her arm injured by a jaguar with filed-down teeth.

Some people tried to make their "pets" more amenable by castrating them, but the unfortunate animals became very fat and did not survive long. Rengger himself brought up a few "tigres," feeding them on milk and cooked meat, and while he was able to implement the observations he had made in the wild, he found it impossible to get the animals into a really tame and affectionate state. Many years later, Hans Krieg had exactly the same experience, finding that his bottle-reared jaguars remained rather surly and irritable. In zoological gardens young caught individuals will, according to Petzsch, get "fairly tame." Jaguars breed from time to time in captivity, but not as often and regularly as lions and leopards.

Cheetah, Hunting Leopard
Acinonyx jubatus
(SCHREBER 1776)

The cheetah, as St. George Mivart pointed out, differs much more from all other cats than any two other cats differ from one another. It is the most stream-lined and long-legged of felines, built entirely for speed. Not for the cheetah the stealthy, patient stalk, the close approach, the sudden spring—in swift pursuit, it catches up with its prey and bowls it over while running flat out.

The cheetah's ancestors must have diverged from the main stem of feline evolution a long time back, most probably at some point during the Pliocene, for the giant cheetah of the early Pleistocene of southern Europe, India, and China was modelled on the same lines as the present-day species. Late Villafranchian specimens show a distinct reduction in size, while late Pleistocene cheetahs from China are almost undistinguishable from modern animals.

The fact that cheetahs could easily be tamed and trained for hunting was realized at a very early date. On a Mesopotamian seal from the third millennium B.C. can be seen an animal led on a leash which is thought to be a cheetah, possibly with a hood over its head. Egyptian tombs and rock-temples contain excellent representations of tame cheetahs, and although they seem to have been in use since the Third Dynasty, the great number of Eighteenth and Nineteenth Dynasty paintings show them at that time almost to have rivalled dogs in their popularity as hunting companions. The Assyrians utilized cheetahs, and so did the Minoans, who probably imported them from Egypt.

In Syria and Palestine the Crusaders saw gazelles hunted with the aid of cheetahs, which they usually referred to as "leopards," and a fifteenth-century king of Armenia is reported to have had a "pack" of a hundred of these animals.

Hunting with cheetahs is usually associated with Eastern countries, but at times this exotic sport enjoyed great popularity among European nobility. There was practically no Italian Renaissance court without hunting leopards, and in 1479, the Duke of Ferrara presented one of his "guepards" to King Louis XI of France, who thanked him most warmly for the much appreciated gift. As shown on numerous paintings, woodcuts, and tapestries, the animals were carried out into the hunting field on horse-back, perched on a pillow behind the handler. They were then released to run down hares and roe-deer.

After conquering the Duchy of Milan, Louis XII took home Lodovico Sforza's "pack" of cheetahs and ran them in the park of the Chateau d'Amboise. Francis I, who can be said to have introduced the glitter of Renaissance Italy into France, delighted in hunting with cheetahs, and so did his son and successor, Henry II.

An Englishman, Fynes Moryson, who visited Prague at the end of the sixteenth century, saw two tame cheetahs of which he wrote: "They were of a yellow colour, spotted with blacke, the head partly like a cat, the body like a greyhound, and when the huntman went abroad, they leapt up behind him, sitting upon the horse like a dog on the hinter parts, being so swift in running, as they could easily kill a hart."

Leopold I, Emperor of Austria, tried to revive the hunting of hares with cheetahs around 1700, but the sport was considered as too sanguinary and found no acclaim. Akbar the Great kept countless cheetahs for coursing gazelles, antelopes, and deer, and Abu Fazil, his chronicler, gives an amusing account of one particular hunt:

> It chanced that they loosed a special cheetah called "Chitr Najan" at a deer. Suddenly there appeared in front of them a ravine which was twenty-five yards broad. The deer leapt into the air to the height of a spear and a half and conveyed itself across. The cheetah in its eagerness took the same course, cleared the ravine and seized the deer. On beholding this astonishing occurrence the spectators raised a cry of amazement, and there was great rejoicing and astonishment. The Emperor raised the rank of that cheetah and made him chief of the cheetahs. He also ordered that as a special honour and as a pleasure to men, a drum should be beaten in front of the cheetah.

It was realized long ago that cheetahs captured adult were more easily trained than those taken as cubs, and Akbar had his animals caught in pitfalls with trapdoors. He trained many of them himself, in a much shorter time, according to Abu Fazil, than was usually required. In India, cheetahs remained a status symbol of nobility until quite recent times, and there was a certain class of men who devoted themselves entirely to the trapping and training of these animals.

Considering how long it has been known to Europeans, it seems strange that Linnaeus did not list the cheetah in the tenth edition of his *Systema Naturae,* published in 1758 and regarded as the basis of scientific nomenclature. It was Schreber who named it *Felis jubatus* in 1776. Naturalists soon discovered the cheetah to deviate in many ways from other cats, and Joshua Brookes, who had an anatomical and zoological museum in London, changed the generic name to *Acinonyx* in 1828.

The pupils are round, and the hyoid is fully ossified as in the so-called "small" cats. The skull is light and thin-boned, high and broad, shortened in its facial part, wide behind the postorbital process and so very convex in the frontal area that it appears domed, raised much higher above the muzzle than in any other cat. The canines are less well developed than those of the leopard. The post-canine spaces, so characteristic of other felids, are lacking, with the anterior upper premolars crowded in between the canines and the second premolars. The upper carnassial is large and very sharp-edged, having the inner cusp greatly reduced in size.

Characteristics. Leopard and cheetah are of about the same length, but the latter stands considerably higher on long, sinewy legs. The body, although deep-chested, is slimmer than the leopard's; the head is smaller and more roundish. The tail is of more than half the length of head and body. The ears are short, broad, and rounded. According to W. Emcke, who studied the young cheetahs born in Krefeld (Germany) Zoo, cubs are able, during the first fifteen weeks, to retract their claws like any other cat. The claws then become partly retractile but the main peculiarity of the cheetah's digits is the absence of the cutaneous lobes which, in other cats, act as claw sheaths. The claws thus remain bared all the time and also show in the animal's spoor. They are blunt and only slightly curved, except for that of the thumb, which is large, sharp, and well curved. With the interdigital webs greatly reduced, the toes can be spread widely. The pads are hard.

The coat is coarse, its colour varying from yellowish grey and tawny to isabelline and bright rufous fawn, paling somewhat on the belly and on the insides of the limbs. Upper lip, chin, and throat are buffy white. The markings consist of round black spots which are not arranged in rosettes. A black line runs from the anterior corner of the eye to the upper lip, a less well defined line or a row of spots from the hinder corner of the eye to below the ears. The backs of the ears are black, tawny at the base and on the margins. The tail is spotted above, with the markings merging into more or less imperfect rings on the posterior part. The tip is white.

Young cubs have the head, neck, and back covered by a long woolly mane of light bluish grey colour. Underneath this mantle, the coat is smoky grey or blackish, indistinctly spotted black. The cloak is reduced within ten weeks, and there remains only a slight mane of wiry hairs on the back of the neck, which, in fully adult specimens, becomes practically invisible. At the age of about three months the colour of the coat turns to tawny with well-defined spots.

Taxonomists have described a number of subspecies, of which eight—two in Asia and six in Africa—are considered valid. There was considerable excitement in zoological circles during the 1920s, when some orange-coloured cheetahs with large spots that tended to merge into longitudinal lines were shot in Rhodesia. Pocock regarded them as representatives of a different species, which he named *Acinonyx rex,* the king cheetah. They are now thought to be mere mutations, analogous to the cases of nigrism and abundism observed in leopards. There have been rumours of "king cheetahs" being seen in the northern parts of the Kruger National Park, and the authorities of the Transvaal Museum managed to locate the skin of one that had been shot near Messina in 1940.

In a letter to the editor of *Nature in East Africa,* H. F. Stoneham reported coming across a black cheetah in the Trans-Nzoia District of Kenya in 1925. Vesey Fitzgerald saw a melanistic individual in what is now Zambia, in the company of a normally coloured animal. Albinism seems to be exceedingly rare, but Jahangir, the "naturalist on the Mogul throne," mentioned a white cheetah that was brought to him at Agra, the first and only one he ever saw. "Its spots which are usually black, were of blue colour," he wrote, "and the whiteness of the body was also inclined to bluishness." A record of incipient albinism has come from Beaufort West.

Measurements. The shoulder height of a cheetah is about 76 to 83 cm (avg. 31 in). Theodore Roosevelt and E. Heller give the following measurements for two East African males: head and body, 1.295 m (4.2 ft) and 1.244 m (4 ft); tail, 73.6 cm (19 in) and 77.4 cm (30 in). Meinertzhagen recorded a Kenya female with a total length of 2.36 m (7.7 ft). A male from eastern Transvaal, measured by Vaughan Kirby, had a total length of 2.03 m (6.7 ft) between pegs, 2.31 m (7.6 ft) along curves, and a tail length of 83.8 cm (33 in). Kirby estimated the average total length of males in that area—over curves—to be about 2.13 m (7 ft), of which the tail would take up 78.7 cm (31 in).

Weights vary from about 40 to 72 kg (avg. 126 lb). Females are somewhat smaller and slimmer.

The measurements of Indian cheetahs as given by Jerdon and others do not differ materially from those of African specimens.

Distribution. On the African continent, cheetahs could originally be found in all suitable regions from the Cape to the Mediterranean. In Asia, the distribution of the species extended through Palestine, Syria, the northern parts of the Arabian peninsula, Iraq, Iran, southern Turkmenistan, Afghanistan, and Baluchistan to Sind, Punjab, Rajputana western Bengal, and central India, south to the Deccan and possibly Mysore. It was never found north of the Ganges, nor east of Bengal. According to Sterndale it was most common at Jaipur and in Hyderabad.

In a revised edition of Sterndale's book, published in 1929, Frank Finn pointed out that the cheetahs used for hunting by Indian princes were now all imported from Africa. He quoted Colonel J. C. Founthorpe as stating: "There is no doubt that the cheetah is now very rare indeed. General Sir Afzul Ul Mulk of Hyderabad told me that there are no cheetahs in the Hyderabad territories—a very large area. A few survive in the Berar districts of the Central Provinces . . . Rajhmar Sadul Singh of Bikaner shot three cheetah out of a bunch of five, or more, which he came across a year or so ago." Frank Finn added: "It is evidently high time that this poor animal were protected, as the lion is in the Gir forest."

Stockley, writing in 1928, regarded the Indian cheetah as very scarce everywhere. It has not been reliably recorded since 1948, and was declared as extinct in 1952. The species is probably extinct in Turkmenistan, where it always was very rare and local, but from Iran comes the good news that cheetahs are holding their own in the eastern deserts, their numbers being estimated as possibly exceeding two hundred.

Harrison considers the cheetah as probably extinct in Arabia, there having been no reliable records since 1950, when four were killed by Aramco employees, one in northern Saudi Arabia, three others near the Saudi, Jordan, and Iraq intersection. The species was last reported from Kuwait in 1949. Writing in 1935, F. S. Bodenheimer mentioned it as still occurring in the Negeb, in Transjordania, and in the Palestinian mountains. He saw many skins, sold by Bedouins from Beersheba. It may have hung on in Jordan and in the Negeb until 1948 or 1949, and there were fairly recent reports of tracks having been seen in the latter area.

In May 1967 a cheetah was shot while stalking sheep in the desert, 15 km (9 mi) north of the 125-km (78 mi) marker on the Cairo-Alexandria road. This incident induced Harry Hoogstraal and several of his associates to search for other recent Egyptian records, and they came across rumours of one having been shot from aboard an oil company helicopter in 1954. That same year, however, another was definitely killed near a checkpoint on the Sidi Barrani-Salûm road. In 1964, a cheetah was reported from the southern edge of the Qattara Depression. The Qattara area may, in fact, be the cheetah's last refuge in the country, for tracks have been noticed in its vicinity on various occasions, and the Bedouins questioned by Hoogstraal were positive about the species still occurring north of the Qara oasis.

Cheetahs have been reported from southern Tunisia and Tibesti fairly recently, but as far as Morocco is concerned, Panouse regards their presence as doubtful. During the 1920s, Strohl reported a dozen captures near Zanaga, while Cabrera found the animal to be well known to the troopers of the Ifni desert police.

In 1934, Shortridge stated the cheetah to be almost, if not completely exterminated in the Cape Province, in Orange Free State, Natal, and in the southern parts of Transvaal, but widely distributed in Botswana and South-West Africa. It has since been reintroduced in the Umfolozi and Hluhluwe reserves of Natal and is reported still flourishing in South-West Africa. In 1960, numbers in the Kruger National Park were estimated at 136, and when I visited this reserve in 1961, Dr. Pienaar, the resident biologist, told me that the species had declined so greatly in recent years as to cause serious worry with regard to its future. One of the reasons for this he thought to be the change of habitat, too much burning having destroyed the open grass lands and brought about a considerable increase of bush. In a radio broadcast from Johannesburg a couple of years ago, the number of cheetahs in the Kruger National Park was stated to be around two hundred. Efforts are apparently being made to strengthen the population by introducing animals from South-West Africa.

Financed by the International Fur Trade Federation, Norman Myers carried out a survey of the cheetah's present status in East Africa. He arrived at the conclusion that the species is already in trouble and will probably be much more so in the near future. This, of course, raises the question: What do we know about the cheetah's former occurrence in the East African countries? The information Paul Matschie of the Berlin Museum was able to give in his writings on the mammals of German East Africa—now Tanzania—was scanty in the extreme, for the naturalist-explorers Boehm and Stuhlmann, on whose notes his work was mainly based, never met with it at all. Two skins in the museum came from Usandawi and Ussukuma respectively, areas situated in the northern part of the country, and there were reports of British sportsmen having encountered cheetahs in the immediate vicinity of Kilimanjaro. The Serengeti Plains, where the species is fairly common, were of course hardly known at that time. In Uganda, the cheetah used to be sparingly distributed through the eastern and northern parts only, and it has now disappeared from many places due to rapid increase of settlement and cultivation. For the present, R. M. Bere reports it as almost, if not entirely, confined to Karamoja.

As far as Kenya is concerned, Sir Frederick Jackson put it down in 1894 as by no means uncommon "on the Kapiti and Athi Plains," while C. H. Stigand reported it in 1913 as "found in small parties on most of the plains of British East Africa," enumerating the Athi Plains, the Uaso Nyiro, the vicinity of Nyeri and the Tana River east of the Ithanga Hills as places where he saw it. Roosevelt and Heller called it a "fairly common species in East Africa." Schillings, who camped for long periods in what is now the Amboseli Reserve, said: "The cheetah, too, occurs in Masailand, but is very rare, and I have only seen it twice."

Writing between the two wars, A. Blainey Percival stated: "Coming abroad by day as his habit is, the cheetah falls easy prey to the gun; hence it is becoming very scarce. At one time cheetahs were common about 9 miles out of Nairobi, but they have been nearly exterminated and few remain. Not many years back I saw a couple near the old Nine Mile Camp."

One is thus left with a definite impression that cheetahs were always local and never very numerous—certainly not as common as lions and leopards.

Today, Nairobi National Park probably has the highest population density of cheetahs anywhere in the world. In the course of about twenty safaris undertaken during the last five years, I have encountered the species regularly in the Amboseli Reserve and in the Serengeti National Park, fairly frequently in the Mara Reserve and occasionally in the Tsavo National Park and in the Samburu Reserve. I have also seen one during a short visit to the Tarangire National Park. Thanks to national parks and game reserves, the cheetah may actually be more common today than it was during the period Percival wrote about.

Habits. The cheetah is an inhabitant of dry, open areas, such as steppes, clayey deserts, semi-deserts, grass lands, orchard-like savannahs, acacia scrub, and light woodlands. Dense forests are never entered, nor does the species occur in thick bush. It is predominantly diurnal, though said occasionally to hunt in bright moonshine. Early sportsmen and naturalists all referred to it as being so shy that its habits could only be studied with great difficulty.

Today's tourists are disappointed if they do not get close-up photographs of cheetahs in the Serengeti National Park. Audrey Moore, who lived in the area for several years between the two wars, only had occasional glimpses of a cheetah family and never obtained any pictures at all. "The grown female, as is the case with most cheetahs," she wrote, "was so timid that it was impossible to approach her." She closed her chapter on cheetahs with the following words: "Of all the bush animals, except perhaps eland, they remain shy and aloof, living by their speed, running down small buck, and stalking ground birds, harmless to man and the larger game, living out their lives quietly; beautiful lithe creatures that are a joy to watch in the freedom of their native bush."

In a book describing his first East African expedition, published in 1924, Martin Johnson captioned one of his pictures: "A tame cheetah—the wild ones went too fast for the camera." On my first visits to the Serengeti National Park in 1949 and 1954, my experiences were the same as Martin Johnson's—the cheetahs "went too fast for the camera." The few which at that time could occasionally be encountered in Nairobi National Park also bounded away the moment they caught sight of a car. During the second half of the fifties, however, cheetahs in Nairobi National Park, in the Amboseli Reserve, and on the Serengeti Plains began to tame down in a most remarkable manner. As more and more families grew up in the various reserves, the youngsters were the ones who first lost the old fear of motor cars, and in 1964 the cubs of one Nairobi Park litter started to come up to cars and to sniff at them with great curiosity.

In order fully to illustrate this incredible change in cheetah behaviour, I shall here describe—from one of my notebooks—an encounter with one especially tame family which lived in Nairobi National Park at the end of the 1960s. On the occasion I am writing about, the three cubs were twenty-two months old, but had not yet separated from their mother. When we came across them, they obviously had had a meal a short time before, their faces still showing traces of blood, but the mother seemed to be fully aware of their healthy appetites, for she paid considerable attention to some hartebeests, among which there could be seen one or two calves. It looked as if she might hunt again, and several cars congregated near by, their occupants hoping to witness the chase.

The female did, in fact, go through the motions of a preliminary stalk, but the hartebeests either spotted her or got her scent. As they gradually drew off, the cheetah mother relaxed and sat down. With the tension of an impending hunt gone, the cubs began to play, running after each other. They were known to regular visitors of Nairobi National Park as the "roof-rack climbing cheetahs," and it did not take long for them to dash toward a sedan and to jump onto it. Two settled down on the roof, their tails hanging down outside the windows, while the third stood on the hood, putting its nose against the wind-screen and pawing the wiper.

From time to time, the three had fun and games all over the car, pushing one another around and jumping off and on, while cameras were clicking on all sides. Suddenly they left the sedan, tore around the cars as if playing hide-and-seek, and then decided to climb upon a Land-Rover that had just arrived. They only stopped their play when the mother began to walk away. As soon as she had gone about 50 to 70 m (avg. 195 ft), they ran after her. One of these youngsters now has a family of her own, and she still occasionally jumps onto a car. No doubt her cubs will begin imitating her in the near future. It certainly is very much easier to observe cheetahs today than it was in Audrey Moore's time.

Cheetahs are usually encountered singly, in couples, or in family parties which may consist of a female and her cubs or of youngsters just having left their mother. Two adult males occasionally team up and roam around in company for a while. Population density has been estimated at one cheetah per 72 km² (28 mi²) in the Kruger National Park, at one per 102 to 127 km² (avg. 44 mi²) on the Serengeti Plain. In Nairobi National Park, which has a surface of 114 km² (44 mi²), twenty-five to twenty-six cheetahs can at times be counted.

In the Serengeti National Park the movements of cheetahs depend very much on those of their preferred prey, the Thomson's gazelle. A female observed by Schaller shifted her hunting ground by almost 12 km (7 mi) just as soon as her cubs were mobile enough. She stayed within a range of about 10 km² (4 mi²) for one and a half months and then moved on again. Females bringing up families in Nairobi National Park are much more sedentary, generally remaining within a certain area until the youngsters are able to fend for themselves. The borders of these hunting ranges are very ill defined, however, and there is a considerable amount of overlap. McLaughlin, who made a study of the Nairobi Park cheetahs, estimated the ranges used by two families to cover 82 (32 mi²) and 76 km² (29 mi²), respectively. Two males were found to roam over 102 km² (39 mi²).

I have always found males to be of rather vagrant habits, much less attached to a home range than male lions usually are. Schaller stated that he had no evidence of any kind of territorial defence, and I can say the same after having watched cheetahs in Nairobi National Park—and elsewhere—for a great many years. They have a tendency toward mutual avoidance, but this operates in a peaceful and very matter-of-fact way on sighting each other, perhaps also on coming across scent marks. There is a certain amount of spraying, although this habit seems to be less developed than in leopards and especially in lions.

As might perhaps be expected of an animal with no marked territorial or social habits, the cheetah does not greatly indulge in vocalization. I have never heard anything resembling a roar, though I have heard cheetahs moan on catching sight of lions. The female uses a chirping sound to call her cubs, which quite often utter a birdlike twitter. A fairly big youngster coming back after chasing a hare called out "puits-puits," and the mother answered with a low "ya." When a female and a cub are licking each other, they often purr, deeply and continuously, and on such occasions there may also be a few very catlike "meaows."

A big male, which walked as if he were following a scent track of sorts, gave vent to a series of calls best rendered as "grr-keow-grrr-keow-yaow-yaow-yaow-grrr-yaow-grrr yaow-kyaow, kyaow, kyaow." The "kyaows" were brought forth with considerable vigour, as could be seen from the contracting of the flanks. It was not possible to follow this cheetah for any distance, but I have a strong suspicion that it might have been after a female.

Cheetahs have large, lively, and very alert eyes. Living in open country they spot their prey a long distance away, and one gets the impression that hearing and smell are of a very minor importance as far as hunting is concerned. According to an observation recorded by E. W. Temple-Boreham, the well-known warden of the Mara Reserve, a cheetah's nose may, however, be keener than is usually assumed:

> Three cheetahs were seen on the edge of a plain near the Barkitabu area. They were obviously hungry, so it was decided to make the experiment of trying to feed them. Part of a Thomson's gazelle was dragged on the end of a rope tied to the back of a car, and the bait was dragged up wind and past where the cheetahs were sitting. They all appeared to be very interested, and one could see them sniffing the air and getting the scent of the drag—which proves that a cheetah's sense of smell is not as dull as people think. As the kill was slowly dragged past them for the second time, two of the cheetah ran out and one actually grabbed the kill, which was then released. The cheetah concerned carried off his prize to the shade of the nearest tree, where he was joined by his two companions, and they all had a good feed.

Scent probably plays a major part in getting the sexes together at mating time.

Despite its doglike build, the cheetah nevertheless moves with true feline grace and elegance. Cubs are good climbers and often play about on trees. Adults like to jump onto fallen or leaning tree trunks to look around, but it is rare for them to do any real climbing.

The appearance of a cheetah causes more excitement among the inhabitants of the veld than that of a lion. I have seen pied crows and fiscal shrikes swoop down at them with persistence and determination, and the behaviour of other animals is well shown by the following notes jotted down while I watched a cheetah crossing an area literally swarming with game:

> Wildebeests, hartebeests, Thomson's and Grant's gazelles not only stare at it, but follow in its wake. From time to time one group or another wheels around and canters away, only to stop and approach again. Four blackbacked jackals suddenly turn up. One of them barks as it becomes aware of the cheetah, two trot along behind it. The wildebeests and hartebeests snort, while the gazelles eventually take flight. The hartebeests are particularly excited, galloping to and fro, gambolling around. Two crested cranes fly over the cat, land nearby and keep pace with it on foot. They jump with uplifted wings when it once turns towards them. At times a regular procession is moving over the plain—the cheetah in the lead, followed closely by the two jackals, with eight or ten hartebeests forming the main body. The cheetah only loses its "retinue" when it finally crosses a deep valley.

Giraffes pay as much attention to a cheetah as they do to a lion and their behaviour may well give warning to gazelles and impalas which, of course, have a much more limited range of vision than the walking watchtowers.

From my own observations in Nairobi National Park, in the Amboseli Reserve and in the Serengeti National Park, the following animals fall prey to cheetahs: Thomson's gazelles, Grant's gazelles, impala, hartebeest, both calves and adults, wildebeest calves, bushbuck, and hare. I have seen them run, without success, after zebra, wart-hog and bat-eared foxes.

The list compiled by Kruuk and Turner for the Serengeti area is fairly similar to this: adult Thomson's gazelles (52%), young Thomson's gazelles (4%), wildebeest calves (22%), adult hartebeests (4%), hartebeest calves (4%), zebra yearlings (4%), hares (4%). An even greater predominance of Thomson's gazelles is shown in Schaller's list: Thomson's gazelles (91%), hartebeests (4%), Grant's gazelles (2.3%), wildebeests (1.9%), impala (1.1%), hare (1.1%), topi (0.8%), dikdik (0.4%). In the Kruger National Park, impala make up 68% of the prey. The kills found in course of one year, 1959, were enumerated as forty-seven impala, two water-buck, one wildebeest calf, six kudu calves, three wart-hog, one roan calf, and five reed-bucks.

It can thus be said that cheetahs mainly prey upon small- and medium-sized antelopes, on the calves of large antelope, and on the odd zebra foal. They will occasionally overpower an adult hartebeest. Stevenson-Hamilton knew of a bull tsessebi and a bull water-buck being killed, but considered both incidents as exceptional.

I have had many opportunities of observing cheetahs in action. On a recent safari to the Serengeti National Park, I watched a female begin to stalk some Thomson's gazelles the very moment she discovered them. The grass was short, there was no cover of any kind, and she advanced in full view of the thomies, moving slowly, on stiff legs, with her head stretched out in front and held below shoulder level. When she ran from a distance of 90 or 100 m (avg. 312 ft), the gazelles had not yet become aware of her presence. They saw her as she was streaking toward them and fled instantly, but she caught up easily and bowled one over by hitting it on the rump with a forepaw. As her victim went down, she grabbed its throat and was still holding it when we drove up to her. She relinquished her grip about five minutes after she had caught the animal and looked around for a few moments before dragging the carcass to the place where her cubs were waiting.

This was a very typical hunt, with everything going off without the slightest hitch. In dealing with somewhat larger and stronger animals, a cheetah may find it less easy to make a quick kill. In the Amboseli Reserve, we once followed a mother with two about half-grown cubs. She was obviously searching for prey, but this did not prevent her from occasionally joining in the youngsters' games. Suddenly, however, she spied some zebras with a small foal. She froze in her stride, watched for a while, and then stalked forward, while the cubs took cover in a patch of Sodom's apple scrub. She disappeared behind some bushes, and we saw the zebras move off rather nervously, without, however, having spotted her. After a short while they returned, but at the same moment a small herd of Grant's gazelles turned up. Next we saw the female cheetah coming around the bushes, her attention now focused on the gazelles. She did not have to do much stalking, for they were moving in her direction, and she ran when they were about 70 m (230 ft) away. The gazelles tried to get away, but she quickly overtook an adult animal and hit it on the rump hard enough to cause a wound. The grantie—a female—fell, but managed to struggle to its feet again. It flashed away in a different direction, and for a couple of seconds it looked as if it might escape. Making an all-out effort, the mother cheetah caught up with it a second time. After having run 200 to 250 m (avg. 246 yd) she was too blown, however, to direct another well-aimed blow at the gazelle's rump. Instead, she simply hurled herself at her quarry, knocking it over through the sheer impact of the collision. She was at its throat before it could get up once more, and at that moment the cubs were already running toward the fallen animal.

The gazelle still moved its legs when we hurriedly drove up, but a few seconds later its struggles had ceased. The cheetah continued to squeeze its neck for several minutes more, and, when she let go, the hair on the gazelle's throat was ruffled, but no blood could be seen. Death had been entirely by strangulation.

Another female pulled her victim to the ground in what might almost be called a "hand-to-hand" tussle. She had settled on a small hillock not far from a forest in Nairobi National Park, with her cubs playing around her, when suddenly she tensed, watching something we could not see. She bounded down from the eminence and went off. The cubs remained behind and stopped playing the moment the mother left them alone.

We followed her, and she crossed the track close to our car, slowly putting one foot in front of the other, her eyes fixed on whatever it was she had spied on the forest edge. There was an expanse of fairly high grass interspersed with scattered bushes between the track and the trees, and we saw her making full use of this cover, going into a half-crouch and keeping low as she moved on. She quickly disappeared from sight, and we now discovered her objective to be a bush-buck, an adult but still youngish male browsing on the bushes fringing the forest. After a few minutes the cheetah reappeared. She ran almost at once, from a distance of only 25 to 30 m (avg. 30 yd), and reached the buck before it really was aware of what was happening. She did not bowl it over at once, however, for we could see the buck's reddish-brown back above the scrub for quite a few moments after she had tackled the sturdy animal. It was impossible to see exactly what was happening, but it appeared that she had grabbed the bush-buck's throat—or perhaps its muzzle—while it was still standing. It once uttered a half-strangled barking or bellowing sound and finally went down, the lush vegetation masking the rest of the drama. A few minutes later we saw the cheetah drag the kill through the high grass. She left it behind a bush, went a few metres, and sat down under a tree, looking around. After some time she moved a short distance in our direction, and we heard her birdlike call. Next moment the cubs came running from about 250 m (820 ft) away. The whole family then went to the bush where the kill lay.

About an hour before she killed the bush-buck, that same female had failed to catch an impala out of a herd which suddenly came in her direction. Having absolutely no cover, she crouched low and dashed at the antelopes when they were only a very short distance from her. She was, however, somewhat half-hearted in her effort and missed, the impala literally "exploding" in all directions, grunting in alarm as they raced away.

Approaching a herd of gazelles in the open, a cheetah apparently singles out one animal and goes for it without letting itself be diverted by any others, even though they might offer a better chance for a kill. I once saw one race along the full length of a line of running thomies, and I expected it to swerve inward suddenly and knock one over, as it could very easily have done. But no—its attention was firmly focused on a gazelle near the head of the line, and the cheetah ran itself to a standstill, trying to catch up with it. We finally found it stretched out in the grass, panting violently, while the gazelles all escaped unscathed.

Randall Eaton, who studied cheetahs in Nairobi National Park, paid some attention to their respiration and found an animal which had been breathing at a rate of 60 a minute while lying in the shade to have a respiratory rate of no less than 156 after having chased, caught, and strangled a wart-hog. This capacity for going through the most amazing fluctuations in the breathing rate must be an essential part of the cheetah's adaptation to speed.

How fast is a cheetah's sprint? In most textbooks the speed attained is given as between 100 and 110 km (avg. 65 mi) per hour, and one manual of mammalian biology even puts it at 148 km (92 mi) per hour. A tame cheetah which was clocked running behind an electric hare reached a top speed of 70.7 (44 mi) on three occasions, while one chased by a car in Kenya has been reliably reported as having done 82 km (51 mi) per hour over 183 m (200 yd). My own observations have long ago made me doubt whether a cheetah ever really exceeds 90 km (56 mi) per hour, and I now find Kruuk and Turner more or less agreeing with this view, although stipulating that somewhat higher speeds may be attained over short bursts. While not quite as fast as some of the more imaginative writers have made it out to be, the cheetah is thus able to run at a speed higher than that attained by a gazelle or an impala. The antelopes, however, are capable of a much more sustained effort. They still have plenty of wind left when the cheetah, after having run a few hundred yards, has to give up the race.

It is customary to compare the cheetah's way of hunting with that of wild dogs, but it seems to me that this comparison is not really valid. Wolves, Indian wild dogs, and African hunting dogs work in packs, and I can vouch for the almost ruthless efficiency of this team effort in the case of the latter species; the cheetah generally runs down its prey as a lone hunter. It has taken to the kind of pursuit characteristic of canids, without, however, also adopting canid social co-operation, and while it has evolved physically to a point where it is faster than any of the wild dogs, the cheetah did not acquire their stamina. Every run after game thus means an all-out effort of the highest order, and if it ends in failure—as it very frequently does—the animal will have to recuperate for half an hour or so, preferably in the shade of a bush or tree, before it is capable of hunting again.

Game animals seem to have a fairly accurate idea of the cheetah's limitations. On the Serengeti Plains I once watched one stalking two Thomson's gazelles, a male and a female, which had settled down to chew the cud on a slight rise of the ground. As usual, the cheetah advanced very slowly at first, but in this case it even lay down each time one of the gazelles looked in its direction, in exactly the same manner a lion or leopard would have done during a similar approach. A passing car attracted the gazelles' attention and made them get up. The cheetah got up, too, watched for a few moments, and then sprinted uphill. It took some moments for the thomies to realize what was coming, but then they darted away at full speed. The cheetah very nearly caught up with one, but it may have been slightly handicapped by having had to run upward—anyway, the thomies got away, and the cat lay down panting after a run of about 300 m (984 ft). The gazelles, however, did not go far. They soon stopped to look back, and when the cheetah walked downhill again, they followed behind in order to keep their exhausted pursuer in sight.

Cheetahs must kill a lot more small "game" than is evident from published lists of prey. In Turkmenistan, according to Ognev, they used to prey largely on small desert mammals and birds. In East Africa they kill ostrich chicks up to a fairly large size, and when ostrich breeding was a paying proposition, farmers lost considerable numbers of chicks to them. It is said that rising birds are occasionally struck down in mid air. I certainly have seen cheetahs strike at vultures in this way, without, however, knocking one to the ground. In the course of one safari, two hares were seen to be caught by cheetahs, both after they had been put up by our cars.

Once, at Amboseli, when a mother with two cubs was moving across an area of scrub consisting of dense, but very low bushes with quite a lot of bare ground in between, one of the youngsters suddenly put up a hare and chased after it. The mother and the other cub immediately joined in the fray, not streaking along as cheetahs usually do, but bounding gracefully over the tops of the bushes. For a while the mother was close behind the madly zigzagging hare, but with so much cover about she finally lost it. The game scout we had along in our car was utterly delighted at the way "Sungura," the hare—which in African folklore plays a part similar to that of Reynard the Fox—had got the better of its pursuers.

I have seen a bat-eared fox chased by a cheetah suddenly turn round and face its pursuer, uttering a series of blood-curdling snarls. The cheetah came to a sudden halt, backed, and then bounded away, with the little fox following for about 10 to 15 m (avg. 43 ft) before it turned and ran in the opposite direction. Repeating this manoeuvre three times more, the plucky canid managed to reach the safety of its burrow.

After killing a small- or medium-sized antelope, a cheetah will usually drag it into the shade of a bush, even though it may only be a scraggy little whistling thorn. In the case of the cheetah mother which brought down a full-grown Grant's gazelle at Amboseli, the two cubs were chewing on the victim before it was completely dead, one near the anus and the other on the left haunch. The mother, although still panting heavily, picked up the prey almost at once and took it to a nearby clump of bush. She was so exhausted, however, that it took her a good twenty minutes to recover to a point where she was able to join the youngsters, who meanwhile had again been busy on the gazelle's rear end, without, however, making any very noticeable inroads. When she did get going at about 8:20 A.M., the female began at the groin and, assisted by the cubs, ate away the skin and flesh of the flank, gradually exposing the paunch. Guts were uncovered as the cheetahs worked their way forward, chewing off rib ends and opening the thoracic cavity from behind. At one moment the female turned the kill over and dragged it a couple of metres, so that the paunch and the guts fell out. One of the cubs scraped up grass and vigorously scattered it over the paunch, an action it repeated several times in course of the next two hours or so. The mother from time to time sat up and looked around, obviously making sure that the kill was not attracting any other predators. No lions or hyenas appeared, but the first vultures came gliding down an hour later, and, as they gradually became more numerous, the cheetahs often looked at them.

The cats fed crouching flat or with hind-quarters elevated, making little use of their forepaws in the process. As the sun gradually moved around the bush, the female several times dragged the kill into deeper shade. She took a rest from eating at about 10:05, but the cubs went on without a pause, even though they already were quite visibly distended. The mother rejoined them at 10:30, but gave up again at 10:45, walked half around the bush and lay down. The cubs, by now really bloated in appearance and with "I'm not feeling too well" expressions on their faces, went on feeding intermittently. The mother returned for one more snack, but soon had enough, and by 11:13 all three cheetahs had retired from the kill, which consisted of not much more than a bloody skeleton. The head was untouched, and the lower parts of the limbs were still covered with skin. The paunch and guts lay where they had fallen, and the thoracic cavity had been completely emptied. Our game scout—who knew the family well—thought that this Grant's gazelle should last the cheetahs for about three days.

A female observed by Schaller, which had two cubs three to four months old, killed twenty-four Thomson's gazelles in twenty-six days. A female with two large cubs caught six thomies during a period of five days. Solitary cheetahs have been found to kill every second or third day, which would amount to a total of about 150 animals taken in one year.

Cheetahs are dirty feeders and always get blood smeared all over their faces. When the meal is over, however, they will lick each other clean in a very short time. Once a cheetah leaves its kill, it usually does not come back. Stevenson-Hamilton, with his long experience of the Kruger National Park, wrote: "I do not think cheetahs care much for carrion. At all events I have never heard of their eating it, and from the manner they neglect their own kills, it is probable that they prefer not only to hunt their meat, but to eat it fresh." Since his time, a few instances of scavenging have been reported from the Kruger Park. I have never seen a cheetah at another animal's kill, nor has Schaller, and he thinks that being so low in the predator hierarchy, cheetahs are in most instances too timid to investigate possible sources of meat.

We have, however, Major Temple-Boreham's evidence that hungry youngsters can be tempted to accept carrion. On one occasion I saw two fairly big cubs stop their play and watch a tawny eagle catching—or finding—something eatable about 50 m (164 ft) away. They got very excited, uttered some tiny little sounds, and then bounded toward the bird. The eagle flew away, and the cheetahs appropriated whatever it had been feeding on, gobbling it up before I could see what it was.

Cheetahs cannot safeguard their kills in the way leopards do, and they frequently find themselves deprived of their hard-won prey by other predators which may have been led to the spot by the sight of

the circling vultures. Schaller states that of 238 kills made by cheetahs in the Serengeti, no less than twenty were taken by lions before
the rightful owners had finished their meal, eleven by hyenas and
one by a leopard. He even had evidence of cheetahs abandoning the
remains of a kill in the face of a solid phalanx of white-backed vultures advancing to within 1 or 1.5 m (avg. 4 ft). I have often watched
cheetahs rush at vultures, scattering them in all directions, but have
never seen them give way to the birds. Jackals, too, are chased away.

One day, in Nairobi National Park, three cheetahs were heading
toward a river-bed, obviously with the intention of settling down for
the hot hours in the shade of the bushes fringing its course. Spotting
some lions on the opposite bank they sat down and eyed them nervously. One uttered a low moaning sound, similar to that of a tom
cat facing a rival. A few minutes passed, and then the cheetahs got
up and began to move away, slowly and with evident reluctance. We
were just preparing to follow them, when a single lioness—which we
had encountered earlier in the day—came toward them in a straight
line from about 500 m (1600 ft) away. The cheetahs had meanwhile
sat down again, looking longingly at the river with its shady bushes.
Whether they really did not see the rapidly approaching lioness or
simply left flight to the last moment, relying on their fabulous speed,
the lioness was able to get to within about 30 m (98 ft) of them. Suddenly she rushed forward and went for the two cheetahs nearest to
her in no uncertain manner. The spotted cats immediately turned
into two yellow streaks. The lioness had absolutely no hope of catching up with them, but she nevertheless pursued the cheetahs for
about 60 m (200 ft). She then turned toward the third cheetah and
chased it just as fiercely. For a moment the distance between the two
animals seemed to narrow, but then the cheetah really got into its
stride and the lioness was left far behind. She soon gave up the chase
and walked toward the river, while the cheetahs disappeared over
the horizon.

On another occasion we saw two youngish lionesses chase a cheetah mother and her three cubs. They almost caught one of the
youngsters, and it was only by a supreme effort that it managed to
escape. The cheetah mother several times let the lionesses get very
close, probably trying to divert their attention from the cubs. It was
only when she knew her family to be safe that she streaked away like
lightning. One of the lion families observed in Nairobi National Park
once managed to surprise and kill a sleeping cheetah, a very old
male whose senses may have been getting somewhat dull. In the
Serengeti National Park, too, a cheetah has been known to be killed
by lions.

One cannot escape the conclusion that in the merciless struggle for survival, the cheetah is up against heavier odds than other members of the cat family. Catching prey is such an effort that after each run it finds itself practically incapacitated for half an hour or so. Forced to hunt out in the open, it is attacked and chased by lions more often than the leopard with its notoriously secretive habits. Unable to safeguard its kills in the way the leopard does, it quite frequently loses them to other predators and has to do more hunting than would really be necessary. Not only for its food, but also for its security, the cheetah depends not on stealth and concealment, but on speed alone, and although it does appear as a masterpiece of streamlined design—and is, in fact, the fastest thing on four legs— one is sometimes left wondering whether adaptation to a very special way of life has in this case not gone just a little bit too far. There have been instances of cheetahs—both in captivity and in the wild— injuring a limb in some all-out sprint, and there are few creatures more helpless than a cheetah with a damaged leg, incapable of catching prey and unable to get away from enemies.

Even pregnancy appears to pose grave problems through slowing down and endangering the magnificent runners. Astley Maberly reports: "Recently, in the Letaba area of Kruger Park, a pair of lionesses were seen (and photographed) deliberately attacking and very severely mauling an obviously pregnant cheetah, who must almost certainly have ultimately died of her wounds, as she could barely limp very far."

I once saw a female, showing every sign of being near to parturition, fail lamentably in an attempt to catch a Grant's gazelle. Everything seemed to be in her favour, only a very short spurt was needed, but she was quite evidently hampered by the state she was in, and the gazelles outdistanced her easily. All these factors must have combined to make the cheetah a somewhat local species and to keep its numbers far below those of leopards and lions. No wonder that it tends to fade away as soon as the scale becomes tipped just a little more to its disadvantage, be it through human persecution or through unfavourable changes of its habitat.

High cub mortality does nothing to help the cheetah in its somewhat precarious status. In the Kruger National Park and on the Serengeti Plains it has been assessed at about 50%. In Nairobi National Park it was around 43% when McLaughlin made his study, and since that time there has been something of an improvement, with several cheetah mothers bringing up large litters with almost no losses.

There probably is no definite breeding season, although births may occur more commonly at certain times of the year than at others. In the Serengeti National Park, for instance, birth months were found to be evenly distributed between January and August. Schaller had no evidence of any litters born between September and December. In Zambia, most births have been recorded from November and March, in eastern Transvaal during the second half of the year.

Several males may follow one female and fight over her, rearing up and hitting each other with the forepaws. Schaller describes courtship as involving a lot of churring and chirping. The female rolls on her back, dashes away, comes back again, and paws at the male. As far as my own observations go, couples stay together for only a very short time. Gestation lasts from ninety to ninety-five days. Litters can number from three to six cubs and the average is probably four. The cubs are born blind and open their eyes after four to eleven days. Their weight at birth varies from 250 to 300 g (avg. 7.8 oz). Two cubs born at the Krefeld Zoo weighed 370 g (13 oz) on the third day and showed a daily increase of 40 to 50 g (avg. 1.6 oz), attaining a weight of 8.33 kg (19 lb) in five and a quarter months. The first cub born in P. Spinelli's private zoo crawled around soon after birth and stood up unsteadily at the age of one week. It walked—still rather wobblingly—when it was twelve to thirteen days old. The three cubs of the second litter stood up on the tenth and walked on the sixteenth day. The first teeth appeared on the twentieth day. Within eighteen days, Spinelli's cubs ate donkeys' meat regurgitated by the mother. Young cheetahs are weaned in about three months in the wild. In captivity they may be suckled until they are five months of age. The milk-teeth are replaced at about 240 days.

Newly born cubs are well hidden in dense, high grass or thick scrub, but they come out fairly soon and begin to follow their mother about at an early age. With their grey cloaks and funny little faces they look truly adorable, even more engaging, if that is possible, than lion cubs. As the mother walks sedately along, they tend to fall behind. At short intervals, however, they chase after her, overtake her, and run in front. If their enthusiasm carries them too far ahead, the female calls "prrr-prrr," and they stop, giving little "peep-peeps" in response. When the mother settles down for a rest, they first climb all over her and demand to be suckled. They may then play about in the near vicinity. The mother keeps an eye on them all the time, and whenever they show a tendency to stray, she utters her "prrr-prrr," which brings them running back immediately.

Watching young cheetah cubs bounding through the grass in that characteristic see-saw gait of theirs, reminds one of honey-badgers, both with regard to colour and to motion. The honey-badger or ratel is probably the most aggressive of African mammals—I have had one "charge" my Land-Rover—and it advertises this fact by wearing a striking livery of white or ashy grey above and blackish brown below. Its area of distribution covers most of Africa and extends through Palestine and Syria to India, thus coinciding to a remarkable degree with that of the cheetah. Could it be that at the time they need it most, young cheetah cubs get a certain amount of protection from this resemblance? Rather far-fetched, you may say. Possibly—though there is a certain amount of evidence to show that the sluggish, absolutely unprotected crested rat of the Kenya forests owes its survival at least partly to the fact that its shaggy black and white coat resembles that of the very well protected African polecat or zorilla.

As the cheetah cubs get older and take on adult colouration and markings, they become even more playful. They chase each other with truly amazing vigour and sometimes they stand up and wrestle, trying to catch hold of one another by the throat. From the age of eleven or twelve weeks onward, one of their favourite games consists in jumping at each other from behind, hitting the partner on the back with a forepaw in exactly the same way they will later hit their victims. The mother often joins in these romps and dashes around with a zest not less than that of her offspring. When the family settles in the shade of a bush, there usually is a considerable amount of mutual licking, not only between mother and cubs, but also between the cubs themselves.

When the mother goes off to chase game, young cubs take cover in high grass or in a patch of scrub and wait until she calls them out or brings the kill back to them. Later on, they sit and watch, ready to run up as soon as a kill has been made.

One morning in Nairobi National Park, the presence of a cheetah was brought to my attention through the panicky flight of a herd of impala. Looking at the cat with our field-glasses, we discovered that she carried a prey in her mouth and was followed by five cubs with cloaks still well visible. The family was moving toward a strip of riverine forest, and we quickly started the car, hoping that we might cut the animals off from cover and get some photographs. This was when the cheetahs of Nairobi Park were still very shy, and the sight of our car made that family run so fast that they crossed the track about 30 m (98 ft) ahead of us. At that moment, the mother dropped her prey, which we now recognized as an impala fawn. She stopped on the edge of the forest and looked round as if she were in half a mind to come back and fetch it, but then decided against it and vanished among the bushes. There was still the possibility, however, that she might return for her kill after having deposited her family in a safe place. We therefore waited patiently. Suddenly, to our amazement, the fawn came alive, got up, and stood, somewhat wobblingly, on its long, stiff legs. As we drove up, it came to the car and let itself be picked up without the slightest struggle. There was not a single scratch on it, and we later released it near the impala herd, none the worse for its adventure.

At the time I was greatly puzzled by the fact that the cheetah mother had not immediately killed the little animal. I now think that she took it for her cubs to practise on, in the same way a domestic cat lets her kittens toy with a mouse. I have since then seen a cheetah mother bring in a young Thomson's gazelle for this very purpose, and from what has been recorded by Schaller, Kruuk, and Turner, this type of behaviour seems to be fairly common on the Serengeti Plains.

By playing with each other or with animals caught by their mother, and through looking on while she chases game, the cubs have their hunting instincts awakened and developed at an early age, and soon they will bound after any hare or other small animal that has accidentally been put up during one of the family's extensive rambles. I once spent a very amusing half-hour watching half-grown cheetahs playing about with youngish wart-hogs. It was nothing very serious, the cats always bounding away at top speed when one of the porkers turned to face them.

Cubs are known to have stayed with their mother for almost two years, but the separation more often seems to take place between the ages of fifteen to seventeen months. Once they are on their own, young cheetahs may at first have a rather difficult time, but experience is quickly acquired. In Nairobi National Park, where females frequently raise litters of four, the youngsters usually remain together for some time, and at least one of these bachelor groups became quite expert at killing adult hartebeests. What an efficient predator the cheetah might have become if, in addition to developing its phenomenal speed, it had also taken on social habits similar to those of the lion. Too efficient, perhaps.

Birth intervals of seventeen, eighteen, and nineteen months have been reported from Nairobi National Park. There is, however, also a record of a female which only mated again when her cubs had attained an age of sixteen months. Having lost her litter, a female will very quickly come in heat again. Maturity is attained early, at twenty-one to twenty-two months, according to observations made in the wild.

In captivity, one cheetah is on record as having lived for fifteen years and seven and a half months. A few have reached ages of ten, eleven, twelve, thirteen and a half, and fourteen years, but as a whole, the species has so far not done very well. Circularizing a great number of zoos, H. van de Werken found that average longevity had been three years, one month, and thirteen days between 1957 and 1961, and five years, one month, and fourteen days between 1962 and 1966. It does at least look as if there were a gradual improvement. Post-mortem examinations revealed liver diseases— especially cirrhosis—feline distemper, tuberculosis, pneumonia, and enteritis as the main causes of death.

Nothing is yet known of longevity in the wild, though one feels that it may prove to be lower than that of lions, tigers, and leopards. Age is sure to seriously handicap the lone sprinter long before it makes itself felt in the lone stalkers, not to speak of the sociable lions where there is always the possibility of eking out an existence on the kills of others.

Cheetahs occasionally become the victims of lions, as we have already seen, and in the Serengeti National Park one was killed by a leopard and taken up a tree. They most probably suffer less from diseases in the wild than in captivity, although they have been known to contract anthrax. A specimen from northern Kenya was found infected with an organism identical to *Eperythrozoon felis,* which causes haemolytic anaemia in domestic cats. The same animal also carried a nematode, *Spirocera lupi,* which can cause damage to blood-vessels. I have never had an opportunity of examining a cheetah for parasites, but a young and very emaciated female killed by a lion in the Serengeti National Park was found infested with ticks of the species *Rhipicephalus carnivoralis.*

Cheetahs are harmless to man. There never has been an unprovoked attack, and the very few cornered or wounded cheetahs which were reported as having charged were probably trying to get away. Kermit Roosevelt rode down on horseback the few specimens required by the Smithsonian Institution. After a mile or two of fast galloping, the cheetah would suddenly crouch flat on the ground, completely done up and offering no resistance at all.

My wife and I saw our first cheetah fairly soon after having arrived in Kenya, when a friend took us to the then quite newly established Nairobi National Park. We chased the animal—something that was banned a long time ago, and very rightly so—and after a short time the cat not only crouched flat as described by Roosevelt, but it also snarled at us in a way I have never again experienced.

Even though some African countries long ago awarded full protection to these beautiful and inoffensive animals, a considerable number of them have been killed for their skins. One of the famous "roof-rack climbing" cheetahs of Nairobi National Park became the victim of poachers, who stoned it to death after having driven it up a tree. They were caught and punished, though their sentence was far below what I would have regarded as adequate.

Edward Hyams has expressed doubts as to the thousands of cheetahs used for hunting having always been wild-caught specimens and not animals bred in captivity. We have, however, the testimony of no less an authority than Jehangir, the son and successor of Akbar the Great who, in 1613, wrote in his memoirs: "It is an established fact that cheetahs in unaccustomed places do not pair off with a female, and my revered father once collected together 1000 cheetahs. He was very desirous that they should pair, but this in no way came off. At this time a male cheetah having slipped its collar, went to a female and paired with it, and after two and a half months, three young cubs were born and grew up. This has been recorded because it appears strange." So keen was Akbar on his breeding experiments that, according to another source, he allowed some to run free in the palace gardens, letting them walk about and hunt after their fashion, but without obtaining the desired success.

The first modern zoo to succeed in breeding cheetahs was the one in Philadelphia, where cubs born in 1956 lived to an age of three months. In 1960, a couple obtained from South-West Africa produced cubs in the Krefeld Zoo. The first to be born was probably eaten by the male. The next two were taken away, but the fourth was left with the mother—now separated from the male—which nursed it properly for two days and then bit off one of its legs. The two surviving cubs were successfully nursed by a domestic cat. Two cubs born in the Arnhem, Holland, zoo were eaten by their parents.

Considering the obvious difficulty in getting cheetahs to breed, it caused something of a stir in 1966 when P. Spinelli had two litters born in his private zoo in Rome, the first of one cub, the second of three. Since then, the zoo in Montpellier, France, has joined the ranks of successful cheetah breeders, and as these lines are being written, there comes the news that Julian Tong, a former care-taker of the Nairobi National Park's Animal Orphanage, has reared five cubs in the Safaripark at Hilvarenbeek, Holland. It certainly begins to look as if a breakthrough has at long last been achieved.

Wild Cats and Man

From the accounts given of the various species it must have become evident that in his physical contacts with wild cats, man has been either a prey, a competitor, or an exploiter. To this can be added various forms of animistic and mythological relationships which have been amazingly widespread through both time and space.

If we disregard the obviously very rare instances of child snatching attributed to the fishing cat, the use of man as a prey is restricted to the big cats. In the case of the jaguar it is uncommon and more or less incidental, but as far as lion, tiger, and leopard are concerned, it cannot be denied that man must be considered as a prey—a rather unusual one, it is true, although the odd individual may become a real specialist in killing humans for food. Opponents of conservation—and amazing as it may sound, there still are some of these types around, even though one cannot quite escape the suspicion that their thickly laid-on *pro bono homo* attitude stems mainly from the fact that destroying wild animals fills their pockets—are busily digging up factual records, overblown jungle tales, and spurious statistics in order to make lions, tigers, and leopards appear as man-devouring monsters, threatening the very existence of Asian and African populations. They are, of course, barking up the wrong tree, for the worst enemy of man is, after all, man himself. Irresponsible motorists alone run up a higher annual tally than lions, tigers, and leopards ever attained, and a lot more humans have been slaughtered in the wars and revolutions of our century than were accounted for by the man-eating cats of the last five hundred years! While admitting the occurrence of man-eating, let us keep away from exaggeration and take comfort from the fact that there usually is a Jim Corbett or Colonel Patterson on hand to rectify the situation. If only one could say the same with regard to human mass-murderers.

In his ceaseless pursuit of game, Palaeolithic man must often have found himself in direct confrontation with other predators, including wildcats, lynxes, leopards, giant tigers, and cave lions. We can be fairly certain that as far as possible he avoided direct encounters with the big cats, while the latter may usually have kept away from the strange, upright creature which went about in hordes

291

and was capable of throwing things. When game was plentiful, there probably existed something like a state of armed neutrality. In times of scarcity, however, hungry cats must have taken the occasional human, while the humans are sure to have done a considerable amount of scavenging from their feline competitors. Having on many occasions seen packs of wolves or hyenas make a big cat relinquish its prey by force of numbers, Palaeolithic men can be assumed to have used similar methods to obtain possession of half-eaten kills.

Humans who never progressed beyond the cultural stage of hunting and food-gathering have scavenged in this way until very recent times and may occasionally do so even today. When Sir J. Edward Alexander, one of the early explorers of South-West Africa, heard that Bushmen regularly robbed lions of their prey, he asked one of them how this was done. The old Bushman took up his assegai and walked to and fro in front of a bush where an imaginary lion was supposed to be tearing to pieces a zebra or an antelope. Brandishing his weapon, he called out to the "lion": "What have you come here for? Have you got anything to eat? You made such a noise I thought you had something. Don't think to come here and quarrel with me, but go off now and get meat." Thus talking he walked around for a while and finally sat down. The puzzled animal usually withdrew, he said, leaving the remains of its prey to him. Another Bushman then started up, spear in hand, and fifty yards in front of the bush sprang about with great animation, shaking his weapon and exclaiming to the imaginary lion: "What have you got there? Cannot you spare me some of it? Be off, and let some stand for me, or I'll do you an injury." He then threw his assegai in a way that it fell half-way to the bush. Some of the Bushmen Alexander came across derived almost their whole sustenance from the lions. Jan Buys, one of his Hottentot companions, upon asking a Bushman what he lived on, received the answer: "I live by the lions." "Well," Jan Buys said, "there is the spoor of three lions before you." "I am following them," was the reply. "I let the lions stalk the game, kill it, and eat a bellyfull. I then go near, throw out my arms and my skins, the lions go away grumbling and I get what they leave. I never kill lions." It is easy to imagine similar scenes taking place in the valley of the Dordogne or among the foothills of the Pyrenees.

In early Neolithic times, domestic animals began to make their appearance, goats and sheep first, followed later on by cattle and horses. As far as the predatory animals, particularly the big cats, were concerned, there naturally was no difference between man's flocks and herds of wild game. They competed with Neolithic farmers and herdsmen for the possession of their livestock as they

had competed for game with Palaeolithic hunters. When man do-
mesticated wild-fowl, geese, and pigeons, the small cats began to raid
his hen-houses where birds could be caught so much more easily
than out in the wild. For thousands of years wild cats, large and
small, have thus been hunted first and foremost because of the damage they did to man's domestic stock.

The necessary and dangerous task of protecting the primitive
pastoral and agricultural communities from the ravages of large
predators usually fell to adventurous elements more inclined to follow the call of the age-old hunting instinct than to turn to the still
relatively novel occupations of tending flocks and tilling the soil.
They were regarded as popular heroes and some became legendary
figures, such as Hercules, Dumuzi-Tanus of Mesopotamia, and Sam-
son of Palestine.

In more civilized societies, however, hunting big cats came to be
regarded as an exciting sport reserved for noblemen and kings. The
hieroglyphic text of a famous scarabaeus tells us that the Pharaoh
Amenophis (Amenhotep) III, who lived from 1405 to 1367 B.C.
killed no less than 102 "fierce-looking" lions during the first ten
years of his reign. The kings who ruled Assyria from the ninth to
the seventh century B.C. were great hunters, too, and one of them,
Ashurbanipal, who called himself "King of the World," described his
exploits in the following words:

> Since I have succeeded to the throne of my father, Adad, the Weather
> God, has sent torrents of rain, Ea, Lord of the Waters that are under the
> Earth, has opened the fountains of the deep, the forests have grown
> enormously, the reeds have shot up in thickets, so that nobody can enter
> them any more. In there, lions have bred in mighty numbers. Through
> the killing of cattle, small stock and man they have become bold. The
> mountain shakes with the thunder of their roars, the game of the plains
> has fled. They constantly kill the livestock of the fields and they spill the
> blood of men and cattle. The herdsmen and the supervisors are weep-
> ing; the families are mourning. The misdeeds of these lions have been
> reported to me. In course of my expedition I have penetrated their hid-
> ing places and destroyed their lairs. For my regal amusement I have
> caught the Desert King by his tail, and on the instruction of my helpers,
> the Gods Nusib and Nergal, I have split his head with my two-handed
> sword.

The Assyrian kings shot lions with arrows from two-wheeled
chariots drawn by three horses, but they did not always "penetrate
their hiding places," as lions for the royal hunt were in actual fact
bred in menageries, transported to suitable places in wooden cages,
and then released in order to give sport to the king and his court.

One would think that the rapid spread of agricultural crops and domestic stock should eventually have made man quite independent of game meat. Today's world population of cattle, not counting water buffaloes, is around 800 million head, while the numbers of sheep, goats, and pigs are assessed at 950, 450, and 300 millions respectively. Of the domestic fowl there must be about 3 billion, making it by far the most abundant bird in existence. Yet hunting continued, especially as a favourite pastime first of nobility and then of the wealthy. Competition for game between man and other predators was, in fact, quite as keen as competition for man's domestic stock. The holders of hunting rights employed gamekeepers not only to protect their preserves for human poachers, but just as much to destroy any predators, furred or feathered, which looked in the least likely to interfere with the game-animals and game-birds they themselves intended to kill. Quantitatively, the stocks of game certainly profited from this policy, among the many victims of which were the forest wildcat and the lynx, but overcrowding and the absence of natural enemies in due course led not only to physical deterioration, but also to increased susceptibility to various epizootics. The gamekeepers eventually found themselves doing the job of weeding out, which formerly had been done more cheaply and efficiently by the animals and birds which they and their employers had contemptuously labelled as "vermin." Wholesale eradication of so-called "vermin" also brought about a tremendous increase of voles and other rodent pests, which had formed the main prey of many of the mercilessly persecuted avian and mammalian carnivores. Some ecological facts of life were certainly being brought home to mankind, but it took an awfully long time for them really to sink in.

In addition to being hunted themselves, some members of the cat family were made to hunt for the human predators. Besides cheetahs, caracals were used fairly regularly, and the ancient Egyptians seem to have trained jungle cats for hunting, without, however, really domesticating them. According to Marco Polo, the Grand Khan of Cathay (China) not only had many "small leopards and lynxes"— cheetahs and caracals—for the purpose of chasing deer, but also made use of tigers, which, in the words of the Venetian traveller, "were active in seizing boars, stags, roebucks and other beasts that are the objects of sport." Tigers may in fact have been used in this way by the Yin and Chou emperors long before Kublai Khan's reign.

Big cats have on many occasions been made to function as executioners. The most highly publicized efforts of this kind have, of course, been those that took place in Roman times, and the picture of ferocious lions, tigers, and leopards racing into the arena and hurling themselves at groups of devoutly praying Christians has been presented ad nauseam in literature, art, and on the movie screen. In reality, after having been confined in dark, underground chambers, the animals must have been very hesitant to enter the glaring daylight of the arena where, in addition, there was absolutely no cover for them, and even if they had been half starved, the roars of the mob and the screams of the victims would most probably have been enough to make them try to slink back into the safety and seclusion of their cages. There is, in fact, plenty of evidence that certain animals, selected because they appeared more "ferocious" than most of the others, were systematically trained as man-eaters. Even so, it was found necessary at times to make the victims move their hands in order to incite the animals to attack.

The custom of having criminals torn to pieces by the big cats has by no means been restricted to ancient Rome. As a spectacle, it was in great favour at many an Oriental court; we hear, for instance, that the King of Pegu in lower Burma "kept a park for lions, tigers and other fierce beasts called 'Leparo,' and it is a sad and daily sight to see criminals devoured by them." Even the relatively inoffensive puma had to play the executioner. In his monograph of the species, Stanley P. Young wrote: "It was one of the animals maintained in the dungeons of the Inca rulers for use in the punishment of treason and disobedience among the Inca people. These dungeons were in many respects not unlike the amphitheatres of the Romans, where the lion was used to dispose of early christian converts."

In thirteenth-century Rome a lions' pit was established near the Capitol, and it is said that Ludwig IV of Bavaria, after conquering the city, had a troublesome monk thrown to the animals. The last of the Capitolian lions was destroyed in 1414, after he had got out of the pit and killed a child.

In 1459, the people of Florence decided to revive the circus games of ancient Rome. After solidly barricading all the streets leading into it, some twenty lions, as well as some wolves and bulls, were released on the Piazza della Signoria. The whole thing turned out to be a tremendous flop, for the well-fed lions had not the slightest inclination to kill bulls or to fight with wolves. After having walked around for some time in a very bored manner, they all lay down together in a shady corner of the piazza.

A similar spectacle was staged on the same square in 1514, of which Joan Barclay Lloyd wrote:

Many "foreigners" came to Florence especially to see the fights. Among them were four cardinals who came up from Rome in disguise. Bears, leopards, stags and other wild beasts were let into the arena, with bulls, horses and dogs. Last of all came two lions. The crowd was frantic with excitement, but the first lion shied away because of the tumultuous noise. When some dogs approached him, the lion seized one with his paw, so that it dropped dead to the ground. He killed a second dog in the same way, but did not attack any of the other beasts. When the lion saw that the other animals would not molest him, he stood quite still and then walked away. The Florentines, however, had made a model tortoise and a model porcupine. Inside were men who wheeled the models all over the piazza. They were armed with lances, which they kept thrusting at the animals to tease them and make them fight more fiercely. Although the lions gave a disappointing performance, the festa was a great success. It was dangerous sport, for many men were injured and three died.

The Roman arena as a place of entertainment has found a successor in the modern circus, in which big cats, especially lions and tigers, but occasionally also leopards and pumas, play a very major part.

The hunting of big cats for sport, instigated by Egyptian pharaohs and Assyrian kings, their use for the chase, as executioners or for pure entertainment, must, of course, come under the heading of exploitation, and this also applies to the killing of felines for the commercial utilization of their pelts.

The wearing of cats' skins as articles of clothing has a very long history. It is sure to go back to the Palaeolithic, but the earliest evidence comes from the Anatolian site of Çatal Hüyük. In this Neolithic settlement, which was a flourishing town by 6500 B.C., paintings of humans dressed in leopard skins—perhaps for ceremonial purposes—have been found in what the archaeologists regard as a "hunting shrine."

A Greek vase dated about 490 B.C. shows Perseus with a spotted skin thrown over his chiton. Leopard pelts were worn by ancient Egyptian priests, by African chiefs, and witch-doctors. In Renaissance Italy they were used to decorate the clothing of the wealthy, and in Tibet they have enjoyed great popularity right up to present times. They also form part of the drummers' parade uniforms in various European regiments.

Some of the Aztec warriors opposing the Spanish Conquistadors were dressed in jaguar doublets, the head-skin drawn up like a hood and the tail hanging down behind. War coats made from the pelts of clouded leopards were popular among the Dayaks of Sarawak, while Abyssinian military leaders and Masai spearmen used to wear lions' manes. Skins of various small cats were much in demand for the piecing together of African karrosses, and lynx pelts have for a long time formed an important item among the furs passing through the trading posts of the Hudson's Bay Company. In Baikov's time, Manchurian hunters found a ready sale for their tiger skins on the markets of Ningouta, Sansin, Ghirin, Mukden, Achikhe, and Tsitsikar, from where they were exported mainly to Peking and Tientsin.

The recent fur craze, however, developed on an international basis and against the background of a world utterly changed from what it had been even a short time ago, with large number of women in a financial position to ape each other's follies, and with hitherto remote areas easily accessible to fur traders. It was the scale of the whole thing, the amount of money involved, the "big business" characteristics, which made it so much more destructive than any of the earlier efforts at exploiting wild cats for their pelts. In 1966, the traders of Iquitos alone exported 15,000 ocelot skins. What a horrifying number of these beautiful and inoffensive animals must have been cruelly trapped and snared over the whole of South and Central America! Shame on the jet-set society which instigated this mass slaughter to satisfy its cravings for luxury and extravagance!

Eating wild cats has, on the other hand, been more or less incidental, without ever leading to any large-scale commercial exploitation of a feline species for food.

The professional hunters of Manchuria made a profit not only from tiger pelts, but just as much from the skinned carcasses which they sold to Chinese apothecaries at about 50 to 75 dollars per 16 kg (36 lb), according to sex and age of the animal and to the part of the body the piece came from. Adult males brought in more than females or youngsters. A one-year-old tiger of 45 to 60 kg (avg. 120 lb), for instance, was sold for only about 100 dollars. From heart, blood, bones, eyes, liver, and genitals, the quack pharmacists manufactured powders and pills which they advertised as cures for a wide range of diseases. The vibrissae, arranged in five rows of about ten hairs each, were particularly valuable, with the longest, situated in the middle row, being the most sought after. Up to ten dollars were paid for the very longest of them all, the seventh counting from the nose. Rolled up and worn as an amulet around the neck, or sewn into the clothes, it was thought to give its owner limitless power over women.

In India, as in China, most parts of a tiger's caracass have their medical uses. The fat, of which 1.8 to 2.7 kg (4 to 6 lb) can be obtained from one animal, is in especially high demand. Lions' fat was considered as an excellent cure against ear-aches, rheumatic pains, and various other ailments by both the Swahili and the Indians living on the East African coast. The Swahili believed—and some may still do so—that the lion carried in its mouth a charm or amulet in the shape of a ball, about the size of a walnut. This, they said, the lion buried whenever it went hunting and scratched up after having eaten and drunk in order to carry it off again. When about to die, he was supposed to spit it as far as possible, to avoid its being found. Whenever a sportsman shot a lion, the porters could be seen anxiously searching all around the body, and from there back to the place where the animal was first seen. A small fragment of the charm wrapped up and worn round the neck was said to make a person immune against attacks by lions and other wild beasts, besides having various other properties.

The story may have originated from the fact that a kind of "bezoar stone" is occasionally found in a lion's stomach, a ball formed out of the hairs he swallows when licking his fur. In course of time, the surface of this becomes as hard as stone and looks as if it had been polished. These "stones" may become as big as a fist, and witch-doctors are always very keen to add them to their supply of medicines.

In discussing the medical and aphrodisiac "qualities" attributed to various parts of wild cats, we have, of course, entered the field of superstition, which, in turn, merges into the shadowy realms of mysticism and mythology. We shall never know what beliefs our Ice Age ancestors held with regard to the big cats they encountered on their hunting expeditions. Paintings and engravings of unmistakable lions have been found on the walls of their cave dwellings, less commonly than those of bears, wild horses, bisons, aurochsen, deer, and various other game animals, but they are there, in the cave of Combarelles, in the Grotte des Trois Frères, in Font-de-Gaume, Laugerie Basse, and Le Combel. One part of Lascaux is known as the "Chambre des Félins," because it contains a group of six or seven lions. A solitary lion's head was discovered in the "Chambre des Gravures."

Palaeolithic hunters must have looked upon cave lions and leopards with considerable awe, and the pictorial representations of big cats may well mark the beginning of a mythical relationship which was to continue for thousands of years.

Primitive man has always regarded himself as closely related to the animal world, so closely, in fact, that in many cases descent from animal ancestors was claimed by tribes or tribal groups. Out of such feelings of kinship arose the concept of totemism which stipulates mystical associations between groups or "clans" of human beings and certain animals. A good account of totemism involving big cats has been given by Gerhard Lindblom, the Swedish anthropologist who spent more than twelve months in East Africa in 1911 and 1912 in order to make a thorough study of the Akamba people. He found the tribe divided into a number of clans, each of which had its special totem animal—lion, leopard, hyena, bush-buck, vervet monkey, baboon, jackal, crow, buzzard, vulture, parrot, and drongo. The clans often were not referred to by their proper names, but by the name of the totem, such as "the clan of the lion," or "the clan of the leopard." Normally, a man was banned from eating his totem animal. If a man of the Lion Clan came upon a dead lion, he was not allowed to take its skin. The rules governing a person's behaviour toward his totem were, however, applied in a reasonable way, and provisions had been made for various exceptions. Thus, a man of the Lion Clan was allowed to kill a lion that attacked him or his cattle, and there was no objection to the killing of leopards and lions penetrating villages at night.

Hearing a lion roar in the dark, one of Lindblom's porters walked out into the bush with a chunk of meat. Questioned by the anthropologist on his return, the man answered: "I belong to the Lion Clan, and I heard a kinsman calling me. He is certainly hungry, perhaps old and feeble, so that he can no longer kill as of old. Is it, then, not my duty to share with him my superfluity, when I sit here by the fire in comfort and have more than I can manage to eat?"

Totemistic association can occasionally take on the form of blood-brotherhood. Turnbull-Kemp, speaking of the leopard said:

> A blood bond between humans and lower animals occurs in both Naga and West Africa. In the West African form the leopard involved is trapped alive and uninjured. Once bound, the leopard is treated with religious respect. Penultimately the worshipper or worshippers make a small incision in the lashed-up leopard and use the resulting blood. Some versions tell of drinking the warm blood from the living beast, others speak of a cut being made in the skin of the worshipper, and a mingling of the blood of man and bound beast. One account tells of the doubtless frightened and furious leopard being seated upright, and even of it being capped or crowned for the ceremony. Finally the probably infuriated but certainly entirely unimpressed leopard is released. It would be interesting to learn how this release is engineered, for the human blood-brother certainly believes in the close, friendly, or even sacred relationship and might be expected to expose himself to a mildly injured and certainly greatly aggravated leopard. For what it is worth, and on the most slender rumour, I consider that the beast wisely is drugged with smoke from burning herbs offered for its delection; but this is simply a personal opinion of the obscure and highly secret West African ceremony. Blood relationship in the Naga Hills is strong enough for it to be

claimed that when the leopard dies, the human blood brother will die as well. Hence the human bloodbrother is said to thresh about if the leopard is hunted closely. For the cynical, there is significance in the fact that death of the human will only occur if he is told of the death of the leopard. If unconscious of the death of his blood-brother, his own life continues. Association with the leopard may be indicated by the face being cut with marks to simulate leopard's whiskers.

From the respect and veneration paid to the totem animal there is only a short step to the adoration of true animal worship, a form of primitive mysticism which must have originated in very ancient times. Baikov tells us that some of the indigenous peoples of eastern Siberia and Manchuria, such as the Golds, Orotchons, and Tungus, used to regard the tiger as a supernatural being to which they offered animal sacrifices. In not-too-far-distant times, whenever a tiger took to killing humans, the shamans ordered a human sacrifice. Some poor wretch was tied to a tree close to one of the tiger's regular beats, and if the feline accepted the offering, the tree was afterward regarded as sacred and decorated with pieces of cloth. This custom was continued after human sacrifices had long ago been given up, and Baikov himself knew of several trees which constantly carried rags torn from the clothes of passing hunters.

There can be no doubt about a fairly elaborate cat cult having been practised in the Neolithic town of Çatal Hüyük, where the fertility goddess has often been found portrayed together with leopards. This may have been done either to symbolize her power over the animal world or because the leopard had become her constant associate. In the "Hunting Shrine," where the earliest paintings of humans clad in leopard skins have been discovered, there were excellent reliefs of leopards, showing the animals with characteristically thrown-up tails and marked with spots correctly arranged in rosettes. Men and women riding on leopards were depicted elsewhere in the settlements, and there is also a stone statue showing a woman sitting on a throne flanked by two big cats, possibly lions.

In Haçilar, a Neolithic settlement about a thousand years younger than Çatal Hüyük, the fertility goddess usually sits on a throne formed by a leopard. Of very special interest are the numerous figurines of women accompanied by leopards and carrying smaller cats, probably wild cats. It may well be that we owe the domestic cat to the cults of Neolithic Anatolia.

While the inhabitants of Çatal Hüyük and Haçilar seem to have made the leopard the main object of their veneration, other peoples of the ancient Near East deified the lion or at least associated it with some of their gods. In Mesopotamia it was Ishtar, the deity of war, who had a lion as her animal attribute. Elsewhere it was often associated with the goddess Cybele, most probably a direct descendant of the fertility goddess of Neolithic Anatolia, which was later to become the "Great Mother" of the Greeks and Romans. In ancient Greece, her priests, wandering about like mendicant monks, frequently had a lion with them and made use of it in their exorcising rites.

There was a widespread tendency to see the lion as a symbol of the sun. The bull having been adopted as a symbol of the moon, the moon bull was thought every morning to be strangled by the sun lion. The temple of the Sun God Amun Ra at Heliopolis was the centre of a lion cult, with sacred lions, which were carefully tended by high-ranking priests who bathed them in perfumed water, salved them, burnt incense for them, and fed them the choicest tidbits to the strains of religious music. There were laws which decreed public mourning on the death of one of these animals, which was then embalmed and entombed with great ceremony. The four lions on the famous Column of Sarnath can be seen to support the chakra wheel, an Indian symbol of law and image of the sun.

The lion did, in fact, become firmly established in the symbolism and mythology of both the religions which struggled for power in ancient India. In early Buddhist art it is often shown between the feet of the Buddha or at the corner of his throne, while in later times, as the "Lion of Sakya," it became the symbol of the Sakyamuni incarnation. In Hinduism, however, Vishnu was thought to take on the shape of Narasinha, the Man Lion, whenever he had to fight some especially fierce adversary. After having overcome his enemy in single combat, he slit his belly, disembowelling him with utmost ferocity.

Among the Chinese, a tiger with face markings forming the letter "Van" used to be regarded as the reincarnation of a human being, usually a king or some other great personage, who had to pay for his sins or the sins of his ancestors.

The superstition of big cats forming suitable receptacles for the souls of the dead—particularly the illustrious dead—has been very widespread. John Roscoe, the missionary-anthropologist, found that the Bahima of Ankole (Uganda) were averse to killing lions, which they assumed to harbour the souls of their former rulers. The wives of the Ankole kings had to be satisfied with rebirth in the shape of leopards, while the souls of princes and princesses were relegated to pythons. Among the Konde people of Ugonde, near the northern end of Lake Nyasa, D. R. Mackenzie recorded a general belief that the spirits of dead chiefs entered into lions and then went about to see how their former subjects were behaving. Friedrich Fülleborn came across similar superstitions in neighbouring areas. The Wanambwe, he tells us, were convinced of their sultans being reborn as lions, while the Wangoni believed in animal rebirth for all souls, with everybody fervently hoping to go through his future existence as a lion. The idea of being reborn as a hyena, however, was exceedingly unpopular.

In Mackenzie's time, the Konde attributed to certain witch-doctors the ability to control lions in order to use them for their own nefarious purposes. Similar beliefs were once widely held in southern Tanganyika. There were, the people said, wizards who, by performing spells somewhere in the bush, could conjure lions out of two sticks, mangy, ugly-looking brutes who did their master's bidding and killed his enemies. When they had performed their allotted task, they were turned into sticks again. Another lion myth from the same area was reminiscent of the "vampire" tales of Eastern Europe. When a man died and his corpse remained flaccid instead of becoming rigid, it was asserted, a watch had to be kept over the grave, for after three or four days the deceased was most likely to dig his way out of the soil in the form of a lion, weak and helpless immediately after emergence and easily killed at that stage, but getting stronger rapidly if left alone. The "vampire" lions were supposed to use the knowledge gained during their existence in human shape for embarking upon successful careers as man-eaters. Finally, there were the real "were lions," or "gluka simba," persons who could turn themselves into lions at will and returned into their human shape again after having satisfied their craving for a cannibalistic feast. Many tribes in Rhodesia and Katanga, as well as the Sara of Ubangi used to believe implicitly in the existence of "were lions."

Livingstone once met a witch-doctor who professed to be able to turn himself into a lion. When the explorer asked him to perform the transmutation, so that he might see and believe in his forces, the old fraud murmured slyly that the change came about, not bodily, but only in the heart.

The jungle people of Sumatra and Java had a firm belief in tiger-men, in "teindakus" and "Ngelmu-Gandogans," who turned into tigers either quite unconsciously or by means of black magic. In Malaya there are deeply rooted superstitions concerning "tiger-kings" able to transform themselves into man, and human wizards having the power to appear in the shape of a tiger.

A legend well-known all over Trengganu, tells of the youngest wife of a man by the name of Hadji Ali, waking up early one morning on hearing her husband approaching the house. Looking at him as he stood half-way up the outside steps, she was terrified to see his head on the body of a tiger. As she watched in horror, the body changed into that of a man, the transmutation ending with the disappearance of the tail. The girl ran away, and nothing would persuade her to enter Hadji Ali's house again, even though he was a very wealthy man. A few weeks later, the village headman took a shot at a tiger and wounded it in a foreleg. The spoor led straight to the house of Hadji Ali, and beneath the floor, raised on stilts according to the custom of the country, the headman could see a pool of blood mixed with water, as though somebody inside had bathed a wound. Hadji Ali's sons prevented him from entering, however, and when he returned with a posse of villagers, he found the house empty and the family gone. A traveller later told the headman that he had found Hadji Ali settled in a neighbouring district, apparently after having suffered some kind of accident. His hand, the traveller said, was gnarled and twisted as if it had been shattered by a shot.

The natives of the Satpura Range in central India have long had a sinister reputation for their alleged power to change into animals and back again into human shape, and the famous—or infamous— man-eating leopard of Kahani was generally assumed to be a member of this tribe. The man in question, Sterndale was told, had one day come with his wife to a jungle glade where some nilgai were grazing. When the woman expressed a desire for some meat, the man gave her a root to hold, with strict orders to let him smell it when he returned. He changed into a leopard, stalked and killed a nilgai, and came bounding back to find that his wife, frightened out of her wits, had fled after throwing away the root. Having searched around for it frantically, but in vain, he pursued his wife and tore her to pieces. Not being able to resume human shape, he afterward continued avenging himself on mankind in general.

Jim Corbett wrote:

> In Garhwal, all kills by man-eaters are attributed to sadhus (holy men), and in the Naini Tal and Almora districts all such kills are attributed to the Bokhsars, who dwell in the unhealthy belt of grass at the foot of the hills called the Terai, living chiefly on game. The sadhus are believed to kill for the lust of human flesh and blood, and the Bokhsars are believed to kill for the jewellery their victims are wearing, or for other valuables they may have on their person.

The leopard of Rudraprayag was naturally declared to be a "were leopard," and this nearly cost a holy man his life. This is how Corbett tells the story:

Incensed at the killing of their relatives and friends, and convinced that a human being was responsible for the deaths, an angry crowd of men seized an unfortunate Sadhu of Kothagi village, Dasjulapatty, but before they were able to wreak their vengeance on him, Philip Mason, then Deputy Commissioner of Garhwal, who was camping in the vicinity, arrived on the scene. Seeing the temper of the crowd, and being a man of great experience, Mason said he had no doubt that the real culprit had been apprehended, but that before the Sadhu was lynched, justice demanded that his guilt should be established. To this end he suggested that the Sadhu should be placed under arrest and closely guarded night and day. To this suggestion the crowd agreed, and for seven days and seven nights the Sadhu was carefully guarded by the police and as carefully watched by the populace. On the eighth morning, when the guard and the watchers were being changed, word was brought that a house in a village some miles away had been broken into and a man carried off. The populace raised no objection to the Sadhu being released that day, contenting themselves by saying that on this occasion the wrong man had been apprehended, but that next time no mistake would be made.

The belief in "were lions" and "were leopards" has often been exploited by secret societies. Ritual murders were made to look like man-eater killings, with the fatal wounds being inflicted by means of iron claws, and the spoor of the presumed culprit faked with a piece of wood carved in the shape of a lion's or leopard's foot. In Tanzania there was a court case connected with "lion men" murders as recently as 1957. Societies of "Leopard Men" were at one time widespread throughout the forest areas of West Africa, from northern Angola and the Congo basin through Gaboon, Cameroon, southern Nigeria, Ghana, Ivory Coast, Liberia, Sierra Leone to Guinea and Senegal. They have received a good deal of publicity, being used to add spice to many a travel book or jungle film, but there also exist a number of serious anthropological studies, like the one by Paul-Ernest Joset, which, in its sober and factual treatment of the subject, makes more horrific reading than any of the more sensationally coloured accounts.

We have so far dealt with the cults, myths, and customs that have sprung up around Old World felines, especially lions, tigers, and leopards. Exactly the same superstitions and beliefs are, however, encountered in the New World, attached, naturally, to the jaguar and puma.

Many Guiana tribes, for instance, regard the jaguar as their ancestor. On the Rio Putumayo, de Wavrin found the Huitotos, Ocayanas, and Boros regarding the "tigre" as a malevolent spirit, a supernatural sorcerer whom it was useless to fight. Evil spirits, the people said, were immortal and could not be killed. In the case of a jaguar actually succumbing to a hunter's spear or arrow, the spirit would live on and continue its evil machinations. He was told that, at the beginning of the twentieth century, the jaguars of the Putumayo were of an unusual boldness, occasionally penetrating communal houses in which up to a hundred Indians might be assembled. As the animal chose its victim and dragged it away, no hand was raised against it, the people contenting themselves with calling out: "Take this child (or this woman)! Keep your prey, eat it! But be satisfied with this one and do not come back. Keep away from us in future!" The similarity with the attitude displayed toward man-eating tigers by primitive Siberian tribes is striking.

The Indians of the Rio Napo believe their medicine men to turn into jaguars after death in order to harry the living. Fighting a jaguar does therefore not mean opposing a spirit, but a man like any other, even though he may have taken on the shape of an animal. A Napo warrior therefore feels not the slightest hesitation about attacking a jaguar. If he himself gets killed or wounded in the encounter, this is not taken as a manifestation of superior powers on the part of the jaguar-wizzard, but merely put down to the luck of the game.

Cat cults have played an important part in all Amerindian civilizations, often in forms quite as twisted and fearsome as anything the Old World has to offer. The Olmecs of Tabasco and Vera Cruz had such a high regard for the "tigre" that Richard Perry wrote of them: "They were more than worshippers. They were jaguar psychotics—deforming their heads in imitation of the great cat's flattened skull and depicting the childlike or Mongolian faces of their images with feline mouths, the lower lips brutally exaggerated." There is, of course, the parallel of Naga tribesmen reproducing the whiskers of their leopard blood-brothers by cutting lines into their faces.

Jaguar worship was a dominant element in the religion of the Zapotecs of Oaxaca, with the citadel of Cosijo, the Jaguar god, perched on top of the hill now known as Monte Alban. The Maya, too, had their Jaguar god, and the big cats were often represented by their artists. Cat gods of one kind or another were, in fact, worshipped from Mexico to Chile, with the puma largely taking the jaguar's place among the Andean peoples. In ancient Mexico nobody doubted the ability of certain individuals to control jaguars or to take on their shape, and the Secret Society of the Nahualists forms an exact counterpart to the "Leopard Men" of West Africa. Its members wore jaguar skins and committed ritual assassinations.

It is at present assumed that man entered America about 30,000 years ago. Before they crossed the Bering Strait, the ancestors of the Amerindians must have been familiar with the giant Pleistocene tigers of China and eastern Siberia. Did the American cat cults evolve from elements brought over from Asia? Or did they develop quite independently in contact with the big cats of the New World, but on lines startlingly parallel to the myths, superstitions, and cults of Asia and Africa? It seems that totemistic and animistic beliefs connected with large and powerful carnivores, especially with big cats, must have originated far back in the Palaeolithic and might well have spread over a large part of the world long before the Neolithic inhabitants of Çatal Hüyük produced their leopard reliefs. The belief in human beings able to change into animals, either through magic or by way of rebirth, may be among the very oldest of mankind's superstitions.

A very pleasant relic of ancient cat worship has been left to us in the shape of the domestic cat. As has already been mentioned, there is evidence of small cats being kept at Haçilar during the sixth millennium B.C., probably as manageable substitutes for the religiously venerated leopards and lions. In Egypt, the domestic cat made its appearance at the beginning of the second millennium B.C., quite possibly as a miniature stand-in for the lion. After a time, however, it became sacred to the Goddess Bast or Pasht and was made the object of a cult of its own. At the death of a cat, the whole household went into mourning. The corpse was embalmed, put into a coffin, and transported to the temple of Bast at Bubastis. One of ancient Egypt's greatest festivals was the solemn entombment of all the cats that had died in the course of the past year. Each cat's "relatives" offered sacrifices to the goddess and provided food and toys for their pet's tomb. The ceremony closed on a somewhat lighter note with a feast, in the course of which considerable quantities of wine were drunk.

In Europe, where lynxes—and possibly forest wildcats as well—had long been associated with the Goddess Freya, vestiges of a cat cult seem to have survived all through mediaeval times, bringing down upon poor Puss the wrath and condemnation of the Church. During the darkest ages of Christianity it became a familiar of witches, a creature of Satan, and in parts of Central Europe it was customary during Lent to kill and bury as many cats as possible. The God-fearing people of the Vosges and Ardennes apparently celebrated the Easter festival by burning cats alive. Puss, however, survived priestly persecution and continued its more or less symbiotic association with man. Today, protected by law, watched over by the Societies for the Prevention of Cruelty to Animals, with an estimated population of twelve million in Britain alone, it can be said to have won the battle.

We can be certain that our Stone Age ancestors were fascinated by the big cats. This fascination, which found expression on Palaeolithic cave walls and in Neolithic shrines, is still with us. Of the tourists who flock to eastern and southern Africa in the tens of thousands, the majority have three animals at the top of their mental check-list—the lion, first and foremost, followed by the leopard and the cheetah. They might not worry too much about not having seen any buffaloes or even rhinos, but they would be greatly disappointed if they were not to see—and photograph—the three cats. No question is asked more often at the entrance to Nairobi National Park than, "Wapi Simba? Where are the lions?" Half the cars you meet in a drive round the park will stop as they come abreast of you, and you will hear the question: "Have you seen any lions today?"—or the occupants will eagerly volunteer information on where they themselves have encountered lions. This, incidentally, applies not only to overseas tourists, for Nairobi residents can sit for hours contemplating those big, magnificent cats.

This new relationship between man and felines—which could easily be extended to tigers in India and to jaguars in some of the Central and South American countries—has so far been quite amazingly peaceful, a fact all the more astonishing if one considers the innane stupidity humans so often display when it comes to dealing with wild animals. The few accidents—very few indeed—have all been due to human carelessness. What, for instance, can one say of three men camping in the middle of the Serengeti in a tent so minute that they have to lie with their heads on the outside? Two lions passing at night were attracted by the three round objects, and one of them began to investigate more closely. A piercing scream induced it to close its jaws—with disastrous results. The unfortunate victim was rushed to Nairobi by air with a fractured skull, but died before the plane could touch down.

A few days before these lines were written, the *East African Standard* ran the following headline: "Woman in minibus clawed by leopard." The news story told of two tourist buses following—"chasing" would probably be a better word—a full-grown leopard until it was caught between the two vehicles. The leopard naturally felt cornered and tried to defend itself. It jumped up at one of the cars, and a lady tourist sitting at an open window had the misfortune of getting her arm and chest badly scratched. The Nairobi lawyer handling the lady's affairs in East Africa was quoted as saying, "Nobody seems to have heard of a leopard behaving in this way before."

Considering the way some drivers of tourist buses have in recent years been harrying the Seronera leopard, these words speak volumes for the patience and the exemplary behavior of the spotted cats. It is up to us humans not to abuse and destroy this mutual trust between man and the big cats which has emerged after millennia of confrontation and exploitation.

Bibliography

Akeley, Carl E. 1924. *In Brightest Africa*. London.

Akeley, Mary L. Jobe. 1937. *Restless Jungle*. London.

Alexander, Boyd. 1907. *From the Niger to the Nile*. London.

Alexander, Sir J. Edward. 1838. *An Expedition of Discovery into the Interior of Africa*. London.

Ali, Salim. 1927. "The Moghul Emperors of India as Naturalists and Sportsmen." Pt. 1. *Journ. Bombay Nat. Hist. Soc.*, vol. 31.

Allen, G. M. 1938. "The Mammals of China and Mongolia." *Natural History of Central Asia*, vol. 11, pt. 1, New York.

———. 1954. "Check List of African Mammals." *Bull. Mus. Comp. Zoology*, vol. 83, Boston.

Allen, J. A. 1924. "Carnivores Collected by the American Museum Congo Expedition." *Bull. Am. Mus. Nat. Hist.*, vol. 47, New York.

Anderson, Kenneth. 1956. *Nine Man-eaters and One Rogue*. London.

———. 1957. *The Black Panther of Sivanipalli*. London.

André, Eugene. 1904. *A Naturalist in the Guianas*. London.

Anon. 1967. "Fun Furs." *The New Yorker*. Reprinted in *Oryx*, vol. 9, no. 3.

———. 1968. "New Mammal Discovered: *Mayailurus iriomotensis*." *Animals*, vol. 10.

———. 1972. "Cheetah in Trouble in East Africa." *Oryx*, vol. 11, no. 6.

———. 1972. "Iran Guards Its Wildlife." *Oryx*, vol. 11, no. 6.

———. 1972. "Project Tiger." *Oryx*, vol. 11, no. 6.

Ansell, W. F. H. 1960. *Mammals of Northern Rhodesia*. Lusaka.

Anthony, H. E. 1928. *Field Book of North American Mammals*. New York–London.

Arseniew, Wladimir K. 1924. *In der Wildnis Ostsibiriens*. Berlin.

Baikov, Nikolai. 1939. *Les Bêtes Sauvages de la Mandchourie*. Paris.

———. 1952. *Le Grand Van: La Vie d'un Tigre de Mandchourie*. Paris.

Bailey, F. M. 1939. "Occurrence of Tiger in Sikkim." *Journ. Bombay Nat. Hist. Soc.*, vol. 41.

Bailey, Theodore N. 1972. "The Elusive Bobcat." *Natural History*, vol. 81, no. 8.

Bailey, Vernon. 1931. *Mammals of New Mexico*. Washington.

———. 1936. *The Mammals and Life Zones of Oregon*. Washington.

Baines, Thomas. 1946. *The Northern Goldfield Diaries*. London.

Baker, Sir Samuel. 1890. *Wild Beasts and Their Ways*. London.

Barclay, Ford. 1915. "The Manchurian Tiger." In *The Gun at Home and Abroad: The Big Game of Asia and North America*. London.

Bates, Henry Walter. 1892. *The Naturalist on the River Amazon*. London.

Baumann, F. 1949. *Die freilebenden Saeugetiere der Schweiz*. Bern.

Bazé, William. 1957. *Tiger! Tiger!* London.

Beaton, K. de P. 1949. *A Warden's Diary*. 2 vols. Nairobi.

Beaufort, F. de. 1968. "Survivance du Lynx dans le Parc National des Pyrénées Occidentales." *Mammalia*, tome 32, no. 2.

Bechtle, Wolfgang. 1972. "Die Wildkatzen des Herrn Professors." *Kosmos*, vol. 68, no. 11.

Beck, Pierre, and Huard, Paul. 1969. *Tibesti—Carrefour de la Préhistoire Saharienne.* Paris.

Beebe, William. 1954. *A Naturalist's Life of New York.* London.

Beelaerts van Blokland, Jonkher M. A. 1964. "Quelques Remarques sur le Lion et l'Aigle comme Figures Héraldiques." Extrait du Recueil du Septième Congrès International des Sciences Généaloques et Héraldiques.

Belt, T. 1874. *The Naturalist in Nicaragua.* London.

Bere, Rennie M. 1962. *The Wild Mammals of Uganda.* London.

———. 1966. *Wild Animals in an African National Park.* London.

Berg, Bengt. 1933. *Meine Jagd nach dem Einhorn.* Frankfurt am Main.

———. 1934. *Tiger und Mensch.* Berlin.

———. 1955. *Meine Abenteuer unter Tieren.* Guetersloh.

Bergman Sucksdorff, Astrid. 1970. *Tiger in Sight.* London.

Besser, Hans. 1915. *Raubwild und Dickhaeuter in Deutsch-Ostafrika.* Stuttgart.

Biddulph, C. H. 1937. "Young Elephant Killed by a Tiger." *Journ. Bombay Nat. Hist. Soc.,* vol. 39.

Bieger, W., and Wahlström, A. 1938. *Die wildlebenden Saeugetiere Mitteleuropas.* Heidelberg.

Bigourdan, J., and Prunier, L. 1937. *Les Mammifères Sauvages de l'Ouest Africain.* Montrouge.

Blackmore, Michael. 1948. *Mammals of Britain.* London.

Blanford, W. T. 1881–1891. *The Fauna of British India and Ceylon: Mammalia.* London.

Blönk, H. L. 1963. *Wildkatzen.* Zutphen.

Bodenheimer, F. S. 1935. *Animal Life in Palestine.* Jerusalem.

Bombay Natural History Society editors. 1921. "A White Tiger in Captivity." *Journ. Bombay Nat. Hist. Soc.,* vol. 27.

Boorer, Michael. 1969. *Wild Cats.* London.

Bourgoin, Pierre. 1955. *Animaux de Chasse d'Afrique.* Paris.

Bourlière, T., and Verschuren, J. 1960. *Introduction à l'Ecologie des Ongulés du Parc National Albert.* Brussels.

Brander, A. A. Dunbar. 1927. *Wild Animals in Central India.* London.

Brehm, A. E. 1925. *Tierleben.* Vol. 4. Leipzig.

Brentjes, Burchard. 1965. *Die Haustierwerdung im Orient: Ein archaeologischer Beitrag zur Zoologie.* Wittenberg Lutherstadt.

Brink, F. H. van den. 1957. *Die Saeugetiere Europas.* Hamburg–Berlin.

Brocklehurst, H. C. 1931. *Game Animals of the Sudan.* London.

Broderick, A. Houghton, ed. 1972. *Animals in Archaeology.* London.

Brooks, A. C. 1962. "Uganda's Small Mammals: The Small Cats." *Wild Life and Sport,* vol. 3, no. 2.

Brown, C. A. 1938. *Claws: The Tale of a Lion.* London.

Brown, C. Barrington. 1876. *Canoe and Camp Life in British Guiana.* London.

Burbridge, Ben. 1928. *Gorilla: Tracking and Capturing the Ape-Man of Africa.* London.

Burchell, William J. 1953. Reprint. *Travels in the Interior of South Africa.* London.

Burmeister, Hermann. 1861. *Reise durch die La Plata Staaten.* Halle.

Burrard, G. 1926. *Big Game Hunting in the Himalayas and Tibet.* London.

Burton, Maurice. 1962. *Systematic Dictionary of Mammals of the World.* London.

Burton, R. G. 1918. "Panthers." *Journ. Bombay Nat. Hist. Soc.,* vol. 26.

———. 1921. "Tigers in Trees." *Journ. Bombay Nat. Hist. Soc.,* vol. 27.

———. 1928. *Sport and Wild Life in the Deccan.* London.

———. 1932. *Les Mangeurs d'Hommes.* Paris.

———. 1933. *The Book of the Tiger.* London.

Butler, A. L. 1914. "Notes on the Lion in the Sudan." In Pease, *The Book of the Lion.* London.

———. 1932. "The Game Animals of the Blue Nile." In Maydon, *Big Game Shooting in Africa.* London.

Büttikofer, J. 1890. *Reisebilder aus Liberia.* Leiden.

Cabrera, Angel. 1960. *Catalogo de los Mamiferos de America del Sur.* Buenos Aires.

Cahalane, Victor H. 1943. "King of Cats and His Court." *National Geographic,* vol. 83, no. 2.

———. 1960. "The American Cats." In *Wild Animals of North America.* Washington.

Caldwell, Harry R. 1924. *Blue Tiger.* London.

Caras, Roger A. 1964. *Dangerous to Man.* Philadelphia–New York.

Carpenter, R. R. M. 1939. "Hunting the Puma." In *North America Big Game.* New York.

Carter, T. D.; Hill, J. E.; and Tate, G. H. 1945. *Mammals of the Pacific World.* New York.

Champion, F. W. 1928. *With a Camera in Tiger-Land.* London.

———. 1929. "Tiger Tracks." *Journ. Bombay Nat. Hist. Soc.,* vol. 33.

———. 1934. *The Jungle in Sunlight and Shadow.* London.

Chapman, Frank M. 1927. "Who Tread Our Trails." *National Geographic,* vol. 52, no. 3.

Cherrie, G. K. 1930. *Dark Trails.* New York.

Child, G. S. 1965. "Some Notes on the Mammals of Kilimanjaro." *Tanganyika Notes and Records,* no. 64.

Chochod, Louis. 1950. *La Faune Indochinoise.* Paris.

Clair, Colin. 1967. *Unnatural History.* London–New York.

Clark, James L. 1939. "The Big Tom of Beaver Dam, Washington." *Natural History,* vol. 44, no. 3.

Clarke, James. 1969. *Man Is the Prey; An Investigation into the Motives and Habits of Man's Natural Enemies.* London.

Colditz, R. von. 1925. *Im Reiche des Kondor.* Berlin.

Condé, B., and Schauenberg, P. 1969. "Reproduction du Chat Forestier d'Europe *(Felis silvestris* Schreber) en Captivité." *Revue Suisse de Zoologie,* tome 76, no. 7.

———. 1971. "Le poids du Chat Forestier d'Europe *(Felis silvestris* Schreber 1777)." *Revue Suisse de Zoologie,* tome 78.

Copley, Hugh. "The Power of Scent in Wild Animals." *Journ. Bombay Nat. Hist. Soc.,* vol. 38.

———. 1950. *Small Mammals of Kenya.* Nairobi.

Corbett, Jim. 1946. *Man-Eaters of Kumaon.* London.

———. 1953. *Jungle Lore.* London.

———. 1954. *The Temple Tiger.* London.

———. 1956. *The Man-eating Leopard of Rudraprayag.* London.

Cotton, W. B. 1912. *Sport in the Eastern Sudan.* London.

Cumming, R. Gordon. 1850. *Five Years of a Hunter's Life in the Far Interior of South Africa.* London.

Cumming, W. Gordon. 1871. *Wild Men and Wild Beasts—Scenes in Camp and Jungle.* Edinburgh.

Cunningham, R. O. 1871. *Notes on the Natural History of the Strait of Magellan and West Coast of Patagonia.* Edinburgh.

D'Abreu, E. A. 1916. "An Albino Tiger from the Central Provinces." *Journ. Bombay Nat. Hist. Soc.,* vol. 24.

Dallet, Robert. 1972. "La Fin des Tigres." *La Vie des Bêtes,* no. 171.

Darwin, Charles. 1889. *Journal of the Researches into the Natural History and Geology of the Countries Visited During the Voyage of H.M.S. "Beagle" Round the World.* London.

David, Ad. 1916. *Jagden und Abenteuer in den Gebieten des oberen Nil.* Basel.

Dekeyser, P. L 1955. *Les Mammifères de l'Afrique Noire Française.* Dakar.

Denis, Armand. 1964. *Cats of the World.* London.

Dorst, Jean, and Dandelot, Pierre. 1970. *A Field Guide to the Large Mammals of Africa.* London.

Drake-Brockman, R. E. 1910. *The Mammals of Somaliland.* London.

Dugmore, A. Radclyffe. 1910. *Camera Adventures in the African Wilds.* London.

———. 1925. "Cats of the Wild." In *Wild Life Illustrated.* London.

Eaton, R. L. 1969. "Hunting Relationship of Cheetahs with Non-prey Species." *Mammalia,* vol. 33, no. 3.

———. 1969. "Notes on Breathing Rates in Wild Cheetahs." *Mammalia,* vol. 33, no. 3.

Edey, M., and Dominis, J. 1968. *The Cats of Africa.* New York.

Edmond-Blanc, F. 1954. *Le Grand Livre de la Faune Africaine et de sa Chasse.* Paris-Brussels-Geneva-Zurich.

Eliez, Annie. 1967. *Le Lion et l'Homme, des Origines à nos Jours.* Paris.

Ellerman, J., and Morrison-Scott, T. 1951. *Checklist of Palaearctic and Indian Mammals.* London.

———, Morrison-Scott, T. C. S., and Hayman, R. W. 1953. *Southern African Mammals 1758–1946.* London.

Emcke, W. 1963. "Bericht ueber Geburt und Aufzucht von Geparden, *Acinonyx jubatus* (Schreb.) im Krefelder Tierpark." *Der Zoologische Garten,* bd. 27, heft 4/5.

Ewer, R. T. 1973. *The Carnivores.* London.

Fawcett, P. H. 1953. *Exploration Fawcett.* London.

Fellner, Karl. 1968. "Erste natuerliche Aufzucht von Nebelparder (*Neofelis nebulosa*) in einem Zoo." *Der Zoologische Garten,* bd. 35, heft 3.

———. 1970. "Einige Bemerkungen zur zweiten natuerlichen Nebelparder–Aufzucht im Vergleich zur ersten." *Der Zoologische Garten,* bd. 38, heft 1/2.

Fend, Werner. 1968. *Tiger vor der Kamera.* Vienna.

———. 1972. *Die Tiger von Abutschmar.* Vienna-Munich-Zurich.

Fengewisch, Heinz-Jürgen. 1968. *Grossraubwild in Europas Revieren.* Munich.

Fenton, L. 1905. "Tigers Hamstringing Their Prey Before Killing." *Journ. Bombay Nat. Hist. Soc.,* vol. 16.

Field, F. 1916. "Hyaena Driving Panther Away from Its Kill." *Journ. Bombay Nat. Hist. Soc.,* vol. 24.

Finn, Frank, 1929. *Sterndale's Mammalia of India. A New and Abridged Edition, Thoroughly Revised and with an Appendix on Reptilia.* Calcutta–Simla.

Fisher, James; Simon, Noel; and Vincent, Jack. 1969. *The Red Book: Wildlife in Danger.* London.

Floericke, Kurt. 1927. *Aussterbende Tiere: Biber, Nerz, Luchs, Uhu.* Stuttgart.

Ford, Alice. 1951. *Audubon's Animals: The Quadrupeds of North America.* London.

Forsyth, J. 1919. *The Highlands of Central India.* London.

Frechkop, S. 1943. "Exploration du Parc National Albert." *Mammifères.* Brussels.

———. 1944. "Exploration du Parc National de la Kagera." *Mammifères.* Brussels.

Frick, Childs. 1939. "Big Game of the Pleistocene." In *North American Big Game.* New York–London.

Frobenius, Leo. 1954. *Kulturgeschichte Afrikas.* Zurich.

Fülleborn, Friedrich. 1906. *Das deutsche Njassa—und Rowuma Gebiet nebst Bemerkungen ueber die Schire Laender.* Berlin.

Gaillard, Dr. 1969. "Sur la Présence du Chat Doré (*Felis aurata Temminck*) et du Caracal (*Felis caracal Schreber*) dans le Sud du Sénégal." *Mammalia,* tome 33, no. 2.

Gee, E. P. "The Size of the Jungle Cat (*Felis chaus affinis*)." *Journ. Bombay Nat. Hist. Soc.*, vol. 39.

———. 1959. "Report on a Survey of the Rhinoceros Area of Nepal, March and April 1959." *Oryx*, vol. 5, no. 2.

———. 1964. *The Wild Life of India*. London.

Geisler, M.; Gropp, A.; Leyhausen, P.; and Tonkin, B. A. 1968. "Cytologische Untersuchungen an Suedamerikanischen Pardelkatzen." *Zeitschr. f. Saeugetierkunde*, bd. 33, heft 5.

George, Wilma. 1969. *Animals and Maps*. London.

Gerber, R. 1968. *Wildlebende Raubtiere Deutschlands*. Stuttgart.

Gesner, Conrad. 1563. *Thierbuch*. Zurich.

Gessi, Romolo. 1892. *Seven Years in the Soudan*. London.

Goldman, E. A. 1920. *Mammals of Panama*. Smithsonian Miscellaneous Collection, vol. 69, no. 5. Washington.

———. 1939 *a*. "The Puma: Description and Distribution." In *North American Big Game*. New York–London.

———. 1939 *b*. "The Jaguar: Description and Distribution." In *North American Big Game*. New York.

Goodwin, George G. 1953. "Lions—the Proud Big Cats." *Animal Kingdom*, vol. 56, no. 4.

———. 1961 *a*. "The Natural History of the Mountain Lion, or Cougar (*Felis concolor*)." In O'Connor, *The Big Game Animals of North America*. New York.

———. 1961 *b*. "The Natural History of the Jaguar (*Felis onca*)." In O'Connor, *The Big Game Animals of North America*. New York.

Gordon, Seton. 1927. *Days with the Golden Eagle*. London.

Greenwood, James. 1864. *Wild Sports of the World*. London.

Grew, J. C. 1910. *Sport and Travel in the Far East*. London.

Grzimek, B. 1973. "Tierleben." *Enzyklopaedie des Tierreichs, Saeugetiere*, bd. 3. Zurich.

Gromier, E. 1936. *La Vie des Animaux Sauvages de l'Afrique*. Paris.

Gudger, E. W. 1925. "Cats as Fishermen." *Natural History*, vol. 25, no. 2.

Guggisberg, C. A. W. 1953. *Unter Loewen und Elefanten*. Bern.

———. 1955. *Das Tierleben der Alpen*, vol. 2. Bern.

———. 1961. *Simba, the Life of the Lion*. Cape Town.

———. 1963. *The Wilderness Is Free*. Cape Town.

———. 1966. *S.O.S. Rhino*. London–Nairobi.

———. 1966–1968. "Beobachtungen an ostafrikanischen Leoparden, *Panthera pardus fusca* (F. A. A. Meyer)." *Jahrbuch des Naturhistorischen Museums der Stadt Bern*.

———. 1969. *Giraffes*. London–New York.

———. 1970. *Man and Wildlife*. London.

———. 1972. *Animals of Africa*. Nairobi.

———. 1972. *Crocodiles*. Newton Abbot.

Hainard, Robert. 1948–1949. *Mammifères Sauvages d'Europe*. 2 vols. Neuchatel.

Hall, E. Raymond, and Kelson, Keith. 1959. *The Mammals of North America*. New York.

Haltenorth, Th. 1937. "Die verwandtschaftliche Stellung der Grosskatzen zueinander." Leipzig.

———. 1953. *Die Wildkatzen der Alten Welt*. Eine Uebersicht ueber die Untergattung Felis. Leipzig.

———. 1957. *Die Wildkatze*. Wittenberg Lutherstadt.

Hanley, Patrick. 1961. *Tiger Trails in Assam*. London.

Harper, Francis. 1945. *Extinct and Vanishing Mammals of the Old World*. New York.

Harris, W. Cornwallis. 1969. Reprint. *Portraits of the Game and Wild Animals of Southern Africa*. Cape Town.

Harrison, David L. 1968. *The Mammals of Arabia.* Vol. 2. London.

Heck, Lutz. 1966. "Ueber den Kaploewen im Staedtischen Museum zu Wiesbaden." *Jahrbuecher des Nassauischen Vereins fuer Naturkunde,* bd. 98. Wiesbaden.

Hediger, H. 1966. *Jagdzoologie auch fuer Nichtjaeger.* Basel.

Hedin, Sven. 1903. *Central Asia and Tibet.* London.

———. 1940. *The Wandering Lake.* London.

Heuglin, M. Th. von. 1874. *Reise nach Abessinien, den Gala-Laendern, Ost-Sudan und Chartum.* Gera.

Hewett, Sir John. 1938. *Jungle Trails in Northern India.* London.

Hewitt, C. Gordon. 1921. *The Conservation of the Wild Life of Canada.* New York.

Hingston, R. W. G. 1920. *A Naturalist in Himalaya.* London.

Hodson, A. W. 1912. *Trekking the Great Thirst: Sport and Travel in the Kalahari Desert.* London.

———. 1927. *Seven Years in Southern Abyssinia.* London.

———. 1929. *Where Lion Reign; An Account of Lion Hunting and Exploration in S.W. Abyssinia.* London.

Hoogerwerf, A. 1970. *Udjung Kulon.* Leiden.

Hoogstraal, H. K.; Wassif, I. Helmy; and Kaiser, M. 1966–1967. "The Cheetah, *Acinonyx jubatus* Schreber." *Egypt. Bull. Zool. Soc.,* vol. 21.

Hornaday, William T. 1927. *American Natural History.* New York–London.

Hornocker, Maurice G. 1969. "Stalking the Mountain Lion—to Save Him." *National Geographic,* vol. 136, no. 5.

Hose, Charles. 1893. *A Descriptive Account of the Mammals of Borneo.* London.

———. 1929. *The Field Book of a Jungle Wallah, Being a Description of Shore, River and Forest Life in Sarawak.* London.

Hoyos-Sprinzenstein, Ernst Graf. 1930. *Mit der Buechse in der Mongolei, in Altai und Thian-Schan.* Neudamm.

Hubert, E. 1947. *La Faune des Grands Mammifères de la Plaine Rwindi-Rutschuru (Lac Edward).* Brussels.

Hudson, W. H. 1892. *The Naturalist in La Plata.* London.

Humboldt, A. von. 1853. *Personal Narrative of Travels to the Equinoctal Regions of America During 1799–1804.* London.

Hunter, J. A. 1938. *White Hunter, the Adventures and Experiences of a Professional Big Game Hunter in Africa.* London.

Hyams, Edward. 1972. *Animals in the Service of Man: 10,000 Years of Domestication.* London.

Inverarity, J. D. 1891. "Notes on the Mammalia of Somaliland." *Journ. Bombay Nat. Hist. Soc.,* vol. 6.

Ionides, C. J. P. 1946. "Some Native Beliefs Concerning Animals." *Journ. E. A. Nat. Hist. Soc.,* vol. 19, nos. 3 and 4.

———. 1950. "Pages from a Tanganyika Game Ranger's Notebook." *Tanganyika Notes and Records,* no. 29.

———. 1954. "Nature Notes (1)." *African Wild Life,* vol. 8, no. 3.

Jackson, F. J. 1894. "East Africa." In Badminton Library of Sports and Pastimes, *Big Game Shooting.* London.

Jaeger, E. C. 1961. *Desert Wildlife.* Stanford, Calif.

Jany, Eberhard. 1967. "Heinrich Barths Mitteilungen zur Flora und Fauna Afrikas (1849–1855)." In *Heinrich Barth, ein Forscher in Afrika.* Wiesbaden.

Jardine, Sir William. 1834. The Naturalist's Library. Vol. 2. *The Felines.* London.

Jeannin, A. 1936. *Les Mammifères Sauvages du Cameroun.* Paris.

———. 1951. *La Faune Africaine: Biologie-Histoire-Folklore-Chasse.* Paris.

———. 1954. "Les Lions et les Panthères." In *Le Grand Livre de la Faune Africaine et de sa Chasse.* Paris–Brussels–Geneva–Zurich.

Jeary, Bertram F. 1936. *Pride of Lions.* London.

Jennison, George. 1937. *Animals for Show and Pleasure in Ancient Rome.* Manchester.

Jerdon, T. C. 1874. *The Mammals of India.* London.

Johnson, Martin. 1924. *Camera Trails in Africa.* London.

———. 1928. *Safari.* New York.

———. 1929. *Lion.* New York.

Johnston, Sir Harry. 1902. *The Uganda Protectorate.* London.

———. 1906. *Liberia.* London.

Joset, P. E. 1955. *Les Sociétés Secrètes des Hommes—Léopards en Afrique Noire.* Paris.

Kauffmann, O. 1923. *Aus Indiens Dschungeln: Erlebnisse und Forschungen.* Bonn–Leipzig.

Kearton, Cherry. 1929. *In the Land of the Lion.* London.

Kennion, R. L. 1911. *By Mountain, Lake and Plain: Being Sketches of Sport in Eastern Persia.* Edinburgh–London.

Kinloch, Alexander A. A. 1892. *Large Game Shooting in Thibet, the Himalayas, Northern and Central India.* Calcutta.

Kirby, F. Vaughan. 1895. *The Haunts of Wild Game: A Hunter-Naturalist's Wanderings from Kahlamba to Libombo.* London.

Kittenberger, Kalman. 1929. *Big Game Hunting and Collecting in East Africa.* London.

Koenig, Claus. 1969. *Wildlebende Saeugetiere Europas.* Stuttgart.

Kolb, Peter. 1731. *The Present State of the Cape of Good Hope.* London.

Kortlandt, A. 1962. "Chimpanzees in the Wild." *Scientific American,* vol. 206, no. 5.

Kratovchil, Josef, et al. 1968. "History of the Distribution of the Lynx in Europe." *Acta Sc. nat. Brno,* vol. 2, nos. 4 and 5/6.

Krieg, Hans. 1939. *Als Zoologe in den Steppen und Wäldern Patagoniesn.* Munich.

———. 1948. *Zwischen Anden und Atlantik.* Munich.

Kruger National Park. 1960. Annual Report of the Biologist 1958/1959. "Koedoe," no. 3.

Krumbiegel, Ingo. 1952. *Der Loewe.* Leipzig.

———. 1954–1955. *Biologie der Saeugetiere.* 2 vols. Krefeld.

Kruuk, H., and Turner, M. 1967. "Comparative Notes on Predation by Lion, Leopard, Cheetah and Wild Dog in the Serengeti Area, East Africa." *Mammalia,* tome 31.

Kuhnert, Wilhelm. 1923. *Im Lande meiner Modelle.* Leipzig.

Kurtén, Björn. 1968. *Pleistocene Mammals of Europé.* London.

———. 1971. *The Age of Mammals.* London.

Lange, Kurt. 1954. "Grosswildjagd im Alten Orient." *Orion,* vol. 9, no. 13/14.

Layard, Sir Henry, 1887. *Early Adventures in Persia, Susiana and Babylonia.* London.

Leakey, L. S. B. 1969. *The Wild Realm: Animals of Africa.* Washington.

Leyhausen, P. 1960. *Verhaltensstudien an Katzen.* Berlin.

———, and Falkena, Maria. 1966. "Breeding the Brazilian Ocelot-Cat, *Leopardus tigrinus,* in Captivity." *Internat. Zoo Yearbook,* vol. 6.

———, and Tonkin, Barbara. 1966. "Breeding the Black-Footed Cat, *Felis nigripes,* in Captivity." *Internat. Zoo Yearbook,* vol. 6.

Lhote, Henri. 1951. *La Chasse chez les Touaregs.* Paris.

Lindblom, Gerhard. 1920. *The Akamba in British East Africa.* Upsala.

Lindemann, W. 1950. "Beobachtungen an wilden und gezaehmten Luchsen." *Zeitschr. f. Tierpsychologie,* bd. 7, heft 2.

———. 1951. "Der Karpathenluchs." *Schweiz. Naturschutz,* vol. 17, no. 2.

Livingstone, David. 1857. *Missionary Travels and Researches in South Africa.* London.

———. 1956. *The Zambesi Expedition of David Livingstone, 1859–1863.* London.

Lloyd, Joan Barclay. 1971. *African Animals in Renaissance Literature and Art.* Oxford.

Locke, A. 1954. *The Tigers of Trengganu.* London.

Loevenbruck, Pierre. 1955. *Les Animaux Sauvages dans l'Histoire.* Paris.

Logan-Home, Major W. M. 1927. "A Panther Treeing Its Kill." *Journ. Bombay Nat. Hist. Soc.,* vol. 32.

Longrigg, J. H. 1921. "Panther in a Tree with a Pig." *Journ. Bombay Nat. Hist. Soc.,* vol. 27.

Lueps, Peter. 1971. "Zwei neue Nachweise der Wildkatze im Kanton Bern (1969, 1970)." *Revue Suisse de Zoologie,* tome 78.

Lydekker, Richard. 1896. *A Hand-Book of the Carnivora.* Pt. 1: "Cats, Civets and Mongooses." London.

———. 1926. *The Game Animals of Africa.* 2d ed., revised by J. G. Dollman. London.

Lyell, D. D. 1932. "The Lion and Leopard." In Maydon, *Big Game Shooting in Africa.* London.

Maberly, C. T. Astley. 1951. *Animals of the Kruger National Park.* 6th ed.

———. 1959. *Animals of Rhodesia.* Cape Town.

———. 1960. *Animals of East Africa.* Cape Town.

———. 1963. *The Game Animals of Southern Africa.* Cape Town.

McCowan, Dan. 1936. *Animals of the Canadian Rockies.* London.

McIntyre, Loren. 1972. "The Amazon—Mightiest of River." *National Geographic,* vol. 142, no. 4.

Mackenzie, D. R. 1925. *The Spirit-ridden Konde.* London.

MacNally, L. 1968. *Highland Year.* London.

Malbrant, R., and Maclatchy, A. 1949. *Faune de l'Equateur Africain Français,* tome 2. Paris.

Martin, Paul S., and Guilday, John E. 1967. "A Bestiary for Pleistocene Biologists." In *Pleistocene Extinctions: The Search for a Cause.* New Haven–London.

Martini, Helen. 1955. *My Zoo Family.* London.

Matschie, Paul. 1895. *Die Saeugetiere Deutsch-Ost-Afrikas.* Berlin.

———. 1898. "Aus der Saeugetierwelt der mittleren Hochlaender Deutsch-Ost-Afrikas." In C. Werther, *Die mittleren Hochlaender des noerdlichen Deutsch-Ost-Afrikas.* Berlin.

Mathews, L. Harrison. 1952. *British Mammals.* London.

Matthews, W. H. "Records of Some Clouded Leopard (*Neofelis nebulosa*) in the Darjeeling District." *Journ. Bombay Nat. Hist. Soc.,* vol. 37.

Maxwell, Marius. 1925. *Stalking Big Game with a Camera in Equatorial Africa.* London.

Mazak, Vratislav. 1965. *Der Tiger.* Wittenberg–Lutherstadt–Stuttgart.

———. 1967. "Notes on Siberian Long-haired Tiger, *Panthera tigris altaica* (Temminck 1844), with a remark on Temminck's Mammal Volume of the 'Fauna Japonica.' " *Mammalia,* tome 31.

———. 1968. "Nouvelle Sous-espèce du Tigre provenant de l'Asie du Sud Est." *Mammalia,* tome 32, no. 1.

———, and Husson, A. M. "Einige Bemerkungen ueber den Kaploewen, *Panthera leo melanochaitus* (Ch. H. Smith 1842)." *Zoolo. Mededelingen,* vol. 37, no. 7. Leiden.

Meinertzhagen, R. 1957. *Kenya Diary 1902–1906.* Edinburgh–London.

Mellis, C. J. 1895. *Lion-Hunting in Somali-Land.* London.

Metcalf, Christine. 1969. *Cats.* London.

Millais, John Guile. 1895. *A Breath from the Veldt.* London.

———. 1919. *Wanderings and Memoires.* London.

Miller, Leo E. 1919. *In the Wilds of South America.* London–New York.

Mitchell, B. L., and Ansell, W. F. H. 1965. *Wild Life of Kafue and Luangwa.* Lusaka.

Mivart, St. George. 1881. *The Cat, an Introduction to the Study of Backboned Animals, Especially Mammals.* London.

Mjöberg, Eric. 1930. *In der Wildnis des Tropischen Urwaldes: Abenteuer und Schilderungen aus Niederlaendisch Indien.* Leipzig.

Moore, Audrey. 1938. *Serengeti.* London.

Morden, William J. 1930. "Saiga Antelope and Long-haired Tiger." *Natural History,* vol. 30, no. 5.

Morris, R. C. 1927. "A Tigress with Five Cubs." *Journ. Bombay Nat. Hist. Soc.,* vol. 31.

———. "Vitality of Bison Mauled by a Tiger." *Journ. Bombay Nat. Hist. Soc.,* vol. 35.

———. "Tiger versus Bison." *Journ. Bombay Nat. Hist. Soc.,* vol. 38.

———. "Distribution of the Hunting Leopard (*Acinonyx jubatus Erxl.*) in South India." *Journ. Bombay Nat. Hist. Soc.,* vol. 38.

———. "Closed Seasons for Big Game—Are They Beneficial? (Breeding Seasons of Indian Mammals)." *Journ. Bombay Nat. Hist. Soc.,* vol. 39.

Mosse, A. H. E. 1913. *My Somali Book.* London.

Mountford, Guy. 1969. *The Vanishing Jungle: The Story of the World Wildlife Fund Expedition to Pakistan.* London.

Mulldoon, Guy. 1955. *Leopards in the Night.* London.

Müller-Using, Detlev. 1954. *Diezel's Niederjagd.* Hamburg–Berlin.

Musselwhite, Arthur. 1933. *Behind the Lens in Tigerland.* Calcutta.

Nelson, Edward W. 1918. *Wild Animals of North America.* Washington.

Novikov, G. A. 1962. *Carnivorous Mammals of the Fauna of the USSR.* Jerusalem.

O'Connor, Jack. 1961. *The Big Game Animals of North America.* New York.

Ognev, S. I. 1962. *Mammals of USSR and Adjacent Countries.* Vol. 3. Jerusalem.

Olrog, Claes Chr. 1955. "Die Jagd der Gegenwart in Sued-Amerika." In *Jaeger, Jagd und Wild in aller Welt,* bd. 2. Muenchen–Hamburg.

Osgood, Wilfred H. 1943. *The Mammals of Chile.* Zoological Series, Field Museum of Natural History, vol. 30. Chicago.

Paasche, Hans. 1907. *Im Morgenlicht.* Berlin.

Pallas, Peter Simon. 1967. *A Naturalist in Russia: Letters from Peter Simon Pallas to Thomas Pennant.* Edited by Carol Urness. Minneapolis.

Panouse, Jean B. 1957. *Les Mammifères du Maroc: Primates, Carnivores, Pinnipedes, Artiodactyles.* Travaux de l'Institut Scientifique Chérifien. Série Zoologie, no. 5.

Patterson, J. H. 1907. *The Man-eaters of Tsavo.* London.

Peacock, E. H. 1933. *A Game-Book for Burma and Adjoining Territories.* London.

Pease, Sir Alfred. 1914. *The Book of the Lion.* London.

Percival, A. Blainey. 1927. *A Game Ranger's Note Book.* London.

Percy, R. H. 1894. "Indian Shooting." In Badminton Library of Sports and Pastimes, *Big Game Shooting.* London.

Perry, Richard. 1964. *The World of the Tiger.* London–New York.

———. 1970. *The World of the Jaguar.* Newton Abbot–New York.

Petzsch, Hans. 1968. *Die Katzen.* Leipzig–Jena–Berlin.

———. 1970. "Kritisches ueber die neuentdeckte Iriomote-Wildkatze (*Mayailurus iriomotensis* Imaizumi 1967)." *Das Pelzgewerbe,* bd. 20, heft 5.

Pike, Oliver G. 1950. *Wild Animals in Britain.* London.

Pitman, C. R. S. 1931. *A Game Warden Among His Charges.* London.

———. 1945. *A Game Warden Takes Stock.* London.

Pitt, Frances. "The Wild Cat: A Highland Gentleman." In *The Romance of Nature.* London.

Pocock, R. I. 1908. "Hybrid Lion and Leopard." *The Field,* April 18.

———. 1908. "The Supposed Lion and Leopard Hybrid." *The Field,* May 9.

———. 1929. "Tigers." *Journ. Bombay Nat. Hist. Soc.,* vol. 33.

———. 1930. "The Panthers and Ounces of Asia," *Journ. Bombay Nat. Hist. Co.,* vol. 34.

———. 1932. "The Leopards of Africa." *Proc. Zool. Soc.* London.

Poeppig, E. 1835–1836. *Reise in Chile, Peru und auf den Amazonenstrome waehrend der Jahre 1827–1832.* Leipzig. (Reprint: Stuttgart, 1960.)

Pollock, T. 1896. *Fifty Years Reminiscences of India.* London.

Polo, Marco. 1946. *The Travels of Marco Polo.* Translated and edited by William Marsden, re-edited by Thomas Wright. London.

Powell, A. 1957. *Call of the Tiger.* London.

Prater, S. H. "Black Tigers." *Journ. Bombay Nat. Hist. Soc.,* vol. 39.

———. 1965. *The Book of Indian Mammals.* Bombay.

Prichard, H. Hesketh. 1902. *Through the Heart of Patagonia.* London.

Psenner, Hans. 1971. *Tiere der Alpen.* Innsbruck–Vienna–Munich.

Reed, Elizabeth C. 1970. "White Tigers in My House." *National Geographic,* vol. 137, no. 4.

Reed, Theodore H. "Enchantress! Queen of an Indian Palace, a Rare White Tigress Comes to Washington." *National Geographic,* vol. 119, no. 5.

Rengger, J. R. 1830. *Naturgeschichte der Saeugethiere von Paraguay.* Basel.

Reynolds, Vernon. 1967. *The Apes: The Gorilla, Chimpanzee, Orangutan and Gibbon— Their History and Their World.* New York–London.

Roberts, Austin. 1951. *The Mammals of South Africa.* Johannesburg.

Roosevelt, Kermit. 1939. "Hunting the Jaguar." In *North American Big Game.* New York.

Roosevelt, Theodore. 1899. *Big Game Hunting in the Rockies and on the Great Plains, Comprising "Hunting Trips of a Ranchman" and "The Wilderness Hunter."* New York–London.

———. 1905. *Outdoor Pastimes of an American Hunter.* New York.

———. 1910. *African Game Trails.* New York.

———. 1914. *Through the Brazilian Wilderness.* London.

———, and Heller E. 1915. *Life Histories of African Game Animals.* London.

Roosevelt, Theodore, Jr., and Roosevelt, Kermit. 1926. *East of the Sun and West of the Moon.* New York.

Roscoe, John. 1922. *The Soul of Central Africa.* London.

Sanderson, G. P. 1912. *Thirteen Years Among the Wild Beasts of India.* Edinburgh.

Sanderson, Ivan T. 1937. *Animal Treasure.* London.

———. 1940. "The Mammals of the North Cameroon Forest Area." *Transactions Zool. Soc.,* vol. 24, pt. 7. London.

Schaefer, E. 1933. *Berge, Buddhas und Baeren.* Berlin.

———. 1961. *Auf einsamen Wechseln und Wegen.* Hamburg–Berlin.

Schaller, George B. 1963. *The Mountain Gorilla.* Chicago.

———. 1967. *The Deer and the Tiger.* Chicago.

———. 1968. "Hunting Behaviour of the Cheetah in the Serengeti National Park, Tanzania." *E. Afr. Wildl. J.,* vol. 6, pp. 95–100.

———. 1969. "Life with the King of Beasts." *National Geographic,* vol. 135, no. 4.

———. 1970. "This Gentle and Elegant Cat." *Natural History,* vol. 76, no. 6.

———. 1971. "Imperiled Phantom of Asian Peaks: First Photographs of Snow Leopards in the Wild." *National Geographic,* vol. 140, no. 5.

———. 1972. "On Meeting a Snow Leopard." *Animal Kingdom,* vol. 75, no. 1.

————. 1972. "Predators of the Serengeti: Parts I, II and III." *Natural History,* vol. 81, pt. 2, 3, 4.

————. 1972. *The Serengeti Lion: A Study of Predator-Prey Relations.* Chicago–London.

Schauenberg, Paul. 1969. "Le lynx, *Lynx lynx* (L) en Suisse et dans les pays voisins." *Revue Suisse de Zoologie,* tome 76, no. 9.

————. 1969. "L'identification du Chat Forestier de'Europe, *Felis silvestris* Schreber 1777, par une methode ostéologique." *Revue Suisse de Zoologie,* tome 76, no. 18.

————. 1970. "Le Chat Forestier d'Europe, *Felis silvestris* Schreber 1777, en Suisse." *Revue Suisse de Zoologie,* tome 77, no. 9.

Schellendorff, F. Bronsart von. 1918–1922. *Afrikanische Tierwelt.* 6 vols. Leipzig.

Schilling, Tom. 1955. *Die Inseln der Tausend Wunder: Jagd auf Sumatra, Java und den Kleinen Sundainseln.* Hamburg–Berlin.

Schillings, C. G. 1905. *Mit Blitzlicht und Buechse.* Leipzig.

————. 1906. *Im Zauber des Elelescho.* Leipzig.

Schmidt, Hans. 1944. *Argentinische Saeugetiere.* San Andres, Argentina.

Schmökel, H. 1957. "Loewen in Alt-Vorderasien." *Orion,* vol. 12, no. 1.

Schweinfurth, Georg. 1878. *The Heart of Africa.* London.

Schwerin, H. J. Graf von. 1971. *Das Raubwild.* Hannover.

Scott, Hugh. 1942. *In the High Yemen.* London.

Selous, F. C. 1890. *A Hunter's Wanderings in Africa.* London.

————. 1893. *Travel and Adventure in Southeast Africa.* London.

————. 1894. "The Lion in South Africa." In Badminton Library of Sports and Pastimes, *Big Game Shooting.* London.

————. 1908. *African Nature Notes and Reminiscences.* London.

Seurat, L. G. 1930. *Exploration Zoologique d'Algérie de 1830 à 1930.* Paris.

Sheldon, Charles. 1930. *The Wilderness of Denali: Explorations of a Hunter-Naturalist in Northern Alaska.* New York–London.

Shelford, Robert W. C. 1916. *A Naturalist in Borneo.* London.

Sherman, George. 1966. *Wonders of the Jungle.* Walt Disney Productions.

Shiras, George. 1936. *Hunting Wild Life with Camera and Flashlight.* Washington.

Shortridge, G. C. 1934. *The Mammals of South West Africa.* London.

Siemel, Sasha. 1952. "The Jungle Was My Home." *National Geographic,* vol. 102, no. 5.

————. 1954. *Jungle Fury.* London.

Simon, Noel. 1962. *Between the Sunlight and the Thunder: The Wildlife of Kenya.* London.

————, and Géroudet, Paul. 1970. *Last Survivors: The Natural History of Animals in Danger of Extinction.* London.

Smithers, R. H. N. 1966. *The Mammals of Rhodesia, Zambia and Malawi.* London.

Smythies, E. A. 1939. "A Battle Royal Between Tigers and an Elephant." *Journ. Bombay Nat. Hist. Soc.,* vol. 41.

Smythies, Olive. 1955. *Tiger Lady: Adventures in the Indian Jungle.* London.

Sody, H. J. V. 1932. "The Balinese Tiger, *Panthera tigris balica* (Schwarz)." *Journ. Bombay Nat. Hist. Soc.,* vol. 36.

Somerville, Augustus. 1962. *At Midnight the Killer.* Calcutta.

Southern, H. N. 1964. *The Handbook of British Mammals.* Oxford.

Spilett, Juan. 1967. "Pesticide Poisoning of Tigers." *Oryx,* vol. 9, no. 3.

Spruce Richard. 1908. *Notes of a Botanist on the Amazon and Andes.* London.

Stebbing, E. P. 1911. *Jungle By-Ways in India.* London.

————. 1912. *Stalks in the Himalaya.* London.

————. 1920. *The Diary of a Sportsman Naturalist in India.* London.

Steinhardt. 1922. *Von wehrhaften Riesen und seinem Reiche.* Hamburg.

Step, Edward. 1936. *Animal Life of the British Isles.* London.

Sterndale, Robert A. 1884. *Natural History of the Mammals of India and Ceylon.* Calcutta.

———. 1887. *Seonee; or, Camp Life on the Satpura Range.* Calcutta.

Stevenson-Hamilton, J. 1932. "Lion and Leopard." In Maydon, *Big Game Shooting in Africa.* London.

———. 1946. "Lions—as I Knew Them." *African Wild Life,* vol. 1, no. 1.

———. 1954. *Wild Life in South Africa.* London.

———. 1954. "Specimen of the Extinct Cape Lion." *African Wild Life,* vol. 8, no. 3.

Stewart, R. R. M., and J. 1963. "The Distribution of Some Larger Mammals in Kenya." *Journ. E. A. Nat. Hist. Soc.,* vol. 24, no. 3.

Stigand, C. H. 1913. *The Game of British East Africa.* London.

Stockley, C. H. 1928. *Big Game Shooting in the Indian Empire.* London.

———. 1936. *Stalking in the Himalayas and Northern India.* London.

———. 1955. "Hochwildjagd in Indien und Pakistan." In *Jaeger, Jagd und Wild in aller Welt.* Munich-Hamburg.

Stone, W., and Cram, W. E. 1902. *American Animals.* New York.

Storey, Harry. 1907. *Hunting and Shooting in Ceylon.* London.

Stracey, P. D. 1968. *Tigers.* London–New York.

Stroganov, S. U. 1969. *Carnivorous Mammals of Siberia.* Jerusalem.

Swanepoel, P. D. 1956. "The Disappointed Lion." *African Wild Life,* vol. 10, no. 4.

Swayne, H. G. C. 1903. *Seventeen Trips Through Somaliland.* London.

Swynnerton, G. H., and Hayman, R. W. 1950. "A Checklist of the Land Mammals of the Tanganyika Territory and the Zanzibar Protectorate." *Journ. E. A. Nat. Hist. Soc.,* vol. 20, no. 6/7.

Taberer, W. M. 1958. "The Rhino and the Lions." *Journ. E. A. Nat. Hist. Soc.,* vol. 23, no. 2.

Talbot, Lee Meriam. 1959. *A Look at Threatened Species.* London.

Taylor, John. 1959. *Man-Eaters and Marauders.* London.

Tegner, Henry. 1971. *A Naturalist on Speyside.* London.

Temple-Boreham, E. W. 1953. "Annual Report 1951." *Game Department Annual Report 1951.* Nairobi.

Thenius, Erich, and Hofer, Helmut. 1960. *Stammesgeschichte der Saeugetiere.* Berlin–Goettingen–Heidelberg.

Tilman, H. W. 1937. *Snow on the Equator.* London.

Tschudi, F. von. 1875. *Das Thierleben der Alpen.* Leipzig.

Turnbull-Kemp, Peter. 1967. *The Leopard.* Cape Town.

Tweedie, M. W. F., and Harrison, J. L. 1965. *Malayan Animal Life.* London–Kuala Lumpur.

Tyrrwhitt-Drake, Sir Gerrard. 1938. "How to Raise Lions." *Zoo and Animal,* vol. 2, no. 9.

Van de Werken, H. 1967. "Preliminary Report on Cheetahs in Zoos and in Africa: Cheetahs in Captivity." *Royal Zoological Society Natura Artis Magistra.* Amsterdam.

Vandivert, William and Rita. 1957. *Common Wild Animals and Their Young.* New York.

Verheyen, R. 1951. *Contribution à l'Etude Ethologique des Mammifères du Parc National de l'Upemba.* Brussels.

Walker, Ernest P. 1964. *Mammals of the World.* Baltimore.

Wallace, Alfred Russell. 1889. *A Narrative of Travels on the Amazon and Rio Negro.* London.

Waller, Richard. 1972. "Tiger Census—How It Was Done." *Oryx,* vol. 11, no. 6.

Wallihan, A. G. 1904. *Camera Shots at Big Game.* New York.

Wallinger, W. A. 1903. " 'Kills' by Carnivorous Animals: Being Some Remarks on the Method of Their Identification." *Journ. Bombay Nat. Hist. Soc.,* vol. 15.

Ward, A. E. 1925. "Game Animals of Kashmir. Pt. 5." *Journ. Bombay Nat. Hist. Soc.*, vol. 29.

———. 1926. "The Mammals and Birds of Kashmir and the Adjacent Hill Provinces." *Journ. Bombay Nat. Hist. Soc.*, vol. 31.

Watson, M. 1950. "The Wild Animals of Teso and Karamoja. Pt. V." *Uganda Journal*, vol. 14.

Wavrin, Marquis de. 1939. *Les Bêtes Sauvages de l'Amazonie.* Paris.

Wells, Eric F. V. 1933. *Lions Wild and Friendly.* London.

Werner, F. K. 1953. "Beitraege zur Freilandbiologie des europaeischen Luchses." *Saeugetierk.* Mitt. 1.

Wethered, H. N. 1937. *The Mind of the Ancient World: A·Consideration of Pliny's Natural History.* London.

Whymper, Edward. 1892. *Travels Amongst the Great Andes of the Equator.* London.

Williams, A. Bryan. 1925. *Game Trails in British Columbia.* London.

Wilmot, E. Cronje. *Always Lightly Tread.* Cape Town.

Wolverton, Lord. 1894. *Five Months' Sport in Somali Land.* London.

Woodyatt, Nigel. 1923. *My Sporting Memories.* London.

Wyatt, A. W. 1950. "The Lion Men of Singida." *Tanganyika Notes and Records,* no. 28.

Ylla. 1958. *Animals in India.* London.

———, and Leakey, L. S. B. 1953. *Animals of Africa.* London.

Young, Stanley P., and Goldman, Edward A. 1946. *The Puma—Mysterious American Cat.* Washington.

Zell, Th. 1911. *Riesen der Tierwelt.* Berlin–Wien.

Zwilling, E. 1939. *Unvergessenes Kamerun.* Berlin.

———. 1949. *Vom Urhahn zum Gorilla.* Giessen.

Index

abundism: cheetah, 269; leopard, 221

African wildcat (*Felis silvestris lybica*), 24, 44; in captivity, 33–34; characteristics, 32; distribution, 32–33; habits, 33–35; measurements, 32; reproduction, 33

albinism: cheetah, 269; jaguar, 249; leopard, 221; lion, 142; tiger, 186

American wildcat. *See* bobcat

Amur leopard (*Panthera pardus orientalis*), 220, 222, 223, 224

Anatolian leopard (*Panthera pardus tulliana*), 219–20, 224

Andean highland cat (*Oreailurus jacobita*), 103, 104

animal worship, 300–1, 305–6

Arabian wildcat (*Felis silvestris iraki*), 33

Asiatic civet cat (*Viverra zibetha*), 84

Asiatic golden cat (*Profelis temmincki*), 75–77

Asiatic steppe wildcat (*Felis silvestris ornata*), 24, 35–36, 101

Bali tiger (*Panthera tigris balica*), 185, 194

Barbary leopard (*Panthera pardus panthera*), 224

Barbary lion, 142, 143

bay cat (*Profelis badia*), 78

bay lynx. *See* bobcat

Bengal leopard (*Panthera pardus fusca*), 220

Bengal tiger (*Panthera tigris tigris*), 184, 190, 191–92

"bezoar stone," in lions, 298

black-footed cat (*Felis nigripes*): characteristics, 40; diet, 41, 42; distribution, 40–41; habits, 41; measurements, 40; reproduction, 41–42

blood-brotherhood, 299–300

bobcat (*Lynx rufus*): characteristics, 59; diet, 61; distribution, 60; enemies, 60; habits, 60–63; hunting methods, 61–62; measurements, 59–60; reproduction, 62–63; territoriality, 60–61; vocalization, 62

Borean red cat (*Profelis badia*), 78

caffer cat, 42

Canada lynx, 49, 53, 59

cannibalism: cheetah, 289; lion, 165; puma, 113; tiger, 215

Cape lion, 142, 143

caracal (*Caracal caracal*): in captivity, 65, 294; characteristics, 64; distribution, 64–65; habitat, 65; hunting methods, 65–66; measurements, 64; reproduction, 66

cars: and cheetahs, 273–74; and leopards, 229–30, 233; and lions, 149

Caspian tiger (*Panthera tigris virgata*), 184, 189, 192–93, 194–95, 202

Caucasian wildcat (*Felis silvestris caucasica*), 26

cave lion (*Felis spelaeus*), 139, 291

cheetah (*Acinonyx jubatus*): in captivity, 266–67, 289, 294; characteristics, 183, 268–69; diet, 274, 276–77, 280; diseases, 288; distribution, 269–72; enemies, 237–38, 282–84; evolution, 21, 266; habitat, 272; habits, 272–74; in history, 217, 266–67; hunting methods, 10–11, 14, 274, 277–84; longevity, 288; and man, 288–89; measurements, 269; reproduction, 284–88, 289; subspecies, 269; tax-

323